LIFE

OF

NAPOLEON.

BY BARON JOMINI,
GENERAL-IN-CHIEF AND AID-DE-CAMP TO THE EMPEROR OF RUSSIA.

"Je fus ambitieux; tout homme l'est, sans doute;
Mais jamais roi, pontife, ou chef, ou citoyen,
Ne conçut un projet aussi grand que le mien."
VOLTAIRE, *Mahomet.*

TRANSLATED FROM THE FRENCH.

WITH NOTES,

BY H. W. HALLECK, LL.D.,
MAJOR-GENERAL UNITED STATES ARMY;
AUTHOR OF "ELEMENTS OF MILITARY ART AND SCIENCE;" "INTERNATIONAL LAW, AND THE LAWS OF WAR," &C., &C.

IN FOUR VOLUMES.—WITH AN ATLAS.

VOL. I.

The Naval & Military Press Ltd

Published by

The Naval & Military Press Ltd
Unit 5 Riverside, Brambleside
Bellbrook Industrial Estate
Uckfield, East Sussex
TN22 1QQ England

Tel: +44 (0)1825 749494

www.naval-military-press.com
www.nmarchive.com

In reprinting in facsimile from the original, any imperfections are inevitably reproduced and the quality may fall short of modern type and cartographic standards.

TRANSLATOR'S PREFACE.

The following translation was made during a seven months' voyage from New York to California, in 1846. It was undertaken partly as a military study, and partly as an occupation during a long and tedious voyage round Cape Horn. After being completed, the manuscript was laid aside for more than sixteen years, and nearly forgotten.

The present war has called attention to military books, and especially to the works of Jomini. No English translation of his Life of Napoleon has ever been published, and it is very difficult to procure a copy in French. Under these circumstances, and to supply a public want, this translation is given to the press, a military friend having kindly offered to supervise the publication, the professional duties of the translator not permitting him to give it the proper personal attention.

During the publication of the fourth volume of the original work, the author's manuscript of the twenty-second chapter was lost, and a very brief narrative of the campaign of 1815 was substituted. The manuscript was afterwards found, and published in another and more elaborate form. The substance of this second publication is incorporated in the translation, the spirit and character of the original chapter being preserved.

With this exception, the translation is almost literal, only a few paragraphs being slightly condensed. These relate to subjects which at the present time are of very little interest. The translator is solely responsible for the Notes, those of the author being nearly all embodied in the text.

Jomini's original maps and plans being deemed too expensive for republication, those of A. K. Johnston's Atlas (which are mostly compiled from Jomini) are substituted.

H. W. H.

WASHINGTON, April, 1863.

CONTENTS.

VOL. I.

	PAGE
SKETCH OF THE LIFE AND WRITINGS OF GENERAL JOMINI	15
PROLOGUE	33

CHAPTER I.

EARLY LIFE OF NAPOLEON;

FROM HIS BIRTH TO HIS APPOINTMENT TO COMMAND THE ARMY OF ITALY.

Plan of the Work—Napoleon's Birth and Parentage—Character and Education—His first Appointment to the Army—France before the Revolution—Summary of the Events of the Revolution—Events of the 17th, 20th, and 23d of June, 1789—Grand Coalition against France—Russia and Poland—War with Austria—The Prussians invade Champagne—The Republic proclaimed—Retreat of the Prussians—Invasion of Belgium—Death of Louis XVI.—War with Spain, Holland, and England—Dumouriez driven from Belgium—He treats with the Austrians—Committee of Public Safety—Sieges of Mayence and Valenciennes—Fall of the Girondists, May 31st—England heads the Coalition—Affairs of Poland—The Ottoman Porte—Situation of France—Energy of the Convention—Carnot appointed to the Committee of Public Safety—Decree for a *levée en masse*—Revolutionary Government—Reign of Terror—Faults of the Allies—They are driven from France—Death of Marie Antoinette—Political Results of the Revolution—Napoleon appointed Chief-of-battalion—His Republican Opinions—Siege of Toulon—He is made General of Artillery—Conquest of Belgium, Holland, and the left Bank of the Rhine—Naval Battle of Ouessant—Insurrection in Poland—

Fall of Robespierre—Peace with Russia and Spain—Fate of the Royal Family—Napoleon employed at Paris—New Insurrections—the Quiberon Expedition—Constitution of the Year III.—Affair of the 13th Vendemiaire—Military Operations of 1795—Napoleon's Marriage to Josephine—His Plan for the Invasion of Italy—Appointed General-in-chief of the Army of Italy.. 35

CHAPTER II.

CAMPAIGN OF 1796 IN ITALY;

FROM THE BEGINNING OF THE CAMPAIGN TO THE PEACE OF TOLENTINO.

Napoleon takes Command of the Army of Italy—State of Affairs in Italy—Napoleon's Plan of Operations—Position and Plan of the Allies—Beaulieu compromises his Left at Genoa—His Centre pierced—Napoleon attacks the Piedmontese—Operations against the Austrians resumed—Double Combat of Dego—Operations against Colli—Napoleon's Proclamation to his Soldiers—The King of Sardinia sues for Peace—Armistice of Cherasco—Napoleon marches against Beaulieu—Passage of the Po at Placentia—Armistice with the Dukes of Parma and Modena—Battle of Fombio—March upon the Adda—Bridge of Lodi—Napoleon enters Milan—The Directory proposes to divide Napoleon's Army; his Resignation—His Address to the Army—Revolt in Lombardy—Definitive Peace with Piedmont—Position of Beaulieu on the Mincio—Passage of the Mincio—Difficult Position of Napoleon on the Adige—Situation and Policy of Venice—Criticisms on Napoleon's Operations—Investment of Mantua—Armistice with Naples—Demonstrations against the Pope—Armistice of Foligno—Troubles in the Imperial Fiefs, &c.—Occupation of Leghorn—Siege of Mantua—Austrians endeavor to save that Place—Approach of Wurmser from the Rhine—Battles of Lonato and Castiglione—Quasdanowich surprised at Gavardo—Attack upon Napoleon's Head-quarters—Second Battle of Castiglione—Second Passage of the Mincio—Wurmser's Retreat into the Tyrol—Close Alliance between France and Spain—Wurmser resumes the Offensive on the Brenta—Objections to this Operation—The Armies in Germany—Battles of Mori, Roveredo, and Caliano—March from Trent to the Gorges of the Brenta—Affair of Bassano—Wurmser marches upon Mantua—Affairs of St. Georgio—Position of the Army about Mantua—New Republics formed—Political state of the rest of Italy—Discussions with Rome—Definitive Peace with Naples—Affairs of Piedmont—Negotiations with Genoa—New Troubles in the Fiefs—Affairs of Corsica—The English occupy Porto-Ferrajo—They evacuate Corsica—Situation of the Armies on the Adige—Alvinzi succors Mantua with a new Army—Vaubois thrown back on Rivoli—Affair of the Brenta—Passage of the Adige at Ronco—Battle of Arcola—Vaubois driven back from Rivoli—Wurmser besieged at Mantua—Reverses of the French

CONTENTS.

in Germany—Descent upon Ireland—Useless Diplomacy—Reënforcements from the Rhine—New Efforts of Alvinzi to save Wurmser—Joubert driven back on Rivoli—Battle of Rivoli—Provera marches on Mantua—Close of the Campaign—Capitulation of Wurmser at Mantua—Expedition into Romana.. 76

CHAPTER III.

CAMPAIGN OF 1797 IN AUSTRIA;

FROM THE CROSSING OF THE TAGLIAMENTO TO THE PEACE OF CAMPO-FORMIO.

Preparations for a new Campaign—The Archduke Charles takes Command of the Austrian Army—Treaty with the King of Sardinia—The Affairs of Venice—Troubles with the States of Terra-firma—Negotiations with Pescaro—Armaments of the Senate—Napoleon resolves to attack the Archduke before he can unite his Forces—Plan of Operations—Passage of the Piave—Affair of Tarvis—The Archduke is reënforced by the Detachments sent from the Rhine—Armistice of Leoben—Operations of Joubert in the Tyrol—Veronese Vespers—Victor suppresses the Insurgents—Condition of the two Armies—Preliminaries of Leoben—Armies of the Rhine—Destruction of the Venetian Republic—Napoleon goes to Milan—Revolution of Genoa—Change of Constitution—Provisional Government appointed—The Disorders continue—Negotiations of Udina and Passeriano—English Affairs—Naval Battle of St. Vincent—Naval Tactics—Mutiny in the British Fleets—Negotiations of Lille—Internal Affairs of France—The eighteenth Fructidor—Foreign Negotiations—Resignation of Napoleon—Cobentzel negotiates on the part of Austria—Napoleon and the Directory—Peace of Campo-Formio—Conditions of this Treaty—Its Results—Revolution of La Valteline—Negotiations with Germany at Rastadt—The Passage of the Simplon asked of the Valois—The Directory foments a Revolution in Switzerland—Proclamation of the Vaudois—Invasion of Berne—Helvetic Constitution—Neutrality of Switzerland and Faults of the Directory—Revolution in Rome—Proclamation of the Roman Republic—Napoleon leaves Rastadt—His Reception at Paris—General Remarks.. 162

CHAPTER IV.

EXPEDITION TO EGYPT;

MILITARY OPERATIONS IN 1798 AND PART OF 1799.

Difficulties of Napoleon's Position at Paris—Origin of the War in Egypt—State of Hindostan—Projects of the Sultan of Mysore, and the Apathy of

France—State of the English Forces—Object of the Expedition into Egypt—Napoleon examines the Port of Antwerp—The Continent again involved in hostile Preparations—Napoleon departs from Toulon—Capture of Malta—Debarkation at Alexandria—March on Cairo—Battle of the Pyramids—Entrance into Cairo—Naval Battle of Aboukir—Results of this Battle—Difficulties with the Porte—Revolt of Cairo—Expedition into Syria—Passage of the Desert, and taking of Jaffa—Resistance of St. Jean-d'Acre—Battle of Mont-Tabor—Continuation of the Siege of St. Jean-d'Acre—Raising of this Siege—Return to Cairo—Debarkation and Battle of Aboukir—Napoleon decides to return to France...................... 204

CHAPTER V.

CAMPAIGN OF 1799;

MILITARY OPERATIONS IN GERMANY, SWITZERLAND, AND ITALY.

Situation of Europe in 1798—Exorbitant Demands of the Directory at Rastadt—Russia in Favor of the Empire—Negotiations of Prince Repnin at Berlin—Embarrassments of Prussia—Views of Austria—Secret Convention between England and Naples—Favorable Chances for Austria—Alliance between Austria and Russia—Policy of the Directory—Affairs of Switzerland—Treaty of Alliance concluded at Paris—The smaller Cantons refuse the Oath of Fidelity—Expedition of Schawembourg against Stanz—The Grisons call upon the Austrians—French Law of Conscription—Consequences of the Defeat at Aboukir and the Declaration of War by the Ottoman Porte—Decree for a Levy of two hundred thousand Men—Embarrassed State of the Finances—Negotiations paralyzed by the Intermission of Spain—State of the Negotiations at Rastadt—England—Russia—Spain—Portugal—Sweden and Denmark—War commenced by the Court of Naples—Joubert seizes upon Piedmont and occupies Tuscany—Ferdinand flies to Sicily—Championnet takes Possession of Naples—Erection of the Parthenopean Republic—The Russians advance toward Italy—The Directory takes the Initiative without Preparation—Massena gets Possession of the Grisons—The Archduke marches against Jourdan—Battle of Stockach—Reverses in Italy—Retreat of the Army behind the Rhine—Attack upon our Plenipotentiaries at Rastadt—Tardy Enterprise of the Archduke—Suwarrow in Lombardy—Grand Naval Expedition of Admiral Bruix—Macdonald's Army evacuates Naples—Suwarrow enters Turin—Massena driven from the Grisons—The Archduke penetrates into Switzerland—Massena evacuates Zurich—The Archduke paralyzed by Cabinet Orders—Macdonald returns upon Modena—Suwarrow attacks him on the Trebia—General State of Affairs—Dissatisfaction against the Directory—Political Operations of Sièyes—Address to the Councils—The Nomination of Treilhard is annulled—Merlin and Laréveillère resign—Consternation at the Result of the Battle of Trebia—Formation of Clubs—Talleyrand is replaced—The Directory close the Manège—New Plan of Operations proposed—Joubert is charged with its Execution—He debouches from the Apennines—Battle of Novi—Massena recaptures the smaller Cantons—Project of the Archduke—New Plan of the Coalition—The Archduke Marches on Manheim—Plan of Suwarrow—Battle of Zurich—Korsakof retires to the Rhine—Suwarrow passes the St. Gothard and marches on the Muttenthal and Glaris—Defeat of the Austrians in this Canton—Difficult Retreat of Suwarrow—Efforts of Korsakof on Winterthour—Movements of the Archduke and Suwarrow—Descent of the Anglo-Russians into Holland—Lecourbe raises the Siege of Philipsbourg—Efforts of Championnet to save Coni.............. 236

CHAPTER VI.

CAMPAIGNS OF 1800 AND 1801;

FROM NAPOLEON'S RETURN FROM EGYPT TO THE PEACE OF AMIENS.

Napoleon's Return from Egypt—Necessity of a Change in the Government—Sièyes had long meditated a Change—Revolution of the eighteenth Brumaire—Project for a Constitution—Consular Government—Napoleon proposes Peace—Fall of Tippoo-Saëb—Maritime Affairs—Continental Armies—Plan of Campaign—Pius VI. and VII.—Project of the Allies on Genoa and Toulon—Massena blockaded in Genoa—Napoleon's Plan of Operations on the Rhine—Carnot Minister of War—Passage of the Alps—The French Army arrested by Fort Bard—Melas deceived—Combat of Chiusella—Napoleon marches on Milan—Passage of the Ticino—Disposition of Melas—Surrender of Genoa—Passage of the Po—Battle of Montebello—Battle of Marengo—Convention of Alexandria—Negotiations of General St. Julien—Disapproved by the Cabinet of Vienna—Negotiations for a Naval and Military Armistice—Kleber proposes to evacuate Egypt—He is forced to conquer at Heliopolis—Important Convention with the United States—The English quarrel with Neutrals—Rupture of the Negotiation of London—Conspiracy of Cerrachi—Expeditions against Ferrol and Cadiz—Resignation of Thugut from the Ministry—Occupation of Tuscany—Preparations on the Continent—Plan of Operation—Brilliant Success of the Army of the Rhine—Armistice of Steyer—Inaction of Brune—Passage of the Splugen—Operations of Brune—Junction of the Army of the Grisons—Armistice of Treviso—Infernal Machine—The Neapolitans beaten in Tuscany—Expedition of Murat against Naples—Armistice of Foligno—Peace of Luneville—Campaign of 1801—English Expedition against Copenhagen—Naval Battle of Copenhagen—Armistice with the Danes and Death of Paul I.—English Descent upon Egypt—Resignation of Pitt—Situation of France—Necessity of a new Religious System—Best means of accomplishing this Change—Chances in Favor of the Reformation—The Concordat—Objections made to it—Fault of my Successors—Negotiations of London—Preliminaries signed—Peace with Russia and the Porte—Acquisition of Louisiana—The Infante of Parma, King of Etruria—Expedition to St. Domingo and Guadaloupe—Provisional Reunion of Piedmont—Affairs of Switzerland and the Cisalpine—Italian Republic—The English—Lord Cornwallis Envoy to Amiens—Debates upon Malta—The definitive Peace—Its Reception in London and France—The Tribunat abolished—Consulate for Life—The Principles of my Works—Solemn Publication of the Concordat—Reunion of Piedmont—Counter-Revolution in Switzerland—Friendly Relations with Russia—Indemnities in Germany.................. 294

APPENDIX.

THE BONAPARTE FAMILY.. 395

LIST OF MAPS

TO ILLUSTRATE

JOMINI'S LIFE OF NAPOLEON.

VOL. I.

1. MAP OF THE VALLEY OF THE PO, to illustrate the Campaigns of 1796–97 and 1800.
2. BATTLES OF LONATO AND CASTIGLIONE, on the 3d, AND AT MEDOLA, on the 5th August, 1796.
3. SIEGE OF MANTUA AND THE AFFAIRS OF ST. GEORGE AND LA FAVORITE, 15th September, 1796.
4. BATTLE OF ARCOLA, 15th, 16th and 17th November, 1796. (1st day, 15th November.)
5. BATTLE OF ARCOLA, 15th, 16th and 17th November, 1796. (3d day, 17th November.)
6. BATTLE OF RIVOLI, 14th and 15th January, 1797.
7. MAP OF LOWER EGYPT AND PART OF SYRIA, to illustrate the Expedition to Egypt and the Campaign of 1798–1801.
8. SIEGE OF ST. JEAN D'ACRE, from 19th March to 21st May, 1799.
9. BATTLE OF MOUNT THABOR, 16th April, 1799.
10. BATTLE OF MARENGO, 14th June, 1800. (1st Sheet.)
11. BATTLE OF MARENGO, 14th June, 1800. (2d Sheet.)

SKETCH

OF THE

LIFE AND WRITINGS

OF

GENERAL JOMINI.

SKETCH

OF THE

LIFE AND WRITINGS

OF

GENERAL JOMINI.

BIOGRAPHICAL SKETCH.

GENERAL ANTHONY HENRY JOMINI was born in the small village of Payerne, Canton of Vaud, Switzerland, on the 6th of March, 1779. His family was of Italian origin, but had for several centuries resided in the Canton of Vaud. Young Jomini received the usual education of young men of his class in Switzerland, and having a desire to enter the military career, steps were taken to place him in the military school of the Prince of Wurtemburg, at Montheliard; that school being transferred to Stuttgard, Jomini, at the age of seventeen, was placed in a banking-house in Paris. In 1798, he was appointed aide-de-camp to Keller, who had distinguished himself in the affair of Ostend. Keller having been superseded by Repond, Jomini lost his position for a time, but was soon afterwards employed by the new appointee, and remained for some time in the employ of the Helvetic minister. After serving in the office of the Secretary of War, with the rank of captain, he was promoted, in 1799, to the grade of chief of battalion.

After the peace of Luneville, in 1801, Jomini returned to Paris to seek military employment, but receiving very little encouragement, he accepted a position in a commercial house. In 1805, Ney gave him a situation on his staff, with the promise of appointing him an aide-de-camp, which promise was afterwards redeemed. He served with Ney in the campaigns of Ulm, Jena, Eylau, and Spain, and was promoted to the rank of chief of Ney's staff, for services in the field. In these campaigns he acquired a brilliant reputation as a staff officer, and as a strategist; but the reputation thus acquired, as is almost invariably the case, created jealousies, and made for the Swiss officer numerous enemies, at the head of whom was Berthier, the Major-General and Chief-of-Staff of the Imperial Army.

After the capitulation of Dupont at Baylen, in 1808, Napoleon determined to direct in person the military operations in Spain, and ordered Ney to join him with the sixth corps d'armée. Colonel Jomini made preparations to accompany Ney in this new field; but the indiscreet admirers of his chief-of-staff had incited the jealousy of the Marshal's wife, by reporting that Jomini had planned or advised Ney's most successful operations. This feeling made his position, for a time, anything but agreeable; nevertheless he served through the campaign, and was sent by Ney to Napoleon, at Vienna, to explain the Marshal's objections to serve under Soult. After the battle of Wagram, he returned with Napoleon to Paris, where they met Ney. The latter was immediately ordered to return to his command, and Jomini was about to accompany him, when he found that Colonel Béchet had been selected by Ney in his place as chief-of-staff, Jomini being assigned to duty in the general staff under Major-General Berthier. Rather than serve under the Prince of Neuchatel, who had always been his enemy, Jomini tendered his resignation, intending to enter the service of the Emperor of Russia. But Napoleon refused to accept it, and placed him on special duty, in Paris, to enable him to write his history of the campaigns in Italy. The progress of his investigations, however, was much impeded in 1811, by Colonel Muriel, Chief of the Dépôt of Archives, who would not permit him to examine any paper without a special requisition and order, designating the particular paper to be inspected.

Meeting the Emperor one Sunday, Napoleon made inquiries in regard to his progress in writing the history of the Italian campaigns. Jomini explained his embarrassments, and was ordered to report in person the next day. He repaired to the palace at the hour appointed, and met the Mameluke, Roustan, passing from the apartment of the Empress to that of Napoleon, announcing the birth of the Prince Imperial. Jomini immediately withdrew; but the Emperor sent for him and reprimanded him for not keeping his engagement. Jomini excused himself by saying that under the peculiar circumstances, he had supposed his Majesty would be too much engaged to receive him. Napoleon's reply was characteristic: " Your conclusion was not logical. If the Empress had continued to suffer, the case would have been different; but as she was safely delivered, the best thing I could do was to let her repose, and attend to my own business." At this interview, Napoleon spoke of Berthier's dislike to him, and asked the cause of this ill-feeling. Jomini replied that he had done everything possible to conciliate the major-general, even offering to dedicate to him his *Treatise on Grand Operations* ; that Berthier consented to accept a simple dedication, but *no letter of dedication*. " He showed bad taste," said Napoleon; "you would have done better to dedicate it to me; I should have been pleased to accept it." Jomini replied that he could not venture to take such a liberty.

When the war of 1812 broke out between France and Russia, Jomini, not wishing to fight against the Emperor Alexander, who had previously offered him a high position in the Russian army, but which Napoleon would not permit him to accept, asked the pacific position of Governor of a province, and was assigned to the Governorship of Wilna. He was afterwards sent to replace General Barbanègre, in the Government of Smolensk, and rendered most valuable assistance to Napoleon in the retreat from Moscow, especially in the passage of the Beresina, at which place he was ordered to select, in conjunction with General Eblé, the points for placing the bridges.

He suffered terribly in this retreat, and several times very nearly perished. When almost on the point of death, he met General Guilleminot, the chief-of-staff of the Viceroy of Italy, who presented him to Eugene as an officer at his service. Eugene received him kindly, but with the significant remark: "What, my poor general, can I do with *you*, when I can do nothing with *myself*?" On his arrival at Stettin, he received orders to join the Emperor at Paris, to assist in the organization of a new army. General Nègre, of the artillery, was the only other officer who received the honor of such an order. Jomini obeyed, but, on his arrival at Paris, his health was such as to confine him for three months to his bed.

He rejoined the army on the day of the battle of Lutzen, and was appointed by Napoleon chief of Ney's staff. He reported to the Marshal, at Leipsic, on the 4th of May. The meeting was embarrassing to both, as neither had asked or expected the appointment. But their old relations were soon renewed, and Jomini distinguished himself at the battle of Bautzen, by the judicious advice which he gave to move on the enemy's right, instead of the left, an opinion subsequently confirmed by the receipt of orders from the Emperor, which had been miscarried. Ney, grateful for the services of Jomini, recommended his promotion to the grade of general of division ; but the old hatred of Berthier prevented this, and, instead of rewarding him for services rendered, the Prince of Neuchatel charged him with incapacity and ordered him in arrest ! This was a little too much for the proud spirit of Jomini, and he resolved to no longer serve under an ungrateful flag. He, therefore, left the French army, and repaired to the head-quarters of the Emperor of Russia, and was received into his service.

The desertion of Jomini from the service of France caused much comment and discussion. His friends defended this act as perfectly justifiable. They said that, in the *first* place, not being a Frenchman, or a French subject, he was under no obligations of patriotism to France. He was simply a soldier of fortune, whose offers of service had been accepted, and that this obligation continued only so long as the two parties agreed. The service itself was not obligatory, nor the term of the engagement for life ; that there could, from the nature of the case, have been no implied understanding, between the parties, of such a character. They said further, that when General Jomini tendered his resignation, and asked to retire from the French service, all obligations on his part ceased, and that subsequently he must be considered as an impressed foreigner, who had a right to desert on the first opportunity. The Emperor having refused to accept his resignation, he remained an unwilling servant, until the ill-treatment of Berthier compelled him, from a sense of self-respect, to desert. That his leaving at the time, and in the manner he did, was in every respect justifiable, and under the peculiar circumstances of the case, entirely unavoidable.

His enemies contended that, having once entered the

French service, he had no right to leave it without the consent of the government, and that, so long as that consent was refused, he was bound to continue in service. That his leaving at the time, and under the circumstances of the case, constituted a real military desertion. Some, moreover, at the time, went so far as to charge him with virtual treason, alleging that he took to the enemy important documentary and parole information.

At this distance of time, and after a full examination of the evidence and arguments on both sides, it is not easy to agree entirely with either party. To hold that an officer, who voluntarily enters a foreign service, is bound to remain in that service against his will and for life, is very unreasonable. On the contrary, it is equally unreasonable to contend that he may leave at any moment he pleases; for instance, to leave the field of battle, and join the ranks of the enemy. If Jomini, after the campaign in Spain, had insisted upon his resignation, and had declined any other voluntary duty in the French service, no one could have blamed him for leaving it on the first favorable opportunity. On the contrary, after Napoleon had refused to accept his resignation, he continued in the willing performance of the duties of his office. Moreover, he accepted promotion to a higher grade and a most confidential trust. Nevertheless it must be admitted that, if anything can ever justify an act like that of General Jomini, in 1813, it was excused by the refusal of his promotion, so earnestly solicited by Marshal Ney, for gallant and meritorious services at the battle of Bautzen, and by Berthier's unjust treatment, and especially by the disgrace of arrest and trial on unfounded charges.

On joining the service of the allies, the conduct of Jomini was in every respect honorable, and proved that he fully appreciated the embarrassments of his position. When asked by the King of Prussia certain questions in regard to the position and numbers of the French troops, he politely declined to answer. The Emperor of Russia, who was present, justified his refusal, and openly approved his delicate sense of honor in regard to the service which he had just left.

The absurd charge that Jomini conveyed to the allies the plans of the Emperor, was forever put to rest by Napoleon himself, in his Autographic Memoirs, dictated at St. Helena. In commenting upon the "History of the Campaign in Saxony," where this accusation was repeated, he remarked: "The author of this book is wrong in charging General Jomini with having conveyed to the allies the secret of the operations of the campaign, and the situation of Ney's corps. That officer did not know the Emperor's plan; the order of general movement, which was always sent to each of the marshals, was not communicated to him, and he did not know what it was. The Emperor never accused him of the crime which is here imputed to him. He did not desert his flag like some others. He had great injustice to complain of, and was blinded by an honorable sentiment. He was not a Frenchman, and there was no love of country to retain him."

During the remainder of the campaign of 1813, General Jomini rendered most valuable service to the Emperor of Russia, by his opinions in regard to military operations. On reaching the banks of the Rhine, he advised against the invasion of France, and in favor of a treaty of peace, honorable to both parties; but Teutonic exaltation at that time would be satisfied with nothing less than the conquest and partition of France. Jomini entered France with the Emperor of Russia, but, on his urgent solicitations, was permitted to return to Switzerland, and was of great service to his native country in saving it, through the influence of Russia, from the intended conquest and subjugation of Austria.

After the occupation of Paris by the allies, and the restoration of Louis XVIII., General Jomini repaired to Vienna in a politico-military capacity, as a Russian officer, and as a representative of his native Canton of Vaud. In these negotiations he greatly exerted himself to secure the liberties of his native country from the rapacity of Austrian diplomacy. It was fortunate for Switzerland at this period, that Jomini, and several other distinguished Swiss, held high positions in the Russian army, and in the councils of the Emperor, who used his power and influence to protect their country.

In 1815 he returned to Paris, with the Emperor Alexander, where he so warmly opposed the execution of Marshal Ney, that it was proposed to strike his name from the list of Russian generals. This act of the allies is a lasting disgrace to their character and cause; and the course pursued by Jomini, on that occasion, constitutes one of the most praiseworthy incidents of his history.

After the peace, Jomini accompanied the Emperor to Russia, and was promoted to the rank of a general-in-chief, that is, a general eligible to the command of an army—a rank next to that of Marshal in the Russian service, which no one can there hold, who has not gained a battle. Thus, Prince Gortschakoff, notwithstanding his brilliant defence of the Crimea, could not be made a marshal, because he had won no battle. Jomini successively received the grand crosses of St. Anne, St. Waldimir, and St. Alexander; assisted the Emperor at the Congress of Aix-la-Chapelle, in 1818, and at the Congress of Verona, in 1823; was made president of a committee for organizing the Military Academy; and was afterwards charged with preparing plans for fortifying and defending the frontiers of the empire. On the accession of Nicholas to the throne, he received many proofs of the confidence of the new Emperor, was appointed aide-de-camp general, and charged with directing the military education of the imperial heir. His health, much broken by his sufferings on the Beresina, was too delicate to withstand the rigors of the climate of St. Petersburg, and he had permission to spend much of his time in Paris and in the south of Europe.

Jomini has two sons and three daughters. His eldest son was aide-de-camp to Marshal Paskewitz, and afterwards left the service to reside at Payerne. The second is first Counsellor of State in the Department of Foreign Affairs at St. Petersburg. His eldest daughter is married in Russia, to a nephew of the Princess Orloff; the second, to a superior officer of the French corps of Engineers; and the third, to a proprietor on the Loire.

NOTICE OF HIS WRITINGS.

To the foregoing sketch of Jomini's life, we will add a brief notice of his published works.

After studying the principal authors on the military art, and comparing their views with those developed by the campaigns of Frederick and Napoleon, Jomini made a scientific analysis of the principles which seemed to lie at the foundation of military operations, which resulted, in 1803, in the preparation of a work entitled a "Treatise on Grand Tactics," in which was set forth his views, with abundant illustrations, from the campaigns of Frederick and of the French Revolution. On reflection, he decided that such a work would not succeed, and in a fit of dejection, he burned the manuscript. Adopting a new plan for the enunciation of his views, he drew up his "*Traité des Grandes Operations Militaires*" ("Treatise on Grand Military Operations"), the first two volumes of which were published in 1804. The fifth volume, including the wars of the French Revolution, was published in 1806, before the third and fourth volumes, in order to incite the interest of the readers, by a recital of recent operations. The other volumes were completed in 1810. The second edition was published in Paris, between 1811 and 1816, in eight volumes. A third edition appeared in 1818, in three volumes, the author having suppressed the first six campaigns of the Revolution, in order to include them in his "History of the Wars of the Revolution," which he was then preparing. The fourth edition of this work appeared in 1857, in three volumes, with an atlas.

This is considered by military critics the most important of all his works, as it embodies the main principles of the military art, with numerous illustrations drawn from the campaigns of the great captains of different ages. All succeeding military writers have borne testimony to the great ability displayed in this work.

In 1811 Jomini began the publication of his "*Histoire Critique et Militaire des Guerres de la Révolution*" ("Critical and Military History of the Wars of the Revolution"), in 15 volumes, with 4 atlases, containing in all 39 plates. This was a work of immense labor, and in some respects it formed the basis of most histories of the same period, which have followed since its publication. The analysis of campaigns and battles, and the critical discussion of plans and military operations, render it of great value to military readers. Its character is scientific, rather than literary, or historical, and, notwithstanding the great ability displayed in it, with general readers it is not popular. The narrative is clear, and the style perspicuous, but the minute details of scientific discussions, render it somewhat tedious as an historical work. The publication was not completed till 1824.

In 1827, Jomini published his Life of Napoleon, under the

title of "*Vie Politique et Militaire de Napoleon, racontée par lui-même au tribunal de César, d'Alexandre et de Frédéric,*" in four volumes, with an atlas of 36 plates. Although published anonymously, the military character of the work plainly indicated its author. It is said, that Jomini originally intended to make it a more complete history of the Wars of the Empire, as a continuation of his History of the Revolution. He was deterred from this by several reasons. In the first place, his position as an old officer of the French army, and as aide-de-camp to the Emperor of Russia, rendered it embarrassing to appear as a public critic of the political and military acts of Napoleon. At least, these criticisms, whether favorable or unfavorable, would be likely to involve him in controversies. In the second place, he could not then have access to official documents, necessary for a full and elaborate history of Napoleon's wars. An anonymous publication would enable him to avoid personal controversies, and to exercise more freedom in the discussion of these great political events.

The other works of Jomini are his "*Tableau Analytique,*" published in 1830; his "*Precis de l'Art de la Guerre,*" published in 1837, and his Treatise "*Sur la Formation des troupes pour le combat,*" published in 1856. His translations, with valuable notes, of Lloyd and Tempelhoff's "History of the Seven Years' War," and the Archduke Charles' "Principles of Strategy," are standard works among military readers. In addition to these works, Jomini has published a number of pamphlets on polemical subjects, and reviews of the military and historical writings of his cotemporaries. In all of these minor publications, he has exhibited great military knowledge, as well as accurate military criticism.

As a military historian, Jomini has no equal, at least, not among the writers who preceded him. And the best of those who have followed him, do not hesitate to acknowledge him as their model and prototype.

The commentaries of Cæsar are of no great military value, for the art of war was then in its infancy, and strategy was very little understood, even by those who are now looked back upon as good generals. In military operations, as in everything else, strong common sense pointed out the same plans of operation as would have been decided upon after the most elaborate scientific discussion. Science tests and approves what genius originates and suggests.

The old military historians, Josephus, Herodotus, Thucydides, Polybius, Sallust, Livy, Tacitus, Plutarch, Arrian, Machiavelli, Montluc, Brantome, Rohan, Montecuculli, Gustavus Adolphus, Turenne, Condé, Feuquières, Santa Cruz, Puységur, and Frederick, described the events of the wars without understanding or attempting to point out the strategic relations of the several movements of the contending armies. Even Guibert, Ménil-Durand, Lloyd, Tempelhoff, Warnery, La Roche Aymon, Bulow, and Dumas, discussed the military operations which they described, in their relation to tactical movements rather than strategic combinations.

The dictations of Napoleon at St. Helena, *Chefs d'œuvre* in their way, are mere fragmentary discussions of historical events, grand in conception, but imperfect in execution. They are valuable studies for experienced generals, but not easily understood by military students, and a mere dead letter to common readers. Napoleon, in criticising Jomini's works, spoke of him in the most complimentary terms; and Jomini, in writing of Napoleon, always held him up as a model of a great captain. On questions of military science, they were fully agreed. While Jomini stated his military problems in scientific language, Napoleon solved them by practical experience.

Since the earlier writings of Jomini first appeared, a very large number of military works have been published, some of them technical books of professional instruction, and others of an historical character.

In the first class, we may mention Xylander, Wagner Decker, Hoyer, Valentini, the Archduke Charles, Muller, Bismark, Boutourlin, Okouneff, Clausewitz, Muffling, Rogniat, Gay de Vernon, Jacquinot de Presle, Rocquancourt, Ternay, Dufour, Augoyat, Bardin, Chambray, Bugeaud, Lallemand, Barre Duparcq, Fallot, Paixhans, Chassaloup, Jacobi, Piobert, Scharnhorst, Thiroux, Choumara, Birago, Bousmard, Carnot, Douglas, Haillot, Carrion-Nisas, Ravichio de Peretsdorf, Macauley, Noizet, Jebb, Laisné, Zastrow, Mahan, Saint-Paul, Mangin, Maurice de Sellon, &c., &c.

In the second class may be mentioned Dumas, Soult, Suchet, Saint-Cyr, Beauvais, Pelet, Koch, Vaudoncourt, Foy, Napier, Regnier, Marmont, Lamarque, Bellune, Charras, Thiers, Belmas, Kausler, Chambray, Savary, Segur, Fain, Siborne, Jones, &c., &c.

Nearly all recent military writers and historians have discussed or criticised the theories and principles set forth in the works of Jomini. It must not, however, be inferred that all, or even a majority of these writers, clearly understood the questions which they discussed, or the principles of the art which they criticised.

Again, Jomini has experienced in his political career much of the fickleness of popular opinion and popular judgment. In his native country he was, at one time, the object of unmeasured abuse, and, at another, of unbounded praise. In France, for some years after he went over to the Russian service, his name was only mentioned with contempt. Afterwards, he was not only honored by the French government, but courted by the literary and military savans of the French metropolis; and the French army, proud of his record of its glorious achievements, claim him as having belonged to its ranks.

Few men of this century have a more wide-spread, or well-earned reputation. His works are read and admired by the soldiers of every country on the continent of Europe, and probably no other author is as much read and studied in the British and American armies.

General Jomini is now about eighty-four years of age, but appears much younger than he really is. At least such was his condition when the translator saw him in Paris, two or three years since.

We will close this biographical sketch of the Life and Writings of General Jomini, with a characteristic anecdote, which will serve to show his remarkable knowledge of military strategy, or what the French call, *strategic intuition*. Having been summoned to the Imperial head-quarters, at Mayence, at the beginning of the campaign of Jena, Napoleon said to him, " I am delighted that the first work which demonstrates the true principles of war, has appeared in my reign. No work like yours is taught in our Military schools. We are going to fight the Prussians. I have called you near me, because you have written on the campaigns of Frederick the Great, because you know his army, and have studied the theatre of the war." Jomini asked for four days to get his horses and equipages from the head-quarters of Marshal Ney, and added that he would join his Majesty at Bamberg. " Why at Bamberg ?" said the Emperor. " Who told you that I am going to Bamberg ?" " The map of Germany, sire." " There are a hundred roads on that map," said Napoleon. " Yes, sire ; but it is probable that your majesty will make against the left of the Prussians the same manœuvre which was made at Donawerth against the right of Mack, and by Saint Bernard against the right of Melas." " Very well," said Napoleon, " go to Bamberg, but don't say a word about it; no one should know that I am going to Bamberg."

The foregoing biographical and bibliographical sketch, is compiled from Major Lecomte's Life and Writings of General Jomini, *Le Spectateur Militaire*, Liv. 126, December 15th, 1861, and biographical dictionaries.

LIFE

OF

NAPOLEON.

PROLOGUE.

Long had the Elysian Fields resounded with the memorable events which marked the beginning of the nineteenth century. The shades of Pitt and Thugut, of Kleber, Moreau, Nelson, Lannes, and the many other heroes slain in battle, had already carried there a thousand different versions of the combinations to which were attributed so many victories and so many defeats. The illustrious inhabitants of these mysterious regions were waiting, with impatience, the arrival of the extraordinary man who had been the principal mover in these events, and who alone could explain them.

Already the news of his exile to Saint Helena, and of the barbarous treatment he received there, gives warning of his approaching end. Already homicidal Fate seizes her scissors * * *, inexorable Atropos cannot suffer so noble a victim to escape. Finally, the fifth of May, 1821, the clear sky of Elysium is suddenly covered with clouds; the angry waves of Acheron, lashed by the unchained winds, give notice of some extraordinary apparition. All, with a common sentiment of interest and curiosity, hasten to the shore. Soon the skiff of the sad and silent Charon is seen approaching; it carries the shade of Napoleon the * * * All press forward to see him; Alexander, Cæsar, Frederick, are in the first rank, and they alone have the right of interrogating him. To the usual felicitations succeed the most weighty questions. *Alexander*, who from the mountains of Macedonia penetrated into India and returned victorious, is astonished at the retreat from Moscow, and seeks to know the cause. *Cæsar*, who died invincible, asks an explanation of the disasters of Leipsic and Waterloo. *Frederick*, so great in reverses, and so measured in his enterprises, wishes an explanation of the prompt destruction of his monarchy, and of its brilliant resurrection in 1813.

Surrounded by this noble Areopagus, Napoleon replies as follows :—

CHAPTER I.

FROM THE BIRTH OF NAPOLEON TO HIS APPOINTMENT TO THE COMMAND OF THE ARMY OF ITALY.

Plan of the Work—Napoleon's Birth and Parentage—Character and Education—His first Appointment to the Army—France before the Revolution—Summary of the Events of the Revolution—Events of the 17th, 20th, and 23d of June, 1789—Grand Coalition against France—Russia and Poland—War with Austria—The Prussians invade Champagne—The Republic proclaimed—Retreat of the Prussians—Invasion of Belgium—Death of Louis XVI.—War with Spain, Holland, and England—Dumouriez driven from Belgium—He treats with the Austrians—Committee of Public Safety—Sieges of Mayence and Valenciennes—Fall of the Girondists, May 31st—England heads the Coalition—Affairs of Poland—The Ottoman Porte—Situation of France—Energy of the Convention—Carnot appointed to the Committee of Public Safety—Decree for a *levés en masse*—Revolutionary Government—Reign of Terror—Faults of the Allies—They are driven from France—Death of Marie Antoinette—Political Results of the Revolution—Napoleon appointed Chief-of-battalion—His republican Opinions—Siege of Toulon—He is made General of Artillery—Conquest of Belgium, Holland and the left Bank of the Rhine—Naval Battle of Ouessant—Insurrection in Poland—Fall of Robespierre—Peace with Russia and Spain—Fate of the Royal family—Napoleon employed at Paris—New Insurrections—The Quiberon Expedition—Constitution of the Year III. Affair of the 13th Vendemiaire—Military Operations of 1795—Napoleon's Marriage to Josephine—His Plan for the Invasion of Italy—Appointed General-in-chief of the Army of Italy.

Plan of the Work.—I will not attempt a complete picture of the important and complicated events of my reign; this immense work can not probably be undertaken till after the great personages who took part, either for or against me, have published their memoirs, developed their views, and explained their actions; it must, therefore, be left to posterity,—to some faithful disciple of the severe Clio. But I will now give an outline of my most prominent actions, of my political views, of my military combinations,—in a word, present myself such as I really was. From this it may be seen how much I have been disfigured by the passions and party spirit of my cotemporaries.*

Napoleon's Birth, &c.—I was born on the 15th of August, 1769, at Ajaccio, in Corsica; my parents were noble,—fortuitous circumstance, to which I attach no importance. *"A captain who renders his country illustrious, and by his own merit rebuilds the throne of Charlemagne, has no need of noble ancestry."* The patrician family from which I sprung, included in its number the Gonfalonier Buonaparte of St. Nicolas, who governed the Republic of Florence towards the middle of the thirteenth century.

Character and Education.—My career has been so astonishing that my admirers have thought to find something extraordinary even in my infancy. They are mistaken. My early life indicated nothing at all remarkable. At ten years of age I was admitted to the school at Brienne, and afterwards to that of Paris. My early education was what is usually given in the military schools of France.†

I succeeded in whatever I undertook, because I wished to do so. My will was strong, and my character decided; this has given me an advantage over all others. The nature of the will depends upon the genius of the individual; it is not every one that can be master of himself. If there has sometimes been an appearance of irresolution in my actions,

---

* The author here acknowledges that he has copied several pages from the pretended manuscript from St. Helena. It is no plagiarism, but an avowed imitation of the original.

† It is worthy of remark, that Wellington, who was born in the same year with Napoleon, received his military education at the military school of Angers in France, about the same time that Napoleon was a pupil at Paris.

it did not proceed from any indecision of character, but it was because my strong imagination presented to me, with the rapidity of lightning, all the various phases of the subject. At school I applied myself to studies that I thought might be most useful to me, particularly to history and mathematics; the former develops genius, and the latter regulates its action. My intellectual faculties expanded without much effort; my conception was quick and lively, my memory strong, my judgment cool and decided. I thought quicker than others, so that I had always time for reflection. In this consisted my depth. My mind was too active to be amused with the ordinary diversions of youth. But I did not, as some have asserted, entirely avoid these juvenile recreations, though I generally found something else to interest me. This disposition often left me to the solitude of my own thoughts, and at length grew into a habit, which continued through all the vicissitudes of my life.

First Appointment to the Army.—Being destined to the military service, I received the commission of lieutenant of artillery four years before the Revolution. I have never received any title with so much interest as I did this. It was then the height of my ambition to wear, at some future day, two epaulettes *à bouillons*, and a general of artillery appeared to me the *ne plus ultra* of human greatness. But if I was not ambitious of power, I was already avaricious of renown; for I conceived the idea of writing a history of the war sustained by Corsica for her independence. I proposed this to Paoli, asking him for the necessary information. Probably, a historian of eighteen years of age, did not inspire him with much confidence, and he paid no attention to the proposition. My mortification at this result was soon indemnified by my promotion to the captaincy of a company. This was in 1789. When the Revolution broke out, my sphere of action seemed to enlarge. It would be superfluous to speak here of the impression first made on me by this great catastrophe; but for the better understanding of the course I afterwards pursued, it may not be amiss to give a simple summary of the events which preceded my promotion to the command of the army of Italy.

France before the Revolution.—No reign ever commenced under such happy auspices as that of the virtuous Louis XVI. Ten years after the ridiculous war of 1756–63, France, by means of her alliances with Austria, Piedmont, Naples, and Spain, held the balance of power on the continent, entirely controlled the Mediterranean, and disputed with the English the supremacy of the ocean. And every thing seemed to promise that, profiting by these close alliances with the half of Europe, she would soon obtain the first rank upon the seas. Her only rival here was England. The alarm has been sounded throughout Europe against my ambition; but my relative power was never so formidable as that of Louis XVI. I occupied more territory, it is true, but this occupation was a hostile one, since it was contested by the half of Europe, and even by a part of the people I had conquered; whereas, under Louis XVI., these same people were voluntarily the allies of France.

Coup d'œil of the Revolution.—The glorious war in America was the first result of this happy position of France; and most probably we should have broken the maritime sceptre of England, had it not been for the unskillfulness of our octogenarian prime-minister (Maurepas,) who knew better how to make puns and madrigals on naval battles, than to direct affairs of state. But, in spite of our faults, England lost her fine American provinces, and was on the point of also losing the Antilles. Unfortunately this war produced results which no one could anticipate. It occasioned debts, and to pay these, it was necessary to include as taxable property, the immense wealth of the noblesse and clergy.

The ministry dared to advise this, but the clergy and nobility refused to submit. Thus, by their own egotism, these noted defenders of the altar and the throne, sapped the foundation of that throne for which they pretended so much devotion. M. Vergennes died at this time, and his successors permitted the English party to get the better of us in Holland, and lost all the advantages of our connection with Austria, by rejecting the projects of Joseph II., and inducing him to form an alliance with Russia. These two errors destroyed all the influence which we had acquired in Europe, through the policy of Choiseul, and the feeble ministry made itself despicable both at home and abroad. The financial embarrassments growing worse, it was thought necessary to have recourse to the *States-general*. Here were opposed the aristocratic classes, who were blinded by their privileges, and a *tiers-état*, who asked the abolition, or at least a modification, of these privileges. From the clash of these interests, which ought to have been avoided, sprung the Revolution. Feudal rights could not be sustained against a *tiers-état* as rich and enlightened as that of France, at the close of the eighteenth century. For twenty years, the Revolution had existed in all minds; in the magistracy, in the nobility, in the army; even in the court itself. The government had become the target for all wounded vanities, and petty ambitions; some opposed to it the aristocratic pride of the Fronde; others, the democratic pretensions of the *Niveleurs*. But had it been in wise and able hands, this effervescence of heads could never have effected a revolution. The political horizon of France was covered with inflammable materials which should have been carefully guarded from the slightest incendiary spark; government, on the contrary, itself applied the match. It brought together the opposing parties, and provoked them to a contest. It mortified the *noblesse*, irritated the people, disputed with the magistrates, humiliated the army, and, to cap the climax of folly, ordered the troops to allow themselves to be maltreated by the populace!

When great public interests are at stake, and a revolution becomes inevitable, a skillful chief should place himself at its head, sacrifice his own life, rather than suffer it to pass certain limits. Revolutions spring from opinions of interests. When interests founded on justice and reason are properly satisfied, opinions become calm of themselves, (if we except religious opinions). But such were not the measures pursued by the ministry of Louis XVI. Opposed by the magistrates and the nobility, it fell into the hands of Necker, who, to form a party for himself, doubled the representative power of the *tiers-état*. This measure was a good one, but the mode of executing it dangerous. The court divided itself into two parties, forming two governments; the one for Necker and reform, and the other opposing both. States-general, assembled with the duplication of the *tiers-état*, and vote *per capita* in a single assembly, could not fail to produce the most fatal results.

Decisive Events of the 17th, 20th, and 23d of June, 1789.— The three orders were to vote separately; the *tiers-état* insisted upon their all voting together and by head, because, being now the most numerous body, this would give them a decided advantage over the others. The *noblesse* and clergy refused, the *tiers-état* constituted themselves, on the seventeenth of June, the *National Assembly*. Their place of sitting was closed against them on the twentieth; they assembled in the *Jeu-de-Paume*, or Tennis court, and took an oath not to separate till they had given a constitution to France. This was the turning point of the Revolution. The King should have dissolved this body, which had now constituted itself the government, in violation of all the laws of the kingdom. If anything could have prevented the

Revolution, it was this measure, executed with firmness, and accompanied with just and necessary reforms. His design was a good one, but he had not the courage to execute it.

On the twenty-third, Louis XVI. goes in person to the Assembly, declares it illegal, and, while making some concessions, orders the deputies to dissolve. The King withdraws, but the deputies do not obey him. The grand-master of ceremonies summons them to leave the chamber. Mirabeau declares that they will leave only when driven out at the point of the bayonet. Instead of forcing obedience, the King permits them to remain, and even orders the clergy and nobility to join them. To Necker, who advised this measure, must be attributed all the evils resulting from it. Many absurd things have been said about the influence of "philosophers and philosophy," in producing the Revolution. If Louis XVI. had taken Mirabeau at his word, it is probable that the States-general had gone home, like their predecessors, and all the Voltaires in the world could not have changed the face of France. But the Revolution was consummated the moment the throne trusted itself in the hands of an Assembly ruled by ambitious demagogues. Mirabeau, Sièyes, and the leaders of the Assembly, escaping the punishment due to state criminals, had only to demolish stone after stone, the monarchical edifice; for them, there was no retreat; they must conquer or die, and they conquered the more easily, as they undertook everything in the name of the government whose authority they had usurped, and by the hands of a mob which they had armed in all the forms of legality.

Too much importance has been attributed, by those who mistake the effect for the cause, to the action of the people in this Revolution. A revolution is soon consummated; it continues but a few days. The mass of the people gradually adopt its measures in proportion as the factions are crowned with success, and menaces from abroad render desperate the situation of the insurrectionary leaders, and force them to unchain the furies of demagogism. *If I had been a minister of Louis XVI., the Revolution would have terminated on the twenty-third of June, 1789. With the same hand that overthrew the enemies of the throne, I would have restored right and justice to the nation.*

Victorious in the events of the seventeenth and the twenty-third of June, the chiefs of the *tiers-état* had little difficulty in effecting the victory of July fourteenth. They were supported by a powerful army of National Guards, and, in a short time, by the troops of the line. Thus far, no great evil had been produced; on the contrary, the substitution of a national government, in the place of a system of court-favoritism, might have effected much good. But unfortunately, the popular leaders now attempted to consolidate their own power, by reducing the royal authority to a mere shadow. This was the great fault which overthrew the state-edifice. There was more reason in attacking the prerogatives of the clergy and noblesse. These classes resisted, but were overthrown by the mass of the people; in this struggle they lost much that really belonged to them, but instead of trusting to time, for a restoration of just rights, they imprudently called in foreign aid, and thus denationalized their cause.

It being rumored that the court was collecting some of its faithful regiments at Versailles, the revolutionary leaders, fearing that the king might escape their power, determined to remove him to Paris, and place him in a situation dependent on the populace. To secure this object, the insurrections of the fifth and sixth of October were incited. Lafayette, at the head of 20,000 National Guards, repaired to Versailles, and the disgraceful excesses committed in the palace cast a stigma upon the character of the Revolution. The King was escorted from Versailles to the Tuileries, by Lafayette, who was there directed to guard his person; for the French guards belonged to the factions, and the body-guards were discharged, so that his guard was reduced to a single regiment of Swiss.

The members of the Assembly, for the better attainment of their object, forbade any interference of the crown in the discussions upon the constitution, limiting it to the simple power of *Veto*. This unfortunate word was borrowed from the Polish Diets, and it is astonishing that the legislators of France had derived so little wisdom from the lessons of history. The *Veto* power was different in the two cases, but it led to the same result—the subjugation of the crown to the tyranny of factions. During all these discussions, the good King, Louis XVI., remained at the Tuileries, a passive spectator of events—more like a criminal than a sovereign. Persuaded by the solicitations of the *émigrés* to join the foreign coalition, he fled from Paris, in April, 1791; but, with his queen and children, was arrested at Varennes; Bouillé offered to rescue him, but the vacillating monarch preferred being led back captive to Paris; he returned to the Tuileries a prisoner, his royal authority being previously suspended. His departure was an error, and his return a calamity.

Having taken the first false step, the Assembly continued to wander further and further from the path of wise legislation. It formed the Jacobin clubs, and allowed their continuance after they were evidently dangerous to public tranquillity. When these took the helm of government, the throne was lost. With great disinterestedness, the Assembly declared its members ineligible to a re-election. This abnegation was worthy of Spartans, but was the height of folly. If eight hundred of the most influential men of France were disfranchised from exercising all public functions, their successors could be found only in the lowest ranks. Against the formal attacks of the new Legislative Assembly upon the throne, were arrayed the coalition and Coblentz; the one to maintain the throne, and the other to profit by its ruin. France was invaded. The revolutionary leaders responded by the cry of vengeance and death.

Grand Coalition against France.—The origin of the grand coalition against France, is still somewhat doubtful, though it is supposed to have begun in the conferences of the Emperor Leopold, and the Count d'Artois, at Mantua. At first it was thought best to resort to an intervention of the princes allied to the royal family, that is, of Spain, Sardinia, and Austria. The Emperor Leopold proposed a Congress of Nations; but the Assembly, influenced by patriotic pride, or perhaps, yielding to a mere temporary effervescence, declared any Frenchman, who should consent to submit the laws of France to the decision of a foreign Congress, to be a traitor to his country. It was afterwards proposed to place Gustavus III., King of Sweden, at the head of the coalition, because, having received assistance from Louis XV. to rescue him from the usurped power of the Senate of Stockholm, he would be the most suitable person to render the same disinterested service to Louis XVI. But, Gustavus having been assassinated, Frederick William, of Prussia, for some unaccountable reason, was placed at the head of the league. It would be difficult to explain why this monarch should wish to interfere in the internal affairs of France. England, of course, was enchanted at the embarrassment of her neighbor, for the greater the internal difficulties of France, the greater the advantages which she could derive from them. Russia, also, rejoiced at this state of affairs, for it left her at liberty to pursue her aggrandizements in other quarters. She expressed a lively interest in the success of the league, but took good care not to appear in the affairs of the west, till she had consummated the partition in Poland.

Russia and Poland.—Towards that partition, Catharine* now directed all her policy. The reformers in Poland acted upon principles the reverse of those in Paris. Instead of weakening the power of the throne which was proclaimed, on the third of May, 1791, hereditary in the House of Saxony, they endeavored to give it that importance which alone could effect its preservation. Those very powers who opposed France for weakening the influence of the crown, attacked Poland for endeavoring to increase it; a contradiction that proves interest to have been the basis of all their actions. Some of the factious nobility, under pretense of securing the public liberty, formed a league, at Targowitz, and implored the intervention of Catharine; guaranteeing the constitution of 1775, she marched an army into Poland for the ostensible purpose of sustaining the constitution, but in reality, to get possession of the important places of the kingdom. The Poles solicited the assistance of Prussia, and Frederick William marched his troops to Thorn and Posen, in order to get these places into his own possession. The wisdom of the confederates of Targowitz may well rival that of the councillors of Louis XVI!

War with Austria.—The National Assembly, certain of a general preparation to invade France, determined to take the initiative. It had many friends in Belgium, where the Austrian yoke had created insurrection, under Joseph II. Explanations were demanded of Austria for her great armaments,

---

* Catharine II., Empress of Russia, was born at Stettin, in 1729. Her father was a Prussian field-marshal. She was married in 1745, to Peter, the nephew of the Empress Elizabeth, whose successor he became in 1761. Peter III., soon became estranged from his wife, on account of her infamous conduct, but Catharine consoled herself with a variety of lovers. A conspiracy, headed by one of her favorites, Orloff, resulted in the death of Peter in prison. Catharine continued to reign till 1792, when she died of apoplexy. "With all the weakness of her sex, and with a love of pleasure carried to licentiousness, she combined the firmness and talent becoming a powerful sovereign. She favored distinguished authors, and affected great partiality for the French philosophers."

but she replied only by menaces. Dumouriez, the Minister of Foreign Affairs, returned these menaces by a declaration of war, and the invasion of the Netherlands; but our armies were betrayed, and defeated by a handful of Germans under Beaulieu, in April, 1792.

The Prussians invade Champagne.—Three months after this, the Duke of Brunswick, at the head of 60,000 Prussians, and 10,000 *émigrés*, and preceded by a proclamation, threatening with fire and sword all who should oppose him, set out from Coblentz, and entered Champagne by Thionville. To facilitate the march of this army, the ministers of Louis XVI., had stripped this frontier of its garrisons, and scattered our soldiers upon the Rhine and the Scheldt. Mallet-Dupan was the agent of the Court for arranging with the enemy the march of the allied armies, and Bertrand de Moleville, then Minister of the Navy, has had the assurance to boast of it; a fact not to be forgotten in history.

The Republic Proclaimed.—The allied armies advanced to the gates of Verdun, and entered that town without opposition. But the manifesto of the Duke of Brunswick, produced results very different from what was expected; in Paris it was answered by the terrible insurrection of August tenth; the throne was destroyed; the provisionary council established; the King shut up in the Temple; the Republic proclaimed, and a national convention convoked to form a charter. The Jacobins elect to this new Assembly their most violent partisans: placed between the armies of Europe and the scaffold, these demagogues plunge deeper and deeper into anarchy; they remove all restraints from the populace, and utterly destroy all social order.

Retreat of the Prussians.—But on the other hand, a noble love of country inflames all generous hearts. Indignant at the menaces of a handful of Prussians, 60,000 volunteers rush to Champagne, whither the provisionary executive council sends Dumouriez with the army of Sedan, Kellerman with that of Metz, and Beurnonville with that of the North. These forces concentrate in the defile of Argonne, which now becomes the Thermopylæ of France. The Prussians in attempting to turn us, are themselves divided, and forced to retreat without scarcely drawing a sword. Custine, departing from Landau, takes possession of Mayence in their rear, and advances upon the Lahn, threatening to destroy the only bridge, that of Coblentz, and thus cut off their retreat. This success saves Lille, whose heroic citizens have bravely sustained a most terrible bombardment.

Invasion of Belgium.—Dumouriez, having thus rid himself of the Prussians, instead of descending the Meuse with his 60,000 men, and cutting off the Austrians in the Netherlands, deliberately advances from Verdun to Valenciennes to attack their line of retreat. Clairfayt and Beaulieu effect their escape, by no other miracle than the stupidity of Dumouriez. Our armies are no less successful in the Alps; Savoy, and the Comté of Nice, are conquered after a semblance of assistance on the part of the Piedmontese. Of all our operations, the ill-directed expedition against the Island of Sardinia is the only failure.

Death of Louis XVI.—The victories of Valmy and Jemmapes, and the conquest of Belgium, completely turned the heads of the Jacobins; the fatal act of the twenty-first of January, was consummated. By destroying a virtuous, but feeble King, they thought to shake off forever the yoke of monarchy, as if the royal victim could have no successors. His death was not only a crime, but a great error; the very terms of the constitution forbade his execution; and, even had he deserved capital punishment, our political and maritime relations with Spain should have caused his life to be spared. But the factious Assembly was incapable of taking any common-sense view of the diplomatic relations of the country.

War with Spain, Holland, and England.—The execution of Louis XVI. could not fail to shatter the very foundations of our political relations. France, recently so brilliantly allied, is put under the ban of all Europe. The Court of Spain, which has heretofore avoided all interference in the war against us, now joins it with the indignant cry of vengeance. Naples and Holland follow her example. The blind demagogues of the Gironde, in their noisy vociferations against the tyrants of Vienna, Berlin, and Madrid, pretend that they can easily overcome them, *since England, the natural friend of freedom, will lend her assistance to the free people of France!* Pitt answers these absurdities by congratulating England, in full Parliament, on the prosperity and greatness that his country is to derive from the internal embarrassments of France! He takes no part in the first campaign of 1792; remains a passive spectator of the tenth of August and the twenty-first of January, and allows the throne to be destroyed, and the unfortunate monarch to be executed; he waits for the quarrel to take a political turn, which very soon occurs. The French having invaded the states of Sardinia and Belgium, and having proclaimed the freedom of the Scheldt, England feigns to join the coalition, merely to guaranty the treaty of Utrecht and as the ally of Holland; but she has lost nothing by this delay, and she soon becomes the head of the war.

Dumouriez driven from Belgium.—At the beginning of 1793, affairs take a different turn; Dumouriez leaves the Austrians on the Roër, near Juliers, when within ten leagues of the Rhine, and commits the still more ridiculous fault of invading Holland, with these forces still on his right and on his communications; he dreams of establishing a republic or a kingdom in the Netherlands, by means of which he can return to Paris, and dictate laws to the Jacobins. He imagines that England and Prussia, intimate allies of the House of Orange, will permit the expulsion of the Stadtholder; that he can create his Batavia, in spite of the reigning sovereign, in spite of France, and even in spite of the coalition! This project forcibly reminds one of the Tales of the Thousand-and-one-Nights. Many think the project a mere invention of Dumouriez after his emigration, and that the threatened invasion of Holland was made by order of the council to support the negotiation of Maret, and to induce England to formally recognize the French Republic. Be this as it may, Dumouriez is soon punished for the wild scheme. The Austrians fall upon his right towards Aix-la-Chapelle and Liege; he returns in haste to fight the battle of Nerwinde; his army reach Valenciennes in great disorder; his expeditionary corps is exceedingly fortunate in escaping to Antwerp, even at the sacrifice of the garrisons left to guard his chimerical conquests.

Treats with the Austrians.—Invectives are thundered against him from the tribune of the Convention. To save himself, he treats with the Prince of Coburg, and threatens to return to Paris at the head of his army. The four deputies, and the Minister Beurnonville, sent to investigate his affairs, are arrested and turned over to the Austrians. His soldiers refuse to obey him, and even attempt to place their general in arrest; they fire upon his escort, and drive him into the Scheldt near Condé, where he joins Coburg. Exposed to the hatred of both parties, he afterwards retired to London, and published his military plans, which have become an object of ridicule for all posterity. Dumouriez was, nevertheless, a man of resource and considerable talent.

Committee of Public Safety.—The occasion of danger to France is seized upon by the Jacobin chiefs to establish a Committee of Public Safety, and to invest it with dictatorial power. Robespierre and Danton are the leaders of this new movement.

Allies lay Siege to Mayence and Valenciennes. — While the events just related were taking place on the Meuse, the King of Prussia crossed the Rhine with strong reinforcements, gave battle to Custine, and laid siege to Mayence, which is heroically defended by Kleber, Meunier, and Aubert Dubayet. The Duke of York and the Prince of Coburg, profiting by the flight of Dumouriez, besieged Condé. Dampierre, in attempting to succor it, is defeated and slain. The allies force the camp of Famars, and lay siege to Valenciennes. At the South the Spaniards under Riccardos invade Roussillon, and the Sardinians enter Savoy; the interior is equally disturbed; the immense military requisitions become the pretext for a formidable insurrection in La Vendée, and 60,000 royalists in arms collect at Nantes and Angers.

Fall of the Girondists. — Danger rather exasperates than frightens the Jacobins. In their eyes moderation becomes treason, and the Girondists, whose brilliant utopian theories overturned the throne, are treated as royalists. On the thirty-first of May the Convention is decimated, and those eloquent declaimers, who have been mistaken for statemen, expiate upon the scaffold the crime of having been too sincerely attached to vain theories. Robespierre, Danton, Marat, and the populace, think themselves the masters of France; but France does not acknowledge their dictation.

England heads the Coalition. — During these violent and frantic operations of the Jacobins, England pursues, with firm and measured steps, the path marked out by her profound policy. Not satisfied with having Russia, Spain, and Holland as her allies, and forcing, with the squadrons of Catharine, Sweden and Denmark to renounce their neutral rights, she sweeps the Mediterranean with the squadrons of Charles IV., and takes into her pay the troops of all powers which will barter their soldiers for money; thus using the spoils stripped from the Nabobs of Mysore, to make flow rivers of European blood! This same government, that the foolish Brissot declared some months before, as the surest support of the French constitution, and that Dumouriez wished to make the arbiter of order in France, had become the head of the coalition against us. Its emissaries were every where preaching crusades against France, with as much fervor as the inspired monks of the middle ages. On the fourteenth of July, at the camp of Mayence, Lord Beauchamp and Luchesini signed a treaty of close alliance between England and Prussia; a treaty of subsidy had already, in April, been negotiated by Lord Elgin with Hesse, for eight thousand men. Lord Yarmouth negotiated a new treaty with Hesse-Cassel on the twenty-third of August, for four thousand men, another with Hesse-Darmstadt on the fifth of October, for three thousand men, and soon afterwards a fourth, with the Grand-duke of Baden. Lord Grenville had concluded a still more important treaty, on the twenty-fifth of April, with the Count de Front, the Sardinian minister, by which Sardinia, for the annual payment of five millions, agreed to keep a standing army of fifty thousand men; on the thirtieth of August, the same English minister formed a treaty of an alliance with the Court of Austria; Lord St. Helens concluded one with Godoy, Duke of Alçudia, and minister of Spain, on the twenty-fifth of May; Lord Aukland with the Stadtholder, and Chevalier Hamilton with Naples, on the twelfth of July. If we add to these treaties the intrigues of Hervey, at Leghorn, of Drake, at Genoa, of Hayles, at Copenhagen, and of Fitzgerald, in Switzerland, we may form some conception of the astonishing activity of the English diplomatic corps, the sophistry of the French government since 1790, and the incalculable danger to which a nation is exposed when its foreign interests are intrusted to a tumultuous assembly. Thus England, holding all the threads of this immense web, managed the affairs of Europe to suit her own will, gave and took away provinces, and even directed the military operations of the other powers by her accredited agents at the different headquarters. To this skilful preparation the Convention opposed its formidable energy, and the ridiculous decree of September seventh, proclaiming Pitt the enemy of the human race!

Affairs of Poland.—We will now direct our attention to the affairs of Poland. Kaminieck, the last and principal strong-hold of the Polish patriots, was surrendered to the Russians, on the second of May, with two hundred pieces of cannon. The southern provinces then gave in their submission, and twelve thousand men swore allegiance to Catharine. This event, and the dispersion of the rest of the army, left no chance for successful resistance. Taking advantage of the factions of the Polish Diet to punish Poland for the domination of the Jagellons at Moscow, and the threats made during her recent war in Turkey, Catharine prevented the reëstablishment of a rival power on her borders by a second partition of the country. While we regret the fate of this brave and patriotic people, we can not fail to admire the perseverance with which the Czarina pursued her objects, and the skill with which she profited by the dissensions of the Poles to increase her own power and territory.

Of the Ottoman Porte.—The Ottoman Porte, through the influence of the coalition, and the *émigrés*, had hesitated, at the close of 1792, to recognize the French Republic. Semonville was sent as ambassador to endeavor to restore our friendly relations with that ancient ally. To reach his destination, it was necessary for this minister to go by Venice, crossing Switzerland and the Valteline. Maret was sent at the same time to the Court of Naples, to treat for the liberty of Marie-Antoinette, and her retention as a hostage of peace. These two diplomatic agents took the road to Coire together; but the government of the Grisons, influenced by the Salis and the Court of Austria, arrested them on lake Maggiore, and, in violation of the law of nations, delivered them to the imperialists, who cast them into the prisons of Mantua, for no other reason than their attachment to republican doctrines. The Barbary powers, influenced by the example of the Grand Seigneur, and the instigations of the English, refused to have any relations with the new Republic.

Situation of France.—If the political situation of France at this moment seems desperate, her military affairs are no less discouraging. From the Alps to the Pyrenees, from the Rhine to the Ocean, from the Rhone to the banks of the Loire, the tri-colored flag is driven back before the numerous but ill-directed hosts of its enemies. Beauharnais, directed to raise the siege of Mayence, arrives too late to prevent its surrender. Custine refuses to risk a battle to save Valenciennes, because his army is composed of recruits. These generals, accused of a want of energy, are led to the scaffold.* But their execution does not prevent Mayence and Valenciennes from falling before the combined attacks of

---

* Viscount Alexander Beauharnais, born in 1760, at Martinique, served with distinction as major, in the French forces under Rochambeau, which aided the United States in their Revolutionary War. At the breaking out of the French Revolution, he was chosen a member of the National Assembly, of which he was for some time President. In 1793, he was general of the army of the Rhine, and afterwards Minister of War. His restoration to military command led to his death. He was the first husband of Josephine Tascher de la Tagerie, who was afterwards Empress of the French. The Marquis Francis de Beauharnais, elder brother of the general, sided with the Bourbons, and joined the army of Condé to fight against the armies of the Republic. He was recalled from banishment by Napoleon, who made him Senator, and afterwards ambassador to Spain. He died at Paris, in 1819.

Count Adam Philip Custine, was born, at Metz, in 1740. He served in the Seven Years War, and afterwards in America, aiding us in our Revolutionary War. He held several important commands in the earlier wars of the French Revolution, but was guillotined under the false charge of treason.—*Encyclopedia Americana.*

Austria, Prussia, England, and Holland. Bellegrade surrenders to the Spanish; La Vendée is on fire, and sixty thousand victorious royalists threaten the Convention in its own bloody halls. Opposition to the demagogues of the Convention arms Bordeaux, Lyons, Marseilles, and Caen. The Austro-Sardinian forces cross the Alps and offer aid to these insurgents. The rest of France, instead of sustaining the Convention, seems ready to throw off its yoke. The army, everywhere inferior to the enemy in numbers, without discipline, and commanded by unskillful chiefs, is upon the point of dissolution; and, as a climax to our misfortunes, our colonies are lost. No government was ever in a more frightful position; never was a nation nearer the brink of ruin.

Energy of the Convention.—But while every human probability seemed to indicate the speedy fall of France, the energy and rage of the Convention increased with every new defeat and every new danger; and the recent partition of Poland, by showing to the French what might be the fate of their own country, produced a still more miraculous effect than the Brunswick proclamation during the preceding campaign. The horrible atrocities of the Reign of Terror, the fear of seeing France humiliated and dismembered, and the powerful motives of patriotism, honor, and independence, all combined to produce the immense results of this campaign. The character of the war was entirely changed. The rights of the *noblesse*, the counter-revolution, and the royal prerogative were no longer the motives of the coalition; nor were the rights of the *tiers-état* the moving power with the republicans. The kings saw anarchy overthrowing all their thrones; the Jacobins saw safety only in anarchy; the former trembled at the fate of Louis XVI.; the latter, at the retributive justice of the blood of their slaughtered victims; the sovereigns saw the revolutionary axe suspended over their heads, like the sword of Damocles; the chiefs of the Mountain could see no escape from the scaffold, but in the ruins with which they covered the soil of France.

The long siege and bombardment of Valenciennes seemed to depress the energy of the Allies, while it animated the courage of the French. Four months had elapsed since the flight of Dumouriez, and still the republican soil, left defenceless by his defection, was scarcely touched. If the overthrow of one of the frontier barriers cost so much toil, when could the Allies expect to reach Paris! The influence of these fortified places, in retarding the operations of the enemy, was well understood by military men, like Carnot, Prieur, Dubois-Crancé, and even those who were unacquainted with the principles of the military art, derived hope from reading the numerous memoirs deposited in the archives of the War Office, on the great efforts which the taking of Lille and Landrecies had cost Eugene and Marlborough. The Allies had now no commander like these great captains, but the French nation, more vigorous than when under the domination of a weak king, only wanted time to display its superior means of defense. Thus, by a mixture of energy, national honor, and the desire of self-preservation, the most intelligent members of the Convention retained some hope of success, and they resolved, either to save themselves with the Republic, or to be buried beneath its ruins. Nevertheless, the fall of the first two frontier barriers, the evacuation of the Camp of Cæsar, and the approach of the Austrians to the gates of Saint-Quentin, soon proved to them that danger was more imminent than was at first supposed. Barrère declared that unless Paris should a second time strike the enemy before Cambray, the country would be lost! Danton carried a decree of death against any soldier who should desert his flag. To avoid the chances of defeat at the new election, and to perpetuate their own power, the

Jacobins obtained the suspension of the charter, and established a revolutionary government in its place.

Carnot a Member of the Committee of Public Safety.—Seeing the necessity of having, at this crisis, the services of men familiar with military affairs, they added on the fourteenth of August, Carnot and Prieur to the Committee of Public Safety. On the same day, the Convention, on Barrère's motion, made the following proclamation to the French people,—a singular compound of bad language and powerful thought.

"To arms, Frenchmen! at the moment when a people of friends and brothers are locked in each other's embraces, the despots of Europe violate your property and lay waste your frontiers. To arms! To arms!! To arms!!! Liberty calls for the aid of all who have just now sworn to defend her. A second time, tyrants and slaves trample upon the soil of a sovereign people. The first time, one half of their sacrilegious armies here found a tomb; now, let them all perish; let their bones whiten on our plains; let them serve as trophies on battle-fields made fertile with their blood. To arms, Frenchmen! cover yourselves with glory the most resplendent, in defending that adored liberty whose first tranquil days will scatter over you, and the generations of your descendants, the germs of wealth and prosperity."

But these proclamations and decrees produced very little effect. Danger daily increased; civil war assumed a more sinister aspect; the authority of the Convention was recognized in scarcely a third of France, and even this portion was exhausted by its former efforts. The leaders, in their despair, resorted to the most frightful system of terror.

Decree for a Levée-en-Masse.—On the twenty-third of August, Barrère ascended the tribune, and proposed the decree of a *levée-en-masse* of the whole French people. This, he said, was the only means that could save the country; having eloquently addressed the Convention on the insufficiency of ordinary measures, in a time of such great danger, he presented the decree in the following words:—

"Until the enemies of the Republic be driven from the territory of France, every citizen shall be in permanent requisition for military service. The young men will march to the battle field; the married men will forge arms, and transport military munitions; the women will make tents and clothes for the soldiers, and attend the sick in hospitals; the hands of children will be employed in making lint for the wounded; and the aged, imitating the example of ancient virtue, will cause themselves to be carried into the public places to animate the courage of the warriors, to inculcate hatred to kings, and the unity of the Republic. Let the national edifices be converted into barracks, the public squares into work-shops, the cellars into manufactories of saltpetre; let the artillery and musketry be used exclusively against the enemy; the fowling-pieces, swords, and pikes will suffice for the service of the interior; let the saddle-horses be furnished for cavalry, the draught-horses for the artillery and provision trains. No man can be replaced in the service for which he is required. Daily will the artist labor at the public work-shops, and the citizen do duty at the head-quarters of his district; every public functionary will be at his post. The Committee of Public Safety will prepare all things for defense, and place at the disposal of the Minister of War the sum of thirty millions. The levy shall be general, and the organized battalion of each district will inscribe on its banner:—*The French people in arms against tyrants.*"

Revolutionary Government.—The decree was voted with universal acclamation. Five days afterwards, the constitution of the twenty-fourth of June was suspended, and the

Revolutionary Government established in its stead. At this crisis arrived the news of the surrender of Toulon to the English and Spaniards. The loss of a place of such vast importance in a maritime, military, and political view, commanding the communications of the royalists of the Rhone, and serving as a base of operations for the allied armies, caused the greatest alarm.

System of Terror.—But the revolutionary energy increases with national disasters. The commune of Paris, directed by Chaumette and instigated by the leaders of the Committee, demands a revolutionary army and twelve revolutionary tribunals with full powers. Barrère proposes these measures in the name of the Committee of Public Safety; and Danton moves that the sum of a hundred millions be placed at the disposal of the Minister of War. These motions are passed into laws, and they announce to the French people that the only means of escaping the revolutionary axe is to fly to the frontiers. Honor can be found only beneath the military uniform, and safety from the guillotine only in the battlefield. Fear of the revolutionary army increases the national forces, and it is now less difficult to procure soldiers than to find generals capable of commanding them. But good fortune supplies the place of skill; and the Allies favor us by adopting the most ill-concerted measures.

Faults of the Allies.—No sooner are they masters of Valenciennes and Mayence, than they adopt the most eccentric lines of operations. The English under the Duke of York march against Dunkirk; the Austrians under the Prince of Cobourg besiege Quesnoy and Maubeurge; the Prussians attack Landau and cover Kaiserlautern; the Austrians under Wurmser force the lines of Weissemburg, take Fort Louis, and threaten Strasburg.

Driven from the French Territory.—Inspired by the genius of Carnot* the Committee directs Houchard to concentrate the army of the North, cut off the English from Furnes, and drive them into the sea. He defeats them at Hondschote, saves Dunkirk, and then overthrows the Dutch at Menin. But he does not drive the enemy into the sea, as directed in his instructions; he is therefore condemned to death for having gained only half a victory and for having attacked in front, when he could have easily reached the enemy's communications. His army under Jourdan marches to the assistance of Mauberge. Cobourg is besieging this place with forty thousand men, and Clairfayt covers it with twenty-five thousand more; the army of observation is cut off and defeated at Watignies, two leagues from the besieging army, which retires in great haste. A part of the victorious army under Hoche flies to the rescue of Landau. It is at first repulsed by the formidable position of the Duke of Brunswick at Kaiserslautern, but Hoche skilfully defiles through the valley of Annweiler against the right of the Austrians, defeating them at Wertheim, Reichskoffen, and Geiersberg, then forming a junction with the left of Pichegru. The Allies are thrown back upon Manheim; and the French forces, by their skilful maneuvers, gain a merited success. Kellerman has reduced Lyons and driven the Sardinians back into Piedmont; Dugommier, with one division of the

* "The royalists and their foreign allies have never been able to forgive Carnot's signal military exploits during the war of the French Revolution; and affected to confound him with Robespierre, as if he had been the accomplice of that monster in the Reign of Terror. Situated as Carnot then was he had but one alternative:—either to continue in the Committee of Public Safety, co-operating with men he abhorred, and lending his name to their worst deeds, while he was fain to close his eyes upon their details, or to leave the direction of the tremendous war which France was then waging for her existence, in the hands of men so utterly unfit to conduct the machine for an instant, that immediate conquest, in its worst shape, must have been the consequence of his desertion. There may be many an honest man who would have preferred death to any place in Robespierre's committee, but it is fair to state that in all probability Carnot saved his country by persevering in the management of the war."—*Edinburgh Review.*

army of Nice, and forty thousand National Guards, has retaken Toulon; Kleber, Marceau, and Canclaux have, by the greatest efforts, subdued La Vendée, where French blood, shed by French hands, was flowing in great torrents.

Death of Marie Antoinette.—But the glory of these victories was tarnished by the crimes of the Jacobins, who did not hesitate to imbue their hands in the blood of the beautiful Queen of Louis XVI. Marie Antoinette, from being an Austrian by birth, and the daughter of Maria Theresa, was charged with having plotted the coalition against France, but even this excuse was unnecessary to Fouquier Tainville and the other tigers of the revolutionary tribunal, for sending her to the scaffold.

Political Results of the Revolution.—France, in spite of her victories, was exhausting the elements of her strength against her natural allies; for, in addition to England, she found herself at war with Russia, Austria, Prussia, the German Empire, Holland, Italy, and Spain; with the United States of America alone, was she at peace. Her old allies, Austria and Spain, were now by the side of England at the head of her most violent enemies. In the meantime, the spirit of liberty and equality was destroying her colonial possessions. At Saint Domingo, the most horrible anarchy prevailed. The partisans of emancipation, enrolling themselves under the English flag, stirred up the mortal hatred of castes, and the populace, maddened by the burning passions of African blood and southern sun, committed horrors even surpassing the ferocious conquerors of the Caribbean Islands.

Napoleon appointed Chef-de-Batallion.—Thanks to the numerous levies, and the consequently rapid promotion, I was proposed, in 1792, as a commandant of a battalion of National volunteers for the Sardinian expedition. I accepted the appointment. They laughed at me for this in the artillery, but I pursued my own course, regardless of their sneers;

and on my return from the expedition I rejoined the artillery, with the rank of superior officer. I was then twenty-four years of age.

His Republican Notions.—Much has been said about my republicanism at this period of my career. It is not strange that a young man, at his entrance into public life, should espouse the maxims which he has learned to admire in the Greeks and Romans. At that time I was sincerely a republican; experience has since changed my opinions. But I have always preserved the idea that strength in the authority of a government may be easily united with the most liberal principles in its administration.

Siege of Toulon.—Previous to the siege of Toulon my life was inactive and insignificant. I was then chief-of-battalion, and served as second in command of the artillery, and in that capacity had some influence upon the results of the siege. In August, 1793, when treason surrendered Toulon and our fleet to the Allies, the white flag was floating over Lyons; civil war was raging in Languedoc and Provence; a victorious Spanish army had crossed the Pyrenees and inundated Roussillon; and a Piedmontese army had crossed the Alps and was at the gates of Chambéry and Antibes. If thirty thousand Sardinians, Neapolitans, Spaniards, and English had united at Toulon, with the twelve thousand "*fédérés*," this combined army of forty thousand men could have been marched upon Lyons, connecting its right with the Piedmontese, and its left with the Spanish forces. But the Allies in taking Toulon did not appreciate the value of their conquest. Six weeks had been spent by the French in collecting forces and material for the siege; and on the fifteenth of October, a council of war was formed at Ollioules with Gasparin, a member of the Convention, for President. A plan of attack, drawn up by the celebrated d'Arçon, for the Committee of Fortifications, was read to the council. I objected to the plan and proposed another more simple. It was probable that the Allies would not abandon twelve thousand men in Toulon, if we could get possession of the two forts which commanded the outer extremity of the entrance to the roadstead. As soon as the communication between the English fleet and the garrison should be cut off, the latter would be obliged to evacuate the place, or become prisoners of war. If this plan had been adopted sooner, it would have been of easy execution, but the enemy had now had time to construct Fort Mulgrave. However, in spite of this unfavorable circumstance, my plan prevailed; and instead of applying ourselves to the destruction of a French town, we effected in one month the desired object. On the eighteenth of December, we entered Toulon, but could save only one half of the squadron, the other half, the arsenal, and ship-yards, being burnt by the implacable enemies of our glory and prosperity.

General of Artillery in the Army of Italy.—By this capture we had done good service to our country.* I was appointed general of brigade, and sent, in the beginning of 1794, to the army of Italy, to command the artillery.† The general-in-chief of this army, Dumerbion, was aged and without genius; his chief-of-staff was intelligent, but of mediocre talent. The operations in the maritime Alps were therefore planned without skill. I proposed a plan for turning the famous position of Saorgio; it succeeded perfectly.

---

* For the details of the siege of Toulon, the reader is referred to the first volume of Napoleon's Memoirs, dictated at St. Helena, and to the report of the engineer Marescot, published in Mr. Pathy's valuable work on sieges.

† The first two months of 1794, were employed by Napoleon in fortifying the coast of the Mediterranean. The military reader will find the general remarks on coast defense in the first volume of Napoleon's Memoirs, well worth reading. Napoleon had no doubts of the capability of forts, when properly constructed, to secure harbors from all attacks by sea. The works built by him effectually prevented any further maritime attacks by the English on this coast. These works, built more than half a century ago, are, of course, somewhat dilapidated at the present time.

I then proposed another for uniting the army of the Alps and that of Italy at Coni, which would have secured to us Piedmont and an easy advance to the Po. But the project was rejected by the staff of the other army, as it required the two armies to be united under a single general. Moreover, the approbation of the Committee of Public Safety, which wished to direct the war from Paris, as the Aulic Council did from Vienna,—would have been necessary for this movement. I made amends for the rejection of this project, by pushing forward the army of Italy as far as Savona, and to the gates of Ceva. This relieved Genoa, which place was now threatened by the allies. Winter, and imperative orders arrested our progress.

Conquest of Belgium, Holland, and left bank of Rhine.— While we were thus wasting our time in the Alps, three hundred thousand French troops inundated Belgium and the Palatinate, defeated the allies at Turcoing, at Fleurus, at Kaiserslautern, on the Ourthe, and on the Roër; drove the English, the Dutch, the Austrians, and the Prussians behind the Rhine, took Brussels, Antwerp, and Maestricht; passed the Waal, and the Meuse on the ice; and entered Amsterdam, Cologne, and Coblentz in triumph. Two other armies under Dugommier, Perignon, and Moncey, after gaining two brilliant victories at Figueras and Saint-Martial, invaded Catalonia and Biscay. And an army of one hundred thousand men succeeded, at last, in putting down the royalists of Britany and La Vendée.

Naval Battle of Ouessant.—But these successes of the French upon land were accompanied by corresponding misfortunes on the sea. France was in great want of provisions, and a large convoy was expected from America, at Brest; a fleet of twenty-five ships of the line, was sent out to facilitate its entrance into port; Admiral Howe, with an equal number of vessels offered battle. Villaret-Joyeuse was persuaded by Jean Bon-Saint-Andrée to receive battle with his inexperienced officers, and sailors ill-disposed towards the Republic. They fought with heroic courage, but without skill. The discipline, coolness, experience, and tactics of the English triumphed over the ill-directed valor of the French. Seven of our vessels were captured or sunk ; and this defeat produced the same paralyzing influence upon our naval force on the ocean, as the burning of Toulon had done upon our fleet in the Mediterranean. Every thing seemed now to presage the loss of our colonies: Martinique was surrendered to the English through the perfidy of Behague ; Saint Domingo had for two years been a prey to servile insurrections, massacres and incendiarism. Thus, the loss of our naval power was fatal to our colonies, and the loss of the colonies reacted upon the navy by depriving it of the great nursery for sailors,—a merchant marine. At the very outset of the war, the naval superiority of England was rendered certain. One would have imagined from our present unskilfulness upon the sea, that many, many centuries had elapsed since the war of 1780, which resulted in the independence of America.

Insurrection in Poland.—During these events in France, the attention of the North was fixed by a drama, less bloody, but not less interesting than our own. Our success had revived the national spirit of the Poles ; they demanded the treaty of Stanislaus, and with his guards at their head broke out in open insurrection. The Russians were driven from Warsaw, Wilna, and the greater part of the invaded provinces. Kosciusko, appointed generalissimo, succeeded in uniting sixty thousand men for the defense of his country, but was obliged to fight against three different armies. Suwarrow, the conqueror of the Turks, was sent by Catharine to subjugate the Poles ; the King of Prussia marched against Warsaw, but was soon forced to raise the siege, and fall back upon Wartha: Kosciusko, menaced by the Russian army of Fersen, marched to give him battle; but, deserted by fortune, he was defeated and made a prisoner.* Other brave Poles succeeded him, but there was neither unity nor energy in their administration. Suwarrow, after two victories over the Polish army, marched upon Warsaw, and carried Praga by assault; the remainder of the Polish army was dissolved, and the definitive partition of Poland crowned one of the most important enterprises of modern policy,—an enterprise reflecting glory upon the genius of Catharine, but disgrace upon the cabinets which coöperated with her.

Fall of Robespierre.—Although the Jacobins had dethroned the tyrant Robespierre, and condemned him and his violent sectaries, Saint Just, Couthon and Lebas to the guillotine, France was still the theatre of the most horrible anarchy; one half of the people were in arms against the other half. The Committee of Public Safety lost all its

---

* Kosciusko, descended from an ancient family in Lithuania, was born in 1756. He was educated in the military school at Warsaw, and afterwards sent to France to study drawing and the military art. On his return he was made captain, but was soon obliged to leave Poland again, in consequence of an unhappy passion for the daughter of Sosnowski. He came to America and soon distinguished himself, under Washington, in the Revolutionary War. He returned to Poland again in 1786, and in 1789 was appointed a major-general. In the campaign of 1792, he distinguished himself against the Russians at Zielence and Dubienka, and at the latter place, under cover of slight field-works, with only four thousand men, repulsed three successive attacks of eighteen thousand Russians. On the submission of Stanislaus to Catharine, he was obliged to leave Poland; but returned again in the revolution of 1794, and was made generalissimo with unlimited powers. Defeated at the battle of Maczicowice, he fell covered with wounds, and was thrown into a state prison. He was released by Paul I., and afterwards visited France, England, and America, (1797). When Napoleon formed the plan of restoring Poland to its place among nations, he proposed to Kosciusko to again take part in the struggle; but the latter declined the offer, being prevented "less by ill-health, than by having given his word to Paul I., never to serve against the Russians." In 1816, he settled at Saleure, where he died, October 16th, 1817, from injuries received in a fall with his horse from a precipice. The women of Poland went into mourning for his loss. His body was removed in 1818, to Cracow, and a monument erected to his memory.—*Encyclopedia Americana.*

efficiency and usefulness, by being made subject to a monthly change of members. In consequence of these absurd measures, Carnot left the direction of the War Department, and the whole interior was soon distorted by the false light of this *magic-lantern of representation.*

Peace with Prussia and Spain.—But the triumph of the moderate party, notwithstanding the instability of its administration, produced a beneficial change in our foreign policy. The exposé, full of wisdom, of Boissy d'Anglas at the tribune of the Convention, marked the return to ideas more moderate, wise, and just; the treaties of Bâle with Prussia and Spain were the result of this change of policy. Frederick William, seeing that he could gain more in Poland than in France, withdrew from the coalition; and the cabinet of Madrid, having declared war merely to avenge the death of Louis XVI., yielded to more wise views of national policy; Spain had imprudently become an accomplice in promoting the English supremacy, from which she had still more to fear than from us.

Fate of the Royal Family.—This general return to moderation acted favorably upon the destinies of the royal family. The Dauphin, called Louis XVII, languished in the dungeon of the temple, and died of a cruel malady, but his sister, the Dutchess d'Angoulême, the only one of the royal family that had not fled from France, was now exchanged with Austria for our arrested ambassadors, and for the Deputies given up by Dumouriez. Louis XVIII. lived in retirement at Verona; the Count d'Artois his brother had gone to England, where he was now preparing an expedition to make a descent upon the provinces of the West, where his partisans were in arms to receive him. The three sons of the Duke of Orleans received from the Directory passports for America; the eldest of these, the Duke de Chartres,* who had distin-

---

* After the execution of his father, the Duke de Chartres assumed the title of

guished himself under Dumouriez, had been living a wandering life in Switzerland under an assumed name; the other two had been detained in Fort Saint Jean, at Marseilles.

Napoleon attached to the Army of La Vendee.—Such was the general state of affairs at the beginning of 1795, when Aubry's famous reorganization of the army left me without employment. I was attached to the staff of the infantry generals serving in La Vendée, but I declined the appointment and repaired to Paris. I was here employed in the bureau of military operations, and charged with drawing up instructions to repair the faults of Kellerman in the Apennines.

New Insurrection in Paris.—After the conquest of Holland the armies had remained for six months inactive behind the Rhine. But the removal of danger did not restore quiet to the interior. The Jacobins, in order to regain the influence which they had lost by the fall of Robespierre, armed the faubourgs against the Convention, invaded its halls, and threatened to burn Paris. The majority of the inhabitants

---

Duke of Orleans, which he retained till 1830, when he became Louis Philippe I, King of the French. His two brothers mentioned in the text were the Duke of Montpensier and Count Beaujolais, the former of whom died in 1807, and the latter about the same time, while on a voyage between Malta and Sicily. When exiled from France, soon after the commencement of the Revolution, Louis Phillippe retired to Switzerland and became a professor in a school at Richenau. He refused to take up arms against his country, and for some time served as an aid-de-camp to General Montesquieu under the assumed name of Corby. He then repaired to the North of Europe and traveled extensively in Denmark, Norway, Sweden, Lapland and Finland. September 24th, 1796, he sailed from Hamburg for the United States, and arrived in Philadelphia after a passage of twenty-seven days. He was here joined by his two brothers who had been released from prison in Marseilles. After traveling through a great portion of the United States they left New Orleans for Havana in the winter of 1798, and then returned to Europe. He lived some time with his two brothers, at Twickenham in England. In 1809 he married the Princess Amelia, daughter of the King of Sicily. He returned to Paris after the restoration and took his seat in the Chamber of Peers, but manifested such liberal sentiments as to render himself obnoxious to the administration. On the abdication of Charles X., after the memorable events of July, he was proclaimed King of the French.

declared for the Convention, and rescued the deputies from the hands of these cut-throats. Pichegru took the command of the troops and disarmed the revolted faubourgs.

The Quiberon Expedition.—This defeat became the signal for partial reactions in the South. The royalists deemed that the moment had arrived for them to strike a decisive blow; all the emigrant corps in the English pay united for a descent upon the Presqu'ile of Quiberon; Count d'Artois placed himself at their head. Hoche, liberated from the chains of Robespierre, and full of energy and activity, took command of the Republican forces. The several detachments of the enemy were driven back into the sea, or forced, after a long butchery, to surrender. The proconsuls of the Convention ordered the remainder to be shot, and among these victims perished two hundred of the *élite* of the old French navy.

Constitution of the Year III.—The monstrous governments of the provisional committees could not long endure. A new charter was drawn up by a commission of the Convention headed by Sièyes. This *doctrinaire* imagined that with a proper balance of powers, the state might be governed by popular elections. His constitution of the year III established a legislative Council of Five Hundred, and a Council of Ancients, as a chamber of revision. One-third of these councils were to be removed each year; and the executive power, confided to a Directory of five members and made completely subordinate to the legislative power, was to be renewed every five years by an annual change of one of its members. This was preferable to the Revolutionary Government, though not less dangerous in its application. It was nevertheless seized, as the last plank of safety, by a nation tired and exhausted by the horrors of the Revolution. The army and a large majority of the Departments accepted the constitution; but the Convention, fearing a defeat at the popular elections, decreed that *two-thirds* of the present members should form a part of the new legislature, and that the relatives of the *émigrés* should be excluded from exercising the legislative functions. This produced a violent opposition in the Sections; and, incited by royalist agents, acting in concert with the Count d'Artois in La Vendée, thirty of the forty-eight Sections rejected the decrees and the deputies, and an armed coalition was formed between the royalists and the National Guards of the insurrectionary districts.

Affair of the 13 Vendemiaire.—The Convention resolved to employ force to execute its decrees; and the Sections determined to compel the dissolution of the Convention. I was then occupied with our foreign wars, and took but little interest in those party squabbles. If Austria had not had an army of one hundred and fifty thousand men at the gates of Strasbourg, and the English forty vessels before Brest, I might perhaps have sided with the Sections; but when a foreign enemy is invading the country it is the duty of every good citizen to sustain the existing government. I was appointed under Barras to command the armed forces against the Parisians. The interest of France was my law. I sent for the artillery from Meudon and collected a force of five thousand men and forty pieces of cannon, a force unnecessarily strong for the suppression of an *émeute*, had not the mob been sustained by cannon and a well armed National Guard. On the thirteenth of Vendemiaire (October fourth,) the *sectionaries* marched against the Convention. One of their columns debouching from Rue St. Honoré was fired upon, and it fled to the steps of the church of Saint Roche. The street was so narrow that I could use but one of my cannon, but with this one I soon dispersed the mob. All was over in half an hour. The column that debouched by the Pont Royal was equally unsuccessful. The affair, so small in itself and which cost only two hundred men on either side, led to important consequences by preventing the

Revolution from retrograding. In gratitude for my services the victorious party made me General of Division. I now burned to enter the field in my new rank, but the Convention retained me in the capital in spite of my wishes.*

Military Operations of 1795.—This detention vexed me the more, as our forces were experiencing reverses on the Rhine, through the incapacity or treason of Pichegru. The

---

* The following is the Duchess d'Abranté's description of Napoleon's personal appearance. "At this period of his life he was decidedly ugly; he afterwards underwent a total change. I do not speak of the illusive charm which his glory spread around him, but I mean to say that a gradual physical change took place in him in the space of seven years. His emaciated thinness was converted into a fulness of face, and his complexion, which had been yellow, and apparently unhealthy, became clear and comparatively fresh; his features, which were angular and sharp, became round and filled out. As to his smile, it was always agreeable. The mode of dressing his hair, which had such a droll appearance, as we see it in the prints of the passage of the bridge of Arcole, was then comparatively simple; for the young men of fashion, whom he used to rail at so loudly, at that time wore their hair very long. He was very careless of his personal appearance, and his hair, which was ill-combed, and ill-powdered, gave him the look of a sloven. His little hands, too, underwent a great metamorphosis. When I first saw him, they were thin, long, and dark; but he was subsequently vain of their beauty, and with good reason. In short, when I recollect Napoleon at the commencement of 1794, with a shabby round hat drawn over his forehead, and his ill-powdered hair hanging over the collar of his gray great-coat, which afterwards became as celebrated as the white plume of Henry IV., without gloves, because he used to say they were a useless luxury, with boots ill-made and ill-blacked—with his thinness and sallow complexion—in fine, when I recollect him at that time, and think what he was afterwards, I do not recognize the same man in the two pictures."

Much ridiculous nonsense has been written about Napoleon's destitute condition at this period of his life. There is not the slightest probability that he encountered any more inconvenience for the want of money, than most young men without fortunes. Besides other small resources, he had the pay of a brigadier-general, which, notwithstanding the depreciation of the currency, must have been sufficient for a man of his prudent habits and simple tastes. We know that at this time he voluntarily supported his brother Louis, and paid his expenses at a provincial military school. Alison says, "that so low were the fortunes of the future Emperor, at this period, that he was frequently indebted to his friends for a meal, which he could not afford to purchase himself." But on the very next page, this historian says, "Above a hundred families during the dreadful famine which followed the suppression of the revolt of the Sections, in the winter of 1795-6, were saved from death by his beneficence."

excesses of the Revolution had disgusted the conqueror of Holland, and he now entered into a correspondence with the *émigrés*. He had been intrusted by the Committee with the supreme command. Jourdan crossed the Rhine, at Dusseldorf, and, advancing to the Mayne, laid siege to Mayence; Pichegru, who commanded ten divisions on the upper Rhine, crossed at Manheim with only two of these divisions, and advanced to Heidelberg, between the two Austrian armies of Wurmser and Clairfayt; they were defeated and driven back upon Manheim, quite fortunate in not being taken prisoners. Clairfayt being thus enabled to unite considerable forces, turned the left flank of Jourdan, and forced him to repass the Rhine at Neuweid. The Austrians afterwards debouched from Mayence against the other three divisions, forming the left of Pichegru, forced their intrenchments, and drove them back upon the lines of Weissembourg. Jourdan had no other alternative, than to fall back upon the Handsruck, and form a junction with the army of the Rhine; but this had already retreated to Landau. It was thought that these faulty operations of this army were due to treason, rather than the want of capacity in its general: perhaps, both of these causes existed. In Italy, our arms were more fortunate; there Schérer, at the head of a portion of the conquerors of the Pyrenees, executed the project which I had drawn up at Paris, in the bureau of military operations. The result was a signal victory at Loano, which put us in possession of the line of the Apennines as far as Savona, and of the sources of the Bormida; but our generals knew not how to profit by this success. The new Directory had just been installed. To the necessity of having some member capable of directing military operations, Carnot[*] owed his reappointment.

---

[*] Carnot was born in Burgundy, 1753. Early exhibiting an uncommon taste for mathematics and military science, he was appointed an officer of engineers. In 1791, he was appointed deputy to the Constituent Assembly. While

Barras* was elected by intrigue, and Rewbel† by would-be-politicians; the other members,‡ were chosen at random. It is a little surprising that Sièyes, the author of this new system, should have been passed over in silence.

Napoleon's Marriage to Josephine.—I was impatient to see the new government organized so that I could be spared from Paris. While waiting here in inactivity I became acquainted with the widow Beauharnais and married her. Many absurd stories have been told about my first acquaintance with Josephine; the facts are these. After the disarming of the Sections she sent her son Eugene, then fifteen years of age, to reclaim the sword of General Beauharnais. This interesting youth shed tears on receiving from my hand the sword of his unfortunate father; the scene affected me, and I went to speak of it to his mother; and became fascinated

---

a member of the Directory, he turned his attention wholly to military affairs, and, in the words of Napoleon, "organized victory." Barras afterwards succeeded in effecting his overthrow and banishment. He was recalled by Napoleon after the eighteenth Brumaire, and made, for a time, Minister of War. He was a firm Republican, and both spoke and voted against Napoleon's elevation to power, but being honest and consistent in his course, his conduct gave no offense. Napoleon did not estimate his talents as high as some others, but he had the highest regard for his character, and on various occasions assigned to him very important duties. In 1815, he was made a Count of the Empire, and a Peer. He died in 1823. He left several scientific and professional works which have some merit.—*Thiers; Napoleon's Memoirs.*

* Barras was born in Provence, in 1755. He was of a noble family. He entered the army at the age of twenty, and served in India. He spent his estate in dissipation, and in the Revolution became the most violent of demagogues. As Director, he was guilty of everything that was base and cruel. After the elevation of Napoleon, by the affair of eighteenth Brumaire, he retired to his estate, and lived in obscurity; he died in 1829.—*Encyclopedia Americana.*

† Rewbel was born at Colmar, in 1746. He was a lawyer of eminence, and a man of honesty and integrity. His talents as a politician, were not great, but he proved himself a useful member of the Directory.—*Thiers; Napoleon's Memoirs.*

‡ These were Lareveillere and Letourneur. The former was a native of Angers, and the latter of Normandy. Both are described by Thiers and Napoleon as honest, well-meaning men, but of ordinary capacity. Letourneur was an officer of engineers.

by the attracting graces which all acknowledged that she possessed.*

Plan for the Invasion of Italy.—I had occasion to see Carnot and speak with him about my old project on Piedmont, which had been rejected in 1794, and also of the plan of invading Italy, which I had drawn up for Schérer. In examining the merits of these projects Carnot had an opportunity to judge of the character of their author. Being exceedingly anxious to obtain the command of an active army, I used every effort to gain the confidence of the government. I laid before the Directors and ministers the following summary of our foreign relations and the effects to be produced by my projected Italian campaign:

Austria, England, the German Empire, Sardinia, Russia, the King of Naples, and the Pope were all leagued against us. Prussia and Spain had treated some months before at Bâle, but their position was equivocal, and their present strict neutrality might be of short duration. Sweden and Denmark had rejected the pretensions of the cabinet of London, and maintained with much energy the true principles of

---

* Alison, to whose distorted vision no act of Napoleon can appear otherwise than criminal, represents his marriage to Josephine to have been founded upon motives of ambition. The charge is so grossly false, and, from the circumstances of the case, so perfectly absurd, as to be hardly worth refuting. No one, unless animated by feelings of the strongest animosity and violent prejudice, could ever think of repeating it. If ever there was a marriage made from pure feelings of love and affection, uninfluenced on either side by considerations of wealth or ambition, it was the union of Napoleon and Josephine. Alison here repeats indirectly a slander first found in the British and Bourbon presses of the lamest character, and afterwards promoted to a place in the no less abusive writings of Scott and Lockhart. The substance of these slanders is, that Barras, with his usual volatility, became tired of his mistress, and embraced an opportunity of disposing of her in marriage to Bonaparte. The latter, to secure the influence of Barras, consented to the arrangement, and received the command of the army of Italy as the dowry of the bride! Such stories repeated at this time do far more injury to their authors than to the memories of Napoleon and Josephine. It may be worthy of remark in this place, that at the time of Napoleon's marriage Barras was the enemy, rather than the friend of Bonaparte. (*Vide the proofs in Notes to Lee's Napoleon.*)

maritime law. The definitive partition of Poland had blotted it from the book of nations. The Ottoman-Porte took no part in European affairs. Portugal, the tributary of England, had at first joined in the expedition of Toulon and the war with Spain in the Pyrenees, but since the treaty of Bâle she had sought to withdraw from a coalition where she could gain nothing but defeats. Our superb colony of Saint Domingo was in a blaze, Martinique had fallen into the hands of the English; our maritime force had been destroyed by the battle of Ouessant, the loss of Toulon, emigration and the troubles of La Vendée. In India we had lost Pondicherry, our last hold in the east; and we had only our old ally, Tippo Saib, Sultan of Mysore, the formidable adversary of the English power. We had on our hands, at the same time, a continental and a maritime war. Perhaps Austria, satisfied with the valuable acquisitions which she had made in Poland, might soon have followed the example of Russia and made peace with us, had not matter foreign from the original cause of dispute been introduced. A great state is always unwilling to relinquish any of its provinces. The recent vote of the Convention for a definitive reunion of Belgium and France, and the ill-success of Pichegru, both combined to render the Cabinet of Vienna less disposed for peace. The state of our affairs on the Rhine was not such as to authorize us to hope for decisive victories in that direction; nor would a war in the German Empire be likely to force Austria to yield to our terms. The most direct means, therefore, of reaching that power was through the States of Lombardy. Under such circumstances the invasion of Italy would be the preferable military operation; especially as it would enable us to humble the smaller princes of Italy who had leagued against us, and would at the same time relieve the Court of Turin, which seemed inclined to treat with us for a separate peace, from the dictation of Austria.

Appointed General-in-Chief of the Army of Italy.—This very simple plan was approved by the Directory, and I was charged with its execution, with the rank of General-in Chief-of the Army of Italy. It was arranged that I should maneuvre by my right to descend by Montferrat upon Lombardy, and direct all my efforts against the Austrians, in order to detach Piedmont from their alliance. The armies of Germany, being reorganized, were to resume the offensive by the end of April, and to attempt the passage of the Rhine. Jourdan commanded seventy thousand men on the Lower Rhine, and Moreau about the same number in Alsace ; the former was to invest Mayence, with thirty thousand men, and advance into Franconia with the other forty thousand ; the latter was to cover Manheim and penetrate into Swabia. These forces were afterwards to unite in the heart of Bavaria. In the meantime I was to detach Piedmont from the coalition, or to dethrone the King of Sardinia, should he refuse to make peace, and then to advance upon the Adige. In fine, the instructions given to me by the Directory were mere copies of those which I had drawn up for the Committee some months before, and whose execution had been so unskilfully attempted by Schérer.*

* For a detailed account of the events of the Revolution, so briefly described in this chapter, the reader is referred to Thiers' History, a work of great ability and impartiality. The great military work of General Jomini, on the Wars of the Revolution, in fifteen volumes, is unsurpassed by any other history of this period. It has served as the basis of Thiers' military criticisms, and is probably the best military history ever written. Alison's work is written with the most virulent prejudice, and exhibits an utter disregard of fact and historical truth.

CHAPTER II.

FROM THE BEGINNING OF THE CAMPAIGN IN ITALY TO THE PEACE OF TOLENTINO.

Napoleon takes Command of the Army of Italy—State of Affairs in Italy—Napoleon's Plan of Operations—Position and Plan of the Allies—Beaulieu compromises his Left at Genoa—His Centre pierced—Napolean attacks the Piedmontese—Operations against the Austrians resumed—Double Combat of Dego—Operations against Colli—Napoleon's Proclamation to his Soldiers—The King of Sardinia sues for Peace—Armistice of Cherasco—Napoleon marches against Beaulieu—Passage of the Po at Placentia—Armistice with the Dukes of Parma and Modena—Battle of Fombio—March upon the Adda—Bridge of Lodi—Napoleon enters Milan—The Directory proposes to divide Napoleon's Army; his Resignation—His Address to the Army—Revolt in Lombardy—Definitive Peace with Piedmont—Position of Beaulieu on the Mincio—Passage of the Mincio—Difficult Position of Napoleon on the Adige—Situation and Policy of Venice—Criticisms on Napoleon's Operations—Investment of Mantua—Armistice with Naples—Demonstrations against the Pope—Armistice of Foglino—Troubles in the Imperial Fiefs, &c.—Occupation of Leghorn—Siege of Mantua—Austrians endeavor to save that Place—Approach of Wurmser from the Rhine—Battles of Lonato and Castiglione—Quasdanowich surprised at Gavardo—Attack upon Napoleon's Head-quarters—Second Battle of Castiglione—Second Passage of the Mincio—Wurmser's Retreat into the Tyrol—Close Alliance between France and Spain—Wurmser resumes the offensive on the Brenta—Objections to this Operation—The Armies in Germany—Battles of Mori, Roveredo, and Caliano—March from Trent to the Gorges of the Brenta—Affair of Bassano—Wurmser Marches upon Mantua—Affairs of St. Georgio—Position of the Army about Mantua—New Republics formed—Political State of the Rest of Italy—Discussions with Rome—Definitive Peace with Naples—Affairs of Piedmont—Negotiations with Genoa—New Troubles in the Fiefs—Affairs of Corsica—

The English occupy Porto-Ferrajo—They evacuate Corsica—Situation of the Armies on the Adige—Alvinzi succors Mantua with a new Army—Vaubois thrown back on Rivoli—Affair of the Brenta—Passage of the Adige at Ronco—Battle of Arcola—Vaubois driven back from Rivoli—Wurmser besieged at Mantua—Reverses of the French in Germany—Descent upon Ireland—Useless Diplomacy—Reënforcements from the Rhine—New efforts of Alvinzi to save Wurmser—Joubert driven back on Rivoli—Battle of Rivoli—Provera marches on Mantua—Close of the Campaign—Capitulation of Wurmser at Mantua—Expedition into Romana.

Napoleon takes Command of the Army.—I left Paris to take command of my army, about the middle of March. The reënforcements which it had received from the Pyrenees, after the peace of Bâle, had been half destroyed, as much by the campaign of Schérer, as by the maladies resulting from a rigorous winter, and the horrible privations to which they had been subjected, amid the arid rocks of Liguria. It counted sixty thousand men, but a third of this number was required to guard Toulon, Antibes, Nice, and the Col-de-Tende, so that its active force did not exceed forty thousand combatants, destitute of everything, except good will. I was now about to put them to the test: for three years they had been fighting in Italy, only because they were at war, but without any military object, and as if merely to satisfy their consciences. This ridiculous manner of carrying on war did not suit me. I wished to captivate general attention by some great achievement, and this I thought myself capable of accomplishing.

State of Italy.—At the risk of repetition, I will describe, briefly, the situation of the peninsula which I was about to invade. Divided, since the fall of the Roman empire, into twenty small rival states, jealous of each other, *Italy* existed only on the map. The good Victor Amadeus III. was king of Piedmont; the marriage of his two daughters to the brothers of Louis XVI., heirs to the throne, attached him, as much as his position, to the house of Bourbon. English subsidies, fear of our doctrines, and his family relations, had precipitated him into the coalition; but the Austrian influence was generally unpopular at Turin; and the minister, Damian de Priocca, although attached to the cabinet of Vienna, only wanted a good opportunity to withdraw from a contest where it was evident nothing could be gained. What, indeed, could the king of Sardinia hope if the coalition should succeed? Could he ask French provinces for the princes of his own family? On the contrary, if the coalition should be overthrown, would it not expose him to lose his states? As Spain, yielding to the irresistible force of national interests, had connected herself with us, it was to be expected that Piedmont would follow her example, as soon as it could be done with security.

The Committee of Public Safety and the Directory had already made two attempts to disengage this power from its alliances; the latter especially, made through the intermediation of the king of Spain, had staggered the monarch, and caused the convocation of a council in which was discussed the question of a separate peace. The Marquis of Silva, a distinguished soldier, had endeavored to draw the council into our favor, by the strongest reasons of civil and military policy. But the king and the minister, Damian de Priocca, adhered to the alliance with the cabinet of Vienna, rather through fear of our doctrines than from any real attachment to the house of Austria. The Marquis d'Albarey described the dangers of the throne with so much warmth that he carried his point over his eloquent adversary. English gold was not without its weight in the balance, for they did not fail to remark that the English subsidies were worth more than all that could possibly be hoped from France.

The house of Austria reigned over Lombardy. A prince of that family governed Tuscany. It was allied to the Duke of Modena, whose only heir had married the Archduke Ferdinand. A grand-daughter of Maria Theresa, sister of the unfortunate Maria Antoinette, occupied the throne of Naples, by the side of the weak and inefficient Ferdinand IV. Her Austrian origin, and the outrage committed on the queen of France, had exasperated Queen Caroline against every thing French. The minister, Acton, born at Besançon, of an Irish family, and ex-officer of the French navy, partook of this hatred on account of some personal misunderstanding which had occurred when he was in the French service. Nothing is more deplorable than to see personal resentment opposing itself to the good of the state; but, unfortunately, nothing is more frequent. Influenced by Queen Caroline and his minister, the king of Naples, who had taken a feeble part in the coalition by sending three thousand men to Toulon, in 1793, and withdrawing them after the evacuation of that place, decided, after much hesitation, to send a strong contingent to the Austro-Sardinian army; a tardy resolution, somewhat difficult to reconcile with previous events, and, indeed, incomprehensible, after the peace which had just been concluded with Spain and Tuscany.

The venerable septagenarian, Pius VI., wore the tiara, and occupied the chair of St. Peter. Our religious dissensions, and the destruction of the Catholic Church in France, had made him an enemy more formidable by his spiritual arms than by the miserable battalions which he could send against us.

The republics of Venice and Genoa, after having disputed for several centuries the commerce of the Black Sea, the Bosphorus, and the Levant; after having fought the memorable naval battles at Caristo, the Dardanelles, Cagliari, and Sapiensa, were now content to carry on a little coast trade under shelter of their neutrality. The first of these, inclosed in the talons of Austria, and having as much to fear from her protection as from our democratic doctrines, ardently desired the continuance of peace. It had just given the strongest proof of this desire by complying with the wishes of the Directory, intimated on the first of March, to order Louis XVIII. from the Venetian territory. This prince had retired to Verona, and published from there, on the death of the Dauphin, a manifesto declaring his accession to the throne of his ancestors. This act of legitimacy, very innocent in itself, had excited the animosity of the Directory. It was much better for France that this prince should remain in the insignificant republic of Venice than to be a refugee in England, or present with the army of the *émigrés*. Since France could not banish him from the European continent, it was best to place him either at Venice or Naples. But the Directory judged otherwise, and knowing the connections which he kept up with the committee of royalists in France, and consulting only its animosity, it demanded of the senate of Venice the same base act for which Louis XV. had been so justly blamed; that of expelling the Pretender from his states.

The procurator Pesaro, an energetic magistrate, worthy of presiding over a better people, alone resisted the mandate. It was carried, however, by an immense majority; and the Republic flattered itself that, by an act of causeless submission, it would secure itself from all danger. Louis, therefore, receiving orders to quit the Venetian States, left for the army of Condé, and afterwards went to Mittau, where Russia, for a time, gave him an asylum more secure than that of Venice. On leaving Venice, he charged the Russian ambassador, Mordwinoff, to erase the names of the Bourbons from the Golden Book of the Republic, and to reclaim the armor of Henry IV., which it had formerly received as a testimony of the affection of that great King. This act, dictated by fear, was no proof of the real sentiments of the Venetian government towards us, but it gave us to understand what we might exact from Venice, if victory should ever conduct us to her gates.

The Republic of Genoa, enclosed, as it were, within the theatre of war, had seen its port violated by the English, in 1793, and its territory, near Oneille, overrun by the columns which, in retaliation, I had directed, in 1794, to turn Saorgio.

These two oligarchies feared the principles which we were propagating, but the mass of the people, especially at Genoa, were much attached to France on account of the great commercial relations between the two countries.

Austria had tried to stir up all the little states of Italy against us; she had endeavored to assemble their deputies at Milan for the purpose of forming an Italian League, over which she might gradually assume a patronage and influence, still more powerful than what she then exercised over the Germanic Confederation; but, the Italian princes, aware of this design, had declined to act upon the question, and limited themselves to furnishing Austria with assistance in men, money, and munitions. Tuscany alone, although governed by an Archduke, had reëstablished relations of friendship with the French Republic, by treating with us immediately after the peace of Bâle.

It will be remembered that General Schérer had gained at Loano, the second of November, a victory over the Austrian army of General Devins; this was a brilliant achievement, due in part to my instructions, and in part to Massena, but from which they were unable to draw any advantages.

Napoleon's Plan of Military Operations.—I arrived at Nice on the twenty-seventh of March. Our recently victorious army was now in a precarious position; perched on the summit of the Apennines from Savona to Ormea, it was too scattered, and its line of communications with France, extending along the shore between the enemy's line and the sea, was everywhere too much exposed. There are two main routes from Nice into Italy; the one which turns to the north by Saorgio, and crosses the great chain of the Alps at Col-de-Tende, is the great road from Turin to Coni; the other, placed on that part of the Apennines which inclines abruptly towards the Gulf of Genoa, runs along the shore, and, between the waves and perpendicular rocks, is sometimes barely wide enough for the passage of a small carriage; this road leads to Genoa, and is called *La Corniche*. The debauch from the coast of Genoa into Montferrat is by the great road of the Bochetta, which runs from Genoa to Alexandria. Between the two mountains, the Col-de-Tende and the Col-de-la Bochetta, which form the great communications between the south of France and Italy, is a third route, that from Oneille to Ceva by Garessio; it is good for artillery. Other more narrow and difficult roads, run from Loano and Savona to Dego, from Savona to Sassello, and from Voltri to Campofreddo. As the army had been in possession of Col-de-Tende, ever since my operations in 1794, it might have descended on Coni, and acted in concert with that of the Alps; but they still persisted in keeping it between Tende and Savona, on the arid rocks of Liguria, where it was impossible to provision it by sea, and where almost every thing must be obtained from Genoa.

This disposition of localities had caused a repartition of the army. The division of Maquart, three thousand men, guarded the Col-de-Tende. The division of Serrurier,* five

---

* Serrurier, (Count Jean Mathieu-Philibert), born 1742, at Laon, was educated for the military service, and obtained the grade of lieutenant, in 1755. He was a major at the commencement of the Revolution. Napoleon raised him to the highest military and civil ranks, making him marshal in 1804, and a senator. He voted for the Provisional government in 1814, but declared for Napoleon on his return from Elba. He died in 1819. Napoleon thus describes his character: "Personally he was brave to intrepidity, but as a general he was not fortunate. He had less enthusiasm than Massena or Augereau, but he far surpassed them both in the modesty of his character, the wisdom of his opinions, and the safety of his intercourse."—*Biographie Universélle.*

thousand men occupied the road from Garessio and Ceva. Those of Augereau,* Massena† and Laharpe,‡ thirty-four thousand men in all, were stationed in the environs of Loano,

* Augereau was the son of a poor fruiterer of one of the faubourgs of Paris. He was born in 1757. He entered the Neapolitan service at an early age; but seeing no prospect of promotion, he retired in disgust and taught fencing at Naples. He was banished thence in 1792 with the rest of his countrymen. He afterwards served as a volunteer in the army of Italy: he distinguished himself in 1794 as general of brigade, of the army of the Pyrenees, and was general-of-division of the army of Italy in 1796. At the day of Castiglione he won many laurels, and afterwards derived his ducal title from that place. "That day," said Napoleon at St. Helena, "was the most brilliant of Augereau's life; nor did I ever forget it." He was made marshal of France in 1804. In 1814 he was one of the first to desert the Emperor, but on his return from Elba in 1815 he again offered his services, but Napoleon refused him as a traitor. Napoleon says that he always maintained good order and discipline in his army, and on the field of battle fought with great intrepidity, but that from defective judgment or want of education he was unfit for a separate command. In politics he was a wild anarchist, and his opinions merited no respect. He died in 1816, leaving a great but tarnished reputation. *Biographie Universelle.*

† Massena (André,) born at Nice, in 1758. His parents were in moderate circumstances, but sufficiently well off, to give him a good education. He entered the army at seventeen, and served as non-commissioned officer till 1786, when he retired from the army and married a woman of property. On the breaking out of the Revolution, he again entered the army as an officer. His promotion was now rapid, and in 1793 he became general-of-division. Napoleon made him Duke of Rivoli and afterwards Prince of Esling. He was made marshal in 1804. He was ever faithful to Napoleon. He died in 1817, less from disease than through chagrin at the conduct of royalists after the second restoration. Napoleon thus describes his character: "He was of a robust frame, indefatigable, night and day on horseback among rocks and in the mountains. In mountain warfare he was particularly expert. He was of decided character and of intrepid courage, full of ambition and self-love. His distinctive characteristic was obstinacy; he was never discouraged. But he neglected discipline, was inattentive to administrative service, and was therefore not beloved by his troops. His dispositions for attack were not skilful, and his conversation was uninteresting: But at the first sound of the cannon, in showers of bullets and in the midst of danger, his intellect acquired its proper force and clearness."

‡ Laharpe (Amédée-Emanuel,) born in Pays-de-Vaud, in 1754. He was a man of fortune and received a good education. In early life he served in the army of Holland but afterwards returned to his home in Switzerland. He was afterwards stripped of his fortune and exiled to France. He entered the French army in 1792, was made general-of-brigade in 1793, and general-of-division in 1795. He was killed at Codogno, in 1796. He was a brave soldier, an able general, of generous feelings, and of unsullied character.

Finale and Savona.* The latter division pushed its advanced guard on Voltri as much to hold Genoa in check as to secure our communications with what the soldiers termed the *nursing mother*. The administrative head-quarters had remained for convenience at Nice, for the last four years; my first care was to remove with it to Albenga, by the difficult road of La Corniche, under the fire of the English fleets. This was sufficient to announce to the army that I was about to occupy myself with its wants and its glory. It was literally an army of Spartans:—In spite of the utter misery to which it had been reduced, it breathed only love of country and military glory. Naked feet and clothes in tatters, far from discouraging our braves, only excited their hilarity.

My plan was simple: I asked of the Senate of Genoa, in reparation for the outrage committed in their port on the frigate La Modeste,† that they should give us passage through that city and the Bochetta, promising that on this condition I would remove forever the war from their frontiers, and secure to them the alliance and protection of the French Republic. If the Senate accepted this offer, I would debouch by Genoa to overthrow the extreme left of the Austrians, throw them back upon Alexandria, take in reverse all the defenses of Piedmont, thus detach her from the imperial

* Thiers thus describes the principal generals under Napoleon's command at this period: "Massena, a young Nissard of uncultivated mind, but precise and luminous amid dangers, and of indomitable perseverance: Augereau, formerly a fencing-master, whom great bravery and skill in managing the soldiers, had raised to the highest rank: Laharpe, an expatriated Swiss, combining information with courage: Serrurier, formerly a major, methodical and brave: lastly, Berthier, whom his activity, his attention to details, his geographical acquirements, and his faculty of measuring with the eye the extent of a piece of ground or the numerical force of a column, eminently qualified for a useful and convenient chief-of-staff."

† The frigate *La Modeste*, had anchored in the port of Genoa, and was moored against the quay. On the fifteenth of October, 1793, three English ships and two frigates anchored in port: an English seventy-four moored along side of the Modeste. The master civilly requested the officer on the quarter-deck of the

alliance, rally upon myself the little army of Kellerman,* and pursue the isolated forces of Beaulieu into the Tyrol. But if they rejected the offer, they would undoubtedly attempt to make a merit of it with the allies who would endeavor by extending their left to cut us off at the Bochetta. This movement would place the mass of the enemy's forces at the two extremes, at Ceva and Genoa, and expose to our attacks an isolated and detached centre.

---

frigate to remove a boat which was in the way of the maneuvres of the English ship, which was readily done by the French. Half an hour after the English captain requested the commander of the Modeste to hoist the white flag, saying he did not know what the tri-colored flag was. The French officer answered this insult as honor dictated; but the English had three platforms prepared which they threw on the ship, and boarded her, at the same time commencing a brisk fire of musketry from the tops and deck; the crew of the Modeste were unprepared for any attack; part of them threw themselves into the water; the English pursued the fugitives with their boats, killing and wounding them. The rage of the people of Genoa was unbounded. *Montholon*, vol. I.

° Kellerman, (Francois-Christophe) was born in Strasburg in 1735. He entered the Conflans Legion in 1752, and served in it during the first campaigns of the Seven Years' War. He passed through all the grades up to the rank of marechal-de-camp, which he attained in 1785. He served under Dumouriez in 1792, and distinguished himself at the celebrated cannonade of Valmy. He next served under Custine, and on the arrest of this officer, Kellerman was also called to the bar of the Convention. But he was more fortunate than his chief; in May, 1795, he was promoted to the command of the army of the Alps and of Italy; he was soon recalled on charges of inefficiency and detained some thirteen months, after which he was restored to his former command. During the campaign of 1796, his army formed the reserve in the Alps. None of his military operations in Italy or in the Alps gave satisfaction, and he was removed from his command and directed to organize the *gendarmerie* in the interior. After the eighteenth of Brumaire, Napoleon made him Senator, and in 1804, Marshal of France, and conferred on him the title of Duke of Valmy. He held under Napoleon several important civil offices; during the campaign against Prussia, he organized provisional regiments at Mayence, in 1818 he commanded the army of reserve in Spain, and in 1813 he collected all the reserves of the army at Metz. His fame may be said to have begun and ended at Valmy; as general-in-chief of an army, he exhibited no great ability. He died in 1820 at the advanced age of 85.

After copying a brief notice of Kellerman from the Encyclopedia Americana, M. Herbert, the translator of Thiers' Consulate and Empire, adds: "He was the *real winner* of the battle of Marengo, changing it, by a single charge of cavalry, from a route to a victory. For this Napoleon never forgave him."

Positions and Plans of the Allies.—The Allies had replaced Devins by Beaulieu, an old man almost eighty, noted for his courage and enterprise, but whose genius had never been brilliant. The reënforcements drawn from Lombardy, and levies made in the states of the king of Sardinia, had made up the complement of his army, and amply repaired the breaches of the preceding campaign. Moreover, the Neapolitan contingent would raise the number to eighty thousand men.

The allies flattered themselves that, with the aid of such enterprises as the British fleets and the Corsican division might make upon the Riviera di Ponente,* they would avenge the affair of Loano, and drive us from Liguria. Happily for us their forces were ill distributed. More than twenty-five thousand Sardinians, under the Prince of Corignan, were so weakened by being scattered over all the heights of the Alps, from Mount Blanc to the Argentière, as to be completely held in check by the little army of the Alps under General Kellerman. The army of Beaulieu and of Colli, from forty-eight to fifty thousand strong, was scattered from

---

And afterwards, he [Napoleon] did not recompense Kellerman, [for his services at Marengo.] No other officer of his distinction but was made marshal of France far earlier than he." It would be difficult to crowd a greater number of errors within the same limits. Francois-Christophe Kellerman was *not* at the battle of Marengo, and unless his *absence* both from the army and from Italy could have exerted a most magical influence, it would be difficult to determine how he was the *real winner* of the victory of Marengo. With respect to Napoleon's influence in preventing his promotion, it may be sufficient to remark that Kellerman was general-in-chief of an army, when Napoleon was a mere subaltern. He held several important commands under Napoleon, but never served under him in the field. But for the services which he had rendered France previous to the opening of Napoleon's military career, the latter loaded him with honors. He was created marshal among the very *first* that were made ; was one of the very *first* appointed to the Senate under Napoleon's Consulate; afterwards make Duke of Valmy, and both himself and family were the objects of Napoleon's kindest regards during his whole life. The Marengo Kellerman will be spoken of in connection with that battle.

* The states of Genoa, on the gulf, were divided into three parts, called *rivieras*, the Riviera di Ponente, the Riviera di Genoa, and the Riviera di Levante.

Coni, and the foot of Col de Tende, to the Bochetta, towards Genoa. The general-in-chief himself had just marched, with the left, upon Voltaggio and Ovada. The centre was encamped at Sassello, and the Piedmontese, who formed the right, were at Ceva. Simple common sense dictated that this spider-web should be pierced by the centre. I made my dispositions accordingly; they were wise, and fortune wonderfully assisted their execution.

Beaulieu compromises his Left at Genoa.—Beaulieu, urged on by the Aulic Council, had determined to take the offensive; and, either informed of my project upon Genoa, or designing himself to get possession of that city, to enter into communication with Nelson and Jervis, who were in these waters with an English squadron, he resolved to move his forces upon that place. The idea was good in itself; and he could have executed it more certainly, and have forced us into a precipitate retreat, had he operated in mass by Ceva against our left. But Beaulieu, who never comprehended a stratagem, resolved, on the contrary, to march directly upon Genoa, with the third of his army, while the remainder annoyed us in front. As early as the 10th of April he himself descended the Apennines, by the Bochetta, at the head of his left wing. I allowed him to drive our little advanced guard from Voltri, while I collected my forces against his centre which had advanced from Sassello upon Montenotte. Three redoubts covered this important spur of the Apennines, which here slope down to Savona. Argenteau assailed these works at the head of ten thousand picked men; he had already taken two of them, and was attacking the most important, with great impetuosity, when the commandant, Colonel Rampon, administered to its garrison, the 32d demi-brigade, the celebrated oath to bury themselves in its ruins rather than to surrender. He, in fact, maintained himself there all day, in spite of numerous assaults, which cost the enemy dear; and he was finally reinforced in the night by the whole division of Laharpe, which bivouacked in rear. The divisions of Massena and Augereau prepare to disengage it.*

His Centre is pierced.—On the 12th Argenteau, who commanded the centre, was attacked in front and rear by superior forces. He was beaten and thrown back upon Dego. This first success was the more important as it disconcerted the enemy; but, in order to gather the full fruits of it, we were obliged to redouble our activity. My whole army was already beyond the Apennines; of the four divisions which composed it, those of Laharpe, Massena, and Augereau marched with me; Serrurier was left at Garessio, to check the Piedmontese.

Napoleon's Attack upon the Piedmontese.—I determined to turn upon these last, in order to effect their entire separation from Beaulieu, and to push them vigorously. The mass of their forces, under the orders of Colli, still held the camp of Ceva, and General Provera, posted in an intermediate position between Colli and Argenteau, occupied the heights of Cosseria. I marched against him at the head of the divisions of Massena and Augereau, leaving Laharpe to observe Beaulieu. On the 13th Augereau carried the gorges of Millesimo, and Provera, beaten and cut to pieces on all sides, was forced to take refuge in the ruins of the chateau of Cosseria. All attempts of the Piedmontese to rescue him having failed, he surrendered on the morning of the 14th, with the fifteen thousand grenadiers under his command.

Operations resumed—Double Combat of Dego.—I was,

---

* In this defence Rampon had only 1200 men, with which he repelled a force nearly ten times as numerous. If the fort had been taken, the army of Napoleon had been cut in two, and "the fate of the campaign, and of the world, might have been changed." Fortifications, though small and unimportant in themselves, if judiciously placed and properly defended, may have a decided influence upon the active operations of an army in the field.

however, obliged to suspend my march against the Piedmontese, for the Austrians, alarmed at the defeat of Montenotte, now sought to concentrate on Dego. But they did it unskilfully; Beaulieu, leaving Genoa and the coast, hastened to Aqui, and sent a part of his left directly across the mountains to join the remains of Argenteau's forces near Sassello. I was not disposed to permit this; after having established Augereau in front of the Piedmontese, I conducted the divisions of Laharpe and Massena, on Dego, and attacked it with vigor. The troops of Argenteau fought bravely, but we were too strong for them; so that they were finally obliged to give up the contest, and retire in disorder on Aqui, leaving twenty pieces of cannon and many prisoners in our hands. Scarcely had we finished with Argenteau, when a new Austrian corps gave us battle on the same ground. It was the corps of General Wukassowich, who was hastening from Volhi by Sassello, with the intention of rallying on Argenteau, whom he supposed to be still near Dego. The brave Illyrian, surprised at finding our troops in the place of those which he expected to join, instantly formed his plan, like a man of activity and courage: far from thinking of retreat, he fell upon the guards of the redoubts of Magliani, carried the work, and drove back the frightened garrison upon Dego. Our troops thought only of pursuing the flying enemy in the direction of Spigno, and had no expectation of being thus attacked on their right and rear. This attack was followed by a moment of disorder, of which Wukassowich boldly took advantage; but his five battalions were insufficient to retrieve the fortunes of the enemy. Massena succeeded, by means of his reserve, in rallying the fugitives and bringing them back to the fight; the division of Laharpe, burning to revenge this momentary reverse, fell in turn upon the enemy, who, being charged by the mass of my forces, was easily overthrown; the shattered remains of his forces considered themselves particularly fortunate in being able to join the *débris* of Argenteau at Aqui.*

Operations against Colli.—Having thus disposed of the Austrians, I again turned upon the Piedmontese with the divisions of Augereau, Massena, and Serrurier. I established Laharpe at San-Benedetto, to protect my right and hold Beaulieu in check. Colli, pressed in front by superior forces, and threatened on his left by the movement of Augereau, who descended the left bank of the Tanaro, was forced to evacuate the camp of Ceva; notwithstanding a momentary success, at the combat of St. Michael, he was driven behind the Cursaglia and the Elero. I closely pursued and defeated him at Vico, near Mondovi, and drove him behind the Stura as far as Carmagnole. On the twenty-sixth, my three divisions united at Alba. One decisive battle would now put me in possession of Turin, from which we were only ten leagues. Nevertheless, the situation of the enemy was far from desperate: it was not, as has been pretended by the poetical Botta, a small river; a brave but conquered army; one place tenable and the other dismantled, forming the barriers of Piedmont; it was the fine position of the Stura, flanked on the right by the important fortress of Coni, on the left by Cherasco, which was secure from a *coup-de-main*, where Colli might have reinforced his army by twenty thousand men, now scattered in the adjacent valleys, and by an equal number from the wrecks of Beaulieu's forces. The allies might have repaired their fortunes by two days of vigor, activity, and resolution; at all events, there was the formidable place of Turin at hand, to receive, in case of reverse, a beaten army, and to that place, Austria could certainly have

---

* "In this action, Napoleon was particularly struck by the gallantry of a chief-of-battalion, whom he made a colonel on the spot, and who ever after was the companion of his glory. His name was *Lannes*, afterwards Duke of Montebello, and one of the most heroic marshals of the Empire."

sent assistance. We feared that they would pursue this course, the more, because Turin could easily brave any means of attack that we possessed, and greatly embarrass us by a prolonged resistance. At this crisis, I sought to incite my army to new victories, to restore its discipline, and strike terror in the hearts of our enemies.

Napoleon's Proclamation to his Soldiers.—The following proclamation was designed to accomplish this triple object:

"Soldiers!—In fifteen days you have gained six victories, taken twenty-one colors, fifty pieces of cannon, many strong places, conquered the richest part of Piedmont; you have taken fifteen thousand prisoners, killed or wounded ten thousand men. Destitute of everything, you have supplied all; you have gained battles without cannon, crossed rivers without bridges, made forced marches without shoes, bivouacked often without bread; republican phalanxes alone are capable of actions so extraordinary!

"The two armies which just now attacked you with audacity, are flying before you; perverse men, who rejoiced at the idea of victory to your enemies, are confounded and trembling. But, soldiers, I will not deceive you; you have done nothing, since much remains to be done. Neither Turin nor Milan are yours: your enemies still trample on the ashes of the conquerors of the Tarquins.

"You were destitute of everything at the beginning of the campaign; you are now abundantly provided. The magazines taken from your enemies are numerous. The siege artillery has arrived. Your country expects great things of you. You will justify these expectations; you all burn to spread afar the glory of the French people, to humble the haughty kings, who thought to put you in chains, and to dictate a glorious peace, which shall indemnify your country for all the sacrifices she has made. When you return to the bosoms of your families, you will say with pride : *I was of the conquering army of Italy.*

"Friends, I promise you this conquest ; but there is one condition which you must swear to fulfil ;—it is to respect the people whose fetters you burst assunder ; it is to repress all pillage made by wicked men incited on by our enemies. Should you not do this, instead of being the liberators of nations, you would be their scourge. The French people would disown you ; your victories, your courage, the blood of your brothers slain in combat, all would be lost, and above all, honor and glory. For myself and the generals who have your confidence, we would blush to command an army that knows no law but force. But, invested with the national authority, I will compel the small number of heartless men to respect the laws of humanity and honor which they trample under foot ; I will not permit brigands to soil your laurels.

"People of Italy ! the French army comes to break your fetters ; the French people are the friends of the people everywhere. Come with confidence to our colors ; your religion, your property, your customs, shall be religiously respected. We make war like generous enemies ; we war only against tyrants who oppress you."

To give greater weight to these measures, the Piedmontese democrats organized at Alba, a committee for distributing addresses among the people of Piedmont and Lombardy, threatening some and encouraging others.

King of Sardinia sues for Peace.—The result exceeded my hopes : the capital was overwhelmed with confusion and terror. The court, regretting its adhesion to the coalition, felt that our impetuous approach threatened it with the most serious danger, by stirring up the numerous partisans of a democratic revolution in Turin, and the other cities of Piedmont. It viewed this danger through the medium of fear.

Although Beaulieu had marched from Aqui to Nizza to join Colli, it thought itself lost beyond hope, and determined to surrender to our mercy; an aid-de-camp came on the part of the king, to ask for peace. This was agreeable news to me; for, in truth, I was somewhat uneasy respecting the course of events at Turin. But I knew the king had hesitated how to act upon the propositions made by France through the mediation of Spain, in the preceding year, and I felt authorized in believing that our presence would increase the credit of our partisans. The same question, again considered on the approach of our victorious phalanxes, was warmly opposed by the Marquis of Albarey and the minister, but Cardinal Costa, the Archbishop of Turin, carried the majority of votes, and decided the king for peace. It is worthy of notice, that the vote of an archbishop accomplished what the military and political arguments of the Marquis of Silva were unable to effect.

This precipitate step of the Court of Turin not only flattered my vanity and ambition, but it extricated me from real difficulty. My success had been brilliant, but the pillage inseparable from the total want of magazines, had given offense to the Piedmontese peasants, and relaxed the reins of discipline in my army. If the king, withdrawing from the Alps a part of the troops of Prince Corignan, had shown himself firm at Turin, as did his ancestor, Victor Amadeus, in 1706; and if the Austrians, reënforced by their garrisons in Lombardy, had seconded his efforts, I might have been driven back upon the sea, and placed in a situation exceedingly critical. Even supposing that I had maintained my position in Piedmont, arrested by the fortresses of Turin, Alexandria, and Valentia, which I was not in a situation to besiege, it would have been impossible for me to advance another step; and the enemy's forces, increased to one hundred thousand men by reënforcements from the Rhine, would have driven me from Italy. But the impetuosity of my march, and my proclamations, striking terror everywhere, gave success to the party which favored peace.

I considered every consequence that could result from this measure of the King of Sardinia; the distance which now separated me from Mantua and the Adige, seemed but a step easily taken. Peace with Piedmont decided everything. If I alone had conquered the two armies united, what could Beaulieu, deprived of his allies, hope to effect against me, when I was reënforced by a part of Kellerman's army of the Alps? The fate of Italy was no longer doubtful; I already contemplated with satisfaction this beautiful country subjected to my laws. I no longer regarded myself as an ordinary general, but as a man called to influence the destinies of Europe; I discovered the immensity of the part prepared for me by fortune; I already lived in history.

Armistice of Cherasco.—I was not authorized, however, to treat for peace, and it was necessary to refer the conclusion of the affair to Paris; but not to suffer my prey to escape, I enchained it by an armistice, which might be regarded as a preliminary treaty; this established us in the heart of Piedmont, by giving us possession of the fortresses of Coni, Alexandria, and Ceva. The king agreed to withdraw from the coalition, and sent the Count of Revel to Paris, to settle the definite conditions of the treaty. Impatient to accelerate this important matter, I gave the Count of St. Marsan, the king's envoy near me, to understand, that so far from desiring to overthrow thrones and altars, we would protect them if they would cease their hostility to France; in a word, that he would gain more by an alliance with us, than by his devotion to the Court of Vienna. Unfortunately their minds were not ripe for such overtures.

I had already done more in fifteen days than the old army of Italy in four campaigns; but my hopes were not yet realized. To rescue this classic country from the Germans, to give the lie to the old proverb that Italy was the tomb of the French :—this was a task worthy of me. I hesitated the less to undertake it as the armistice exposed to our attacks the isolated army of Beaulieu, which had already proved too feeble to arrest me in Lombardy, notwithstanding the reënforcements it had found there.

Napoleon marches against Beaulieu.—The next day, after the signature of the treaty, I marched my four divisions upon Alexandria. Beaulieu had already repassed the Po at the bridge of Valencia, which he had destroyed. The mass of the Austrian forces took position at Valeggio, on the Agogna, and pushed forward detachments upon the Sesia, and the left of the Ticino.

Passage of the Po at Placentia.—Wishing to deceive Beaulieu respecting my intentions, I had inserted in the armistice a clause which allowed me to cross the Po, with my troops, in the environs of Valencia. This stratagem succeeded to perfection. Beaulieu thinking me foolish enough to attack him in front on the Ticino, when I could act with greater advantage on his rear, directed his whole attention upon the space between the Agogna and Valencia. In order to confirm his error, I pushed forward a detachment upon Salo, making a feint to pass the Po at Cambio. Under cover of these demonstrations, the army turned to the right, and rapidly descended the river. To accelerate this march I myself conducted the advanced guard. We arrived at Placentia on the 7th of May, closely followed by our divisions in echelons. I felt the importance of hastening the enterprise, in order not to allow the enemy time to prevent it. But the Po, which is a river as wide and deep as the Rhine, is a barrier difficult to overcome; we had no means of constructing a bridge, and were obliged to content ourselves with the means of embarcation which we found at Placentia and its environs.

Lannes,* chief-of-brigade, crossed in the first boats with the advanced guard. The Austrians had only two squadrons on the other side, and these were easily overthrown. The passage was now continued without interruption, but very slowly. If I had had a good pontoon equipage, the fate of the enemy's army had been sealed; but the necessity of passing the river by successive embarkations saved it. This enterprise, though, for the above reason, it did not entirely succeed, was not one of the least remarkable circumstances of my first campaign.

Armistice with Dukes of Parma and Modena.—This passage lasted two days; but I profited by the delay to conclude an armistice with Parma, by which the duke purchased his neutrality at the price of ten† millions of francs, munitions and horses for the artillery and cavalry, provisions for the army, and, what was of greater value, a good number of *chefs-d'oeuvre* of painting and sculpture, selected from his galleries.‡ The Duke of Modena had fled to Venice, but the

---

* Lannes (Jean,) was born at Lecture, France, in 1769. He received a good education in the college of his native city, and was intended for the bar or the church; but his father having lost his property by becoming security for a friend, young Lannes began the trade of a dyer. On the first requisition of 1792 he was sent to the army of the Pyrenees, with the rank of sergeant-major. This changed his career. After the peace of Bâle, in 1795, he returned to his home with the rank of chief-of-brigade; but at the opening of the campaign of 1796, he joined Napoleon as a volunteer. His life now became a continual scene of actions the most brilliant, which won for him the love of his general, the gratitude of his country, and the admiration of the world.

† This is probably a misprint for *two*, the actual amount of the contribution levied.

‡ An immense amount of ink has been wasted by English writers, in defamation of Napoleon, for the course pursued towards the Duke of Parma. It will be sufficient to remember that this prince had repeatedly rejected offers of peace made by France, and was now to be punished as a vanquished foe. Under the circumstances this punishment was not severe. The Spanish ambassador, whose offer of mediation had been rejected by Parma, confessed that the French had been very moderate. Alison, following Scott and Lockhart, says, "it is impossible to condemn too strongly" these forced contributions from the galleries of the arts. His reasoning is not founded on fact. In the first place, very few of the master-pieces taken from Italy were in their original places, or in the possession of their original owners. We need hardly mention the Apollo Belvidere

regency which he had instituted, hastened to conclude an armistice with me on the same conditions as Parma. These conditions were rather hard, especially on the Duke of Parma, whose quality of Infanta of Spain seemed to entitle him to a better treatment. But he had turned a deaf ear to all the overtures made to him, even after my victories of Montenotte. We now punished him for his attachment to our enemies.

Battle of Fombio.—Beaulieu, receiving intelligence of my passage at Placentia, maneuvred to oppose it. This octogenarian general, instead of falling with vigor on that part of my forces which had already crossed the river, took only half-way

the Dying Gladiator, the Venus, the Laocoon; the Bronze Horses, first carried from Corinth to Constantinople, thence to Venice, &c. In the second place, they were as safe, and certainly as accessible, in the public galleries of the Louvre, as scattered through the palaces of the petty princes of Italy. In the third place, works of art which, by private individuals, are made commodities of bargain and sale, and transported according to their caprice or interest, could hardly suffer indignity by being made the subjects of treaty stipulations. As for their being taken as exotics where they would not be rightly appreciated or understood, as asserted by Alison, it is needless to refute so absurd a reason. Alison quotes Napoleon's words at St. Helena as a *confession* of guilt. By following Alison's reference, it will be found that Napoleon's remarks are wholly in *justification* of the course he pursued!

Lee, in his Life of Napoleon, deems these forced contributions not only justifiable by the laws of war, but as highly creditable to Bonaparte. "This measure," says he, "lent a grace and refinement to his warfare, which, reflecting lustre on the French arms, harmonized the rudeness of military fame with the softer glories of taste and imagination. The homage of other conquerors, for the master-pieces of art, had been shown by seizing with avidity, or leaving with indifference, such specimens as the chance of war placed within their reach. The arm of victory had transferred from Corinth to Constantinople, and thence to Venice, the famous horses of bronze. In later times, Frederick the Great, though twice in military possession of Dresden, left untouched, and almost unnoticed, the objects collected in the royal gallery. The livelier sympathy of Bonaparte for the efforts of genius, rendered it impossible for him to desecrate or neglect its creations. What had hitherto been subjects of military rapine, princely exchange, selfish display, or private acquisition, he elevated into considerations of national compact, and means of public relief and refinement, receiving, as compensation for territory which he might have occupied, and treasure which he could have exacted, a small selection of Italian paintings. This proceeding, which evinced equal respect for talent and humanity, and opened a higher sphere of glory for the arts, made the magic of Correggio's pencil turn aside from his country the ravages of war."

measures which were entirely insufficient to accomplish his object. He rested his left on the Adda without abandoning the Ticino on which he rested his right. On the eighth of May, General Liptay, who commanded his left, established himself at Fombio opposite my advanced guard. I supposed that Beaulieu was advancing with his *corps de bataille*. It was therefore necessary to attack Liptay immediately, to avoid having at once on my hands the great mass of the enemy's forces. I gave the order to General Lannes who executed it with that vigor and impetuosity which has since so illustrated his glorious career. Liptay was defeated, separated from Beaulieu, and thrown back on Pizzighettone. On the very night following this affair Beaulieu arrived on the ground where his lieutenant had just been defeated, and attacked the division of Laharpe at Codogno. The advanced posts were surprised, and the *generale* beaten at Codogno: in the confusion which followed, General Laharpe* was killed by some of his own troops, but not before the Austrians had been compelled to retire. Beaulieu, not satisfied with having divided up his army, now so scattered his own corps between the Po and the Adda that he had only three battalions of disposable troops. Seeing himself in presence of superior numbers, he thought to concentrate his whole army on Lodi where the Adda was crossed by a bridge. His right, which was still at Pavia, had to gain Cassano. This he could not have accomplished, had it not been for the unfortunate delay in the passage at Placentia caused by the want of a proper ponton equipage.

March upon the Adda.—Although the road to Milan was now open to my troops, the possession of this important city

---

* Laharpe was an officer of distinguished bravery and much beloved by his troops. "It was remarked," says Hazlitt, "that during the action of Fombio, on the evening preceding his death, he had appeared absent and dejected, giving no orders, seemingly deprived of his usual faculties, and overwhelmed by some fatal presentiment." The whole army mourned his loss.

could not be otherwise than precarious, so long as the enemy maintained himself behind the Adda.* It was necessary, therefore, first to drive him to a greater distance. I marched on Lodi with my grenadiers and the divisions of Massena and Augereau. One division was left before Pizzighettone to mask this place and cover my right. Ignorant that the enemy had already withdrawn the forces on the Ticino to the main body in rear of the Adda, I directed Serrurier to march on Pavia to secure my left.

The Bridge of Lodi.—We arrived at Lodi on the tenth. Leaving General Sebottendorf with ten thousand men to defend the Adda, Beaulieu had already retired to Crema with the main body of his forces. The enemy had secured the bridge of Lodi, which was over one hundred yards in length, by twenty pieces of cannon placed at the extremity. The occasion furnished an opportunity for stamping by some bold stroke the character of my individual actions, and I did not let it escape. The affair might be attended with the loss of a few hundred men, but even should I be defeated it could not have the least influence upon the result of the campaign. We easily routed a battalion and some squadrons of the enemy from Lodi, and pursued them so closely as to prevent their destroying the bridge. I immediately formed my grenadiers in close column and threw them upon the bridge. But assailed by a murderous storm of grape they were staggered for a moment, when my generals threw themselves at the head of the column, and carried it by their examples. At the same time a number of the soldiers let themselves down from the bridge upon an island where they were less exposed to the fire of the enemy, and finding the second arm of the

---

* Alison says, "on the tenth Napoleon marched towards Milan, but, before arriving at that city, he required to pass the Adda." This betrays great ignorance of the theatre of war. Napoleon was already on the same side of the river as Milan, but he turned his back upon that city, in order to drive the enemy beyond the Mincio.

river fordable, they deployed as tirailleurs to turn the Austrian line. The main body of the grenadiers now charged across the bridge, overthrew everything that opposed its passage, captured the batteries and scattered the battalions of the enemy. Sebottendorf retreated on Crema with a loss of fifteen cannon and two thousand men. This was merely an affair of a rear-guard, but still it was a brilliant one.*

Napoleon enters Milan.—The immediate consequences of the combat of Lodi were the occupation of Pizzighettone, and the retreat of Beaulieu upon the Mincio. I pursued him no further. For the past month my troops had been incessantly in motion, and they now required repose. Moreover my presence was necessary at Milan. I therefore established the division of Serrurier at Cremona, and with the remainder of the army took the road to the capital, where I made my triumphal entrance on the fifteenth of May. A deputation, headed by the respectable Melzi, came to meet me at Lodi, and I was received by a numerous National Guard dressed in Lombard colors, and commanded by the Duke Serbelloni, lining the streets quite to my quarters. Joy seemed universal; and France herself could not have paid me higher honors even by voting me a triumph.

For the security of our conquests it was essential to establish the republican system there, and to connect these countries with France by common principles and common interests. In other words, the ancient regime was to be destroyed and equality substituted in its place, for that is the entering-wedge of revolution. I myself was not tainted with the doctrines of our propagandism, but as they made us enemies

---

* Historians, ignorant of the military art, have sought to magnify the importance of this affair of Lodi. As a mere trial of skill and personal bravery, it was one of which Napoleon and his soldiers may well have been proud, but as a piece of generalship it does not deserve to be mentioned with the days of Arcola. It had no strategic relations with the campaign, and merely served to encourage the French soldiers and give them confidence in the individual bravery of their general.

of the few, I thought also to make with them friends of the multitude. But the Italian nobility were so much less removed from the people than in most other states that it was not impossible to reconcile them to political equality. I feared the clergy and their retainers, and foreseeing resistance from this quarter, I resolved either to conciliate them by concessions or to crush them by military power, but without any insurrections of the people.

Project for dividing the Army; Napoleon's Resignation.—On hearing that I had marched upon Milan, the Directory transmitted an order to divide my army into two parts, giving the command of that in Italy to Kellerman, to observe the Austrians on the Mincio, while I, with twenty-five thousand men forming the army of the South, was to march upon Rome and Naples. This division of the forces, just as we were about to encounter the vast resources of the House of Austria, was the height of absurdity. I refused to submit to it, and to save the army from certain destruction, tendered my resignation. But while waiting for the action of the Directory upon my letter, I determined to drive Beaulieu into the Tyrol.

Address to the Army.—Calling upon my troops for new enterprises, I addressed to them the following proclamation, which is too intimately connected with the history of the times to be omitted here:

"Soldiers! you have descended like a torrent from the summit of the Apennines; you have overthrown and dispersed everything that opposed your progress. Piedmont, delivered from Austrian tyranny, has yielded to its natural inclination for peace and for a French alliance: Milan is yours, and the republican standards wave over the whole of Lombardy. The Dukes of Parma and Modena owe their political existence to your generosity. The army which menaced you with so much pride, no longer finds a barrier to protect itself against your arms. The Po, the Ticino, and the Adda, have not checked your progress a single day; these boasted bulwarks of Italy have been crossed as rapidly as the Apennines. Such a career of success has carried joy into the bosom of your country; fêtes in honor of your victories have been ordered by the national representatives in all the communes of the Republic; there, your parents, your wives, your sisters, your lovers, rejoice at your success, and glory in their connection with you.

"Yes, soldiers! you have, indeed, done much;—but much still remains to be done. Shall posterity say that we knew how to conquer, but not how to profit by a victory? Shall it be said that we found a Capua in Lombardy? I already see you run to arms; for you, days of repose are but days lost to glory and to honor! Let us march! We have yet enemies to conquer, laurels to gather, injuries to revenge! Those who sharpened the poignards of civil war in France, who basely assassinated our ministers, burnt our vessels at Toulon,—let them tremble; for the hour of vengeance has struck!

"But the people of all nations may rest in peace; we are the friends of every people, and especially of the descendants of Brutus, Scipio, and the other great men whom we have for models. To restore the capital, to replace there with honor the statues of heroes who have rendered it immortal; to rouse the Romans from centuries of slavery—such will be the fruit of our victories; they will form an era in history; to you will belong the immortal glory of having changed the face of the most beautiful part of Europe.

"The French people, free, and respected by the whole world, will give to Europe a glorious peace; which will indemnify her for all the sacrifices she has made for the last six years; then you will return to your homes, and your fellow-citizens will say of each of you in passing, *He was of the army of Italy."*

I well understood the men with whom I had to deal. I knew that eloquent words would excite unbounded enthusiasm in the ardent minds of the French soldiers. I knew that they would produce at Rome and Naples the same effect as they had already produced at Turin, animating the courage and heroism of my men, while they petrified my adversaries with fear.

Before beginning new exploits promised to my soldiers, I attended to the interior administration of Lombardy. The citadel of Milan, from its proximity to the city, had not only a powerful influence on that city, but, so long as it remained in the hands of the enemy, rendered our position in Lombardy more or less dependent upon the success of our arms in the field; I therefore determined upon its reduction. Before leaving Milan for Lodi, I caused the material for this siege to be prepared at Alexandria and Tortona, and to be immediately directed upon Lombardy.

Revolt in Lombardy.—My triumphal reception in the capital gave me good reasons to think that the Italians would really second my operations. I had caused the churches and the property of the nobility to be carefully respected, and I therefore had a right to expect some gratitude from these two privileged classes. But I soon learned that my moderation had calmed neither their fears nor their hatred. The very day that I left Milan to march against the Austrians the tocsin was sounded in rear of my army. The peasantry of the country, excited to fanaticism by their priests, rushed to arms, seized upon Pavia, and the citadel in which I had left a garrison. The least hesitation on my part might have caused a general insurrection. I instantly turned about, and with three hundred horse and a battalion of grenadiers, marched in all haste to Pavia, which had now become the head-quarters of the rebellion. Having in vain summoned them, through the Archbishop of Milan, to return to order, and to give up the guilty, our grenadiers forced the gates and entered the city, which was now given up to pillage. Here clemency to the insurgents would have been criminal towards my army. It is sometimes necessary to shed a little blood in order to prevent a greater effusion ; to have pardoned these perfidious wretches, who had seized the poignard, even before the sounds of their acclamations had died away, would have exposed my brave soldiers to the horrors of new Sicilian Vespers.* I caused the municipality to be shot, and order was restored. In the meantime the army had continued its march against the Austrians on the Mincio.

Definitive Peace with Piedmont.—I had just learned that

---

* Under the reign of Charles of Anjou over Naples and Sicily, a project for the expulsion of the French was formed between Giovanni di Procida, a noble of Salerno, Pope Nicholas III., King Peter of Aragon, and Palæologus, Emperor of Constantinople. To favor this project, an insurrection was incited among the Sicilians. March 30th, 1282, at the hour of vespers, on Easter Monday, the inhabitants of Palermo flew to arms, and fell upon the French, who were all massacred. Women and children were not spared, and even the Sicilian women with child by Frenchmen were murdered. Messina and other towns followed the example of Palermo. This massacre is called the *Sicilian Vespers.*

To prevent a repetition of these horrible massacres, Napoleon resorted to the severe but decisive measures mentioned in the text, and for which he has been so much censured by the English historians. Alison compares the conduct of the inhabitants of Pavia, to that of the French peasantry in 1814, when Napoleon called upon every citizen to take up arms in defense of his country. The cases are essentially different. Pavia had already submitted to the French, and exhibited for them every mark of friendship. While treating them in this way they drew the poignard of the assassin. But the French peasantry rose in open war to repel the invaders of their country—the right and duty of every people. There is not the slightest justification for their cold-blooded execution by the Allies. The inhabitants of Pavia undoubtedly deserved severe punishment, but this did not entirely justify the pillage of the city. "Pavia," said Napoleon, at St. Helena, "is the only place I ever gave up to pillage. I had promised the soldiers twenty-four hours; but at the end of three, I could bear it no longer, and put an end to it. Policy and morality are equally opposed to the system." Thiers says, that being scarcely a thousand men, the French, in the short time allowed them, could do no great mischief in so large a city as Pavia. The houses of two illustrious votaries of science, Volta and Spallanzani, were purposely spared from plunder—an example honorable to both parties.

a definitive peace had been signed at Paris on the fifteenth of May, with the King of Sardinia. The latter had engaged to leave us in possession of Alexandria and Tortona during the war, to raze Susa, La Brunetta and Exiles, and also to establish a line of posts by Mont Cenis and l'Argentière. I wished to connect this prince to the Republic by the ties of interest and alliance, so as to strengthen our hold in Italy and enable us to act with more vigor against the Austrians. But it was difficult to induce Victor-Emanuel to desert his ancient allies so abruptly, and we, therefore, were obliged to satisfy ourselves with removing him from the list of our opponents, leaving the rest to the action of time.

In less than one month I had turned the line of the Alps, gained three battles, detached Piedmont from the coalition, taken twelve thousand prisoners, opened a direct communication with France by Savoy, and obtained possession of a fortified base for future operations; but all this was only the introduction to still greater victories.

Position of Beaulieu on the Mincio.—After the defeat of Lodi, Beaulieu did not venture to halt either behind the Oglio or the Chiesa. The strong line of the Mincio, however, flanked as it was on the left by the Fortress of Mantua, and on the right by Lake Garda and the Tyrol mountains, seemed to him a sufficient barrier for his protection, and he there established his army, its left at Goito, its centre at Valleggio and its right at Peschiera, a small place belonging to the Venetians. As the wings were supported by fortifications, it would not have been prudent to direct the attack upon them; I therefore resolved to force the centre at Valleggio, and, in order to induce the enemy to draw off his forces from this point, I at the same time made a demonstration upon Peschiera, threatening his line of communication with Austria by the Tyrol.

Passage of the Mincio.—On the thirtieth of May, I arrived at Borghetto with the main body of my forces. The enemy's advanced guard on the left of the Mincio was repulsed, and driven across the bridge of Borghetto, one arch of which they destroyed. I ordered its immediate repair, but being exposed to the fire of the enemy, the work necessarily advanced slowly. The grenadiers became impatient and some fifty of them threw themselves into the Mincio, and, holding their fire-arms over their heads, began to wade with the water up to their shoulders. Fearing a repetition of the affair of Lodi, the enemy retreated towards the Tyrol, giving us an uninterrupted passage of the river. I followed him with the division of Serrurier on Villa-franca, and Augereau directed his division by Castel Nuovo to turn Peschiera, while Massena remained at the bridge of Borghetto. Beaulieu still endeavored to remain firm upon the heights between Villa-franca and Valleggio; but upon learning the movement of Augereau's division on Peschiera, he thought that I purposed cutting him off from the Tyrol, and in consequence retired beyond the Adige, ascending the right bank of that river, by Dolce, as far as Caliano. A part of his left ascending the Mincio suddenly appeared at my headquarters, where I had only a feeble guard. I had merely time to save myself by the gardens and to rejoin the troops of Massena, who soon swept away the enemy, in turn very much astonished at the sudden appearance of our forces. The remainder of this wing detached at Goito entered into Mantua, whose garrison was now increased to more than thirteen thousand men.

Investment of Mantua.—However great my desire to pursue the fragments of Beaulieu's army, I did not deem it safe to do so, for I was not sufficiently strong to enter into the heart of the Austrian States, while our other armies still remained beyond the Rhine. I had run over, rather than conquered Italy, and the possession of Mantua alone could consolidate our establishment here.

Difficult Position on the Adige.—Although nothing had thus far been able to arrest my victorious march and the expulsion of Beaulieu from Lombardy, nevertheless all might yet change ; the enemy's forces seemed to increase in proportion as mine diminished. I had swept over this vast basin of the Po which separates the Apennines from the Maritime and Tyrolese Alps, more rapidly even than I had hoped, and now my impetuous arrival on the Adige presented a crowd of new combinations. The petty princes of Italy, dazzled by the brilliancy of our achievements, had subscribed to armistices most flattering to us ; but the King of Sardinia and the Dukes of Modena and Placentia, had not, in laying down their arms, become our friends. The people of Lombardy were far from unanimous in our favor ; the Court of Rome was stirring up rebellion in our rear ; and Naples might second these operations by thrusting forward its army upon Ancona or Sienna. Corsica was in possession of the English, who were stirring up discord on the continent ; and, although Tuscany had signed a treaty with us at Paris in 1795, it was to be feared that the Cabinet of St. James might throw ten thousand men into Leghorn to rally in our rear this imposing mass of enemies. I had only forty-five thousand combattants ; Mantua had a garrison of over twelve thousand Austrians ; Beaulieu and the Tyrolese had thirty thousand men in the valley of the Adige, and thirty thousand on the march from the Rhine upon Inspruck to form a junction with the others.

Situation and Policy of Venice.—To this picture which is far from being overdrawn, it must be added that Venice alone could incline the balance against us. She had granted a military road to the Austrians from the Tyrol to Milan, and in pursuing our enemy we had encroached upon her territory ;

of this she had no right to complain ; but in seizing and arming the arsenal of Peschiera and the Fortress of Verona, and in making requisitions upon her provinces for the support of our army, and in propagating sentiments of independence, we had necessarily given offense to the Venetian Government. This was no fault of mine ; circumstances forced it upon me ; I had no other means to support my army, and self-defense rendered necessary the occupation of the posts which I had siezed.

If Venice had really wished to preserve her neutrality, she ought, as soon as Beaulieu had retired behind the Po, to have formed a cordon of twenty thousand men on the Mincio, abandoning the right bank to the operations of the belligerents, and declaring war upon the first who should trespass upon the remainder of her territory. Pesaro proposed this, and urged the Senate to form an armed neutrality. But this ancient queen of the Adriatic, and entrepôt of the East, that in the league of Cambrai had singly braved all Europe, and in the wars of Charles VIII., Louis XII., and Francis I., had held the balance of power in Italy, for the last two centuries had been buried in a lethargic sleep. Its maritime power had been on the decline ever since the discovery of the Cape of Good Hope, and its land power since the surrender of the Morea to the Turks by the peace of Passarowitz. The population of the Republic was three millions, and its revenues some thirty millions ; its land forces consisted of seven regiments of infantry and six of cavalry, amounting to twelve thousand men ; the people of the main-land were like the Swiss, organized as militia ; but unlike the soldiers of Alviana, these miserable troops could be compared with no others than those of the Pope. The Republic trusted mainly for its security to foreign mercenaries whom its wealth enabled it to keep in pay. Its fleet consisted of fourteen ships-of-the-line, and six of the second class lying at Corfu and

Venice; and from the superb arsenal and ship-yard of the latter place, ten other vessels could have been immediately prepared and armed. But, if instead of this navy, which had been prepared against the Turks, Venice had now possessed a good army, events might have assumed a very different aspect. This proud oligarchy, which once thought to honor Henry IV. by inscribing his name upon the golden book of its nobles, was fallen into decay. It feared our democracy not less than our bayonets, and had equal dread of Austria, whose eagle was already enclosing it in his talons. It vainly hoped to save the vessel of state by allowing it to drift at will, between the two dangerous rocks—a course utterly absurd in such times of great peril.

Although this enemy was not very dangerous in itself, yet as an auxiliary to a strong Austrian army, and as a place of refuge for an English squadron, it was of much greater consideration, and I felt considerable anxiety respecting the part Venice would take. The Senate rejected the noble proposition of Pesaro, and by resolutions characteristic of its unworthy spirit, appointed two proconsuls, Foscarini and Sanfermo, with full powers to govern the provinces on the mainland, and to maintain relations of friendship with the two belligerents. The disgraceful surrender of Verona, two days afterwards, proved the wisdom of the Senate in the choice of its agents!

Criticisms on Napoleon's Operations.—Some eloquent writers have blamed me for not having masked Mantua and pursued Beaulieu into the Tyrol. If I have ever merited blame, it is not for having been too circumspect. I have already mentioned the dangers we encountered on our arrival upon the Adige—viz.: eighty thousand Austrians and Tyrolese, including the garrison of Mantua and the corps approaching from the Rhine; the Pope and his influence; Naples, as yet undecided, but capable of bringing thirty thousand men to the attack; the English—Corsican division, threatening to debark in Tuscany; the King of Sardinia, dissatisfied with a peace precipitately signed; Venice, still discussing the question of peace and war; such were the obstacles I had to encounter, with a force of less than fifty thousand combatants. It is somewhat amusing, that my critics, in spite of all this, would have me rush into the heart of the Austrian monarchy. Charles XII., with all his rashness, would never have attempted such foolhardiness. I adopted the only suitable course, that of imposing on our enemies, and confirming our doubtful allies, by assuming the attitude and language of a conqueror. This required much activity and decision of character, and no one ever exhibited these qualities in a higher degree than I did on that occasion.

Investment of Mantua.—I directed all my attention upon Mantua, convinced that its fall alone could render my army available, and enable me to assail Austria without danger from the south of Italy. Our siege artillery being still employed against the citadel of Milan, we merely made an investment of the place. To do this effectually, it was necessary to be master of the whole course of the Adige. The fortress of Verona was the key to the river, and the base of any system of operations upon this line. The Austrians had, either by permission or by force, obtained possession of Crema and Peschiera, two places, which, like Verona, belonged to the Venetians. As an offset to this, I summoned Verona, and the feeble Foscarini, making use of his full powers, surrendered up the place on the first of June. This precious acquisition secured to us three fine bridges across the Adige; and the bastioned work, and two strong castles perched on the last heights of the Tyrol, hermetically closed the valley on the left of the river. While waiting for artillery necessary for the siege of Mantua, I closed the debouches from the fortress, so that eight thousand men could secure its investment; while Serrurier was charged with this operation, Augereau remained as a corps of observation on the lower Adige towards Legnago.

Armistice with Naples.—Fortunately for us at this crisis, our political horizon began to clear up. Ferdinand IV., of Naples, wearied with a war which was bringing him large pecuniary losses without any real advantages, and, induced by the example of the King of Sardinia, and the solicitations of the King of Spain, now asked to treat, and sent for this purpose Prince Belmonte-Pignatelli to my head-quarters. He arrived just after the defeat of Beaulieu, in the plains of the Mincio. I granted him an armistice, on condition that the Neapolitan contingent immediately withdrew from the Austrian army, and returned home. The details of the treaty were to be settled at Paris, between the Directory and the Neapolitan minister. These negotiations, for reasons of which I am ignorant, were protracted for more than six months. The peace was, nevertheless, very important to us, for our embarrassments would have been very great, had this prince, whose states could furnish and support fifty thousand troops, continued to act against us. The geographical position of his kingdom enabled him to attack us with advantage; in the same country, and under less favorable circumstances, Hannibal had made war for ten years against the Roman Empire; but, fortunately for us, Naples now produces no Hannibals.

Demonstrations against the Pope.—After the treaties of peace with the kings of Sardinia and Naples, our only enemy in Italy was the Pope. With Naples against us, I had opposed any attack being made upon Rome, but now a single column might be sent against Ancona with perfect safety. I therefore determined, during the blockade and siege of Mantua, to humble the majesty of the Tiara before that of the Republic. The division of Augereau passed the Po at Borgoforti, and marched upon Bologna, where I arrived on the 19th of June. With a population of only sixty thousand, this city contained more learned men than any other city in Italy. Had the remainder of the peninsula possessed the same intelligence and energy of character as the citizens of Bologna, Italy would have become, ere this, a very respectable power. I promised its Senate the independence, territory, and consideration, of which it had been stripped by the Pope. The whole city seemed intoxicated with joy. In fifteen days it organized a National Guard of three thousand men, who were often of great use to us. Ferrara, also, gave in its submission without the least opposition.

Armistice of Foligno.—While these things were occurring at Bologna and Ferrara, a second column left Placentia, and entered Tuscany. The court of Rome was in the utmost consternation at these demonstrations. It solicited an armistice, which was granted, the 24th of June, on condition that it yielded to us the Legations of Bologna and Ferrara, and received a garrison in the citadel of Ancona. This peace was of vital importance to France, but I made it in violation of the orders of the Directory, who never calculated either distance or obstacles, but expected, at the same moment, to revolutionize Rome, Naples, and Florence; and, with seven or eight battalions, to conquer all Italy. What it now directed me to undertake, with only fifty thousand men, itself attempted, three years after, with one hundred and twenty thousand men, and ended in the loss of all our Italian possessions. Having terminated the affair with the Pope, Augereau was directed to return to the Adige, after first having punished the inhabitants of Lugo and its environs, who, at the instigation of the priests, had taken arms against us, to the number of three or four thousand.

Troubles in the Imperial Fiefs.—Troubles also occurred, at this time, in the Imperial Fiefs, and in the states of Genoa.

Bandits organized between Alexandria, Novi, and the Bochetta, and, joined by Austrian prisoners who had effected their escape, attacked and massacred our soldiers. I directed Faypoult to demand satisfaction for these things, and to cause the Marquis of Girola, who was suspected of being the agent of this mischief, to be driven from Genoa. Arquata had now become the focus of the revolt, and Lannes was sent there, with a few battalions, to destroy the rebels and sack the place.

Occupation of Leghorn.—The presence of our troops in Tuscany gave me an opportunity to execute the Directory's orders for the occupation of Leghorn. It was executed with so much rapidity and secrecy, that fifty loaded vessels were surprised in the port. And even had this prize escaped us, we should still have made a rich capture in the goods of English merchants. As Tuscany had strictly preserved her neutrality, nothing but extreme necessity could justify so high-handed a measure. As this port, directly opposite Corsica, and occupied by ten thousand British troops, could readily become a *point d'appui* to the English, and enable them to stir up a revolt in our rear, and to cut off our communications, self-security required these severe and decided measures. I garrisoned Leghorn with my own troops; but I treated the grand-duke with all the respect due to his noble character, and to his rank as a prince of the House of Austria, and heir of the good Leopold.*

These expeditions much strengthened our influence in the interior of the country; and the fall of the castle of Milan,

---

* The view taken of this affair by Alison is entirely erroneous. The neutral power, being unable to protect itself from the operations of the English at Leghorn, Napoleon was perfectly justifiable in the course he pursued. Such is the law of war. The grand-duke took no offense at the occupation of the French. His minister, Monfredini, acknowledged that the English had been more masters of the port than the grand-duke himself.

on the twenty-ninth of June, confirmed the wavering Lombards in our favor.

Siege of Mantua.—The capture of several fortified towns, in these expeditions, and the reduction of Milan, had furnished us with a sufficient park of artillery to undertake the siege of Mantua, and I therefore directed my entire attention to that object. The trenches were opened on the eighteenth of July. Serrurier's division, ten thousand strong, was charged with the works of the siege. The remainder of the army constituted the corps of observation between the Adige and Lake Garda. Augereau, with eight thousand men, formed the right at Legnago; Massena, with fifteen thousand, constituted the centre at Rivoli and Verona; General Sauret, with four thousand, formed the left at Salo; while the reserve, of six thousand, was posted between the right and centre. These dispositions enabled me, by interior concentric movements, to bring the whole of my troops to bear upon either side of the Mincio, according as the enemy should develop his forces. His numbers had been too much increased to expect him to longer remain inactive.

Efforts of Austria to save Mantua.—The cabinet of Vienna, justly alarmed at my progress, resolved to put a stop to it, by sending against me a new army and a new general. Marshal Wurmser left Manheim with twenty thousand men of the *élite*, and superseded Beaulieu. The Austrian combined army, assembled at Trent the last of July, amounted to sixty thousand combatants. This superiority of numbers seemed to ensure victory, and my adversaries began to triumph at my approaching overthrow. Their calculations seemed well formed, but the result proved that they had left out the relative value of the two commanders-in-chief—an important item in the estimate.

Approach of Wurmser from the Rhine.—Wurmser debouched from the Tyrol the last of July. Quasdanowich carried twenty-five thousand by the right of Lake Garda on Salo and Brescia; while the marshal, with the remaining thirty-three thousand descended the Adige in three columns. I learned at the same time, that Sauret had been thrown back upon Desenzano, and Massena expelled from Rivoli. This information, discouraging as it might seem to one less familiar with the science of war, gave me the strongest hopes of success. The enemy, by dividing his forces, gave me an opportunity to penetrate between the two parts of his army, and beat them separately. But the success of this depended upon the utmost promptness; the slightest hesitation on my part would have given Wurmser an opportunity to unite with Quasdanowich on the Mincio. I left everything in order to prevent this reunion. I raised the siege of Mantua, leaving one hundred and forty cannon in the trenches; and I soon had to rejoice that I had taken this measure in spite of the prejudices which existed against it. A general of artillery might make it as much a point of honor to preserve his battery as his flag; but the point of honor for a general-in-chief is success. A council of war was assembled to discuss this measure. In all armies there are some generals intelligent, but timid, others brave, but uneducated; the truly valuable are those who unite these two qualities. In this council there was the usual difference of opinion; Kilmaine and the more discreet advised against the project; but, Augereau, animated by a noble ardor which he never after exhibited, declared that he would not rest till he had given battle with at least his own division. Encouraged by this, I determined to risk everything for success, and accordingly gave orders to attack the Austrian column, which had just taken Brescia. The divisions of Massena and Augereau, with a reserve, on the evening of the thirtieth, united between Peschiera and Goito. One half of the division of Serrurier on the left of the

Mincio rejoined Augereau, and the other half passed the Oglio at Marcaria.

Battles of Lonato and Castiglione.—The next day I passed the Mincio to attack Quasdanowich. The enemy was repulsed from Lonato, Brescia, and Salo. I established my army on the Chiesa, and Quasdanowich fell back upon Gavardo. The faults of the Austrians could have been repaired by Wurmser, on the thirty-first of July, after the taking of the Montebaldo, had he passed the Mincio under Peschiera to reach Lonato. He then would have effected a junction with Quasdanowich, and have forced me to regain, in all haste, the Ticino or Placentia; after this, he could easily have made a victorious entry into Mantua. But the Austrians never knew the value of time. They devised wise projects, and then failed by wrong calculations of time and distance. Wurmser, instead of joining Quasdanowich, went first to make a triumphal procession at Mantua, and crossed the Mincio at Goito, as late as the evening of the second of August, on his way to Castiglione. This gave me full time to defeat his lieutenant, and drive him from Ponte San Marco, Lonato, and Brescia. But I could not cut him up very much, on account of the mountains of Gavardo, which favored his retreat. I hoped to take my revenge on Wurmser, himself. The third of August, Augereau carried his division and the reserve on Castiglione; Massena directed his division on Lonato, and at the same time, to induce Quasdanowich to continue his retreat, I ordered General Guyeux to defile on Salo and threaten his communications with the Tyrol. The operations of this day were somewhat singular, but on the whole favorable to us. I had thought to direct my attack upon Wurmser, but on the contrary it fell upon the left of Quasdanowich, who was trying to renew his junction by Lonato. For this purpose he had resumed the offensive and, as usual, in several columns. That of the

Prince of Reuss had to descend by Salo ; Ocskay marched from Gavardo direct upon Lonato ; Ott on Desenzano. General Ocskay attacked the advanced guard of Massena and caused him some loss. My arrival with the main portion of the division restored the equilibrium. We carried Lonato, and lively pursued the retreating enemy. Happily for them the Prince of Reuss, who had reached Salo before Guyeux, finding no one there, fell back upon the road taken by Ocskay, and assisted in rallying his men. But this fortuitous accident worked wonderfully in our favor the next day. Quasdanowich resumed his first position at Gavardo with all his columns, except some detachments which had lost their way, and remained in the mountains near Lonato. The same day Augereau attacked and defeated the advanced guard of Wurmser, at Castiglione.

Quasdanowich surprised at Gavardo.—I had yet gained only a partial success, but this had strengthened my central position and afforded means to renew my operations. I reserved my strongest efforts for Wurmser who was advancing by Gurdizzolo on Castiglione. But as his march was slow, and as I had still to wait for Serrurier from Marcaria, I resolved to employ the day of the fourth in more completely routing Quasdanowich. General Despinoy, reënforced at Brescia with three thousand men from the army of the Alps, received orders to advance by Sant-Ozetto on Gavardo. St. Hilaire was detached from Massena to assist Guyeux, who was to move from Salo on Gavardo. The effect of these attacks surpassed my most sanguine hopes, the Austrians, hearing that Prince Reuss had found no one at Salo the night before, thought themselves secure on this side, and directed all their attention upon the road to Lonato. Favored by this circumstance and by the nature of the ground, Guyeux and St. Hilaire got in rear of the enemy without being perceived. Assailed thus unexpectedly in reverse, the Austrians retreated by the road of the Val-Sabbia upon Riva. This movement relieved me for the time from all attacks of this corps.

Attack upon Napoleon's Head-quarters.—But if fortune had greatly favored my operations at this important juncture, it had also exposed me to great personal danger at my head-quarters. I had remained at Lonato, with only one thousand two hundred men, after the departure of the division of Massena. Suddenly the city was surrounded by a corps of the enemy, who summoned me to surrender. Fortunately, I preserved my presence of mind and determined to substitute audacity for strength. I made so many threats to the enemy's general that he immediately laid down his arms and surrendered with his two thousand men and four cannon. This was the advance guard of Quasdanowich, which in making a reconnoissance for forming a junction with Wurmser had crossed the columns of St. Hilaire and Sauret. This occurred at the very instant that my troops surprised the enemy at Gavardo; but the results were different in the two cases: the first was the capture of the attacking force without loss; the other the retreat of twelve or fifteen thousand Austrians from a most important position.

Second Battle of Castiglione.—The first success of these operations was to be decided on the fifth of August. Wurmser, still wedded to the system of detachments, had sent one in the direction of the Lower Po and left another to blockade Peschiera. With the remaining twenty-five thousand men he took post between Solferino and Medolano. The divisions of Massena and Augereau, and the reserve which I had united at Castiglione, together formed a force equal to that of the enemy. The arrival of the division of Serrurier inclined the balance in our favor. In order to give time for this last division to debouch by Gurdizzolo on the enemy's rear, and reach the field of battle, I at first merely sought to preserve my line without giving any decided character to the affair. As soon as the troops of Serrurier came in sight near Cavriana, I seriously engaged my right and centre. His left being outflanked and on the point of being driven back upon Lake Garda, Wurmser deemed it best to order a prompt retreat, and to repass the Mincio, leaving in my hands twenty pieces of artillery.*

Second Passage of the Mincio.—A junction with Quasdanowich was the only thing Wurmser wanted to establish himself firmly on the Mincio and to maintain his communications with Mantua. In order to prevent these results I resolved to attack the enemy again the next day, notwithstanding the barrier which separated us. While the main body of my army checked the Austrians on the Mincio towards Valeggio, Massena crossed this river at Peschiera, and fell upon the enemy's right wing opposite this place.

Wurmser's Retreat into the Tyrol.—The intrenchments which the enemy had just commenced were soon carried and his troops put to flight. Wurmser, seeing his right wing forced and his communications with the Tyrol threatened, abandoned the Mincio and retreated up the Adige as far as Alla. He left in Mantua a garrison of fifteen thousand fresh troops. We pursued him to the Tyrol, and by the twelfth of August regained possession of all the posts on Lake Garda, which we had lost by the offensive movement of Wurmser. The division of Serrurier resumed the operations at Mantua, but having lost all our siege artillery, we could only maintain the blockade. Wurmser had now resumed his position in the Tyrol with a loss of ten or twelve thousand men and fifty cannon. The theatre of his defeat was

---

* It has been said that during these extraordinary six days, Napoleon never once took off his boots, nor lay down upon a bed. He was almost constantly on horse-back, and Thiers says that he killed five horses with fatigue. He would not intrust any one with the execution of his orders, he was determined to see everything, to verify everything, to animate all by his presence.

the same as that where Prince Eugene had so well succeeded over Vendôme in the celebrated campaign of 1705. If the operations in the two cases be compared, it will be found that I manœuvred much more skilfully than the general of Louis XIV. Although he had Mantua on his side, while it was against me, he operated so unskilfully as to lose his footing on the Adige and the Mincio, and to allow Prince Eugene to turn his left by transporting his infantry in boats across Lake Garda on Gavardo ; this movement required not less than six days, and in half that time I should have destroyed an army attempting such an enterprise in my presence.

Close Alliance between France and Spain.—France now began to gather the fruits of these victories. The government of Spain was not satisfied with a mere treaty of peace with us. Seeing the danger to which Spain would be exposed, if England should triumph upon the seas, they desired to preserve our colonial and maritime power as a safe-guard for other nations. Should we fall, it was evident that Spain could no longer support her colonies or maritime influence, but would become, like Portugal, a mere tributary to proud Albion. Animated by these wise and politic sentiments, the Cabinet of Madrid was willing to forget the natural sentiments caused by the Revolution, and form with France a treaty of offensive and defensive alliance. A treaty containing nearly all the clauses of the celebrated family compact was signed at San-Ildefonso on the nineteenth August, 1796. This event contributed to our advantage in many respects, particularly in its influence upon the conduct of the Sardinian and Neapolitan governments.

Wurmser renews the Offensive on the Brenta.—No sooner had the Austrians entered the Tyrol than they received reënforcements sufficient to again outnumber us. Under these circumstances it was not to be expected that they would suffer us to quietly continue the siege of Mantua. Wurmser had received positive orders to relieve that place, and he now thought to accomplish this object by simple manœuvres. Davidowich was to cover the Tyrol with twenty thousand men scattered from the environs of Feldkirch to Roveredo, while Wurmser himself with the remaining twenty-six thousand, should descend the valley of the Brenta to debouch on Porto Legnago and the rear of my army.

Faults of the Plan.—The Austrian general, supposing my views as narrow as his own, judged that the only course I could pursue would be to fall back behind the Mincio, and that he would in this way liberate Mantua, by the single effect of his combinations. But I was not a man to be intimidated by vain demonstrations; and I could have outgeneraled him, even if his unfortunate blunders had not immediately placed him in my power. My good fortune rendered no great efforts on my part necessary. Having received a reënforcement of six thousand men, at the moment the enemy began his false manœuvre by the left, I resolved to penetrate into the heart of the Tyrol, and effect a junction with the army of the Rhine, conformably to the proposition I had made to the Directory, after the peace with Piedmont.

The Armies in Germany.—Emboldened by my victories, and the success of the armies of the Rhine and of Sambre-et-Meuse, at the opening of the campaign, the Directory had renewed the plan of 1703, in which Louis XIV. and the Elector of Bavaria had failed. This of the Directory was still more difficult than that of Louis XIV., for then Bavaria was closely allied with France, and the French army, not, as now, foolishly scattered from the Danube to Bamberg, was seconded by the valiant Charles Theodore and his brave troops, and opposed only by Prince Eugene of Savoy and Marlborough, the German armies acting merely as auxiliaries; the operations of Louis XIV. were, therefore, more excusable than those proposed in 1796.

In order to execute this plan of the Directory, Jourdan advances from Dusseldorf and Neuwied, on the Lahn, so as to draw the enemy on the lower Rhine; he gains two victories at Altenkerchen. The archduke hastens to meet him, and forces Jourdan to fall back, at the moment when my victories induce the Cabinet of Vienna to withdraw Wurmser from the upper Rhine, and to send him into Italy. Moreau, being now opposed only by the corps of Starray, passes the Rhine at Kehl, on the twenty-fourth of June, and on the twenty-eighth beats the Austrian general at Renchen. The archduke returns in all haste from the lower Rhine, gives battle on the sixth of July, at Ettlingen, is turned by the left, and forced to continue his retreat to the Danube; he again attacks Moreau at Neresheim, but his line being too much extended, he is defeated, and crosses the Danube, at Donawert, on the thirteenth of August. During this interval, Jourdan, favored by the success of Moreau and the departure of the archduke, has again advanced upon Frankfort, and, leaving General Moreau to observe Mayence, with twenty-five thousand men, has continued his march up the Main by Schweinfurth and Bamberg. This direction was too eccentric, and it soon became necessary for him to fall back by Nuremberg, towards Amberg, in hopes of forming a junction with the army of the Rhine. This last army, after the battle of Neresheim, advanced on Ulm and Munich. It now had to extend its left, to form a junction with Jourdan, and to throw, by its right, a strong detachment on Innspruck. To require a single army to pursue two objects, so far separated, was the height of absurdity; for, after these two eccentric detachments, Moreau had hardly a skeleton of an army. If Jourdan had fallen back from Aschaffenbourg upon Donawert, and Moreau had carried his forces, *en masse*, upon the

Lech, between Augsbourg and the mountains, we might have swept the Tyrol in concert, and all three have united on the Inn. But there was no concert of action; the Archduke Charles fell upon the isolated army of Jourdan, and defeated it, on the twenty-third of August, at Amberg, and, on the second of September, at Wurtzbourg; and Moreau, whose right was already near Bregentz and Leutkirch, compromised by the retreat of the army of the Sambre-et-Meuse, instead of penetrating the Tyrol, was compelled to seek safety in retreat.

Combats of Mori, Roveredo, and Caliano.—I was still ignorant of Jourdan's defeat, and Wurmser's movement on Bassano, when I advanced against him in the valley of the Adige. I directed on Roveredo the divisions of Augereau and Massena, which were now posted at Verona and Rivoli; these were to be joined on their march by the division of Vaubois, debouching from Salo by the west shore of Lake Garda. These forces could hardly fail to defeat the single corps of Davidowich, which was guarding the Tyrol, and scattered in many detachments. On the fourth of September Wukassowich, who commanded his advanced guard, was driven from Mori by the manœuvres of Vaubois and Massena, and compelled to fall back, first upon Roveredo, and afterwards upon Caliano, where he united with the main body of the corps. Davidowich himself, assailed by superior numbers at Caliano, was forced by my brave soldiers to yield this formidable pass. Seeing that nothing could withstand our impetuous attacks, the enemy sought safety in flight, leaving in our hands twenty-five cannon and two thousand prisoners. Davidowich having rallied his forces behind the Lavis, as it was important to remove the enemy from the vicinity of Trente, I ordered him to be attacked by Vaubois. The Austrians attempted in vain to defend the passage of the Lavis, and were driven upon Salurn and Neumark.

March from Trente by the Gorges of the Brenta.—I now learned, for the first time, the movement of Wurmser, on the Brenta. So far from being intimidated by this, I derived the strongest hope of a decisive victory. *An army, separated into two parts, whose centre I cut, overthrow its right, and turn its isolated left!!! What better could I desire?*

The occupation of Trente was so much the more important as it opened to us the head of the valley of the Brenta, and exposed the rear of Wurmser. I took care not to let so fine an opportunity escape me. Instead of attempting to form a junction at Innspruck with the right of Moreau, (from whom I had received no intelligence), I determined to profit by the enemy's false movement, and prevent his destroying the remainder of our troops before Mantua. On the sixth, I directed Massena and Augereau by Levico, in the valley of the Brenta, in order to mask this movement and check Davidowich; Vaubois remained on the Lavis. On the morning of the seventh the advanced guard of Augereau encountered at Primolan a detachment of three battalions of the enemy, closing the passages of the gorges of the Brenta. After a pretty close contest, this detachment, driven from Primolan and fort Covolo, and outstripped by a regiment of dragoons which closed the defile, was surrounded and forced to surrender. We advanced as far as Cismona.

Affair of Bassano.—Wurmser had already reached Bassano; but seeing that, instead of trembling for my own communications, I had marched to cut off his, he was at a loss whether to advance or recede. Of all parts he chose the worst possible—that of waiting the event at Bassano. His army was established on the heights in front of the city, with the advanced guard at Solagna and Campo-Lungo. At seven o'clock on the morning of the eighth, we attacked this advanced guard, and drove it back in disorder on Bassano, and carried the town by force. The enemy knew not which way to turn; Wurmser, with the left of his *corps-de-bataille*, retired on Fonteniva, where he passed the Brenta, and marched upon Vicenza. Quasdanowich, with the right, being unable to reach the Brenta, directed his course toward Friouli. In this affair we captured two thousand prisoners, thirty cannon, and an immense train.

Wurmser marches upon Mantua.—Wurmser now had remaining only fourteen thousand men, entirely disorganized, and scattered through a country whose communications were all in our hands; under such circumstances, I hoped to compel him to surrender; I therefore manœuvred to close all the outlets. Augereau marched on Padua; Massena on Vicenza, and General Sahuguet, who commanded the division of Serrurier, received orders to take advantage by the difficult topography of the country between Legnago and Mantua, to prevent Wurmser from approaching that place. My measures seemed well taken; but a fault of Sahuguet prevented me from obtaining complete success. Wurmser had gone from Vicenza to Legnago; not imagining that my troops, after the great fatigue they had endured, could possibly make other forced marches, he thought it safe to allow his troops to repose at Legnago during the day of the tenth. This delay ought to have been fatal to him; Massena had passed the Adige at Ronco, on the evening of the tenth, after encountering the greatest difficulties for want of a suitable equipage.* He succeeded at last in putting himself in a position where he could cut off the Austrians from the road to Nogara. This advance guard set off on the morning of the eleventh; but deceived by a guide, instead of going directly to Sanguinetto, where it could easily have anticipated the enemy's column, it was conducted to Cerea. It there encountered the advanced guard of Wurmser, who had begun

---

* This is the second important operation of Napoleon, that failed for want of good bridge-equipage. Placentia was the first.

his march on the morning of the eleventh, after having first left a garrison of seventeen hundred men at Legnago. The Austrians being the most numerous, our troops were repelled with loss, and Wurmser succeeded in marching his column without further obstacle on Nogara. I was somewhat vexed at this check, but still was satisfied that Wurmser could not escape; I knew that Sahuguet was at Castellaro, with the most positive orders to destroy the bridges of the Molinella, and by this means arrest the progress of the enemy. Unfortunately, he forgot the bridge of Villa-Impenta; Wurmser took advantage of this last means of escape from the certain ruin I had prepared for him, and shut himself up in Mantua. I never pardoned Sahuguet for so gross a fault, which deprived me of all the fruits of the victory of Bassano. The garrison of Legnago, blockaded on the left bank of the Adige by the division of Augereau, and on the right by a brigade of Massena, capitulated on the twelfth.

Affairs at San-Georgio.—Wurmser had flattered himself that he would raise the siege of Mantua at the head of twenty-six thousand men; he was now driven with twelve thousand vanquished troops to seek refuge there, and he himself to submit to a siege. At first he encamped his troops between San-Georgio and the citadel. This position would enable them to act offensively against our besieging army, and to make sorties for provisions. I therefore determined to force them to enter within the walls of the town, from which they could not easily, on account of the topography of the environs, debouch against us. The main body of my forces was therefore directed on Mantua. Some partial advantages gained over Sahuguet and Massena on the thirteenth and fourteenth, inspired them with a fatal security. A general sortie being made by all the garrison on the fifteenth, I attacked them with all my forces: on the right

Sahuguet was posted at La Favorite; on the left, the division of Augereau marched from Governolo by Castellaro, on San-Georgio; on the centre, Messena took a covered position near Due-Castelli. Wurmser, seeing himself assailed on the two wings, supported them with strong detachments from the centre; seeing this part weakened, I suddenly threw forward the division of Massena, which, meeting no serious resistance, penetrated as far as San-Georgio, and carried that place at the point of the bayonet. This cut off the retreat of the Austrian right, which now sought safety by penetrating in the direction of the citadel. Wurmser having lost two or three thousand men, shut himself up within the walls of the place.

Position of the Army about Mantua. — Entrusting the blockade of Mantua to General Kilmaine,* who had under his orders the old division of Serrurier, eight thousand strong, I placed the rest of my army in observation before the Tyrol; it would have been useless and imprudent for me to penetrate into this region after Jourdan had fallen back, under the cannon of Dusseldorf, and Moreau under those of Kehl; this useless invasion would have allowed Wurmser to escape. I then stationed Massena, with ten thousand men, at Bassano; Augereau with nine thousand, at Verona; while Vaubois, with ten thousand, remained on the Lavis.

---

* Kilmaine (Charles Jennings), was born in Dublin, of a noble family. He emigrated to France with his father, when very young, and entered the army at the age of fifteen. He was exceedingly fond of military studies, and early distinguished himself for his knowledge of the military art. He came to America with M. de Baron as lieutenant, and served in our Revolutionary War. He saw much service in the earlier wars of the French Revolution, and received rapid promotion. He greatly distinguished himself in the campaign of 1796. He died in 1799. Napoleon thus describes his character: "He was an excellent cavalry officer, possessing coolness and *coup-d'œil*, and was well suited to command on parties of observation, and all such delicate commissions as required discernment, sagacity, and presence of mind. In the campaign of Italy, he rendered important services to the army, of which, but for his ill-health, he would have been one of the principal generals."

Add to these **my reserve of** cavalry, and it will be seen that **my available force did** not exceed forty thousand combatants.

The presence of a small army in Mantua ought to augment the trophies we hoped to gain from this conquest; but the reverses which our arms had encountered on the Rhine, gave us good grounds to fear that the Austrians might reënforce their army in the Tyrol and the Friouli, and renew their efforts to deliver it. In that case, the presence of Wurmser with twenty thousand men in our rear, might become an object of much solicitude. As a climax to our ill-luck, my army encountered the autumnal fevers of the marshes about Mantua; and the southern horizon of Italy began to be overcast.

New Republics formed.—Convinced, however, that Austria would not immediately trouble me, I gave all the month of October to the interior organization of Italy. The threatening invasion of Wurmser had again revived the hopes of Rome, and they no longer troubled themselves with executing the conditions of the armistice of Bologna. To disembarrass ourselves of this power, it was necessary in turn to negotiate and to threaten. Ercole III., Duke of Modena, had fled to Venice with his treasures. This last descendant of the house of Este* belied his name in every respect; he was a man of breeding and taste, but a sordid avarice obscured all his faculties. The Archduke Ferdinand was his heir, and this

---

* This was one of the most illustrious families of Italy, and traced its origin to those petty princes who governed Tuscany in the time of the Carlovingians (tenth century). In the contests of Guelfs and Ghibelines, the Marquises of Este became leaders of the Guelf party, and acquired the territories of Ferrara and Modena. The house was afterwards celebrated for its magnificent patronage of distinguished men, and several of its dukes acquired the reputation of statesmen and warriors. Alfonso I., and his wife Lucretia Borgia, both occupy a prominent position in the history of the sixteenth century. Ercole III., the last Duke of Modena, Reggio, and Mirandola, married his only daughter, Maria Beatrice, to the Archduke Ferdinand. The House of Este was definitely deprived of its sovereignty by the **treaty of** Campo-Formio, October 17th, 1797.

of itself was enough to make him our enemy. The regency instituted in his absence was hostile to us, and I, therefore, determined to destroy it; the people of Reggio were on our side, and required no stimulus to revolt. We occupied without obstacle the fortified place of Modena, and our troops effected a revolution there.

I felt the necessity of creating a new state in Italy; but my plans for the regeneration of that country were not yet matured. Nothing is more difficult than to unite ten states of separate interests into one. The simple question of choosing the capital would excite local feelings and interests. For the time, it would have been sufficient for my purpose to revive the Lombard power, in order to oppose an antique Italian glory to the House of Austria. But to speak of a kingdom, or even a duchy to the Rewels and Barras, had been to compromise me without any advantage; these gentlemen wished to republicanize everything. I therefore laid the basis of several provisional republics,—the Cisalpine, the Cispadane, and Transpadane. They were democracies, for it would then have been imprudent to speak to my soldiers about founding aristocracies; but I succeeded in preserving something of *préséance* to the nobility and clergy, in order to conciliate these classes. Bologna and Ferrara formed a Transpadane Republic, Modena and Reggio united formed the Cispadane. It was best to give them this organization for the present, because it suited the contracted notions of the plebeians of these cities, and facilitated the arrangements necessary to secure peace. Milan gradually adopted the idea of a general regeneration in Italy. The fear of being given up to Austria on a treaty of peace, cooled the Lombards, and, in fact, I did not wish to compromise too seriously the people of these provinces; it was enough to sow the seed, in order to gather the fruit after the war. It was sufficient for me that Lombardy should organize some paid legions which, with the National Guards of the republics of the Po, would preserve order in the interior, and render available a part of the garrisons which I had left there.

Political State of the rest of Italy.—These measures were the more prudent as the affairs of the remainder of Italy presented an aspect not very encouraging. The negotiations with Naples were still under discussion, and the policy of Piedmont uncertain. Victor Amadeus might remember the influence which his ancestor had acquired, by declaring, in 1705, against Louis XIV, when his armies were on the Adige against those of prince Eugene. The same motives now existed, and, the circumstances being the same, he might hope to obtain like results. The environs of Genoa were far from quiet, and the Senate, beset, it is said, by the solicitations of Faypoult, had some hand in the troubles of the Imperial Fiefs. The Pope, recovered from his terror, no longer thought of peace. Venice, by declaring against the new republics, could give a dangerous turn to the war. Fearing to rouse the Lion of St. Mark, I sought, in concert with the Directory, by propositions skilfully offered, to attach to us the old republic, whose slightest effort, in the critical situation of affairs, was capable of inclining the balance on the side of our enemies. Who knew but the present Doge, in imitation of the Morosini, Dandolos and Alvianis, might put himself at the head of twenty thousand men and assist the imperialists in expelling from Italy that handful of men who had just excited so many conflicting interests? Would not such an act have decided the fate of Mantua, encouraged the King of Naples, and also the King of Sardinia, whose country, covered with a triple line of posts, was ill-disposed towards us? To determine the vacillating Senate to throw itself boldly into the arms of France, by painting to it in turn the dangers to which it was exposed on the one side by propagandism and on the other by the ambition of Austria; and, in case of refusal, to quiet it with promises and to prolong its lethargy by protestations of friendship, till it could be overthrown by a popular revolution; such were the means to which I resorted in order to accomplish my objects. But the result did not answer to my first hopes. In vain did the Minister Lallement exhaust all the arguments of diplomacy; neither the proposition of a quadruple alliance with the Porte, Spain and Naples, nor the fear of the encroachments of its redoubtable neighbors, nor the dependence of Austria and England, could break the impassable policy of a body already struck with paralysis in all its parts. Trusting in its own weakness, it required all the entreaties of such men as Pesaro to induce the Senate to order a levy of Sclavonic soldiers, and the armament of a flotilla for the defense of its lagoons; measures of interior security of which no foreign power had a right to complain, but which in the present state of affairs caused us much anxiety. The coincidence of these armaments with the refusal of the Pope to sign the treaty of peace, and the arrival at Rome of the Marquis del Vasto, charged by the King of Naples to form an offensive and defensive alliance between the two states, caused me to think that I should soon have to contend with an Italian league, unless the Directory hastened its negotiations with Naples. I urged it to make peace with that power at any price, as it was the only means of forcing the rest of the Peninsula to terms.

Discussions with Rome.—Pius VI continually protested his love of peace, but he partook too much of the hatred which the cardinals and secretary of state had vowed against our democratic principles, to willingly close the negotiations with the severe conditions which I had imposed upon him; he prolonged them in hopes of finding, sooner or later, an occasion for breaking them off with eclat. The first success of Wurmser and the momentary raising of the blockade of Mantua, revived the hopes of the pontifical government; it confided in these temporary successes so much as to charge the prelate Lagreca to endeavor to retake Ferrara, and succeed, under different pretexts, in eluding the articles of the armistice. It had been specified that no eclesiastic should be sent to treat definitively of peace; but in violation of this clause, the prelates Petrarchi and Vangelisti had been sent to Paris. Such a want of faith on the part of Rome was calculated to destroy all confidence, and the French government, refusing to recognize these two agents, ordered them to quit Paris in twenty-four hours. The nuncios and legates of Ancona and Romana conducted themselves as declared enemies of the French army. Finally, the Holy See was negotiating a close alliance with the cabinet of Vienna and asking of it officers for the papal troops. Informed of these malevolent dispositions I was preparing to put an end to them, when the operations of the imperial armies forced me to dissemble my resentment and to turn my whole attention to the Adige. The Pope, after the dismissal of his agents, sought to renew negotiations at Florence. The prelate Galleppi, the Domincan Soldati, and the Chevalier d'Azzara, the Spanish ambassador who had just been mediator in the ill-observed armistice, presented themselves to the commissioners Salicetti and Garreau, but it was impossible to come to an understanding. These last required the Pope to withdraw and declare null the bulls published against France since the Revolution; that he should close his ports to the English, and make reparation for the murder of Basseville.* Carrying their inflexibility to the last degree, they presented

* In 1793, a popular commotion was caused in Rome by the display which some young French artists made of the tri-colored flag; the carriage of Basseville, the French envoy, was attacked in the street, his house was broken into, by the mob, and he himself, unarmed and unresisting, was cruelly assassinated. He was thrust through the abdomen with a bayonet, and dragged through the street, holding his bowels in his hands.

to his plenipotentiaries a treaty in sixty-four articles, declaring that it must be adopted or rejected as it was, as they were not authorized to enter into any discussion. This method of treating, wholly unprecedented even in the Revolutionary diplomacy of 1793, produced an injurious effect. Galleppi returned to Rome. So powerfully had the success of the Austrians operated upon all minds that the Pontifical government, thinking the deliverance of Italy near at hand, not only rejected the propositions submitted to it, but suddenly passed to hostile preparations ; the armistice was disregarded ; the money sent to pay the contributions was recalled, and new amounts raised in all the States of the Church. The novenas, prayers, processions, bulls, in a word all that could influence the hatred of an ignorant and superstitious multitude was put in operation in order to increase the recruits of the Papal army. But these means, so powerful in the fifteenth century, had now lost their magic ; the mass of the people limited themselves to the offer of vows and prayers for the success of so just a war ! Some of the princes, through fear of losing their priviliges, were compelled to join in the preparations. The Constable Colonna raised a regiment of infantry, the Prince Gustiniani offered one of cavalry. But these were not sufficient to form an army ; indeed they could hardly raise eight thousand men ; but they flattered themselves that Naples would furnish thirty thousand.

In the mean time Chevalier d'Assara, interposing the mediation of Spain, succeeded in retarding the explosion, and, in these trying circumstances, rendered us eminent services. The French envoy, Cacault, on his side, contributed, by his impassable countenance, to avoid an open rupture, which at this epoch might have had for us the most fatal results.

Definitive Peace with Naples.—These troubles were at last happily dissipated by the definitive treaty signed at Paris, the tenth of October, between the French Republic and the court of the Two-Sicilies. The conditions were very mild, compared with those imposed upon the Pope and Piedmont. This moderation was due, without doubt, to the great distance of the kingdom of Naples, the difficulty of carrying on war against it, and to the urgency of getting rid of an enemy whose army alone exceeded my own. If we had continued hostilities, the Neapolitans could have sustained Rome, and, in concert with the English division of Corsica, advanced upon the Po with forty thousand men, rendering the conquest of Italy still doubtful. But, after the treaty, they would no longer trouble themselves about Lombardy; Rome would be left to its own troops; the English would not alone attempt anything in Tuscany, and nothing would interfere in the ulterior military operations against Austria. The Directory, yielding at last to my solicitations, supported by Carnot, abated its pretensions, in order to facilitate the treaty. The court of Naples merely engaged to remain neutral, to ferret out the authors of the crimes of 1793, to promise to France a reciprocal treaty of commerce, to recognize the Batavian republic, and to renew with it ancient relations.

Affairs of Piedmont.—If the definitive peace concluded with Ferdinand, on the tenth of October, rid us of a troublesome neighbor, the death of the king of Sardinia, about the middle of the same month, seemed likely to produce a vexatious change in the policy of the court of Turin. The new king, Charles Emanuel, had declared for peace, and had favorably received the propositions of alliance made by Poussielgue, but he had put in a condition that they should cede to him Lombardy, and the Directory had obstinately refused every arrangement of this nature. It was therefore to be feared that this prince, desirous of signalizing his accession to the throne, would seek to restore the lustre of his power by acquisitions equal to the provinces lost by his predecessors, in this war. The refusal of France, leaving him no hope of obtaining indemnities in that quarter, he would naturally join the coalition as soon as there was any hope of his recovering his lost provinces. This resolution seemed so much the more probable, as the lesser powers usually range themselves on the strongest side, especially where fear is united with the manifest interest of the state. This uncertainty of our relations with Piedmont made me strongly sensible of the necessity of making sure of Genoa. If Piedmont should change her policy, we would then have neither a base of operations nor a line of retreat; the possession of Genoa would procure both. I was not now in a situation to obtain this by force, and, moreover, we had no motives for hostile measures with that power.

Negotiations with Genoa.—The first success of our arms had closed the port of Genoa against English vessels, in reprisal for hostilities committed by them, in 1793, against French ships. The Senate refused, for a long time, to recognize the Count de Girola, the envoy of the emperor, under the pretext that he had excited insurrection in the Imperial Fiefs. The Genoese people were well disposed towards France, on account of the intimate commercial relations between the two countries, and the Senate had given such proofs of its moderation as ought to have satisfied us; but this was not sufficient for my safety, or the ambition of the Directory; we wished Liguria to make decidedly common cause with France. The presence of the English minister, Drake, the reports he circulated respecting the designs of the English upon the rear of our army, the seizure of the frigate *La Modeste*, and other offenses, of which Genoa was not guilty, seemed plausible grounds of complaint. Thinking it best to assume an imperious tone, I dispatched, at the moment when embarrassments of all kinds were troubling me on the Adige, an aid-de-camp to the Doge, with a list of grievances, for which I asked reparation; threatening, in case of refusal, to march on Genoa. But the moment was not propitious. Faypoult demonstrated that an untimely explosion might spoil all; besides, the news that the Directory were treating at Paris, with the republic, turned aside the blow; and, waiting for a proper opportunity for the execution of my designs, I exacted new sums of money. On the ninth of October a treaty, stipulating the payment of four millions, the shutting of the port to the English, free passage to our troops and convoys destined for the army of Italy, transformed Genoa into a French place-of-arms.

Troubles in the Fiefs.—The peasants of the Imperial Fiefs, instigated, as some say, by the agents of Faypoult, and, according to others, by Count Girola, opposed this treaty, and organized new insurrections. The Fiefs of St. Marguerita, situated advantageously in the valley of the Scrivia, was the focus of the revolt. They had assembled there escaped prisoners of war and deserters, for the purpose of afterwards sending them to the Tyrol, by Sestri di Levante. There was a depot of arms and munitions, which they drew in secret from Genoa. Wurmser, informed of their movements, wished an officer should be charged with their direction; but again, on this occasion, he was anticipated; the French sent some movable columns into the Fiefs, scattered the assemblage, took hostages, and got possession of the arms. With the exception of the Barbets, who disturbed the passage of the Apennines, all the north of Italy was tranquil, thanks to the presence of the little army of Kellerman.

Affairs of Corsica.—The possession of Corsica became daily more difficult and onerous to the English. The declaration of war by Spain rendered their situation in the Mediterranean perilous, and exposed this colony to the attack of two powers well provided with the means of making descents; moreover, they had much to fear from the inhabitants, the major part of whom remained sincerely attached to France. Even the

Paolists, deceived by England, had already committed many acts of hostility against the viceroy.

English Occupation of Porto-Ferrajo.—Lord Elliot, convinced that it was not the interest of Great Britain to preserve, by force of arms, a station were the population was so irritable, had been for some time preparing to evacuate the island. Hearing of the occupation of Leghorn by the French troops, and the preparations made at Toulon for an expedition, he felt the urgency of the English occupying Porto-Ferrajo. This maritime, military and commercial station, for England, united almost all the advantages, without the inconveniences of Corsica. The Tuscan commandant was therefore summoned on the tenth of July; and in retaliation for our occupation of Leghorn, he permitted the English to occupy the forts in conjunction with the troops of the Grand Duke.

Evacuation of Corsica.—Elliot soon had reason to congratulate himself on this arrangement. The discontent of the Corsicans continued to increase; the glory reflected upon them by my victories, and the reception of the Corsican patriots in France, contrasted too strongly with the treatment received by their compatriots from the English, to say nothing of the old national hatred, not to incite all the inhabitants to throw off their yoke. The number of these patriot refugees at Marseilles and Leghorn increased daily, and the intelligence they maintained with those who had at first ranged themselves under the banners of England, announced that the moment of insurrection had come. An order of evacuation from the admiralty to the governor prevented an actual outbreak.

In the meantime, I myself was endeavoring to lend assistance to my compatriots; I charged General Gentilli to make at Leghorn secret preparations for an expedition. On the other hand, the government had directed at Toulon the preparation for an armament necessary for this enterprise ; the Spanish squadron of Langara, leaving Carthagena with twenty-five vessels, seemed certain of success. As soon as Gentilli got wind of the dispositions of the English for a retreat, he embarked General Casalta with a small detachment of troops-of-the-line, and some armed refugees. This officer, braving the enemy's cruisers, and combating the elements, arrived, in spite of every obstacle, in Corsica, on the nineteenth of October. The next day he was joined by a considerable number of patriots with whose assistance he attacked Bastia. Master of the heights commanding the city, and protected by the inhabitants, he summoned the garrison of the fort to surrender ; the English reached their vessels, but their rear guard, composed in part of the regiment of Dillon, lost several prisoners. Saint Florent and Ajaccio were soon surrendered, and in a few days the island returned to the empire of which it formed a part.

Situation of the Armies on the Adige. — These political revolutions, armistices, and interior expeditions, filled up the interval between the combat of San-Georgio and the battle of Arcola. The main body of the French army remained during these two months about Mantua, and in observation on the Brenta and the Adige. Epidemic fevers had filled my hospitals, and diminished considerably the number of combatants ; reënforcements arrived too slowly to enable me to make any advance. The Austrians, on the contrary, made vast preparations for a new trial of arms.

Alvinzi comes to succor Mantua.—By the middle of October, the forces of Davidowich's corps was increased to near twenty thousand men. The corps of Quasdanowich which, after the defeat of Bassano had retired to Gorizia, was also increased to about twenty-five thousand men. The permanent organization of the Croats into regiments had produced a part of these forces, and the rest had been drawn from the northern Tyrol after the retreat of the armies of the Rhine, or had been recruited in the interior. General Alvinzi, appointed commander-in-chief of all these forces, repaired to the corps of Quasdanowich and took the offensive, directing himself by Bassano on Verona, where he hoped to effect a junction with Davidowich, who had received orders to descend the Adige. My position was extremely difficult ; I could not advance to meet Alvinzi without leaving Verona, and consequently enabling Davidowich to drive back Vaubois, to unite with Wurmser under Mantua, and thus establish on my rear an army superior in number to all the forces which I could collect. On the other hand, I could not concentrate the mass of my forces on Roveredo without leaving open to Alvinzi the road to Mantua, which, in an inverse sense, would effect the same results. Nor could I well concentrate on Verona, for the communications between Alvinzi and Davidowich would then be reëstablished by the valley of the Brenta. It was almost as necessary for me to prevent the junction of these two generals, as the union of one of them with Wurmser. I therefore was obliged to adopt a middle course.

Vaubois driven back on Rivoli.—Vaubois was too inferior in numbers to effectually defend the access to Trente. By making him take the offensive, I thought to intimidate Davidowich : I was deceived. The second of November Vaubois obtained some advantages at St. Michael, in the valley of the Adige ; but turned himself on the right by the valley of the Lavis, he was obliged to fight in retreat the next day, in order to reach Calliano. Davidowich entered Trente on the fourth. The same day, the army of Alvinzi arrived at Cittadella and Bassano. At the approach of the enemy, Massena fell back by Vicenza to Montebello. The communication between the two parts of the enemy's army, now seemed certain ; but as in changing their general the

Austrians had not changed their system of strategy, they still continued to act separately. Davidowich marched on Calliano, and Alvinzi prepared to attack Verona, by Vicenza. I determined to repeat, from right to left, the manœuvre which, from left to right, had succeeded so well against Wurmser; that is, I determined to defeat Alvinzi and drive him behind the Piave, and then ascend the Brenta to assail the rear of Davidowich.

Affairs of the Brenta.—I advanced towards the Brenta with Augereau and Massena; I already found the enemy on this side of the river. On the sixth, Massena attacked, at Carmignano, the left of Alvinzi which was commanded by Provera. His right, under the orders of Quasdanowich, was attacked the same day at Lenova by Augereau. We obtained only a partial success. Provera repassed the Brenta and Quasdanowich approached Bassano without our having been able to seriously injure them. The enemy was stronger and better prepared to receive us than I had expected. On the other hand I learned that he was closely pressing Vaubois in the valley of the Adige. It was necessary to renounce my projects, for I felt the importance of calling to me Vaubois and Kilmaine. On the seventh, I took the road to Verona. Alvinzi followed me and arrived on the eleventh at Villa-Nova. Vaubois, attacked at Calliano, sustained a hard fight. On the sixth and seventh he maintained his position; but fearing to be turned by the right, he retired on the night of the seventh and eighth to the Corona. I hastened with all speed to this division, harangued the 39th and 85th which had failed at Calliano, and threatened to inscribe on their flags that they were no longer worthy to be of the army of Italy. They swore to conquer or die.

Combat of Caldiero.—In the meantime I was closely pressed; and I determined to fall again on the army of Alvinzi. On the eleventh I left Verona, with Massena and

Augereau, and the next day attacked the enemy in position at Caldiero. A violent north-east hailstorm in the face of our soldiers, and the strong position of the enemy, rendered our efforts utterly useless; we were repelled with loss.

Passage of the Adige at Ronco.—I returned to Verona in a critical condition; my forces were everywhere too weak. Fortune seemed decidedly against us. But I had heretofore profited by her favor; I now wished to prove to the world that I could conquer with fortune against me. Any other general would have repassed the Mincio, and lost Italy. But my future hopes would have died with the loss of my conquests. It was necessary to risk all for all. I resolved to pass the Adige below the left of Alvinzi, in order to threaten his rear. This was a hazardous course; but it was the only one that left me any chance of success. Alvinzi, in advancing upon Verona by the route of Caldiero, had, on his right, impracticable mountains, on his left, the Adige, and in front, a strongly fortified town. The ground which he occupied was thus inclosed on three sides, and offered no other outlet than the defile of Villa-Nova. In crossing to Ronco I approached this outlet, and forced the enemy to fight with his line faced to the rear, in order to open to himself a passage; finally, I placed my inferior army in marshy ground, where the enemy could give battle upon three dykes, and where I had all the advantage of the defensive, joined to the individual superiority of my soldiers.

Battle of Arcola.—I withdrew General Kilmaine from the blockade of Mantua, with two thousand men, and confided to him the defense of Verona, which place it was indispensable for us to maintain, in order to close the passage of the valley of the Adige to Alvinzi, and prevent him from joining Davidowich. With the divisions of Massena and Augereau, and the reserve of cavalry, in all about twenty thousand men, I left Verona on the fourteenth for Ronco, where I threw a bridge across the Adige. Some have thought that I ought to have crossed at Albaredo, in order to avoid the Alpon, its marches, and the defile of Arcola. It is true I should, in this way, have more easily gained Villa-Nova, but I was not strong enough to recklessly throw myself upon the only route of Alvinzi; I could merely threaten it, without quitting the support of the Adige; and at the same time, it was necessary for me to maintain my connection with Verona and the division of Vaubois. The movement by Albaredo was too long to accomplish this triple object, and it was, by far, too dangerous to give battle on the Alpon, at Villa-Nova, with my front to the rear, in order to face Verona. I therefore passed the Adige at Ronco, on the fifteenth of November. The ground which separates it from the Alpon was entirely inundated: over this there were only three dikes. Massena took the one on the left, which runs nearly parallel to the Adige, as far as Porcil. Augereau took the centre dike, leading to the bridge of Arcola, over the Alpon. A brigade of Croats, detached as flankers from the left, defended this last point. These troops made the best use of the advantages of ground to repel the attacks of Augereau. This circumstance, which I could not foresee, was near becoming fatal: the resistance of the Croats gave Alvinzi time to hasten to their assistance. The Austrian general, fearing that his retreat might be cut off, sent Provera, with six battalions, against Massena, to Porcil, and, with the main body of his army, fell back upon San-Bonifacio. The unforeseen opposition at Arcola did not prevent me from persevering with my project. If I could not reach Villa-Nova by the left bank of the Alpon, I could act by Porcil more directly on Alvinzi's line of retreat; but it was necessary to be master of the village and defile of Arcola, in order to secure my right, and to avoid being taken myself in this *cul-de-sac*. I again tried to carry the bridge. The greater part of my generals had been wounded in leading on their men. I now threw myself at the head of my grenadiers; but it was all useless. Possibility had limits even for my troops. The head of the column was broken, and most vigorously repulsed. In the midst of this disorder I was thrown from the dike into the morass, and ran imminent risk of being made prisoner: Belliard charged with a company of grenadiers and rescued me. Towards evening the Austrians abandoned Arcola, at the approach of a brigade which I had thrown across the Adige, by the ferry of Albaredo, and which advanced by ascending the left of the Alpon. But it was now too late, and I did not wish to run the risk of passing the night with my troops crowded together in the morass, and exposed to the enemy's army, which was now deployed between San-Bonifacio and San-Stefano. Moreover, it was possible that Vaubois might be driven to Bussalingo, and, in that case, it would be necessary for me to make a forced march, in the night, on the Mincio, in order to join him at Mantua; but this I could not possibly accomplish without taking the precaution of repassing to the right of the Adige, in the day-time. This I did, leaving on the left bank troops merely sufficient to guard the bridge.

It was now too late to act upon the rear of Alvinzi; but I had, at least, succeeded in removing him from Verona. This circumstance only postponed my defeat, unless I could throw him completely back upon the Brenta. This it was necessary to effect at any sacrifice. Certain that Vaubois had not been molested, on the fifteenth, by Davidowich, we repassed to the left of the Adige on the morning of the sixteenth. The Austrians having occupied Albaredo, Arcola, and Porcil, now advanced against our bridge; we drove them back. Massena entered Porcil, and throwing back one of his brigades on the centre, cut off, on the dike, a column of fifteen hundred men. Augereau again advanced upon

Arcola; here the operations of the previous evening were repeated, and we sustained considerable loss, without being able to carry the bridge. At night we recrossed the Adige, for the same reason as on the previous day.

But all this ill success did not discourage me. Davidowich had attacked the Corona on the sixteenth, and got possession of Rivoli. Vaubois had retired in good order on Bussalingo and Castel-Novo. It was now very important for me to force Alvinzi to retire beyond Villa-Nova, so as to open a direct communication with Verona, for the assistance of Vaubois. The third time I renewed the attack; and I would have renewed it ten times more, if I had not succeeded. I felt that the preservation of Italy was necessary for my political existence. I preferred dying at the head of my army, to commencing a retreat which I knew would destroy all the fruits of my preceding exploits. On the seventeenth, at the break of day, my troops again took the road to the bridge. Fortune seemed decidedly opposed to me. At the moment of effecting the passage one of the boats of the bridge sunk. This unfortunate accident would have deprived me of all chance of success had not the address and zeal of my pontoniers extricated me from the difficulty. When the bridge was repaired, my army crossed the river and again drove back the enemy to Porcil and Arcola. But as this was no longer the principal point of attack, I now limited myself to sending General Robert against it with a demi-brigade of Massena's division. Massena himself moved with the other demi-brigade against Porcil. The rest of the division remained in reserve near the bridge. If the enemy should profit by his superiority over Robert, I was ready to make him repent it. Augereau's division had orders to throw a bridge over the Alpon near its mouth in order to act against the left of the Austrians and take Arcola in reverse.

The Austrians, being reënforced at Arcola, took the offensive, routed General Robert, and pursued him quite to the bridge. This was just what I wished, for it was important to cut up the enemy's forces as much as possible before attempting the passage of the Alpon. Their deep column, proud of a first success, encountered the main body of Massena's division, at the same time that the troops I had concealed in the reeds fell upon the flank of the column, cutting off three thousand men and driving the remainder back in disorder upon Arcola. This was the decisive moment. The division of Augereau having at last succeeded in constructing its bridge, crossed the stream and came up in front of the left wing of the Austrians which rested its left on a morass. I had expected to turn this obstacle by means of eight hundred men from Legnago; but as they had not yet made their appearance, I thought to impose on my enemies by making a feint against the flank. I therefore ordered an officer to gain the point of the Austrian wing with twenty horsemen and some buglers. This *ruse* produced its effect. The Austrian infantry lost that *aplomb* which they preserved till then. Augereau profited by this to force it back, and the opportune appearance of the small garrison of Legnago in rear of the enemy, precipitated his retreat towards San-Bonifacio. The division of Massena then debouched by Arcola and San-Gregorio. Alvinzi, who had not been able to arrest us upon ground the most favorable for the defensive, did not attempt to risk a battle in an open country with an army already reduced to about fifteen thousand combatants. On the eighteenth he retired to Montebello.* I had lost almost as many men as the enemy; I had not defeated him, but I had gained the means of turning against Davidowich.

---

* In speaking of this movement Alison says, "It was so apparent to all the Austrian army that this retreat was the result of a secret understanding with the French general, and with a view to the negotiation which was now depending, that they openly and loudly expressed their indignation. One colonel broke

Vaubois driven from Rivoli.—This general, who for eight days had amused himself before the intrenchments of the Corona, had at last attacked Vaubois on the sixteenth. He gained no great advantage on the first day, but on the second Vaubois, threatened to be turned by the right, evacuated his position and fell back behind the Mincio, crossing the river at Peschiera. On the eighteenth Davidowich advanced to Castel-Novo, and I now resolved to make him pay dearly for his slight success. I sent my reserve of cavalry in pursuit of Alvinzi and with the main body of my infantry fell back from Villa-Nova to Verona and made a triumphal entry into that city by the gate of Venice, three days after having mysteriously left it by the gate of Milan. The inhabitants, and my soldiers, astonished at manœuvres which they could not comprehend, regarded me with equal admiration. Massena recrossed the Adige at Verona and marched upon Villa-Franca, where he expected to meet Vaubois, who had again crossed the Mincio at Borghetta. These two divisions were to attack Davidowich in front, while Augereau marched from Verona by the mountains on Dolce in order to cut off his retreat. Davidowich barely escaped a complete overthrow by hastening to regain Roveredo; his rear-guard was much cut up. Alvinzi, on his side, seeing that he was pursued by cavalry only, returned to Villa-Nova. But I had now finished with Davidowich, and was preparing to debouch anew by Verona on the left of the Adige. Alvinzi, being isolated,

---

his sword in pieces, and declared he would no longer serve under a commander whose conduct brought disgrace on his troops. Certain it is that Alvinzi, during this dreadful strife at Arcola, had neither exhibited the capacity nor the spirit of a general worthy to combat with Napoleon." The object of these remarks is evidently to diminish the glory acquired by Napoleon in this victory. Never was a battle harder fought by the Austrians, and to attribute Alvinzi's retreat, after seventy-two hours' fighting, to a secret understanding with Napoleon, is too absurd to merit comment. Alison's account of this battle is wholly chimerical, but where errors so abound it is hardly worth while to point out the details.

did not venture to take the field, but fell back behind the Brenta.

Wurmser besieged in Mantua.—During these stirring events upon the Adige, Wurmser had remained quietly in Mantua. Alvinzi, at the beginning of his operations, had calculated that he could not arrive before Mantua till the twenty-third, and had engaged Wurmser not to make a sortie till that day. But as things did not turn out exactly as the enemy had hoped, he found that Kilmaine had already returned before the place. The besiegers were therefore in a situation to repel any operations of the besieged.

Reverses in Germany.—These events were the more fortunate for France, as the armies in Germany had been forced to retreat to the Rhine. I have already said that the Archduke Charles had wisely resolved to throw the main body of his army on Jourdan, certain that, if he beat him at Franconia, he would force him upon Mayence, and compromise Moreau, who had advanced as far as Munich. With these dispositions he could hardly fail of success. And if, after his victory at Wurtzburg, on the third of September, he had thrown himself on the communications of Moreau, sending only some twenty thousand men in pursuit of the *débris* of Jourdan, the army of the Rhine must have been lost. Moreau, but feebly troubled, made his retreat in good order, while the Archduke was operating on the Lahn. Our armies prepared to defend Kehl and Dusseldorf; the Archduke concentrated all his means on the upper Rhine, to retake Kehl, but Moreau and Desaix most skilfully defended it till the middle of January. As a climax of contrariety, the Directory replaced Jourdan*

---

* Jean Baptiste Jourdan was born at Limoges, France, in 1762. He entered the military service in 1778, and fought in America. He distinguished himself in the early wars of the French Revolution, and in 1793 became general-of-division, and held several important commands, but was soon after promoted by Napoleon to the office of governor of Piedmont. In 1803 he was made gen-

by Beurnonville,* a man very much inferior to his predecessor. Although reënforced by twenty thousand men from the superb troops which, for two years, had occupied Holland, and by twenty-five thousand who had blockaded Mayence, he remained inactive for two months, with eighty thousand men against twenty-five thousand Austrians. This inaction was the more censurable as it took place in November and December, when the affairs of Moreau and myself were the most critical; I had then just experienced my severe losses upon the Brenta, at Caliano, and at Arcola.

Descent upon Ireland.—Venice having rejected our alliance, it became necessary to adopt some plan to relieve ourselves from our critical position. I most strongly urged the Directory to send forces sufficient, not only to support myself, but to overthrow Wurmser, and attack the heart of the Austrian monarchy. The Directory, at first, sent me one division, drawn from the army of the Atlantic coast; but the troubles excited in the south, by the royalist reaction, caused a part of them to be retained in Provence, and General Rey brought to me hardly six thousand men, while they might easily have sent me twenty-five thousand, had it not been for the expedition which was sent, at this inopportune moment, against Ireland. My object now being merely to speak of what concerns myself, rather than to trace a history of the events which took place at a time when I was not at

---

eral-in-chief of the army of Italy, and in 1804 marshal of France. He served in many of Napoleon's wars, and espoused his cause in the final struggle of 1815. He was an honest, upright man, and showed considerable ability as a general, but never gained a very high reputation. He died in 1826.—*Encyclopedia Americana.*

* Pierre Riel de Beurnonville, was born in 1752, at Champignole. He was made general in 1792. He saw much service, but never distinguished himself as a general. Between 1791 and 1793 he is said to have been present in no less than one hundred and seventy-two engagements. Napoleon employed him principally on diplomatic services. He died in 1821.—*Biographie Moderne.*

the head of affairs in France, I will not stop to investigate what was then occurring in Ireland, nor to give the details of Lord Malmesbury's negotiations at Paris. I will merely say, that the Directory, meditating an expedition of twenty-five thousand men under Hoche, in order to give to four millions of Irish Catholics a point of support which might shake the English power, neglected, for this important but untimely object, to send me the reënforcements which might have been withdrawn from the coast. Nothing was more natural than to attempt this expedition to Ireland, after having made peace with Austria; but it was imprudent, with our small forces, to attempt to dictate terms at the same time at Vienna and Dublin. Hoche left Brest on the fourteenth of December, but his squadron was dispersed by storms; his isolated vessels had the good luck to escape the English and regain their ports; his soldiers, debarked at the beginning of the following campaign, went to restore victory to the banners of the army of Sambre-et-Meuse, and, after one whole year's delay, joined the army in Italy.

There is a division of opinion respecting the degree of importance, and chance of success, of this expedition to Ireland. There is no doubt, however, that an expedition of this kind, seriously occupying England, might have prevented her from sending forces into the two Indies. Many military men have thought that the object was to maintain a long and determined contest with a nation full of energy and patriotism, rather than merely to land a few divisions; and that France had no chance of success while inferior upon the sea; that the feeble army of Hoche, after having forced the court of St. James to resort to the national levies, and finding itself consumed by a hundred battles, would have been obliged to sign a treaty of evacuation, or to reëmbark its scattered forces. Admitting this supposition as the most probable, it follows, that instead of retaining twenty-five thousand of the *élite* of Britanny for so long a time, and turning them afterward upon the coast of Ireland, it would have been more wise to send five or six thousand of them, with skilful chiefs, to Tippoo-Saib, and the other twenty thousand to me, so as to secure the defeat of Wurmser and Alvinzi, under whose attacks I had three times been reduced to the very brink of destruction. The elements of an Irish insurrection would continue for a long time, so that there was no reason why the Directory might not adjourn its projects to a time when, freed from the continental war, it could attempt an expedition without compromising the success of its arms. In the actual state of things, it seemed more urgent to deliver India, and to dictate peace to Austria, than to excite a civil war on the banks of the Shannon.

Useless Negotiations.—The protracted negotiations with Malmesbury could lead to no conclusions, for England would not sanction the change of government in Belgium till the consent of Austria was obtained. Clarke was therefore sent to ask at Vienna the conclusion of an armistice, and to propose sending negotiators to Bâle or Paris. He presented himself for this purpose at my head-quarters, but the success of the Archduke in Germany had so raised the hopes and pretensions of the House of Austria, that they would not permit him to pass the outposts. An event of the highest importance, which had just occurred in the north, might also change the state of affairs on the continent. The great Catharine had, by sudden death on the seventeenth of November, closed her long and illustrious career; her son, Paul I., succeeded her. This prince, singular in everything, might adopt a policy entirely opposite to that of his mother, either profiting by the commotions in the west to make war upon the Turks, or taking part himself in the affairs of France. In the uncertainty that then existed on these questions, the cabinet of Vienna thought best to send the Baron de Vincent to meet Clarke. They commenced a discussion on the fourth of January, at Vicenza, on the proposition of opening negotiations, and on the necessity of first concluding an armistice for the armies of Germany and Italy. Peace presented too many subjects for discussion to be settled definitely at an outpost, and the conditions of an armistice offered in the case no less difficulties. I showed Clarke that if any communication was allowed with Mantua, all the advantage would be on the side of Austria, for famine must soon force its surrender; but Austria insisted that the garrison should be supplied with provisions during the suspension of hostilities. Of course they could not agree. M. de Vincent, a negotiator without powers, returned to Vienna to submit the propositions of France, and his cabinet sent Clarke to the Imperial Minister near the Court of Turin. In this interval, Malmesbury, not having been able to agree to the first article of the negotiation, left Paris, under the suspicion of having been sent merely to learn the object of the preparation made at Brest for the expedition to Ireland. We therefore had now only to think, on our part, of maintaining ourselves in our present position till the arrival of reënforcements, and on the side of Austria, to redouble activity and energy to save Wurmser.

Reenforcements from the Rhine.—The government, which undoubtedly had little hope of success in the negotiations of Clarke, convinced by my picture of the dangers of my position, and by the contest at Arcola, that I was within a hair's breadth of being driven from Italy, determined to take more decided measures : the five divisions of Bernadotte and Delmas, drawn from the armies of the Rhine, and directed in mid-winter across the Alps, would increase my army to seventy-five thousand men. This grand detachment would in no way compromise the armies of Germany, which had now retired under the cannon of Strasburg and Dusseldorf, and besides had been strongly reënforced by fresh troops from Belgium and Holland. Moreover, this would remove the decisive theatre of war to the point where the enemy was most vulnerable. In waiting the realization of these fine, but far-off hopes, I employed the month of December in hastening the organization of the interior of Italy, and guarding against Venice, which seemed more and more ill-disposed toward us as our dangers increased by the unfavorable changes of the war. I felt that, since I could not persuade her to join our interests, it was the wisest course to embarrass her to such a degree as to deprive her of the means of injuring us. For this purpose, and at the same time to cover the left flank and rear of my army on the side of the Valteline, I caused to be occupied the important château of Bergamo, which is perched on the last slope of the Alps toward Lombardy. Patriotic societies, established at Brescia, Bergamo, and Crema, scattered everywhere the seeds of democracy, always so flattering to the multitude. I had gone to Bologna to regulate the affairs of the two little Cispadane and Transpadane Republics, and to menace the Pope, and force him to execute the articles of the armistice, when I learned that Alvinzi had advanced with a new army to raise the siege of Mantau.

New Attempt of Alvinzi to save Wurmser.—My work seemed as unstable as that of Penelope; its destruction seemed the natural result of the constant reënforcements sent by the cabinet of Vienna to the army in Italy, and of the as constant neglect of the French Directory to sustain my efforts. They treated me at Paris as Hannibal was treated by the Carthaginian Senate. At the end of December, Alvinzi's forces were again increased to more than forty thousand men, and it was necessary to contend a fourth time for the possession of Mantua. While waiting for the promised reënforcements from the Rhine, I learned that Alvinzi had resumed the offensive, and I therefore flew to the Adige. My army occupied the following positions : Serrurier's division before Mantua ; Augereau on the Adige, from Verona to Legnago ; Massena at Verona ; Joubert, with a fourth division, at the Corona and Rivoli. Each of these four divisions numbered about ten thousand men. General Rey was at Desenzano with a reserve of four thousand men. The enemy advanced at the same time upon my centre and both wings by Roveredo, by Vicenza, and by Padua. Not knowing on which of these routes the enemy had directed the main body of his forces, I determined to remain in my present position until he should develop his projects. On the twelfth of January, the column which had advanced by Vicenza approached Verona, and drove back the outposts of Massena. But the main body of this general's division having debouched by St. Michael, the enemy was repulsed with loss. This fact convinced me that this could not be the main body of Alvinzi's army.

Joubert is driven back on Rivoli.—The next day, in the afternoon, I received the news that General Joubert, pressed in front by superior forces, and menaced on both flanks by strong columns, had been obliged in the morning to evacuate the position of the Corona, and fall back upon Rivoli, whence he expected to continue his retreat upon Castel-Novo. I had no longer any doubt of the enemy's plans. It was evident that the column of Vicenza, and that which had been directed on the lower Adige, were merely diversions made to facilitate the march of the principal corps on the valley of the Adige. It was necessary, therefore, to oppose to this corps the mass of my army. I left Verona immediately with the divisions of Massena, leaving at that place only about two thousand men to check the column of Vicenza ; I, at the same time, sent orders to Rey to move from Salo on Rivoli, where I had resolved to collect the mass of my forces.

I was convinced, from Joubert's report, that Alvinzi, following the usual foolish plan of the Austrians, and not content with weakening his forces by the detachments thrown on Verona and Legnago, had also divided those he had with him. I knew that in occupying the plateau of Rivoli, where the different paths through this mountainous country united, I should be able to act in mass against columns separated by insurmountable obstacles. Not to lose the advantages of such a position, I ordered Joubert to maintain himself at all hazards in advance of Rivoli till my arrival. I had not been deceived respecting the dispositions of Alvinzi. On leaving Bassano, this general had sent Provera with eight thousand men on Legnago, and Bajalich with five thousand on Verona, while he himself, at the head of thirty thousand men, debouched by Roveredo, on the Corona. This force was now subdivided into six columns. Three of these, forming in all twelve thousand men, attacked Joubert in front, while General Lusignan, with another of four thousand men, was to turn our left by passing the western slope of the Monte Baldo. Quasdanowich, with a fifth column of eight thousand men, was to assail our right, he moving along the road on the right of the Adige; the artillery and cavalry, as they could not be employed in the mountains, were directed to follow this last column. Finally, Wukassowich, with the sixth column of four thousand men, descended the left bank of the Adige, and moved on Chiusa. To form an idea of these absurd movements, it should be remembered that the crest of Monte Baldo cut off all communication between the column of Lusignan and those of the centre, that these were equally cut off from the column of Quasdanowich by the impracticable summits of San-Marco, and that the Adige separated Quasdanowich and Wukassowich.* Moreover, all these

* Alison, in speaking of these dispositions of the Austrians, says, "*The plan was ably conceived, and had nearly succeeded;* with a general of inferior ability

columns were obliged to pass the mountains without cannon, while I, placed on the plateau of Rivoli with artillery, could receive them as they arrived in succession. It was evident that, if the slightest accident should prevent them from all arriving at the same moment, I should be sure of victory.

Battle of Rivoli.—When my orders reached Joubert, near midnight, he was in full retreat; but he immediately returned to his position at Rivoli, which very fortunately the enemy had not had time to occupy. I arrived there after midnight; the weather was clear and beautiful, and, as the unclouded moon silvered the precipices of Monte Baldo, we could distinguish the lights of the five separate camps of the enemy. On the morning of the fourteenth I made my dispositions: the main body of Joubert's division marched on Caprino, San-Giovanni, and San-Marco, against the Austrian centre, while a demi-brigade, placed in the intrenchments in rear of Osteria, covered my right and held Quasdanowich in check. Massena, who was rapidly advancing, received orders at the same time to debouch a demi-brigade in order to oppose Lusignan. The combat now became warm; Joubert was too weak, and his left began to fall back. Seeing this, the right, under General Vial, also retrograded; but the 14th of the line kept its place admirably at the centre, and enabled me to reëstablish affairs. I hastened to the left and directed to its support the column of Massena, which had just arrived. The enemy was repulsed, and our left established on the heights of Trombalora. But the critical moment was not yet over: my right was hotly pursued by the Austrians, who

---

to Napoleon, and troops of less resolution than his army, it unquestionably would have done so." How admirably qualified such a judge of strategy must be to criticize the military operations of Napoleon! In support of this absurd opinion, Alison refers to "Thiers, viii., 5, 13; Napoleon, iii., 414; Jomini, ix., 275." Now it happens that each of the three authorities, here referred to, condemns most unequivocally the positions of the Austrian general. In fact there is not the slightest foundation for the opinion of Alison.

descended the heights of San-Marco. Quasdanowich had at the same time forced the intrenchments of Osteria, and his column began to descend the plateau of Rivoli. On the other side Lusignan, master of Coserman, was moving by Affi upon my rear.*

I was now completely surrounded, but, far from losing courage, I saw that if I could overthrow Quasdanowich I should have nothing to fear from Lusignan, who would advance only to his own destruction. Quasdanowich was obliged to defile by a very deep ravine enfiladed by our batteries. No sooner had the head of his column appeared upon the plateau than it was assailed on the flanks by infantry and in front by cavalry, which the intrepid Lasalle led to the charge. The enemy was broken and thrown back into the ravine. The disorder had already become great when one of our shells blew up a caisson in the middle of the ravine, which was crowded with Austrians; this produced the most frightful scene of confusion; infantry, cavalry, and artillery retreated pell-mell by Incanale. Having disposed of Quas-

---

* Alison says, "At this perilous moment, the presence of mind of Napoleon did not forsake him. He instantly, in order to gain time, sent a flag of truce to Alvinzi, proposing a suspension of arms for half an hour, as he had some propositions to make in consequence of the arrival of a courier with dispatches from Paris. The Austrian general, ever impressed with the idea that military were to be subordinate to diplomatic operations, fell into the snare: the suspension, at the critical moment, was agreed to; and the march of the Austrians was suspended at the very moment when the soldiers, with loud shouts, were exclaiming, "We have them! we have them!" Junot repaired to the Austrian headquarters, from whence, after a conference of an hour, he returned, as might have been expected, without having come to any accommodation; but, meanwhile the critical period had passed; Napoleon had gained time to face the danger, and make the movements requisite to repel these numerous obstacles." In confirmation of this statement, he refers to "Jomini, v. iii., 282, 283; Thiers, viii., 518; Napoleon, iii., 416." Neither of the authors referred to confirms, in any degree, this statement; indeed, their accounts of the battle preclude any possibility of its truth. It is a pure invention of a prejudiced mind, wishing to diminish the brilliancy of the victory by making it the result of petty trickery. Alison's account of this battle is unworthy of the slightest confidence. He was either incapable of understanding it, or wilfully misrepresented the facts.

danowich I directed all my efforts to sustain Vial, who was now in full retreat. The Austrians had pursued with too much imprudence. Two hundred horsemen. which I threw against them, so completely routed them that Alvinzi could rally the broken remains of the centre only behind the Tasso. This is a striking example of what marvelous effects may be produced by the smallest troop if engaged at the proper moment. My victory was decisive ; but to make it still more so, I desired the destruction of Lusignan. This general, fearing no serious resistance, had established himself on Monte Pipoli in order to completely cut off my retreat. I had secured my rear by opposing to him a part of the division of Massena, who kept up the combat till the arrival of Rey. The head of Rey's column having finally debouched by Orza on Lusignan's rear, this last general found himself surrounded at the very moment that he had thought to envelope me : his corps was completely destroyed, and he regained Monte Baldo with only a few hundred men.

Provera marches on Mantua.—The very night of this battle, I learned that Provera, forcing the centre of Augereau's division which was scattered along the Adige, had succeeded in crossing the river at Anghiari on the evening of the thirteenth, and marched toward Mantua. It was very important to prevent him from raising the siege of that place. Thinking Joubert and Rey strong enough to oppose the broken remains of Alvinzi, I immediately set off with the division of Massena for Roverbella, where I arrived on the evening of the fifteenth. On the fourteenth Provera had reached Nogara without encountering any opposition ; but Augereau, having had time to unite the main body of his division at Anghiari, had fallen upon his rear-guard, and cut it to pieces, and at the same time burnt the bridge over the Adige. On the fifteenth, Provera arrived before Mantua; he thought to enter by the faubourg of San Georgio, but finding it intrenched and occupied by us, he could open no communication with the place. Not yet despairing of being able to open a passage, he, the next day, made an attack on the side of the citadel. But I had here prepared for him an unexpected reception. On the sixteenth, at five o'clock in the morning, Provera attacked the post of La Favorita, and Wurmser that of St. Antonia. Serrurier, aided by the reenforcements which I had sent him, succeeded in defending these posts. Wurmser retired into the place, but Provera did not get off so cheaply; attacked in front by Serrurier, on the left by the garrison of San-Georgio, on the right by a part of the division of Massena, which I had directed against him, while the division of Augereau, debouching by Castellaro appeared on his rear, and finding no means of escape, he laid down his arms with the five thousand men he had left. While these events were taking place at Mantua, Joubert, on the fifteenth, moving some columns rapidly by the reverse of Monte Magnone and Monte Baldo, succeeded in turning the flanks of Alvinzi's retreating army. These centre columns, deprived of the assistance of Quasdanowich and Lusignan, with their line of retreat cut off, and hemmed in by the precipice of the Corona, were almost completely destroyed before reaching Ferrara: nearly five thousand men were taken prisoners.

Close of the Campaign.—After having finished with Provera, I moved upon the Adige. Alvinzi had lost more than half his army. The remains of his forces were marched behind the Piave, and the defense of the Tyrol intrusted to General Laudon with about eight thousand men. The Austrian rear-guard was everywhere defeated. At the beginning of February, my army had resumed the same position it had occupied previous to the battle of Arcola; Joubert on the Lavis, Massena at Bassano, and Augereau at Citadella.

Such was the celebrated battle of Rivoli, in which we

made twenty thousand prisoners with only thirty thousand combatants. Our legions had crowned themselves with glory, and had surpassed the so much vaunted rapidity of the legions of Cæsar. The same troops which had left Verona and fought near St. Michael on the thirteenth, had marched all night to reach Rivoli, fought there all the next day of the fourteenth in the mountains, returned to Mantua on the fifteenth, and captured Provera, who thought them defeated amid the rocks of the Corona.

Wurmser capitulates at Mantua.—Mantua capitulated on the second of February; the starving garrison had already consumed the flesh of all their horses, and large numbers had been carried away by disease. There were still remaining about thirteen thousand men under arms, who, having surrendered as prisoners of war, were conducted to Trieste to be exchanged. The number of sick was not less than seven thousand. We here found the siege artillery which we had abandoned before the battle of Castiglione, and three hundred and fifty other pieces upon the ramparts and in the arsenal.

Expedition on Romagna.—While I had been engaged with Alvinzi, the court of Rome, seduced by the instigations of my enemies, had broken the armistice made in June last, raised extraordinary armaments, and given the command of them to General Colli, who was sent for this purpose by the cabinet of Vienna. It was now necessary to punish Rome, both as an example to others, and to get rid of a troublesome enemy. For this purpose I formed a new division, giving the command of it to Victor. It reached Imola on the second of February. The campaign was neither long nor bloody. A corps of four thousand of the Papal troops attempted to defend the Senio, but was overthrown with great loss. On the ninth Victor arrived at Ancona, and captured twelve hundred more prisoners. Our advance-guard took possession of Notre Dame Loretto and its famous treasure. On the eighteenth we advanced to Tolentino. All was now consternation at Rome. I was master of all the States of the Church, but I did not wish entirely to destroy the power of the Pope; indeed, in the present situation of our affairs this would not have been so easy as some have imagined. We were obliged to pursue a cautious course of conduct toward the courts of Madrid and Naples, both of which were interested in preserving the power of the Pope; independently of this consideration, it would have been imprudent to weaken our army by detaching from it the forces requisite for garrisoning our conquests: and I was not foolish enough to commit such a fault, when about to begin a decisive campaign into the heart of Austria. I therefore wrote to Rome to propose a settlement of our differences. They were eager to send me plenipotentiaries. The negotiations were short, inasmuch as they had merely to sign such conditions as I saw fit to dictate. The peace was concluded at Tolentino on the nineteenth. The Pope confirmed the cession of Avignon, of the Comtat, of the Legations of Ferrara and Bologna, and of Romagna, and agreed to pay a contribution of thirty millions of francs. These conditions were too humiliating to the Head of the Church not to make it an irreconcilable enemy; and still not hard enough to destroy its power to injure us. I knew this well, but it was not in my power to do otherwise; state policy then belonged to the Directory, who wished to humble the Pope and brave the thunders of the Vatican, without once reflecting upon the advantage of converting it into an ally or an instrument: and considering my present critical situation on the Adige, I deemed it best to carry out the views of the government and relieve my army of a troublesome neighborhood.*

* This campaign of Napoleon is minutely described in Jomini's Wars of the Revolution, in Thiers' History, in Napoleon's Memoirs dictated at St. Helena, and

in Lee's Life of Napoleon, a work of much merit, by a young American. It is greatly to be regretted that Mr. Lee left his work incomplete.

Alison pretends to give due credit to Napoleon for the great military genius displayed in this campaign, but the praise is faint and most unwillingly and grudgingly given. The results are attributed, he thinks, in a great measure, "to the admirable character, unwearied energy, and indomitable courage of the troops which composed his army." The condition of the army, at the beginning of the campaign when Napoleon took the command of it, seems to have been forgotten. The success of the Republican arms is evidently very annoying to this staunch royalist; but he takes consolation in looking forward to the events of 1814 and 1815, and closes his remarks with the reflection that "*Aristocratic firmness in the end asserted its wonted superiority over Democratic vigor; the dreams of Republican equality have been forgotten, but the Austrian government remains unchanged, the French eagles have retired over the Alps, and Italy, the theatre of so much bloodshed, has finally remained to the successors of the Cæsars.*"

CHAPTER III.

FROM THE PEACE OF TOLENTINO TO THE CLOSE OF THE CAMPAIGN OF 1797.

Preparations for a new Campaign—The Archduke Charles takes Command of the Austrian Army—Treaty with the King of Sardinia—The Affairs of Venice—Troubles with the States of Terra-firma—Negotiations with Pescaro—Armaments of the Senate—Napoleon resolves to attack the Archduke before he can unite his Forces—Plan of Operations—Passage of the Piave—Affair of Tarvis—The Archduke is reënforced by the Detachments sent from the Rhine—Armistice of Leoben—Operations of Joubert in the Tyrol—Veronese Vespers—Victor suppresses the Insurgents—Condition of the two Armies—Preliminaries of Leoben—Armies of the Rhine—Destruction of the Venetian Republic—Napoleon goes to Milan—Revolution of Genoa—Change of Constitution—Provisional Government appointed—The Disorders continue—Negotiations of Udina and Passeriano—English Affairs—Naval Battle of St. Vincent—Naval Tactics—Mutiny in the British Fleets—Negotiations of Lille—Internal Affairs of France—The eighteenth Fructidor—Foreign Negotiations—Resignation of Napoleon—Cobentzel negotiates on the part of Austria—Napoleon and the Directory—Peace of Campo-Formio—Conditions of this Treaty—Its Results—Revolution of La Valteline—Negotiations with Germany at Radstadt—The Passage of the Simplon asked of the Valois—The Directory foments a Revolution in Switzerland—Proclamation of the Vaudois—Invasion of Berne—Helvetic Constitution—Neutrality of Switzerland and Faults of the Directory—Revolution in Rome—Proclamation of the Roman Republic—Napoleon leaves Radstadt—His Reception at Paris—General Remarks.

Preparations for a new Campaign.—The brilliant victory of Rivoli, the fall of Mantua, the evacuation of Corsica by the English, the treaties of peace with Naples and Rome, and the approach of large reënforcements, had at last completely changed the face of affairs in Italy. Having now the means of definitely securing the possession of the country, I determined to make the Emperor tremble even in his own capital. The divisions of the army of the Rhine having arrived in the course of March, I saw myself at the head of seventy-five thousand men. It required, however, about twenty thousand men to garrison the fortifications and to observe the south of Italy. With the remainder of my forces I moved forward. In order to second my operations, the Directory ordered Moreau to repass the Rhine at Kehl, and Hoche, after having reorganized the army of the Sambre-et-Meuse, to advance anew on the Main.

Archduke Charles commands the Austrian Army.—The cabinet of Vienna had adopted the same idea as ourselves about transferring the theatre of war into Italy; but not till after the taking of Kehl by the Archduke Charles and the defeat of Alvinzi at Rivoli. It was therefore the middle of January when this illustrious prince and able general set out to cross the Tyrol, with three divisions of select troops, to oppose me in Italy.*

---

* The Archduke Charles (Louis de Lorraine) of Austria, son of the Emperor Leopold II., was born at Vienna, in 1771. Already at the age of twenty-two he had acquired a high military reputation under the prince of Cobourg, in the campaign of 1793. In 1796 he was made field-marshal of the German Empire, and took command of the Austrian army on the Rhine. An outline of his operations in that campaign is given in the text. When sent against Napoleon, in 1797, the latter remarked to Macsfield: "Your cabinet has sent against me three armies without generals; now it sends a general without an army!" After the campaign of 1799, the Archduke was, by intrigue, removed from the army and sent into Bohemia in a kind of honorable exile. After the disasters of Hohenlinden and Marengo, he was recalled to favor and placed at the head of the War Department. In 1805 he opposed Massena in Italy, but was absent from Germany at the overthrow of the Austrian monarchy on the field of Austerlitz. In the campaign of 1809, he commanded the Austrian army and was wounded at the battle of Wagram. He was afterward made governor and captain-general of Bohemia, and retired to the country. He was the ablest of all the generals that opposed Napoleon. His many virtues and noble character endeared him even to his enemies. Napoleon always spoke of him in terms of high admiration. He ranks high as a military writer. His principles of strategy, illustrated by the campaigns of 1796 and 1799, were published in Vienna in 1813

Treaty with the King of Sardinia.—The events which I have just narrated had rendered our position as strong, comparatively, as it had formerly been precarious and hazardous; but it must, nevertheless, be observed, that the king of Sardinia, who was not our ally, might, on the least reverse to our arms, become our enemy. I had often urged the Directory to offer him conditions sufficiently advantageous to induce him to form with us a treaty of offensive and defensive alliance. I had myself taken the responsibility of signing, at Bologna, on the sixteenth of February, a treaty with the Count of Balbo; but the Directory, jealous of its prerogatives, refused to ratify it, and the whole matter was referred to General Clarke at Turin. The arrangement was not terminated till the eighth of April, after the armistice of Leoben had rendered it unnecessary, and even then it was not ratified at Paris. Had we obtained a timely succor of ten thousand Piedmontese, my army would have been increased, by the divisions of Bernadotte and Delmas, to ninety thousand men, and my rear perfectly secured as far as the Adige by the troops of our allies.

The Affairs of Venice.—Venice was the only power whose restless spirit gave us cause for apprehension; war was ravaging her states of *terra-firma*, and the people, excited against us, were only waiting for an opportunity to rise. But democratic propagandism had proselytes, both at Brescia and Bergamo. The patriots of these cities demanded to be united with Lombardy, and a revolution broke out there just as I was about to enter the Friouli. This revolution, enkindled by Adjutant-General Landrieux, was rather the work of the Directory than of myself; but, as it suited my purposes, I did not interfere with it. The reason of this was obvious; should the democrats succeed, they would reënforce

and 1819, in seven volumes, with valuable maps and plans.—*Biographie Universelle.*

my army and fight for my party; should they fail, the hostility of the oligarchy would justify me in destroying it. I was ready to adopt whatever course was best calculated to secure our hold in Italy. If I loved France, I nevertheless had not entirely forgotten my Italian origin; my heart was fixed upon regenerating a nation so interesting from its ancient reminiscences. But to obtain peaceably the cession of the Milanese by Austria, who had already yielded Belgium, it was absolutely necessary to have some equivalent to offer her for at least one of these countries. Should Venice give us cause for declaring war against her, she might possibly serve as the victim of our combinations of state policy.

Troubles in the States of Terra-firma.—The government of Venice weighed less heavily on the lower than on the higher classes. There is no domination so absurd as for a single city to rule a whole nation, at least when that city gives the notables of the country no suitable part in the government. In this case it was not an odious oligarchy, like that of Berne or of the city of Venice; it was an aristocracy like that which existed at Rome after the right of citizenship had been given to the Latins; in a word, it was the only reasonable form of a republic. If the Senate had made a timely grant of some thirty new places of senators to the influential families of Brescia, Bergamo, Verona, Vicenza, Padua, and Treviso, we should have lost our influence over the people of the States of *terra-firma*. But, instead of scattering the impending storm by timely concessions, they opposed all changes, excited the peasants of the mountains of Salo against Brescia, and sent to their support General Fioravanti. Salo fell into the hands of the enemy, but was soon retaken by the patriots, with the aid of our soldiers and the Cisalpines. At the same time the Senate armed eight or ten thousand Sclavonians, reënforced its troops, and equipped a formidable flotilla to cover the lagunes.

Negotiations with Rome.—In the present situation of our affairs, it was necessary to either attach Venice to ourselves, or else to paralyze her power. The Senate sent Pesaro to me to enter into explanations respecting the troubles of Brescia. I endeavored to prove to him that it was for the interest of Venice to frankly accept our alliance, and make certain modifications in the government; I gave him to understand that it would be useless to side with our enemies, by declaring for Austria, for, in less than a fortnight, I could drive the imperialists from the Friouli, and invade La Carinthia.

The Senate prepares for Defense.—The Senate had decided upon its course. It hated us too much to embrace our cause; and it had too great a fear of our power and dread of Austrian influence, to throw itself into the arms of Austria. Its courage was that of the poltroon: it thought to impose upon us by preparations for defense and by stoutly swearing its absolute neutrality. I was not fool enough to be duped by this neutrality, which would last so long as victory inclined on our side, but on the slightest loss in the Noric Alps, twenty thousand Venetians, with a *levée en masse* of peasants, would fall upon our rear, destroy our depôts, and cut off our retreat. I should have felt no alarm at this state of things, if the Directory had settled the treaty with the King of Sardinia; for, in that case, the Piedmontese contingent would enable me to leave ten or twelve thousand French troops to neutralize Venice. But the court of Turin wished to have guaranteed to it all or a part of Lombardy, and the Directory was unwilling to bind itself so as to be obliged to make this a *sine qua non* of peace with Austria. This conduct was childishness, for such a clause is always eventual: *à l'impossible nul n'est tenu;* and we had on the right bank of the Po the means of indemnity in case of need.

Napoleon takes the Initiative against the Archduke.—In the mean time the Archduke had repaired in person to the

Piave, and was there waiting for three divisions which he expected from the Rhine by the Tyrol or the valley of the Drave, but which were still afar off. Bernadotte and Delmas had joined my army some eight days, when the Austrian succors were still crossing Bavaria. Thus finding myself prepared for action before the enemy, I deemed it best to profit by the circumstance, and to begin the attack without waiting to settle matters with the Venetians. Victor,* whose division still remained at Ancona superintending the execution of the treaty with the Pope, received orders to return to the Adige, where he could cover my communications. I now entered the field with the divisions of Massena, Bernadotte, Serrurier, and Augereau (the latter being at this time commanded by General Guyeux), amounting in all to thirty-eight thousand men. I gave to Joubert the divisions of Delmas, Baraguay-d'Hilliers, and that which he himself had commanded at the battle of Rivoli; these together amounted to seventeen thousand combatants.

Plan of Operations.—Starting from the Mincio as a base, there were two lines of operations which could be pursued

---

* Victor (Perrin Claude) Duke of Belluno was born at La Manche in 1766. He entered the army in 1781, and received his discharge in 1789. In 1792 he served as a volunteer, and was promoted to the grade of chef-de-bataillon. In 1793 he distinguished himself under Napoleon at the siege of Toulon, and served under him in the campaigns of 1796-7, where he acquired a brilliant reputation and was promoted successively to the grades of general-of-brigade and general-of-division. In 1799 his division rendered important services on several occasions. At the battle of Marengo he commanded a *corps-d'armée*, and for his gallant services on this occasion he received a Sabre of Honor. He immediately afterward passed to the Batavian army, and in 1805 was sent as ambassador to Denmark. He joined the army in Prussia in 1806, and was wounded at Jena; in 1807 he was promoted to the command of the first *corps-d'armée*, and contributed mainly to the victory of Friedland. Napoleon made him a Marshal of France on the field. After the treaty of Tilsit he was made Governor of Berlin and most of Prussia. In 1808 he commanded the first *corps-d'armée* in Spain. He greatly distinguished himself in the campaigns of 1812, 1813 and 1814. After the restoration of the Bourbons, he held several important offices, and continued in favor till the overthrow of their government in 1830.

against the hereditary states of Austria: the first, to the north by the valley of the Adige, or the Tyrol; the second, to the east by the Friouli and the Carniole. These two lines formed a right angle with its vertex at Verona. As the enemy occupied both of these lines, it was impossible to confine myself exclusively to either without being exposed in flank and rear to the enemy's corps descending the other. As the Tyrol was the most favorable for defense, and led less directly into the heart of the hereditary states; and, moreover, as its narrow valleys would not permit me to develop my forces, I chose the line of the Friouli. Nevertheless, it was impossible to advance on Udina without being exposed in rear to an enemy debouching from the Tyrol. It was therefore preferable not to form a permanent double line of operations, but to push a strong corps upon the upper Adige to check the enemy in the Tyrol; and then to draw their corps toward the main army by the valley of the Drave, which nature seemed to have traced for such a movement. But the extent of these movements rendered the operation very delicate and complicated. If, however, this configuration of the country had some chances against us, it also had some in our favor; for should the enemy wish to defend the Friouli by parallel positions behind the Piave, the Tagliamento, the Isonzo, his line would then rest on the coast near his left wing, and his only line of retreat would lie in rear of the right wing. Therefore, the slightest manœuvre turning this right wing would cut off his line of retreat, and drive him into the Adriatic. On these facts I based my plan of operations. The greater portion of Alvinzi's scattered forces had taken position on the Tagliamento; the corps of the Tyrol, commanded by generals Kerpen and Laudon, was behind the Lavis and the Noss; in the centre, the brigade of Lusignan, at Feltre, kept open the communication between the two principal corps. The total of the

Austrian army did not then amount to more than thirty-five thousand men, the reënforcements of the Rhine not having yet arrived; there should be added, however, to this number a few thousand Tyrolese armed for the defense of their firesides; but these fought only on their own mountains.

Passage of the Piave.—My army began to move on the tenth of March. With the main body of my troops I advanced directly toward the Tagliamento. Massena marched on Feltre in order to drive back the brigades of Lusignan, and threaten the right wing of the Archduke. Lusignan retired ascending the Piave; on the thirteenth, his rearguard was attacked and overthrown at Longaro and he himself taken prisoner. Massena, satisfied with having thrown the Austrian brigade on Cadora, fell back on Spilimbergo and Gemona, so as to turn, nearer, the right of the Archduke and to get possession of the important route of Poteba, of which I feared the enemy might profit to retire on Villach. On the sixteenth I reached Valvasone, on the Tagliamento. The Archduke had already begun a retreat, leaving merely a rear-guard on the river, which was fordable. My columns rushed into the stream, overthrew the enemy, and pursued him on the road to Palmanova. The Archduke divided his forces: he himself fell back on Goricca; one of his columns commanded by generals Gontreuil and Bayalitsch, with a great part of the material, moved by Cividale and the valley of Natisona on Caporetto; General Ocskay, who commanded the brigade of Lusignan, covered the road from Villach to Chiusa-Veneta. The Isonzo, from its source to Goricca, runs between two chains of mountains almost impracticable on the side of Krainburg. Could I succeed in there inclosing the army of the Archduke, I would make it for him the Caudine Forks. For a moment I had strong hopes of doing so. Massena, in ascending the Fella, was in position to drive Ocskay beyond the Tavis and get possession of the debouches of the Isonzo on Villach. I myself manœuvred against the left flank of the Archduke, to push him into the valley of the Isonzo, the two extremities of which were in my possession. The enemy's left was covered by the city of Gradisca, which was then occupied by four battalions. On the seventeenth, Bernadotte attacked this place in front, while Serrurier, passing the Isonzo between that city and Montfalcone, took it in reverse; the garrison capitulated. I then ascended the left bank of the Isonzo with Serrurier and Bernadotte; Guyeux moved by Cividale on Caporetto. Inclining to the right by the valley of Vippach, I hoped to cut the enemy off from the road to Czernita, or to force him to plunge into the valley of the Isonzo, by Canale or Caporetto.

Affair of Tarvis.—The first object of the Archduke was to avoid any decisive battle till after the arrival of his troops from the Rhine; he therefore took good care not to wait for me to complete my movement, but fell back in all haste by Czernita and Adelsberg on Laybach. I sent Bernadotte in pursuit, and turned my own efforts against the column of Gontreuil and Bayalitsch. This, at least, could not escape me. Embarrassed by the convoy that accompanied it, and pursued by Guyeux and by Serrurier, who was ascending the Isonzo, it was also checked in front by Massena. This general had forced the gorges of the Ponteba, occupied Tarvis, and driven Ocskay on Wurtzen. Gontreuil tried in vain to open a passage by Tarvis; and was driven into the gorges of Ober-Preth, where he and Bayalitsch were surrounded, and forced to lay down their arms. We captured nearly four thousand prisoners, twenty-five cannon, and four hundred baggage-wagons. On the twenty-eighth, I united at Villach the divisions of Massena, Guyeux, and Serrurier. Bernadotte had pursued the Archduke by Laybach; as a flank movement to our march, he pushed forward some light troops on Trieste to seize upon the resources of that flourishing city, an acquisition of value for further operations.

Archduke reenforced from the Rhine.—The Archduke, who, from Laybach, had marched by Klagenfurth on St. Veit, was there joined by the first reënforcements from Germany. I wrote a letter from Klagenfurth to this prince, deploring the calamities of a war which could no longer be justified, and sought to incite in his noble heart a desire for peace. He replied that he had no power to make treaties, but that he had no less desire than myself to put an end to the horrors of the war.

Armistice of Leoben.—The Archduke, however, did not consider himself strong enough to give battle. At my approach he retired to Neumark, and on the thirtieth I arrived at St. Veit. On the second of April Massena forced the gorges of Diernstein and beat the enemy's rear-guard at Neumark and Hundsmark. The grenadiers which had come from the Rhine were defeated in these two rencontres. The Archduke continued his retreat on Vienna. On the fifth I arrived at Judenburg. Two days after, the Austrians, who had had time to send my letter to Vienna and receive an answer, asked an armistice for the purpose of negotiating a treaty. I consented to it with joy; my position was more brilliant than solid. I did not consider myself strong enough to attempt decisive measures against the Austrian monarchy; for the armies of the Rhine and the Sambre-et-Meuse, notwithstanding the superiority they had acquired since the departure of the Archduke, did not move from their cantonments on the left of the river, and I therefore could not, for a long time to come, hope for any assistance from them : at the moment I believed they designed to sacrifice me by leaving me alone to fight the combined armies of the enemy; and moreover I had much reason to fear for my communications.

Operations of Joubert in the Tyrol.—Joubert began with

success : after having beaten Kerpen and Laudon separately, the first on the Lavis the twentieth of March, and the second at Neumark on the twenty-second, he had advanced to Brixen. Kerpen fell back on Sterzing, and Laudon into the valley of Meran. But the picture was soon changed. The Tyrolese are a warlike, independent, and religious people; the Austrian government had taken good care to convince them that we were the enemies of religion; moreover, the ravages inseparable from war had greatly exasperated them against us. At the call of Count Lehrbach they had rushed to arms. More than ten thousand of these now joined Laudon and enabled him to resume the offensive by descending on Botzen in the valley of the Adige. Joubert was strong enough to fight them, if he had wished to fall back; but, after the affair of the Tagliamento, I had sent him orders to retire on La Carinthia. Although surrounded by enemies he thought it time to unite with me by passing through the valleys of the Rienzi and the Drave. On the fifth of April he left Brixen and moved by Prunecken and Lientz on Villach : a bold march, which he executed through an insurgent country, and without loss. The Tyrol being now evacuated by us as far as Trente, Kerpen marched by Rattenberg and the valley of the Salza on Muhrau in order to form a junction with the Archduke. Laudon, reënforced by the Tyrolese militia, descended the Adige, overthrew the feeble detachments which covered it, and moved toward the *terra-firma* of Venice, where all was in fermentation.

Veronese Vespers.—The Senate, exasperated by the events at Brescia, which I have already mentioned, thought only of vengeance. The approach of Laudon was the signal for a general insurrection of the peasantry, whom the oligarchists, and more especially the priests, had incited against us. A repetition of the Sicilian Vespers took place at Verona; all Frenchmen found in the city were massacred. General Balland, who commanded there, retired into the castle, with three thousand men. He was there besieged, on one side by Laudon, and on the other by the insurgents and a corps of Sclavonians, commanded by General Fioravanti, whom the Senate had sent from Venice. But when Laudon heard of the armistice of Judenburg he returned into the Tyrol.

Victor reduces the Insurgents.—The Venetians, abandoned to themselves, were unable to resist a corps of about fifteen thousand men which General Victor had collected, by uniting his division and the several garrisons of the posts in Lombardy, under the orders of Kilmaine. Fioravanti surrendered, and the insurgents were all dispersed.

Condition of the two Armies.—In the mean time I was ardently endeavoring to conclude a treaty of peace. Independently of the above-mentioned events, which gave me just apprehensions for my communications, I saw with uneasiness that the fate of the war was to be decided under the walls of Vienna, by a battle, where the chances would not be in our favor. It is true that the junction of Joubert and Bernadotte had again given me an army of fifty thousand combatants; but the armies of the Rhine were still inactive one hundred and fifty leagues in my rear; the archduke, sustained by the *levée-en-masse* of Hungarians, and the volunteers which the danger of the capital could not fail to rally to his aid, would still be able to oppose me with superior forces.

Preliminaries of Leoben.—I had a greater reason for not wishing again to jeopardize my reputation, as, at this juncture, the glory of making a general peace would be greater than that of a triumphal entry into the capital of the emperor. I determined to negotiate for peace, and in this I was fully seconded by the cabinet of Vienna. The precipitation with which it entered into these negotiations plainly showed the fear with which I had inspired it. I took advantage of this fear to dictate terms. On the eighteenth of April the preliminaries were signed at Leoben, where I had established my head-quarters.

Armies of the Rhine.—At this very time Hoche passed the Rhine at Neuwied, at the head of a superb and well organized army. After a series of victories over the inferior army of Werneck, he entered Frankfort on the twenty-third of April. Moreau passed the Rhine at Kehl, with the same success, and Starray, unable to arrest his progress, was driven back to Radstadt. Had these two passages been executed a month sooner, they would have given a decisive turn to the war, by carrying one hundred and twenty thousand men on the Inn ; which would have secured to the Republic a still more advantageous peace, and, perhaps, have saved Venice.

Destruction of the Republic of Venice.—I now evacuated the hereditary states, and marched my army into the Venetian territory. This movement had the air of being made as a mark of good feeling toward the emperor ; but, in fact, I was anxious to secure my communications. The hostile proceedings of the Senate of Venice, much as they had annoyed me previous to the armistice, now were truly fortunate for me. At Leoben I had promised Austria indemnity for the loss of Belgium and Lombardy ; but I should have been at a loss for the means of doing this had not the hostility of the Venetians furnished an occasion for making a conquest of a part of their states. On the sixteenth of May my troops occupied Venice, through the assistance of a democratic revolution, instigated by Villetard, the secretary of legation. The oligarchic government was dissolved. The Venetian patriots flattered themselves that I would permit them to establish a democratic government. But it was now too late ; their fate was subordinate to the progress of the negotiations for a definitive peace. I had at first hoped to preserve the republic by selecting indemnities in the Friouli ; but the turn of the negotiations did not permit it. At most I hoped it would be merely a loan to Austria, and that, on the first opening of hostilities, we could obtain its restitution. If this be weighed in the balance of severe justice, it can not be denied that the Venetians were sacrificed. But the scales of Themis are not the usual tests of national policy. Venice had rejected our alliance; her hatred of us had not been disguised; to the intrigues of Brescia she had responded by a horrible insurrection: war was declared; and the conquest was legitimate.

If the question had been merely to occupy the states of *terra-firma*, the war had been declared and ended in a single day; but the situation of Venice, surrounded as she was by water, secured her from our attacks. Two hundred armed boats or galleys and numerous frigates prevented our approach. It was necessary to proceed with caution lest we might cause Venice to throw herself into the arms of the English, and make of this place a port impregnable in the hands of the Islanders. Our only hope of success was to neutralize, by the aid of party spirit, all its dispositions for defense. Such was the object of the movement instigated by Villetard and resulting in the provisional government. This ruse was intended to spare the blood that would necessarily be shed in a forcible conquest, and to prevent Venice from falling into the hands of maritime enemies. In this light it should be judged of by posterity. Our detractors have represented it as an act of felony. The manes of our soldiers butchered at Verona, and of Captain Laugier assassinated by the Sclavonians in his own vessel in the port of Venice, will pardon, or at least palliate our conduct, especially when it is remembered that we entered Venice with the intention of preserving the Republic by giving it some compensations on the right bank of the Po. Moreover, Venice could not be more astonished at being transferred into the hands of Austria, than were the Republics of Dantzic, Elbing and Thorn, at being made Prussians. The declarations of moralists do not change the course of events in this world. The historian Botta, after quoting with admiration the philippics of the priests, calling upon the people to assassinate us, reproves us for treating these men as enemies! Such is history!

Napoleon goes to Milan.—After these events I established my head-quarters at Passeriano, near Udina, where I waited for the Emperor's plenipotentiaries, in order to arrange the definitive conditions of peace. I had signed at Montebello, on the twenty-fourth of May, with the Duke of Gallo, a preliminary convention, in order to accelerate the progress of the negotiations. The cabinet of Vienna having refused to ratify this, I repaired to Milan in order to hasten the organization of the Cisalpine Republic, annexing to it all the countries that naturally belonged to it, and thus to show to Austria her limits. Modena, Reggio, Bergamo, Ferrara, and Bologna were annexed to Lombardy, forming together a single state of nearly three millions of inhabitants. I was satisfied with the indications of a revival of public spirit; already the Italians began to consider themselves as good soldiers as the Germans; I had elevated their moral character in calling upon them to share the glory of our destinies.

Revolution of Genoa.—I profited by my sojourn at Milan to direct the democratic revolution which overthrew the Genoese oligarchy and made the Ligurian innovators entirely dependent upon us; the Valteline was added to the Cisalpine Republic, whose existence was solemnly proclaimed on the ninth of July. Three centuries' constant intercourse between France and Genoa, had made the latter a kind of French port; we had more partisans there than in any other city. The oligarchists alone, from fear of democratic tendencies, inclined to our enemies. The Directory, desirous of destroying aristocratic influences in all the surrounding states, could not overlook Genoa, the nearest and most important of all. In July, 1796, it directed me to demand satisfaction for certain griefs which it pretended to have against the Senate; but being then too much occupied with Wurmser, I was obliged to content myself with pecuniary satisfaction. Nevertheless, the agents of the Directory, instigated by the ambassador Faypoult, neglected no opportunity to extend the influence of the democratic party, whose progress was so rapid that the Genoese Senate soon saw itself threatened with the same fate as that of Venice.

A tennis party became the subject for a popular insurrection; on the ninth of May, the multitude disarmed the troops of the line, took possession of the gates, and appointed a committee to demand reforms of the Senate, which, too weak to make resistance, promised such changes in the constitution as should be deemed necessary. Some patricians, more bold than others, eight days afterwards, stirred up an insurrection among the colliers and peasants of the neighboring villages; a violent reaction followed; the parties fought in the streets, and the Senate triumphed. I had gone from Montebello to Milan when I heard this news. I regarded Genoa as the most important acquisition which could be made to France for the consolidation of my work in Italy. *This great fortress, perched upon rocks against which it would be exceedingly difficult to construct regular works of siege, might be the key of Lombardy as we possessed neither Piedmont nor, as yet, the route by the Simplon.* It was then of little consequence to me whether Genoa was ruled by a patrician Doge, or by a band of plebeian conspirators; what I wanted was that *French* influence should predominate, and as our banners were the banners of democracy, it was necessary to side with that party. I sent one of my aids-de-camp to Genoa to consult with Faypoult and take cognizance of all the details of the affair.

Change in the Genoese Constitution. — Called upon by the deputies of the Senate to decide these matters, I at first demanded the liberation of the French and the chiefs of the revolutionary party, and the arrest of the leaders of the reaction. Some days after, the deputation of the Senate, accompanied to Milan by Faypoult, signed with me at Montebello a convention putting an end to the Genoese oligarchy. This singular compact, in which the French Republic appeared as the mediator between the Senate and the Genoese people, contained twelve articles, the first of which recognized the sovereignty of the people. The legislative power was confined to two representative councils, one of three hundred, and the other of one hundred and fifty members. The executive devolved upon a Senate of twelve members, with the Doge at its head. These latter, and the senators, were nominated by the two councils. Until the new government should be installed, the authority was confided to a commission of twenty-two members, presided over by the present Doge.

This form of government was not at all appropriate to the situation and character of the Genoese. Indeed it was impossible for this little republic to be governed by a representative body of four hundred and fifty unpaid members, without substituting the aristocracy of wealth (which is the most objectionable of all aristocracies), for that which we had just abolished. But I then paid but very little attention to these matters; I regarded Liguria as an indispensable addition to France, and these changes in its constitution as temporary, and calculated rather to facilitate this annexation, than permanently to ameliorate its condition. Nevertheless, the little council the next day ratified the convention of Montebello by a vote of fifty-seven to seven. From that moment the council and the colleges ceased their functions and surrendered their authority to the Doge and the provisional commission.

Napoleon appoints a Provisional Government.—Nothing was said in the convention of Milan about the appointment of the provisional government, but as I was not in the habit of leaving things half done, I myself appointed the members, selecting the most distinguished democrats; and on the thirteenth of June, the Doge was required to convoke this commission.

The Disorders continue.—Although there was still some fermentation among the lower classes, a part of whom were still armed, yet the revolution was effected with order; in the evening the Golden Book was burnt by the democrats on the place of Aquaverda. The next day a decree of the provisional government abolished the noblesse and all feudal rights; the armorial bearings on the doors of hotels were destroyed, and, as such popular movements are never exempt from excesses, sacrilegious hands dared to break the colossal statues of those Dorias who were formerly the pride of the Genoese name.

While the legislative commission was engaged in forming a constitutional compact, I directed General Duphot to organize a corps of six thousand Ligurians to be added to the number of our auxiliaries. But the oligarchists were not yet completely reduced: a committee assembled at Pisa, organized in the month of September the insurrection of the *Riviera di Levante,* and of the Bisagno. General Duphot marched against the insurgents, but was driven back into Genoa; they even got possession of Fort Eperon. But reënforced by the inhabitants of the Ponente, the Genoese democrats, and some French troops from Tortona, Duphot finally triumphed over all their efforts, notwithstanding the instigations of the Durazzos, the Dorias, the Spinolas, and the Pallavicini. This was the last effort of a government really prudent, and friendly disposed toward France. The victim of revolutionary dogmas, some have thought it might have avoided its ruin by admitting, in 1796, a tenth part of plebeian senators and forming an alliance with France. It owed a slight sacrifice to the opinion of the age; and if, after the concession, it had fallen, the odium of it would have rested upon its enemies. Nevertheless, the Directory looked as much to its independence and neutrality as to its form of government. We desired Genoa as a base for our operations in Lombardy, so long as the direct passes of the Alps were not in our possession.

Negotiations of Udina and Passeriano.—The congress with Austria was first appointed to meet at Berne, but was afterwards changed to Udina, where I treated with Meerfield and Gallo. The Directory, jealous of its prerogatives, sent General Clarke as an adjunct in these negotiations, and gave me orders which must have been a great obstacle to an agreement, had not the cabinet of Vienna itself retarded the negotiations immediately after the preliminaries had been signed. The counter-revolutionists, with Pichegru, Villot, and Imbert-Colomès at their head, had so far succeeded in the elections, as to have a strong party in the councils. A violent contest took place between the executive and legislative powers; the latter, instead of assisting the operations of the government, threw all possible obstacles in its way. These internal difficulties revived the hopes of our enemies.

Affairs of England.—The situation of our affairs with England also exercised a considerable influence upon the negotiation. The great genius of its prime minister could not save this power from receiving rude shocks in the course of this year. Ireland was in insurrection; and although Hoche's expedition failed to attain its object, still it raised the hopes of the insurgents to such a degree, as to render it necessary for the government to employ force to repress them. Truguet was not discouraged by the ill-success of Hoche. The peace of Leoben had restored all his activity. He had at Cologne a superb army, which in a few weeks could be upon the shores of the Channel. They thought to make the English tremble for their own firesides. The assistance of Spain and Holland, with their respectable naval forces, seemed to give promise of success. Spain, especially, might have added much weight to the scale, if the gold of Mexico had sufficed to procure good workmanship in her ship-yards, and a better organization and stronger emulation among her sailors. Those colossal men-of-war, the pride and predilection of Spaniards, were, for the most part, bad sailers, and required better officers than theirs to manœuvre them.

Battle of Cape St. Vincent.—Nevertheless, the junction of the combined fleets in the Channel could not fail to produce great results; for the bond of union between Ireland and England was on the point of rupture. The British admiralty made every exertion to extricate itself from this embarrassment. Lord Bridport blockaded Brest; Duncan watched the Texel; and Jervis, who was in the Tagus, watched the movement of the Spanish fleet. This fleet of twenty-seven ships and ten frigates, under Admiral Cordova, an officer celebrated in the war of American independence, sailed from Carthagena, passed the strait and raised the blockade of Cadiz. Jervis had only fifteen vessels, but, full of noble confidence, he met the Spaniard half way. The battle was fought off Cape St. Vincent. The English admiral surprised the enemy, pierced his line, cut off nine of his vessels, defeated them, and captured five of his large men-of war. Nelson, to whom much of this victory is attributed, signally distinguished himself in this battle.

Naval Tactics.—The Spaniards, eighteen of whose vessels had not even entered into the engagement, shamefully fled to

Cadiz. Jervis owed his triumph to the application of the same principles which I had adopted at Montenotte, Castiglione, and Rivoli. On land, as on the sea, the first talent of a commander is to paralyze a part of his adversary's forces, and concentrate all his own on the decisive points. It is astonishing that no French admiral ever knew how to apply this simple rule, and that all of them fought in parallel order, vessel to vessel, which is in formal opposition to the first principles of the art. Suffern is the only one who made the proper manœuvre, and he owed it to chance.

After this check the Spanish naval power was completely paralyzed. Jervis, with his force increased to twenty-one vessels, swept the Mediterranean, and the English even blockaded and bombarded Cadiz. Nelson attacked Teneriffe, but was repulsed, with the loss of an arm. In the Antilles Admirals Harvey and Abercromby captured from the Spaniards the important post of Trinidad, which offered a point for attacking the continent of South America. But less fortunate at Porto-Rico, the latter officer was repulsed with loss.

Mutiny in the British Navy.—Thus all things were not prosperous with proud Albion; but even at the moment of victory, she was on the brink of ruin. A frightful insurrection broke out in the two great fleets of the Nore and the Texel. The mutiny was carried to such a pitch that the sailors took command of some of the vessels; and the fear of punishment getting the better of their patriotism, might have induced them to steer for our ports for safety. Fortunately for England no one thought of it, and this mutiny, produced by a discussion about pay, was suppressed by a wise union of force and concession, supported by all the powerful resources of discipline and patriotism.

Negotiations of Lille.—These events, so well calculated to cause terror in London, joined to the certainty that Austria was in favor of peace, and that Holland and Spain might yet concert with our fleet at Brest a descent upon Ireland— all these things combined to stagger the English government. The suspension of specie payments by the bank, and the rejection of the fiscal measures of Pitt, added much to the effect produced by the mutiny in the navy. Under these circumstances the minister deemed it necessary to gain time and to negotiate a treaty of peace, afterward either executing or breaking it, as might best suit his purpose. He sent Malmsbury, on the fourth of July, to Lille to enter into negotiations with Maret, Letourneur, and Pleville-Lepelley. The first named of these alone conducted the negotiation and met with unexpected success; the instructions of the Minister, Charles Delacroix, were an almost incredible tissue of absurdities. They demanded the restitution of the vessels taken at Toulon, or an equivalent, and also, under the name of restitution, the surrender into our hands of Jersey, Guernsey, and even Gibraltar. Besides this it was necessary to treat for France, Spain, and Holland, which rendered the negotiation a very delicate and complicated affair. Maret had too much intelligence to undertake such a mission till a change in the Directory had replaced Delacroix by Talleyrand, who left the negotiator without restraints. Thanks to his moderation and skill, the affair was most ably conducted; and he obtained for France the restitution of all her colonies, an indemnity for the vessels taken at Toulon, and even the renunciation of the title, *Roi de France*. These two last concessions were mere bagatelles, but they flattered the spirit of the time. He obtained for Spain the restitution of all her colonies except Trinidad. As to Holland, the restitution of all her colonies, without exception, was promised, but Malmsbury having observed that he could not return to the English people without preserving, for the sake of appearance, some of their trophies, it was agreed that the port of Trincomalo should be declared neutral and be occupied alternately by an annual English and Dutch garrison. The English garrison was then in possession, and it was understood that no change would take place. It is worthy of observation that in this discussion Malmsbury wished to retain the Cape of Good Hope, and offered St. Helena in exchange, but Maret declined the offer. He corresponded with me through the intervention of Clarke, and we should have effected a general peace, had it not been for the tricks of Rewbel, the avowed leader of the war party.

Affairs of the Interior.—18th Fructidor.—I was no less thwarted by the obstacles constantly thrown in my way by the Minister Rewbel, than by the influence exercised by the councils upon the resolutions of the cabinet of Vienna. Foreseeing the possibility of a new rupture, I urged the ratification of the treaty made some six months before with the King of Sardinia, and which the Directory, contrary to all reason, had rejected. But I was again disappointed; and in my discontent, I complained bitterly to those whom I thought my friends in the Directory. It was represented to me that the republican party was likely to fall even by the hands of the constituted authorities, who, transformed into blind instruments of the *reactionnaires*, were divided into two distinct factions. Each party sought to attach to itself a distinguished general. The royalists had gained Pichegru and were now manœuvring to secure Moreau. Another party sought Hoche. My glory having excited the jealousy of many members of the Directory, they were desirous of raising up one of my rivals to balance the influence which I had acquired with the public. I determined to side with the republicans, and sent General Augereau to the Directory at Paris to take command of its troops there. Barras and his colleagues, who were in a position to know these things, assured me of the existence of a plot to overthrow the republic, and papers found in the *portefeuille* of Count d'Antragues, minister of Louis XVIII., seized at Venice, confirmed these reports. The more I engaged in political affairs, the more I was convinced of the necessity of terminating and regulating the revolution; it was the offspring of the age, and could not retrograde without the cost of oceans of blood and the humiliation of France. I therefore fully concurred in the affair of the eighteenth Fructidor, which destroyed the constitution of the year III., the offspring of Utopians, who, as a balance of power, had introduced into the state a system of perpetual squabbling, which must necessarily impede the progress of affairs. If this *coup-d'état* led to the exile of Carnot, Barthelemy, and the fifty-three Deputies, and the gratification of mere personal animosities under the cloak of public good, the fault is to be attributed to those who deceived me; it did not depend upon me to direct its course and lead it to more beneficial results.

Foreign Negotiations.—The newly organized Directory, with Talleyrand* in place of Charles Delacroix, as minister of foreign affairs, did not show itself much more skilful or pacific than before. The first result of the change was the breaking off of the negotiations at Lille, where Treilhard and Bonnier had succeeded Maret and Letourneur. They imperiously refused all the demands of England, and revived the

---

* Charles Maurice de Perigord, prince of Talleyrand, was born at Paris in 1754. At the breaking out of the Revolution, he was bishop of Autun, but he soon left his profession and became one of the most rabid politicians of that age. His first diplomatic mission was to England; after this he was exiled, but returned as soon as the decree of banishment was repealed. He filled many important diplomatic missions under Napoleon, who raised him in 1805 to the dignity of sovereign prince of Benevento. In 1814 and 1815 he favored the Bourbons, and at the Congress of Vienna did every thing in his power to unite the Allies against Napoleon. He joined Louis XVIII. at Ghent, and returned with him to Paris. In 1830 he was sent to London as ambassador from the new government of Louis Philippe. He died in 1838. His diplomatic talent was very great, but his reputation for intrigue is much higher than that for honesty. —*Encyclopedia Americana.*

discussion of subjects which had already been agreed upon by their predecessors. Thus the swaggering vanity of Rewbel and Merlin rejected the only opportunity that occurred of arresting, by a favorable maritime peace, the threatening increase of English power on the ocean. A similar result was near being produced at Passeriano. The eighteenth Fructidor produced, on the part of France, no other change in the negotiations than the recall of Clarke,* and my being left in sole charge. The Directory refused to ratify the alliance with Sardinia, as if this treaty was to rescue a victim from its ambition. This body now opposed the cession of Venice, on the ground that it might increase the maritime power of Austria, whereas it had formerly assented to this, in the hope of gaining Mantua. It even carried its pretensions so far as to refuse all indemnity in Italy.

Napoleon Resigns.— Disgusted with the opposition and apparent distrust of the Directory, I sent in my resignation on the twenty-fifth of September, a few days after having notified the plenipotentiaries that if peace were not signed by the first of October, I would then treat only on the basis of *uti possidetis*. Uncertain what result would be produced by this declaration, I sought to detach Bavaria and Wirtemberg from Austria, and sent to them, under different pretexts, General Desaix, whom curiosity had brought into Italy. But

---

* Clarke (Henri Jacques Guillaume) Duke of Feltre, was born at Landrecies in 1765. He was educated at the Ecole Militaire of Paris, and entered the army in 1782, and attained the grade of general in the early wars of the Revolution. Under Napoleon he acted mostly in a diplomatic character, and was rewarded for his services with the title of Duke of Feltre. He was an industrious, laborious man, and a good administrator. After the restoration, he became a servile flatterer of the Bourbons, and enjoyed considerable favor at court. His chief foible was pride of descent; he spent much of his time in hunting up old family documents, and sought to prove himself related to half of the faubourg St. Germain. His conduct as minister of Louis XVIII. did much to blast the reputation he had previously acquired under Napoleon. He died in 1818.— *Biographie Universelle.*

surrounded as he was by the agents of Austria, it was impossible for this officer to succeed in his mission.

Cobentzel takes part in Negotiations.—The moment the imperial deputation received the news of the eighteenth Fructidor, they dispatched General Meerfield in all haste to Vienna. As the Emperor could no longer hope any thing from a royalist reaction, he immediately sent Meerfield back with Count Cobentzel, who was furnished with more positive instructions. Henceforth the negotiations progressed with less interruption. But Austria did not appear any more pliant; far from renouncing Mantua, which had been assured to her in the preliminaries, she now demanded Venice, the Legations, and the line of the Adda. Indignant at such pretensions, I contested even Dalmatia and Ragusa, of which she had already taken possession. The Directory did not confine itself to these menaces: it formally declared, as its *ultimatum*, to limit Austria by the Isonzo, and to send her for an indemnity to the secularizations in Germany—a circumstance that seemed to render the rupture inevitable.

Napoleon and the Directory.—In the mean time the Directory, seeing the danger of accepting my resignation after the services I had rendered the republic, sent an agent to me to enter into satisfactory explanations. Having determined to continue the war, it felt that it still had need of my sword, and it now conceded every thing which it had formerly refused. The army of Italy was reënforced by three demi-brigades and a regiment of cavalry; more than eight thousand *requisitionnaires* joined the skeletons of my infantry; I was also promised a *remonte* of sixteen hundred horses; it also submitted the treaty of alliance offensive and defensive with Piedmont for the ratification of the councils; finally, as a proof of its condescension, Kellerman was removed and the ambassador Cacault was recalled from Naples, because I had previously shown dissatisfaction at their conduct.

Peace of Campo-Formio.—I did not wait the effect of all these resolutions; but, encouraged by the secret mission of Bottot, and pretty certain of the sanction of the Directory, I determined not to limit myself by the instructions of the ministers, who would have produced the same results at Passeriano as at Lille. After the usual form of high demands, made with the design of more easily obtaining the object desired, I decided abruptly to close without any further authorization. Many reasons contributed to produce this result. Our army in Italy was in a flourishing condition, and had a good base of operations in Osoppo and Palmanova; but the season was too far advanced for a campaign in Carinthia, and by allowing the Emperor the winter for organizing his forces, we would risk all the advantages of the initiative. Besides, the position of the respective armies was not in our favor. The Austrians were near the centre of their power, in the neighborhood of their magazines and dépôts, with their flanks secured on the one side by Croatia or Hungary, and on the other by the Tyrol, all warlike provinces, ready at a moment's warning to second military operations. We, on the contrary, had every thing to fear for our rear; Naples was ready to embrace the first opportunity to give vent to her hatred; Venice wished to remove us from her neighborhood; and the King of Sardinia, whose treaty of alliance had been rejected by the council, might take this occasion to declare against us. Moreover, Austria had opposed to me the main body of her forces, while the mass of ours was still on the Rhine, some two hundred leagues behind my army, which, for a month or more, would be obliged to sustain the whole weight of the war. In fine, the rupture of the Directory with England, the incoherence of the plans adopted by the government in case of war, made it my duty to be less exorbitant in my demands, and to consent to the double cession of Venice and Salzbourg. Therefore, on the seventeenth of October, when everybody was expecting a renewal of hostilities, peace was signed at Campo-Formio.*

Conditions of the Treaty. — The treaty consisted of twenty-five articles patent, ceding Belgium and Lombardy, (Mantua included), and consenting to the limits of the Rhine and the Alps; the States of Venice were ceded to Austria as far as the left bank of the Adige, with the fortress of Verona and a fixed arrondissement. The provinces of Brescia and Bergamo, situated on the right bank, were given to the Cisalpine Republic, and the Ionian Islands to France. Fourteen secret articles, more important in some respects than the treaty itself, specified the limits of the Republic and the disposition to be made of the resulting territory. Should the Diet refuse the cessions on the left of the Rhine, the Emperor promised to give no support to the German Empire: the free navigation of this river and of the Meuse was promised: France consented to the acquisition by Austria of the

---

* When the French *ultimatum* was made to Cobentzel, he positively refused to receive it, preferred a new trial of arms, and charged to Napoleon's obstinacy the blood that would be shed in the new contest. Upon this Napoleon, with great coolness, although he was much irritated at this attack, arose, and took from a mantelpiece a little porcelain vase, which Count Cobentzel prized as a present from the Empress Catharine. "Well," said Napoleon, "the truce is at an end, and war is declared; but remember, that before the Autumn, I will shatter your monarchy as I shatter this porcelain." Saying this, he dashed it furiously down, and the carpet was instantly covered with its fragments. He then bowed to the congress and retired. The Austrian plenipotentiaries were struck dumb. A few moments afterward, they found that as Napoleon got into his carriage he had dispatched an officer to the Archduke Charles, to inform him that the negotiations were broken off, and that hostilities would commence in twenty-four hours. Count Cobentzel, seriously alarmed, sent the Marquis of Gallo to Passeriano, with a signed declaration that he consented to the ultimatum of France. It was on signing the treaty on the following day, October seventeenth, that Napoleon directed the first article acknowledging the French Republic to be stricken out. "The French Republic," said he, "is like the sun; they who can not see it must be blind. The French people are masters of their own country; they formed a Republic; perhaps they may form an Aristocracy to-morrow; and a monarchy the day after. It is their imprescriptable right; the form of their government is merely an affair of domestic law."—*Montholon.*

country of Salzbourg, and that she might receive Innviertel from Bavaria, and the city of Wasserbourg on the Inn. Austria ceded the Frickthal to be given up to Switzerland, the Imperial Fiefs for Liguria, and the Brisgaw to the Duke of Modena in exchange for his states which had been amalgamated with the Cisalpine Republic. France agreed to yield the Prussian states between the Rhine and the Meuse. Indemnity was promised in Germany to the princes who had been dispossessed on the left of the Rhine, the same as to the Stadtholder. In fine, article VII. left an opening for still further partitions, in stipulating that *if one of the contracting powers should make any acquisitions in Germany, the other might make equivalents.*

Results of the Treaty.—This was a glorious peace, and might have been lasting; it was glorious inasmuch as it secured to France Belgium, the line of the Rhine and of the Alps, Mayence, great influence in Italy, and the Ionian Islands—an important possession which might secure to us the key of the Levant and afford immense maritime advantages; it might have been lasting, because it gave Austria ample compensation for the provinces she had ceded to us. Being now separated from Piedmont by the Cisalpine Republic, Austria had suffered to pass into our hands the influence over the house of Savoy and northern Italy; but her own territory, contiguous to the Adige, with Verona, Legnago, and Venice, gave her a much better base for future operations against this part of Italy. Peace ought, therefore, to have appeared to her so much the more advantageous as she had, as it were, been rewarded for her defeats. Beaten at Jemmappes, Fleurus, Juliers, Loano, Ettlingen, Montenotte, Lodi, Castiglione, Bassano, Arcola, Rivoli, she had, nevertheless, rounded off her territory by an addition of three millions of inhabitants; she had exchanged her distant provinces of Belgium for Galicia, which was bordering on her own frontiers; she had received the states of Venice in exchange for Lombardy, with which she could hold no communication except by passing through foreign territory; she had exchanged the port of Antwerp, blasted and ruined by the closing of the Scheldt, for that of Venice, which was much more advantageous to her commerce and to her political power. As to France, she had additional reason to rejoice at this peace, inasmuch as the English had just gained a great naval victory; Duncan had, on the eighteenth of October, at Camperduyn (Camperdown) on the coast of North Holland, beaten and destroyed half of the Dutch fleet, and this important success might raise an additional obstacle to a maritime peace, and also increase the difficulty of trading with Austria. But the highest passions were excited, and they did not fail soon to involve the two hemispheres in a new conflagration. The mania of propagandism which had seized upon the Directory, the want of any fixed system in our foreign policy, the hatred borne by all foreigners to our republican institutions, could not fail, in a short time, to provoke a new war.

Revolution of La Valteline.—Scarcely had the treaty of Campo-Formio been signed, when new elements of discord began to rise: the revolution of the Valteline was the beginning. This country, subject to the Ligues-Grises, had strong motives for wishing its emancipation; it was properly a part of Italy, as it spoke the same language, was situated on the southern slope of the Alps, and drew all its grain from Italy. Its inhabitants, excluded from all political functions, very naturally desired an order of things that would give them some part in the government. An insurrection was incited against the Grisons; these called for the mediation of France. France answered by annexing the Valteline to the Cisalpine Republic. The sterile advantage of extending the territory of this republic to the high Alps, caused the danger of this junction of the Valteline to an Austrian province to be overlooked. In fact, the French Republic, certain of the friendship of the Swiss, ought not to have given to a state, whose existence was as precarious as that of the Cisalpine, rights which might some day revert to the ancient possessors of Lombardy. The Valteline, united to the Grisons, closed the access of Switzerland on the side of the Tyrol, diminished the influence of Austria over the Helvetic valleys, secured the Cisalpine frontier, and perfectly covered the line of French troops called to fight on the Adige. To unite this province to a state formerly Austrian, was to establish a direct contact between the upper Tyrol and the communications of the French army, to open the route of the Tonal and the Breglio by Sondrio on Milan, in fine to give the key of the Rhetian Alps to Austria, if she should ever regain possession of the Adda.

Negotiations at Rastadt. — Austria had made peace only on her own account; it was still necessary to treat with the Empire. This crowd of petty German principalities were of themselves incapable of carrying on the war, and a treaty with them would have been a mere formality, had it not been necessary to obtain their assent to the cession of the left bank of the Rhine in favor of France, and of Salzburg and Innviertel in favor of Austria. Moreover, it was necessary to indemnify the princes who had lost territory by these arrangements. A congress was assembled at Rastadt to settle these minute and complicated questions. I repaired thither as the head of the French legation; the other members were Bonnier and Treilhard; but I soon perceived that the discussions, being no longer supported by victory, were taking a deplorable turn which did not at all suit me. I was too much accustomed to decide authoritatively to have sufficient patience for a long and minute investigation. I therefore left Rastadt, having first provided by a military convention for the execution of the treaty of Campo-Formio, so far as concerned the transfer of Mayence to our troops and the evacuation of the other places of the Rhine by the imperialists.

Passage of the Simplon asked of the Valois.—To consolidate as much as possible the young republic which I had created, I had, on leaving Italy, demanded of the Valois free passage by the Simplon for the troops returning to France. I was desirous to possess this upper valley of the Rhone which offered us the most direct communications with Milan, especially at a time when Piedmont, still independent, might range herself on the side of our enemies. The Swiss very properly declined acceding to a demand which destroyed the system of their neutrality. The Directory, already designing to revolutionize that country and to draw it within its own meshes, was now only the more inclined to execute its imprudent project.

Directory foments Revolution in Switzerland.—Rewbel and Talleyrand had formed the project, it is said, of surrounding France by petty democratic republics, either to cover our frontiers by separating them from Austria, or to form a federative system capable of balancing new coalitions. They flattered themselves by this singular means to create a new system of political equilibrium, not between the masses of powers, but between the dogmas of governments! To think of defending the French Republic against European monarchies by surrounding it with a girdle of petty democratic states, was a piece of Utopian diplomacy destitute of the first principles of common sense. These feeble states, instead of avoiding points of direct contact with Austria, would keep us in continual altercation; as they could only exist under the protection and patronage of France, we would be obliged to mingle in all their frontier difficulties with Austria. A Cisalpine custom-house officer could, therefore, bring about a war as easily as the *nez coupé* of the English Jeffreys had between George II. and Louis XV. Our alliance with Spain and our friendly relations with Prussia showed that it was very easy to acquire weight in the real balance of Europe without attaching to it any *doctrinaire* ideas : these in international policy have but little weight, and are more often a pretext than an object.

Conformably to this absurd project of the Directory, Mengaud was charged with stirring up at Bâle, Arau, and Zurich, a revolution in which France could interfere as she had done at Genoa. Mangourit was doing the same among the Valois ; and similar effects were easily produced in the *Pays-de-Vaud*, which had been ceded to the canton of Berne, in 1565, under the guarantee of France.

Reclamation of the Vaudois.—With better foundation for their demands than the Valtelines, or the bourgeois of *terrafirma*, and all those who demand their part of inalienable political rights, the Vaudois wished to obtain from the Bernese the same prerogatives which they had enjoyed under the Dukes of Savoy. This was no body of politicians demanding equality, it was an enlightened people demanding, for their notables, the part in public affairs which belonged to them by treaties. France was the guaranteeing power, and therefore she possessed the right of intervention ; but instead of doing this nobly and in good faith, she did it in a reprehensible and underhand way.

Invasion of Berne.—The Vaudois rose in insurrection, drove away the Bernese magistrates (*baillés*), and called to their aid the division of Massena, which was then cantoned in Savoy, on the banks of Lake Geneva. This division entered the country in the early part of January, under the orders of Brune, and advanced as far as the borders of the *Pays-de-Vaud*. The Bernese assembled in all haste a corps of twenty thousand militia on the Sarine. The Senate of

Berne, distracted by internal dissensions, and paralyzed by a powerful French party, decided to make concessions : it promised to revise its constitution in the course of a year, and to admit a number of deputies representing the ancient subjects of Vaud and Argovie. The more reasonable of the Vaudois were disposed to accept these concessions, but the majority rejected them : in times of revolution, every thing is suspected and unsatisfactory ; and these advantages, which really exceeded their most sanguine hopes at the outset, now appeared insufficient to the sectaries of liberty and equality, who wished all or nothing. Moreover, pacific concessions did not at all suit the views of the French Directory, who wished to profit by the frenzy of its partisans to subject all Switzerland to its influence, and to establish a central government which should be under its own domineering control. It required Berne to disband its army and to give pledges of its sincerity. The old *avoyer*, Steiger, a venerable magistrate, very different from the degenerate oligarchists of Venice and Genoa, preferred the resort to arms. Berne, showing herself as great in the moment of danger as she had been moderate in the beginning of the difficulties, most nobly answered to this appeal. The combat soon began: Schawembourg penetrated from Bienne on Soleure and on Berne with a division of the army of the Rhine, while that of Brune was driven back on the Sarine. They nevertheless formed a junction the next day at Berne. A superb arsenal and a treasure of twenty millions became the prey of the avaricious conquerors, who were much more occupied in enriching themselves with the Bernese spoils, than in sustaining the political rights of the Vaudois, for which they pretended to fight.

Helvetic Constitution.—A uniform constitution was concocted by Talleyrand, Ochs, and Laharpe, to bind into one bundle the uncivilized democrat of the little cantons and the proud oligarchist of Berne. It was necessary to employ artillery to impose upon the Swiss this pact of the united Helvetic Republic. I had been a warm partisan of the Vaudois; I had even advised that their just demands be sustained by diplomacy, and by an imposing demonstration; but I was indignant at the ulterior conduct of the Directory toward the Swiss. In driving these mountaineers into the arms of Austria, we lost all support to our armies on the Adige, and Italy became subject to the masters of the Rhetian Alps, which take in reverse all the lines of the Adige, the Mincio, and the Ticino. We were certain to pay dearly for this error, which cost us, in 1799, all Italy to the Var.

Neutrality of Switzerland.—The question of Swiss neutrality was connected with the highest combinations of European policy. The German Empire, Austria, France, and Italy, were equally interested in preserving this neutrality. Without it the line of the Rhine was a vain barrier, and the Alps no longer secured France and Italy from invasion. By possessing Switzerland, France weakened instead of strengthening her power; for the slightest success of the Austrians on the banks of the Var opened to them the access of the Jura, and enabled them to attack the soil of France by the only vulnerable point of her frontier. The same reasoning applies to Italy; with the neutrality of Switzerland, France, then mistress of Mantua, of Pizzighettone, and the fortresses of Piedmont, had a very decided advantage over the imperialists, reduced as they were to the walls of Verona and to the ramparts of Palma-Nova. But destroy the prestige of this neutrality, and the least success obtained in Switzerland by an imperial army, would destroy all defense in Italy, and force the French army to fall back in order to arrest the enemy on the confines of Dauphiny, or on the banks of the Rhone. The plans of the Directory, in destroying the neutrality of Switzerland and violating that territory, were, all things considered, the height of folly. In considering the increase thus given to the French line of defense, we are not to regard the mere circular extent of a hundred leagues, but the permanent contiguity of a line running from Venice by Trente and Lake Constance to the marshes of Friesland and the North Sea. This space being cut by the mass of the Alps, and the centre neutralized, each of these isolated fractions would necessarily present an independent line of operations. One might, therefore, select on either of these wings a strategic point most suitable for his operations, without being troubled with what was passing at the accessories. For example, operations by the left to cover the Rhine, would be carried on between Strasburg and Mayence without any danger to the other extremity along the sea or on the neutral line. If operations were directed by the right for the protection of Lombardy, the defense would be entirely confined to the line of the Mincio or the Adige. If, on the contrary, the Swiss territory be included in the front of operations, the line of defense would extend from the Adriatic to the mouths of the Yssel, and for this entire extent of three hundred leagues every point would be exposed to an attack. The lines of the Adige and the Rhine (between Strasburg and Mayence) would then be only secondary fractions, subordinate to other operations; and, should the combatants be drawn into Switzerland, the occupant of this country, reduced to defend himself there, would be obliged to cover Bâle, Schaffhausen, Rheineck, St. Gothard, the Simplon, and Mont-Cenis, without being able to dispense with imposing forces on the Rhine and the Po. Thus the defensive power, having its forces cut up into twenty separate corps, would be greatly exposed to an active and enterprising opponent, who, by the rapidity of his movements, might multiply his assailing forces. Indeed, the following campaign did not fail to prove that, although the salients Schaffhausen and the

Simplon offer strategic advantages for a simple passage, Switzerland, as a field of operations, should never be included in the plan of a campaign. This truth is fully demonstrated by the events of 1799, and the operations of 1805 and 1809. With my title of mediator, and the powerful influence I possessed in Switzerland, I could have taken possession of that country with impunity, but interest directed me to leave it intact. However highly I valued two or three debouches, I knew how to render them subordinate to the calculations of policy, and I have proved that a route may always be found for manœuvring on the communications of the enemy, without trampling under foot national rights, and destroying the equilibrium of European states.

Revolution in Rome.—A few days before the fall of Berne, Rome had surrendered to Berthier. My brother Joseph had been named ambassador near the Holy See. All Italy was then in a fever: it was a strife who should plant the first tree of liberty. Naples was also in fermentation, and the prisons were insufficient to contain all who were arrested on suspicion. Rome could not, in this revolutionary excitement, forget entirely her former greatness: all who, in the country of Cicero, of Emilius, and of Brutus, could read their alphabet, threw off the monastic and pontifical yoke to bring back the glorious days of the consular government, and, strange as it may seem, a part of the clergy partook of these sentiments. Since the peace of Tolentino harmony had been but partially established: Joseph felt that he must act with prudence. The partisans of France exhibited a desire to reëstablish the Roman Republic, but he persuaded them from the project. Being afterward indirectly informed that a conspiracy would break out on the twenty-sixth of December, he thought to give proof of his loyalty to the Holy See by frankly reporting the facts to the Cardinal Secretary of State, Doria. But these princes of the church were too much prejudiced against us to appreciate such an act of kindness. They redoubled their watchfulness and severity, but, in spite of all their precautions, an insurrection actually broke out on the twenty-eighth, in the vicinity of the palace of France ; the multitude invaded the enciente of its jurisdiction, crying out : *Long live the Roman Republic ; Long live the French Republic.* Charged upon by the gendarmes and the trabans of the Pope, this crowd took refuge under the portico of the palace, which it was impossible to prevent. They were pursued and fired upon even in the courts.

Proclamation of the Roman Republic.—This act was a violation of the law of nations. Young General Duphot, an officer of merit, affianced to one of my sisters, rushed out, sword in hand, to defend an asylum regarded as sacred, and was basely murdered, being pierced with many balls. The quality of the offender adds to the heinousness of the offense. Such an act on the part of the *sbirri* of the Pope could not be passed over unpunished. Berthier marched upon Rome, and encamped, on the tenth of February, at the head of two divisions under the walls of the castle St. Angelo. Five days after, at the foot even of the Quirinal, was heard the cry of Roman Liberty, a cry that had not been uttered in the vicinity of the capital since the famous conspiracy of Rienzi. The people assembled in the Forum, like their illustrious ancestors, drew up a declaration of their enfranchisement, and proclaimed their consuls, a senate, and tribunes. It was a ridiculous parody of the Rome of the Scipios ; but these magic words struck the minds of the rest of Europe, and if the Directory had been more skilful, and better advised in the choice of its agents, it might have drawn immense advantage from it. Berthier, yielding to the wishes of the people, marched at the head of his grenadiers to the capital, and there proclaimed the recognition of the Roman Republic.

The Pope had no other alternative than to abdicate; and what was exceedingly annoying to Pius VI., this revolution took place on the fifteenth of February, the twenty-fifth aniversary of his pontificate, and three days after, to return thanks for the abolition of his sovereignty, and the reëstablishment of the Roman Republic, *a solemn Te Deum was chanted in St. Peter's by fourteen Cardinals!* On the twentieth of February the Pope left Rome, never to return; Berthier gave him an escort. He repaired to the Carthusian Monastery of Pisa, where he remained till the thirtieth of April, 1799, when he was transferred to France. The conquest of Rome became an unfortunate affair by the ulterior faults which followed it, and the great extension it gave to our line of operations. The government of Rome should have been organized, and a small corps left for its defense, the rest of the army being withdrawn to the line of the Adige. This rich city was overrun by military chiefs, who were not very delicate in their distinctions of *meum* and *tuum*, and more particularly by numerous depredating civil agents, who fell upon the treasures of St. Peter like a cloud of vampires. The army was left without food or pay, while these rascally civilians were swimming in gold; it mutinied, as the British seamen had done a year before, and if a military revolt is ever susceptible of excuse, it certainly was under such circumstances. Massena, who had succeeded Berthier, was forced to leave the army, which he could not recall to duty, and which accused him (unjustly, perhaps,) of not only tolerating these abuses, but even of participating in them. Two such events as the invasion of Rome and Switzerland were more than sufficient to put an end to the peace of Campo-Formio; indeed, under the circumstances, that treaty could be little more than a truce.

Napoleon's Reception at Paris.—While these events were preparing a new storm, my new title of general-in-chief of the army of England, and still more, the project of an expedition into Egypt, called me from Rastadt to Paris. I could not better celebrate my return to the capital than by bringing there the ratification of peace. Therefore, I was received with transports bordering on delirium. All hearts opened to hope; the wounds of *La Patria* were about to be healed; with her glory raised to the clouds, France was about to reëstablish her political relations on both continents, and, sooner or later, force England into a peace which would secure our conquests; industry, the arts, commerce, would then take the impetus which the Revolution seemed calculated to impress: in a word, every thing seemed to promise a rich and prosperous future. The Directory, giving me a formal audience on the tenth of December, at the Luxembourg, proclaimed me *the man of Providence, one of those rare prodigies which nature bestows upon the human race only at periods far remote*. France did not fail to echo the pompous eulogy of its president. I was forced to take refuge under the modest garb of a member of the Institute in order to escape the importune acclamations of a people always enthusiastic in its admiration and ever ready to change its object. The authorities were emulous in giving testimony of national gratitude. A committee of the Council of Ancients passed an act presenting me with the estate of Chambord and a grand hotel in the capital; but the Directory, alarmed at the proposition, refused its assent.

General Remarks.—During the two years that I had commanded in Italy, I had filled the world with the *éclat* of my victories; the coalition had been dissolved; the Emperor and the princes of the empire had formally recognized the French Republic; all Italy had submitted to our laws and influence; two new republics, like the French, had been created; England alone remained in arms, but she had manifested a desire for peace, and the fault of its not being signed rested with the Directory. To these great results in the external relations of the Republic, must be added advantages gained in its interior administration and in its military power. At no time had the French soldiers shown so decided a superiority. It was due to the influence of the victories in Italy, that the armies of the Rhine and the Sambre-et-Meuse had been able to carry the French standards to the banks of the Lech. At the beginning of 1796, the Emperor had one hundred and sixty thousand troops on the Rhine, ready to invade France. Our brave but undisciplined armies were then scarcely capable of securing the fortified lines of defense, much less of making conquests. The victories of Montenotte, of Lodi, etc., carried the alarm to Vienna; they forced the Aulic Council to recall from its armies in Germany Marshal Wurmser, the Archduke Charles, and more than sixty thousand men, thus establishing the equilibrium there, and enabling Moreau and Jourdan to resume the offensive. More than one hundred and twenty millions of extraordinary contributions had been raised in Italy; one half of this had supported my army, and the other half, transmitted to the treasury of Paris, had assisted in providing for the expenses of the interior and the support of the armies of the Rhine. In addition to all this, the treasury owed to my victories an annual saving of seventy millions, which, in 1796, was required for the support of the armies of the Alps and of Italy. Considerable provision had also been made in hemp and ship-timber, and the vessels captured at Genoa, Leghorn, and Venice, had greatly increased our naval force at Toulon. The National Museum had been enriched by *chefs-d'œuvre* of the arts from Parma, Florence, and Rome, which were valued at more than two hundred millions. The commerce of Lyons, Provence, and Dauphiny had begun to revive the moment the great *debouche* of the Alps was opened. The naval forces at Toulon, reorganized and reënforced by the squadrons of Spain, now ruled the Mediterranean, the Adriatic, and the Levant. Happy days seemed assured to France, and for these she was indebted to the conquerors of Italy.

CHAPTER IV.

NAPOLEON'S EXPEDITION INTO EGYPT.

Difficulties of Napoleon's Position at Paris—Origin of the War in Egypt—State of Hindostan—Projects of the Sultan of Mysore, and the Apathy of France—State of the English Forces—Object of the Expedition into Egypt—Napoleon examines the Port of Antwerp—The Continent again involved in hostile Preparations—Napoleon departs from Toulon—Capture of Malta—Debarkation at Alexandria—March on Cairo—Battle of the Pyramids—Entrance into Cairo—Naval Battle of Aboukir—Results of this Battle—Difficulties with the Porte—Revolt of Cairo—Expedition into Syria—Passage of the Desert, and taking of Jaffa—Resistance of St. Jean-d'Acre—Battle of Mont-Tabor—Continuation of the Siege of St. Jean-d'Acre—Raising of this Siege—Return to Cairo—Debarkation and Battle of Aboukir—Napoleon decides to return to France.

Difficulties of Napoleon's Position at Paris.—My brilliant reception in the capital was sufficient to flatter the vanity of the most modest, and to incite the least ambitious. It was evident that I could aspire to every thing in France. Nevetheless the moment had not yet arrived to profit by this popularity; it was necessary to wait until the Directory should entirely destroy its own influence. France had proclaimed me her hero; but this was not sufficient, and to become the head of the state, it was necessary to be its saviour and restorer. However great my claim to the national gratitude, it did not give me the right of overthrowing an established government to which I owed my rapid advancement and a part even of my glory: it would eventually destroy itself by its own incapacity and the disasters it would bring upon France ; then only could I appear on the stage as the saviour of my country. I knew well what would be the inevitable course of events. It was only necessary to leave the silly heads of the Directory to their own measures ; for, independently of the weakness of the individuals composing this body, it could not, from the nature of things, continue a long time. Either the Directory would attempt to seize the dictatorship, like the Committee of Public Safety, or it would itself fall a prey to anarchy, like the Executive Council of 1792 ; in either case, its fall was inevitable.

Origin of the War in Egypt.—Nevertheless the part I had to play was embarrassing. They had conferred upon me the pompous but illusory title of general-in-chief of the army of England. This was a mere bugbear, by which the cabinet of London was not to be duped ; there was nothing prepared at that epoch to give to the project any reality ; all that could possibly be done was to throw some twenty or thirty thousand men into Ireland : an enterprise, advantageous without doubt, but not suited to my ambition. I was too important a personage to remain with folded arms at Paris. Although the Directory had mingled its acclamations with those of all France, I knew that Rewbel and Merlin were secretly opposed to me : under a pretext of a hierarchy of powers, they censured the resolution which I had taken of my own accord ; they accused me of having treated with Austria instead of marching upon Vienna, which, in their opinion, would have secured the revolution of Germany, and given Rewbel the pleasure of fabricating a few democratic republics from the *débris* of the Holy Empire ! This was, according to them, the most infallible means of securing the triumph of the principles and the preponderance of France over all her neighbors. They supposed an empire like Austria could be revolutionized as easily as Rome or Milan, or rather they were ignorant that no one could be less disposed in favor of their Utopian theories than the subjects of the court of Vienna. Their shallow declamations against me were scandalous. It was necessary for me to take some step; for every day the most opposite factions knocked at my door: now, the royalist agents sought to demonstrate to me the impossibility of continuing the republican system in France, and to induce me to restore the monarchy; now, the most ardent sectaries of the Republic came to complain of the assaults of the Directory upon liberty, and to urge me to act the Gracchus. I was therefore obliged to make common cause with the Directory, or to join in the conspiracy against it. I was unwilling to do either. The only reasonable course for me to pursue was to absent myself, and to do so with *éclat*. I knew that to keep the public attention fixed on me it was necessary to attempt something extraordinary. Many anonymous letters, very well written, had already been addressed to me, warning me of the difficult part which I had to play in France. One of these letters advised me to form a state for myself in Italy, as Dumouriez had thought to do in Holland. But I was not foolish enough to do this. I shall allude to this proposition again.

I had spoken vaguely during the negotiations of Campo-Formio of a project on Egypt, although I had then no idea of taking charge of it myself. Talleyrand had also mentioned it. On my return, I offered to put it in execution. As the results might be immense, the enterprise seemed worthy of my ambition. Of course the majority of the Directory received with delight a proposition for ridding themselves of a pacificator whose popularity they feared. They were therefore enchanted to see me thus anticipate their wishes by a voluntary exile. Some statesmen wished to retain me, endeavoring to convince me that I was called by the circumstances of the time to take the helm of affairs.

I replied that the pear was not yet ripe, and that I was going to win new titles to their confidence.

We had no very accurate idea of what was passing in the East, for the loss of Pondicherry and the European embarrassments of the Republic had withdrawn attention from that quarter. But we remembered that Tippoo-Saëb, chief of the empire of Mysore, founded by Hyder-Ally with the assistance of France, had proposed to Louis XVI., in 1788, to drive the English from India, if France would assist him with eight thousand European troops, and with a good number of officers to lead his forces ; and that Louis XVI., on account of the internal troubles of France, had not accepted a proposition which would have embarrassed him with a maritime war at the moment when he was threatened with a revolution. Finally, we knew that the English, to punish Tippoo for this message, had assisted the Nizam against him, and, having besieged him in Seringapatam, had forced him into a treaty in 1792, stripping him of half his dominions. We therefore had reason to expect some support from the Sultan of Mysore. We also knew that the Mahrattas, although enemies of the Mogul and Mussulman race, were equally hostile to the English East India Company, and that it might be possible to find among them the elements of a powerful alliance. But to appreciate fully the expedition into Egypt, it will be necessary to speak more particularly of the real state of India prior to that epoch.

State of Hindostan. — The Tartar prince Aureng-Zeb, contemporary of Louis XIV., extending the conquests of his predecessors, founded in the centre of India the Mogul empire, with a population of not less than fifty millions, a revenue of nine hundred millions, and an army of eight hundred thousand men. This immense empire was divided into numerous provinces governed by Subadars and Nabobs. This conqueror died in 1707 ; and such is the miserable condition of the despotic dynasties of the East, that his successors, in the short space of forty years, harassed by their own vassals and attacked by the Persians under the terrible Thamas Kouli-Kan and by the Mahrattas, were compelled to ask the aid of Europeans, and to surrender to them several provinces. The story of the revolutions and counter-revolutions that have taken place within the last fifty years in the *presqu'île* of the Ganges, seem more like Arabian tales than history. Passing over the details of these contests, we will look merely at the general results.

It was not till the middle of the eighteenth century that the British East India Company, appreciating the system proposed by the skilful Dupleix, for France, began to take part in the quarrels of the native princes. Here, as in Europe, the British policy was *to divide and conquer*. At one time sustaining the Hindostan princes against Mussulmans of the Mogul dynasty, and at another taking the part of the latter against the natives, if these seemed too strong, this Company succeeded in appropriating to itself the most important parts of the territory of both its *protegés* and its enemies. At the epoch of the French Revolution, India was divided into five principal states: those governed by Mussulman princes were at the south; Mysore, subject to Tippoo-Saëb; at the north, Mogul, subject nominally to Schah-Alloun, but in fact to his principal officers; still further north, Zeman-Schah reigned over the Afghans, who inhabited Candahar and Cabul. By the side of this kingdom lay that of Beloochistan, inhabited by a warlike and savage people. In the centre of the *presqu'île* was the empire of the Mahrattas, founded by Sevaji, an Indian prince, who, having maintained himself in possession of the kingdom of Sattara, afterward succeeded in capturing the greater part of the conquests of the Moguls in the Deccan. Soon after his death all the petty tributary princes rendered themselves independent of the great rajahs who succeeded him, and whose authority was successively circumscribed to the fortress of Sattara. Feigning to recognize the right of this family to the crown, the Peishwah, its prime minister, obtained absolute power over the northern part of the *presqu'île* where he founded the kingdom of Poonah. Madaji-Schindiah did the same in the north and east. This able man, conquering the army of Ismaël-Beg, and succoring Schah-Alloun against the ferocious Golaem-Cadir, succeeded in reëstablishing the preponderance of the Mahrattas in the states of Mogul, where he exercised supreme authority in the name of the emperor, to whom he left only the palace and a small income ; sole heritage of the colossal power of Aureng-Zeb. Madaji-Schindiah had been seconded in his operations by a European corps, or one organized and instructed in the European manner by a Savoyard officer named Boigne. This celebrated Mahratta died in 1794 ; and his nephew, Dowlut-Row, without inheriting his talents, pursued his system, preserved his preponderance over the Mogul, and succeeded in extending it, in 1796, as far as the states of the Peishwah, placing Bodje-Row, whom he held entirely under his tutelage, on the throne of Poonah. General Peyron had succeeded Boigne in the command of the army of Schindiah, composed of five brigades of European organization, thirty-four thousand well disciplined infantry, and a very large force of cavalry. A third Mahratta state, governed by the Rajah of Berrar, extended to the north of the Deccan : although less powerful than the two preceding, it was one of the most formidable members of the confederation. The family of Holkar reigned over Malwa, and twenty other petty feudatory princes, independent of these, had diaghirs, a kind of dotation. It thus appears that the Mahratta people formed a numerous confederation, much like the German Empire, differing from it only in the nature of Eastern organization and

Eastern institutions. The Hindoo confederation presented, in fact, the singular spectacle of a great hereditary rajah possessing vast dominions without authority, and surrounded by two great dignitaries who, not satisfied with making their power hereditary, did not scruple to divide among themselves the domains of the prince from whom they received the investiture. Still more to be pitied, the emperor of the Moguls distributed crowns without the power of retaining one, for, properly speaking, he was a sovereign without subjects; a despot incapable of making himself obeyed, he sold to adventurers the right of exercising absolute authority in his provinces; poor, though all the money of Hindostan was stamped with his image; he prided himself in having great kings for his tributaries, though he depended upon their generosity for his own support.

The finesse of Lord Clive, the profound Machiavellism of Hastings, and the wise policy of Lord Cornwallis had successively been directed to connect the Company with the complicated interests of these states, and to intermeddle in their differences with an appearance of loyalty. Always appearing upon the scene as an umpire, this Company was enabled to arrange the conditions of treaties to suit its own interests; it aided the weaker power against the stronger for the double purpose of profiting by the spoils of the latter and of removing all obstacles to its own ambition. Thus, by the aid of the Mahrattas and the Nizam, it had, in 1792, conquered Tippoo-Saëb, whom it could not forgive for having sent ambassadors to Louis XVI. with proposals for expelling the English from India. Two years after, the Mahrattas in their turn attacked the Nizam, overrun the country with two hundred thousand men, without any efforts on the part of the English Company to succor this prince, whom it held under its tutelage. Either dissatisfied with this conduct of the Company, or aspiring to independence, he had confided to an officer named Raymond the care of organizing, in the European manner, an army of fifteen thousand men, and gave him, for their pay, the revenue of a rich province.

Projects of the Sultan of Mysore.—Tippoo-Saëb, since the unfortunate treaty of Seringapatam which had deprived him of half his empire, had thought only of vengeance. France, distracted by anarchy and discouraged by the loss of Pondicherry, seemed to have forgotten the advantage it might derive from the hostile disposition of the people of Hindostan against the English Company. Not a vessel, not a man had been sent to India; and from the carelessness of the governors of the Isle-of-France, one would suppose that the very existence of the two *presqu'îles* of the Ganges had been entirely forgotten. At the end of 1796, Truguet had thought of sending assistance to the Sultan of Mysore, but his project was based on the possibility of forming battalions of negroes in the plantations of the Isle-of-France, and its execution was never even begun. A few adventurers were on the eve of doing what Louis XVI. and the Committee of Public Safety had neglected. Rippaud, a Corsican, cast away on the coast of Mangalore, was taken to Tippoo-Saëb, and by relating the victories of the Republican armies in Europe, excited in that chief the hope of obtaining succor from the ancient allies of his father. He sent an ambassador to the Isle-of-France with a project of alliance to be submitted to the Directory; a project so well combined that it would have done credit to the best European diplomatist. The reply of Governor Malartic shows that it was not appreciated by him; he, however, sent to the Sultan thirty non-commissioned officers, artillerists, and artisans, who were estimated at a high price, but who disgraced the French uniform by their revolutionary extravagances, and furnished a pretext to the English Company to assail the Sultan of Mysore. We have reason for believing that the Directory were never well informed of what took place on this occasion. Nevertheless Tippoo did not stop here: seeking to allay the rivalry of the Mahrattas, he sought to arm the Peishwah and Schindiah against the Company; and carrying his views still further he sought the alliance of Zeman-Schah. The joint forces of these several states might amount to fifty thousand men armed and disciplined as Europeans, and three hundred thousand soldiers of the native organization. If the tumultuous impetuosity of the Mahrattas, the chivalric bravery of the Rajpootas, and the unbridled ambition of the chiefs, had been so directed as to act in concert for the deliverance of India, no doubt this formidable coalition would have soon triumphed over the English, particularly if a French division, commanded by an able general, had served to regulate the operations of these combined forces.

State of the English Forces. — The English East India Company had then for allies only two or three subaltern nabobs and the Nizam; still this last, in sending the English battalions of its guard to throw themselves into the hands of Raymond, gave reason to think that it would return sooner or later to the policy of its predecessor, who had fought under the flag of Hyder-Ally. But the Company had now become redoubtable in itself, for each of the three Presidencies of which it was composed formed veritable empires. The first of these, including Calcutta, Bengal, the coast of Orissa, and the rich valley of the Ganges as far as Oude, was the centre of the general government, and was equal to the mother country in power and wealth. The second, composed of the possessions of the Deccan about Madras, had its seat of government in that city. The third, established at Bombay, united the establishments of Malabar and Surat to the factories of the Persian Gulf. The joint forces of these Presidencies amounted to twenty-five thousand Europeans and sixty thousand well organized Sepoys.

Object of the Expedition to Eygpt.—Such was the state of India when I undertook to open a direct communication with that country. I was convinced that this was the shortest way to reach the heart of England, for at this epoch India was every thing to her, excluded as she was from the greater part of the American continent. The expedition to Egypt had three objects: 1st. To establish on the Nile a French colony, which, without resorting to slave labor, might supply the loss of St. Domingo and all the sugar islands; 2d. To open to our manufacturers new outlets in Africa, Arabia, and Syria, and to furnish to our commerce all the productions of this part of the world; 3d. To furnish a base of operations for moving an army of fifty thousand men on the Indus, and of raising the Mahrattas, the Hindoos, the Mussulmans, in a word, all the oppressed people of these vast countries. An army, one half of Europeans and the other half of the people of the burning climates of the tropics, transported by ten thousand horses and as many camels, carrying with them provisions for fifty or sixty days, and water for five or six, and a doubly furnished train of artillery with one hundred and fifty field-pieces, would reach the Indies in four months. The desert is no obstacle to an army abundantly supplied with camels and dromedaries. This expedition would give an exalted idea of the French power; it would draw public attention to its chiefs; it would surprise Europe by its boldness—these motives were more than sufficient to induce me to attempt it.

Egypt, it is true, was tributary to the Ottoman Porte, who was one of the oldest allies of France, and who, since the age of Francis I., had made common cause with her. But the Mameluke being the true master of the country, and in open revolt against the Grand-Seignior, we had reason to believe that the Divan, already fully occupied with war against Passwan Oglu, Pacha of Widdin, and against the

Wechtabies, and so weak as to be unable to reduce a large body of insurgent pachas, would not blindly join our enemies for the mere shadow of suzerainty, which, if necessary, we could acknowledge as well as the Mamelukes. We had every reason to expect, with a skilful negotiator, to succeed in convincing the Divan of our friendly disposition.

Napoleon Inspects the Port of Antwerp.—Full of confidence in the results of my mission, I urged forward the preparations for my departure. But in order to distract the attention of the enemy from the ports of the Mediterranean, where every thing was in full activity, I profited by my title of general-in-chief of the army of England to make an inspection of the ports of the coast. Having gone as far as Antwerp, I saw in the superb basin of the Scheldt the important advantages that might one day be derived from this position: it had upon me the same effect as the beautiful Neva had upon Peter the Great.

New Troubles on the Continent.—In the mean time the political horizon of the continent was again overcast. After my departure from Rastadt, the congress had broken off the discussions upon the conditions of peace with the German Empire. The French plenipotentiaries had difficulty in obtaining the cession of the left bank of the Rhine, for it overturned the constitution of that empire by absorbing the three electorates of Mayence, Treves, and Cologne. But the great powers, having tasted the benefits of secularization, hoped to make acquisitions at their convenience. Austria thought to secularize the archbishoprics of Saltzbourg, Passau, and Trent; Bavaria, the bishoprics of Franconia (Wurtzbourg, Bamberg, Aichstedt); Prussia, those of Munster, Paderborn, etc. These powers, therefore, definitely agreed to the line of the Rhine. It was a vain formality, for the Directory, in its presumptuous career of propagandism, was already embroiling the whole continent in new difficulties. England took advantage of these difficulties to form a new coalition, and sounded the alarm at the same time at St. Petersburg, at Vienna, Berlin, Turin, in Tuscany, and at Naples. It was generally believed that the Empress of Russia, at the moment of her death, was about signing a treaty of subsidy with England. Already an imperial ukase had ordered a levy of one hundred and thirty thousand recruits; whether these preparations were intended for taking part in the continental contest, or for the conquest of Turkey, or to punish the young Gustavus of Sweden for his rupture of the contract of marriage with the grand duchess Alexandrina, they announced the approach of great events. But the Emperor Paul, in ascending the throne, instantly changed the affairs of the north. He revoked the levy, and directed his whole attention to the internal affairs of his vast empire. These pacific demonstrations had an immediate influence upon the Russian finances, the price of paper money even exceeding its nominal value. But the whimsical character of the emperor gave hope to the cabinet of London that he might yet be induced to join in the war against France, and no means for obtaining this object were left untried. At this time an event took place at Vienna, which might serve, in some degree, as an index of the popular feelings of the Austrians, and of the present sentiments of the government. Bernadotte, our ambassador at Vienna, had raised the tricolored flag on his hotel in celebration of a victory over the Austrians. The hotel of the embassy was attacked by an irritated populace, and the flag seized and burnt; Bernadotte left Vienna the next day. The Directory at first wished to declare war, and to place me in command; but I persuaded it from such a course, demonstrating that Bernadotte was in the wrong, and that Austria, if resolved on war, would have avoided such a hasty and immature act.

Nevertheless there were other circumstances which indicated new difficulties. I, therefore, wished to defer my departure, but the Directory having settled the affair of Bernadotte, insisted; and placed in the alternative of ruin or obedience, I complied. The Directory, delighted at getting rid of me, granted all my requests. I prepared my departure in profound secrecy; this was necessary for its success, and added to the singular character of the expedition. Never were such formidable preparations better disguised.

Departure from Toulon.—I repaired to Toulon on the tenth of May, 1798. On the nineteenth, I set sail with thirteen ships of the line, six frigates, and transports for twenty-five thousand troops. I was joined at sea by the squadrons from Bastia, Genoa, and Civita-Vecchia, with seven or eight thousand men who also belonged to the expedition. On the ninth of June, we reached Malta.

Taking of Malta.—I had maintained an understanding with a small number of French officers, more devoted to their country than to this knighthood, already falling to decay; the Order had made no preparations for defense; nothing was ready to oppose us, and if we had not taken possession, it is certain that the English would have done so, for this post was essential for our communications with France. I feared lest some measure of their former glory might induce the knights to defend themselves, which might have retarded, and perhaps defeated, my expedition: fortunately for us they surrendered more readily even than I had hoped, and thus placed in my hands one of the strongest works in Europe.

Debarkation at Alexandria.—After having left a good garrison at Malta with the necessary instructions for its defense, I continued my voyage with rare good luck. The English fleet in pursuit crossed our course without meeting us. It arrived at Alexandria before us; but Nelson, hearing that we had not been there, went in search of us on the coast of Syria. We reached Alexandria on the evening of the thirtieth of June. I commenced the debarkation the same night at the anchorage of Marabou, and the next day I marched on Alexandria with the part of my army which had already debarked. A column followed the shore of Marabou, and made an attack on the side of the New Port. Two others turned the city, and assailed it on the side of Pompey's Pillar and the gate of Rosetta. A numerous population manned the walls and the towers of the city of the Arabs. My artillery had not yet been landed; nevertheless our columns carried the first enciente by assault; the new city and the forts capitulated the same day. The possession of Alexandria gave me a secure footing in Egypt. The debarkation continued without obstacle. My army, thirty thousand strong, was divided into five divisions under the orders of Generals Kleber,* Desaix,† Reynier,‡

* Kleber (Jean Baptiste) was born at Strasbourg in 1754. His parents were poor, but his early education was attended to by the curate of a village of Alsace. He was admitted, while still young, into the military school of Bavaria, where he completed his education and was commissioned in the army of the Electorate. He afterward resigned and returned to France. He entered the French army in 1792 and distinguished himself at the defense of Mayence. He served in the following campaigns, and had already acquired a brilliant reputation when he started on this expedition, which has immortalized his name.

† Desaix (Louis Charles Antoine) was born at St. Hilaire-d'Ayat, in 1768. He was educated at the military school of Effiat, and at the age of fifteen, entered the army as sub-lieutenant. He early distinguished himself for his enthusiastic love of study. His promotion was very rapid, for we find him a brigadier-general in 1793; in 1794 he was made general-of-division and greatly distinguished himself with the northern army, and also, in 1796, with the army of the Rhine. He joined Napoleon in Italy in 1797. A mutual attachment was instantly formed, which continued till the death of Desaix on the field of Marengo.

‡ Reynier (Jean Louis Ebenezer) was born at Lausanne, in 1771. He received a scientific education to prepare him for the profession of engineer. He entered the military service in 1792, and was made general-of-brigade in 1794. He had greatly distinguished himself previous to the campaign in Egypt. He served in the south of Italy during the campaigns of 1805 and 1806. He served in Spain, and also under Napoleon, in the campaigns of 1809, 1812, and 1813. He was made prisoner at the battle of Leipsic, and died in the beginning of 1814. He was the author of several works on Egypt.

Bon,* and Menou;† my cavalry, amounting to three thousand men, had only three hundred horses; the remainder were to be mounted in this country.

March on Cairo.—To give the Mamelukes no time to concert means of defense, it was essential to push forward rapidly the conquest of Egypt. The *élite* of their forces was composed of cavalry, the most redoubtable in the world; their infantry were merely militia, inferior in every respect to our soldiers. Success depended on the rapidity of our attacks and the consternation produced by our victories. The crusaders had failed against Egypt because theirs was a war of religion, carried on against the entire masses of Islamism. This danger was now to be avoided. Thanks to the revolts and independence of the Mamelukes, the Mussulman population was divided; we came as the friends of the Porte and thus gained a good part of the Turks. Victory is always the surest means of making partisans; by offering at the same time the laurel and the olive, we might gain those who were inclined to peace, and whom the violent administration of a warlike horde rendered very unhappy. St. Louis had required four months to reach Cairo, and had there halted; I would reach there in fifteen days and immediately push forward to other conquests.

* Bon (L. A.) born at Romans in 1758, first entered the army in 1775, but after some years' service in the colonies retired to civil life. He again entered the army in 1792, and in 1794 was made general-of-brigade. He distinguished himself in the Italian campaigns of 1796 and 1797, and won great admiration by his bravery and skill in Egypt. He was killed at the siege of St. Jean-d'Acre. His widow and family were afterward most liberally provided for by Napoleon.

† Menou (Jacques François) was born in Touraine in 1750. He was of a noble family and was a *maréchal-de-camp* in the army before the revolution. He was a politician of some distinction, but had seen little service; he owed his place in the army of Egypt rather to political influence than to military merit. After the death of Kleber he became the commander-in-chief, but was utterly incompetent to the duties of his station. After his return to France, he received from Napoleon several political appointments, but was no longer employed on military service. He died in 1810. *Biographie Universelle.*

I left Alexandria on the sixth of July ; and directed my march across the desert upon Rahmania, where I was rejoined by Kleber, who had marched by Rosetta, taking possession of this place. On the way we first encountered the Mamelukes, a part of whom were repulsed by my advanced guard under Desaix. We now ascended the Nile, and pressed forward toward Cairo.

Combat of Chebreiss.—But before reaching the capital of Egypt it was necessary to fight. On the thirteenth of July, we encountered Mourad-Bey, the most courageous of all the Mameluke chiefs, who was posted, with four thousand horsemen, near the village of Chebreiss, with his right flank covered by a flotilla. Nothing can compare with the beauty of the *coup-d'œil* presented by this African cavalry ; the elegant figures of the Arabian horses, relieved by the richest trappings ; the martial air of the riders, the variegated brilliancy of their costumes, the superb turbans enriched with their plumes of office ; all together presented to us a spectacle new and peculiar. The Turkish cavalry, which is really very fine, is, however, far from equal to that of the Mamelukes. The combat began between the flotillas ; ours, which, in ascending the Nile, kept pace with our march, was first attacked by the enemy. To disengage it, I attacked Mourad-Bey. I adopted the order of battle used by the Russians against the Turks, each division being formed in squares enclosing the equipages, and the few cavalry which I possessed. These squares were disposed in echelons so as to flank each other. In vain did the Mamelukes present themselves against the different sides of the squares ; at last, harassed by the fire of my artillery, they fell back toward the capital.

Battle of the Pyramids.—On the twenty-first of July, we arrived in sight of Cairo ; we had seen the pyramids for some days. The aspect of these wonderful monuments of antiquity, braving the storms of ages, and now surrounded by the superb cavalry of the Mamelukes caracoling in the plain, excited in the breasts of my soldiers a mingled feeling of astonishment and pride. I profited by this to raise their enthusiasm to the highest pitch, addressing them in words as lasting as the Pyramids themselves:

"Soldiers! you have come to rescue Egypt from barbarism; to bring civilization into the East; and to save this beautiful land from the yoke of England. Forty centuries are looking down upon you from the tops of these monuments!"

Mourad-Bey had armed the village of Embabeh with artillery, and the intrenchments with militia, supported by six thousand Mameluke and Arabian cavalry. I advanced with my squares. Desaix and Reynier were to extend their line, the right in advance, so as to cut off all communication from Embabeh to the upper valley of the Nile, while the divisions of Bon and Kleber should attack the front of the intrenchments. The Mamelukes seeing Desaix in march, attacked him in great numbers; but all their brilliant charges failed against the intrepidity of the French squares. Never were charges better made, or better sustained: but the vigor and ardor of these famous Mameluke horsemen even augmented the disorder in their own ranks; unable to penetrate our squares they sought to die in the attempt. At the left the intrenchments of Embabeh were carried by our troops, and the enemy, seeing himself shut in between our line of squares and the Nile, fled toward Upper Egypt, except fifteen hundred men who were drowned in the river; and their camp and forty pieces of artillery fell into our hands.

Napoleon enters Cairo.—This brilliant victory cost me only two hundred men *hors de combat*, and it opened to me the gates of Cairo, which I entered on the twenty-fifth. Ibrahim-Bey, who commanded the Mamelukes of the right bank of the Nile, fell back on Belbeis. Mourad-Bey, with those of the left bank, took the road to Upper Egypt. I sent Desaix in pursuit. This able general with his small force established himself in Upper Egypt, and checked the operations of Mourad-Bey, who, always beaten, but never discouraged, renewed his attacks with admirable constancy. To complete our conquests it was necessary to dispose of Ibrahim-Bey. I left Cairo on the seventh of August with the divisions of Reynier, Menou, Kleber, and the cavalry, directing my march on Belbeis. Ibrahim retired toward the desert of Syria; I continued the pursuit. On the eleventh my cavalry overtook and defeated his rear-guard at Salchich. Ibrahim escaped, with about a thousand cavalry, across the desert to Gaza. I left Reynier at Salchich with orders to fortify this post as a protection to Egypt on the side of Syria. The division of Kleber was directed on Damietta, the possession of which rendered me master of all the shore. With the division of Menou I returned to Cairo.

Naval Battle of Aboukir.—But all my hopes were marred by the fatal event at Aboukir, which was caused by neglect to obey my orders. I had several times directed that our fleet should be withdrawn into the old port of Alexandria, or if that could not be effected, to immediately set sail for France. It was pretended that the canal leading to this port was too shallow for our vessels of the line, but the soundings made by my orders proved that a seventy-four-gun ship could pass. Brueys thought the operation hazardous, and preferred the open sea to a possible blockade in port. He, therefore, made preparations to sail for Corfu or Toulon. While ranged in close order in the harbor of Aboukir he was attacked on the evening of the first of August. Nelson pierced his ill-arranged line, and destroyed the left, while the right was obliged to remain an idle spectator of the combat. The battle continued thirty-six hours, and ended in the destruction of three quarters of our fleet. Admiral Brueys, by a glorious death, expiated his fault, which proved so fatal to the French navy.*

* Alison endeavors to attribute to Napoleon all the faults of the battle of Aboukir, but, notwithstanding his erroneous statements and garbled quotations, his documents prove the very reverse of what he asserts. The account given by Jomini, in the text, is perfectly correct. Napoleon urged upon Brueys, time and again, the importance of securing his fleet in the harbor of Alexandria; he sent engineers to make the soundings at the entrance, suggested to the naval commander the use of water camels or butts on which to float his larger ships over the bar; Brueys wished to take position in Aboukir Bay, where he could secure his line by land batteries. But on the twenty-sixth of July, he had determined to follow Napoleon's advice, and wrote to him that he would enter the port. On the thirtieth Napoleon wrote to Brueys, "I am induced to believe that you are by this time safely in the port." The battle was fought on the first of August.

With respect to Alison's charge, "that the only real culpability in the case is imputable to Napoleon, in having endeavored, after Brueys' death, to blacken his character," in his report to the Directory, it may be remarked that it is not true. The report states nothing but what is given in his previous correspondence with Brueys. He says that the Admiral had neglected his advice, which was actually the case, but he speaks of his error in the mildest possible terms. Indeed, he and Brueys were personal friends, and it was to this friendship that Napoleon attributes Brueys' unwillingness to sail for Corfu till he could hear from him at Cairo. This looks much more like excusing his faults than like "blackening his character." The following is Napoleon's letter to Madame Brueys on her husband's death: "Your husband has been killed by a cannon ball, while fighting on his quarter-deck. He died without suffering; the death the most easy and the most envied by the brave. I feel warmly for your grief. The moment which separates us from the object we love is terrible; we feel alone on the earth; we almost experience the convulsion of the last agony; the faculties of the soul are annihilated; the world is seen only through a vail which distorts every thing. We feel as if nothing longer binds us to life; that it were far better to die; but when after these first and unavoidable throes, we press our children to our hearts, tears and more tender sentiments arise; life for their sakes becomes tolerable. Yes, madam, they will open the fountains of your heart; you will watch their childhood, educate their youth; you will tell them of their father, of your present grief, of the loss which they and the republic have sustained in his death. After having resumed the interest in life by the cord of maternal love, you will, perhaps, feel some consolation from the friendship and warm interest which I shall ever take in the widow of my friend."

For further information on this subject, the reader is referred to Gourgaud, vol. ii., Norvins, vol. i., and to Thiers' History of the Revolution. Alison rests his assertions on such absurd authorities as Bourienne, and an anonymous work called "*Mémoires d'un Homme d'Etat*," neither of which, however, confirm his most important statements against Napoleon. These have no other origin than his own imagination.

Fatal Consequences of this Event.—Although this catastrophe changed the chances of our expedition, still we were not without hopes of success. We could maintain ourselves in possession of the country if we should succeed in attaching the inhabitants to our cause. With money, arms, and officers, we could recruit our legions as well as the Mamelukes. All my efforts were now directed to this object. But to this there were two opposing obstacles: the first was the maritime blockade, which prevented any commerce of exportation, the true source of that country's wealth; the second was the religion. The Koran directs the extermination of idolaters, or subjects them to pay tribute; it allows no obedience or submission to an infidel power. In this it is more favorable to a military spirit than the Christian religion, which directs us to render unto Cæsar the things which are Cæsars, and declares that the empire of Jesus Christ is not of this world. We have already said that in the tenth, eleventh, and twelfth centuries, the dogmas of Islamism had raised up immense obstacles to the crusaders in Syria, for the war being one of religion, was necessarily one of extermination, in which millions of Europeans were destroyed. If such a spirit had animated the Egyptians in 1798, we should have been lost; my little army, incited by no fanatical zeal, and already disgusted with the country, could not have held out six months against a population of several millions of exasperated Mussulmans. Fortunately for us the intercourse between the Egyptians and Europe had destroyed the influence of these precepts of the Koran. Religious hatred had not been carried to fanaticism, as in the tenth century. I therefore did not despair of conciliating the Imans, the Muftis, the Ulemas, and all the ministers of the Mussulman religion. The French army, since the revolution, was indifferent to all forms of worship; even in Italy, they never went to church. I took advantage of this circumstance to persuade the Mussulmans that my soldiers were so many cenobites, disposed to embrace Mohammedanism. The Christians of different denominations in Egypt, who were quite numerous, wished to profit by our presence to get rid of the restrictions imposed on their worship. I opposed this, and took care to maintain religious affairs on the same footing as they were. Every day, at sunrise, the Scheiks of the Grand Mosque came to my house; they overwhelmed me with marks of their regard, and I held long conversations with them on the life of the Prophet and the contents of the Koran. I assisted at many of their ceremonies, and, by respecting their usages and their belief, succeeded in inspiring them with great confidence.

Difficulties with the Porte.—By the same system, I used every effort to calm the Porte. On landing in Egypt, I had sought to prove that there was no reason for its taking umbrage at my expedition, as I had come to chastise the rebellious Beys, to destroy the English commerce in the Indies, and to render Egypt the entrepôt of the East. I hoped that Talleyrand would repair to Constantinople for the same object; but the old fox feared the Seven-Towers; confiding his mission to a subaltern he found pretexts for staying at Paris, and thus left an open field for the ministers of Russia and England. Nevertheless the Porte still hesitated to declare openly against us; but the destruction of our fleet soon removed its doubts. On the first of September, Ruffin, our *chargé-d'affaires* at Constantinople, was conducted to the Seven-Towers, and war was declared. Up to this time I had conceived well-grounded hopes for the success of our project of colonization. Egypt, except an occasional incursion of the Mamelukes, appeared tranquil. The savans who had accompanied my expedition were exploring this antique cradle of civilization; scientific establishments, formed under their direction at Cairo, contributed to drive away the ennui which one is so apt to feel in a strange land; some of these learned men assisted in forming armories, founderies, powder manufactories, and all the military resources furnished by the arts. But the rupture with the Porte clouded our happy prospects.

Revolt of Cairo.—The news of this event now spread through Egypt and caused a general fermentation. The chiefs of the Mussulmans having declared against us, we were now only *Christian dogs*, and to exterminate us was meritorious service. A serious revolt broke out at Cairo on the twenty-second of October. General Dupuis, who commanded there, and some three hundred of our officers and soldiers, were strangled. It became necessary to resort to severe punishment; my troops who were encamped about the city penetrated there and made a great carnage of those who were found armed. After two days of massacre tranquillity was restored, and the quelling of the sedition seemed to consolidate our power in Egypt. Desaix had just completed the subjugation of Upper Egypt, gaining, over the remains of the Mamelukes, the victory of Sediman.

Expedition into Syria.—Our repose was not of long duration; I learned that the Turks were assembling an army in Natolia to enter Egypt by marching along the eastern coast of the Mediterranean. Djezzar, pacha of St. Jean d'Acre, was already collecting magazines for this army, and preparing to furnish it a reënforcement of troops collected in Syria. The best means of disconcerting these projects was to destroy the preparations before the Ottoman army could come to the support of Djezzar. I therefore resolved to march into Syria with such of my troops as were not absolutely necessary to guard the coasts, and to maintain tranquillity in Egypt during our absence. On the tenth of February I left Cairo with the divisions of Bon, Lannes, and the cavalry. On the seventeenth I reached El-Arich, where I found the divisions of Reynier and Kleber, which had come from Salchich and Damietta. Reynier had already carried the village of El-Arich by assault, but the fort still held out. This little fort might, for a long time, have resisted our means of attack, but fortunately the garrison capitulated on the twentieth.

Capture of Jaffa.—Although the total force of my expedition did not exceed thirteen thousand men, still I was obliged to make them march by isolated divisions across the desert which separated us from Syria, so as not to exhaust the wells, our only resource in this arid country. After forty-eight hours of the most fatiguing march, we reached the plain of Gaza. All the army united near this city, which had been evacuated by the enemy, leaving us in possession of its great magazines. On the third of March we reached Jaffa. The garrison was numerous and disposed for defense. I established batteries against the outer wall. On the seventh the breach was found practicable, and the city carried by assault. We captured on this occasion two thousand prisoners, who very much embarrassed me. The weakness of my army did not allow me to detach an escort to guard them; on the other hand, they could not be released on parole, for they did not consider it binding; moreover a part of them had already been discharged at El-Arich, on their promise not to again serve against us, and were now taken in arms. Knowing of no other course to pursue, I caused them to be shot. I did this with great repugnance; but as the barbarians treated Christian prisoners in this way, and gloried in sending their heads to Constantinople, I felt the less scruple in the course I was forced to pursue. My enemies have not failed to reproach me with this action, which, judged of by the rules of civilized warfare, is not justifiable, but which the laws of retaliation, and of necessity, in the difficult circumstances in which I myself and my army were placed, will perhaps excuse it in the eyes of posterity.*

Resistance of St. Jean d'Acre.—Djezzar-Pacha had taken every means for the defense of St. Jean d'Acre, which place was invested on the eighteenth of March. The fortifications of

---

* Thiers, in speaking of this event, says, "that when Napoleon summoned the commandant of Jaffa to surrender, the latter replied *by cutting off the head of the messenger!* The place was then carried by storm after extraordinary exertions, and having no means of disposing of the prisoners without allowing them to return and swell the enemy's ranks, he decided on a terrible measure, *the only cruel act of his life.* Transported into a barbarous country, he had involuntarily adopted its manners." Alison gives the following version of this affair. "When the prisoners were assembled, a council of war was summoned to deliberate on their fate. For two days the terrible question was debated, What was to be done with these captives? and the French officers approached it without any predisposition to cruel measures. But the difficulties were represented as insurmountable on the side of humanity. If they sent them back, it was said, to Egypt, a considerable detachment would be required to guard so large a body of captives, and that could ill be spared from the army in its present situation; if they gave them their liberty, they would forthwith join the garrison of Acre, or the clouds of Arabs who already hung on the flanks of the army; if they were incorporated unarmed in the ranks, the prisoners would add grievously to the number of mouths, for whom, already, it was sufficiently difficult to procure subsistence. No friendly sail appeared in the distance to take off the burden on the side of the ocean; the difficulty of maintaining them became every day more grievous. The committee, to whom the matter was referred, unanimously reported that they should be put to death, and Napoleon, with reluctance signed the fatal order. It was carried into execution on the tenth of March."

These circumstances greatly palliate, though, of course, they can not fully justify the act. The opportunity thus offered to Alison to blacken the character of Napoleon is too good to be lost, and he accordingly proceeds to give him what he calls "his deserts;" such phrases as "atrocity," "foul deed," "iniquitous and atrocious act," "execrable deed," etc., are most unsparingly applied.

It may be interesting to the unprejudiced reader to compare Alison's remarks in this place with his labored defense of Hastings for the cold-blooded murder of Nuncomar, for the horrible Rohilla war, carried on under his direction, and for the cruel treatment and robbery of the princesses of Oude. In the former case, Macaulay says, "a man was unjustly put to death in order to secure a political purpose." In the second case, "Mr. Hastings put down by main force the brave struggles of innocent men, fighting for their liberty, "he folded his arms and looked on, while their villages were burned, their children butchered, and their women violated." "More than a hundred thousand people fled from their homes to pestilential jungles, preferring famine and fever, and the haunts

the place consisted in a wall flanked by towers and surrounded by a ditch. But our means of attack were not even sufficient for the reduction of these slight obstacles, for Sidney Smith, commanding the English cruisers, had captured the siege-train which I had sent from Alexandria by sea, and put it in battery against us. The trench was opened on the twentieth of March. Djezzar, under the direction of a French engineer and a French artillerist, made a most des-

---

of tigers to the tyranny of him to whom an English and a Christian government had, for shameful lucre, sold their substance and their blood, and the honor of their wives and daughters." "The finest population of India was subjected to a greedy, cowardly, cruel tyrant." To extort money from the princesses of Oude they were seized and imprisoned at Tyzabad. "Their two male attendants," continues Macauley, "were, by orders of the British government, seized and imprisoned, ironed, starved almost to death, in order to extort money from the princesses. After they had been two months in confinement their health gave way. They implored permission to take a little exercise in the garden of their prison. The officer who was in charge of them stated, that if they were allowed this indulgence, there was not the smallest chance of their escaping, and that their irons really added nothing to the security of the custody in which they were kept. He did not understand the plan of his superiors. Their object in these inflictions was not security, but torture; and all mitigation was refused. Yet this was not the worst. It was resolved by an English government that these two infirm old men should be delivered to the tormentors. For that purpose they were removed to Lucknow. What horrors their dungeon there witnessed, can only be guessed. Food was allowed to enter the apartments of the princesses only in such scanty quantities that their female attendants were in danger of perishing with hunger. Month after month this cruelty continued, till at length, after twelve hundred thousand pounds had been wrung out of the princesses, Hastings began to think that he had really got to the bottom of their revenue, and that no rigor could extort more. Then at length the wretched men who were detained at Lucknow regained their liberty. When their irons were knocked off, and the doors of their prison opened, their quivering lips, the tears which ran down their cheeks, and the thanksgivings which they poured forth to the common Father of Mussulmans and Christians, melted even the stout hearts of the English warriors who stood by." These are the words of an impartial English writer, long years after the events had transpired. Alison justifies these proceedings on the ground of the "overbearing pressure of state necessity." Hastings, he says, "did evil that good might come of it," and he, therefore, has no words of censure for him, only the most unbounded praises for his "firmness and ability," his "great achievements," his "far-seeing wisdom and patriotic disinterestedness." His deeds, he says, "originated in overbearing necessity." Verily, circumstances alter cases! "It is your bull that has gored my ox."

perate defense. My first assault on the twenty-eighth, having failed, the hopes of the besieged were increased.

Battle of Mont-Tabor.—From my posts of observation at Saffet and Nazareth, I received intelligence of the approach of an army from Damascus and Palestine. To check this hostile force, I dispatched toward the Jordan two small corps of observation, Kleber, with his division, to Nazareth, and Murat, with a detachment of about two thousand men, to Saffet. A few days afterward I learned that the enemy had passed the Jordan at the bridge of Giz-el-Mesania, and that Kleber would be attacked. I flew to his assistance. I left the camp before St. Jean d'Acre on the fifteenth of April, followed by the division of Bon and the cavalry: the next morning I arrived near Mont-Tabor in sight of the enemy, who, with the great mass of his infantry, occupied the village of Fouli. Their cavalry of about twenty thousand horse, inundated the celebrated plain of Esdrelon, where the division of Kleber, formed in two squares, and entirely surrounded, maintained its position with admirable bravery. My arrival was a thunderbolt to the enemy: already discouraged by the invincible resistance of Kleber's squares, they did not venture to fight my fresh troops, but precipitately fled. We carried the village of Fouli with the bayonet, and the Ottoman army, utterly routed, fled across the Jordan at the bridge of Giz-el-Mesania, and retired on Damascus. This singular victory had such a marvelous effect upon the enemy that he did not venture to trouble our army again during the siege. I left Kleber at Nazareth, and with the rest of the troops returned to Acre.

Continuation of the Siege.—The siege was pushed with obstinacy, but with little success. The Turks, directed by Philippeaux[*] and Tromelin, and assisted by the English of

---

[*] Philippeaux was an emigrant engineer-officer of great merit and distinction; he had been a schoolmaster of Napoleon at Paris, and had studied with

the squadron of Sidney Smith, defended themselves with great valor. The place had already sustained five assaults when a flotilla, fitted out at Rhodes, and having on board the famous corps of Hussein-Pacha, came to reprovision the port. Seeking to anticipate this succor, I directed, on the eighth of May, the sixth assault to be made. Again we were repulsed. There seemed no further hope of carrying the place. By obstinately continuing the siege, I might risk the safety of my little army. I was therefore obliged to prepare to retreat. But I was so little accustomed to reverses that I could not retire from this enterprise without making one more attempt. Kleber had just rejoined me; his troops were fresh; I flattered myself that they might assist me in carrying a place whose open breaches presented some chances of success. On the morning and evening of the tenth of May, I renewed the attack for the seventh and eighth times. The ardor of my troops seemed to have acquired new strength; but nothing was capable of shaking the obstinate intrepidity of the besieged.*

Raising of the Siege.—On the twenty-second of May, I raised the siege and directed my march to Egypt. On the way we laid waste all the country, both to supply ourselves with provisions for crossing the desert and to deprive the

him the science of engineering. Tromelin was an artillery officer, also in exile. He afterward returned to France and asked service under Napoleon. The latter gave him a colonel's commission, saying to him, "I only ask you to injure my enemies as much as you did me in Egypt."

* Napoleon received during the siege an affecting proof of devotedness. While he was in the trenches, a shell fell at his feet; two grenadiers who observed it, immediately rushed toward him, placed him between them, and raising their arms above his head, completely covered every part of his body. Happily the shell respected the whole group; nobody was injured. One of these brave grenadiers afterward became General Dumesnil, who lost a leg in the campaign of Moscow, and commanded the fortress of Vincennes, at the time of the invasion in 1814. The capital had been for some weeks occupied by the allies, but Dumesnil still held out. Nothing was then talked of in Paris but his obstinate defense and humorous reply when summoned by the Russians to surrender: "*Give me back my leg, and I will give up my fortress.*" (*Las Casas.*)

Turks of the means of following us to the frontiers of Egypt. I was obliged to leave behind all who could not follow us. There were fifty men sick of the plague who could not move with the army, and who must be left to the ferocious Djezzar. I caused opium to be administered to them to relieve them from their sufferings. In this I did wrong: but yielding to a natural feeling of humanity I did to them what, in similar circumstances, I could wish done to myself. In this action, from which I could derive no possible advantage, I had no idea that I was furnishing to my enemies matter for calumnious interpretations.* I ought to have left these unfortunate men to the mercy of the Turks, since such was the hard lot which destiny had reserved for them.

* It is believed that the author has here fallen into an error, which does not appear in his great scientific History of the Wars of the French Revolution. In the retreat from Syria, Napoleon showed every care for his sick, giving up, for their transportation, the horses of his artillery and his staff; he himself gave the example to his officers of marching on foot. From Jaffa, three separate detachments of sick were dispatched for Egypt; the first under Colbert, by sea, directed on Damietta, the other two by land, on Gaza and El-Arich. About fifty or sixty, declared incurable, could not be taken with the army, for want of means. Napoleon suggested to his physician Desgenettes, that it would be more humane to give them opium than to leave them to the cruelties of the Turks. But the proposition was rejected and not again alluded to. Napoleon said at St. Helena, that he would have advised this course if the case had been that of his own son. This circumstance furnished grounds for believing that opium was actually administered, and the report was most industriously circulated by the English. But it has since been disproved by the highest authority and indisputable evidences. Even Alison dares not venture to assert its truth, but expresses a fear that it *may* have been so. His language is as follows: " At Jaffa he visited the plague hospital, inviting those who had sufficient strength to rise, to raise themselves on their beds, and endeavor to get into litters prepared for their use. He walked through the rooms, affected a careless air, striking his boot with his riding-whip in order to remove the apprehensions which had seized all the soldiers in regard to the contagious nature of the malady. Those who could not be removed were, it is feared, poisoned by orders of the general; their numbers did not exceed sixty; and as the Turks were within an hour's march of the place, their recovery hopeless, and a cruel death awaited them at the hands of those barbarians, the moment they arrived, the painful act may perhaps be justified, not only on the ground of necessity, but of humanity."

This story was first circulated by Sir Robert Wilson, with all the horrible

Return to Cairo.—Returning into Egypt, I marched to Cairo with the main body of my forces, and reached that place on the fourteenth of June. Kleber returned to Damietta. I left a strong garrison at Cattieh. In the mean time Desaix had finished the subjugation of Upper Egypt, the battle of Semanhout having completed the ruin of the Mamelukes.

The ill success of my Syrian expedition had made me still more sensible of the necessity of influencing the people through the instrumentality of the ministers of Islamism. I proposed to them to publish a *fetam*, directing the people to take the oath of obedience to the general-in-chief. The proposition startled them, and an old man replied to me: Why do you not turn Mussulman with your whole army? A hundred thousand men would then flock to your banners, and being disciplined by you, you could with them restore the Arabian power and conquer the entire East. I opposed to this the necessity of circumcision and abstinence from wine. But they said that an accommodation could be made with Heaven: that a man might drink wine and still be a good Mussulman, provided that he doubled his good works. I then caused to be drawn the plan for a mosque more grand than that of Gemil-el-Azar, under the pretext of raising a monument to the conversion of the army; but in fact I wished to amuse them and gain time. The *fetam* of obedience was given by the Scheiks, who declared me the friend of the Prophet, and especially protected by him. The report was generally cir-

---

details which his ever-fruitful imagination could suggest. To give the account the greater probability, he asserted that he possessed indisputable evidence, which would soon be produced. It, however, never appeared. Dr. Desgenettes and others afterward completely refuted the story, and at this day none but a rabid English tory or a Scotch libeler would think of attaching the slightest credit to it. For a very important and detailed account of Napoleon's treatment of his sick, the reader is referred to Dr. Desgenettes' "*Histoire Medicale de l'Armée d'Orient.*"

culated that in less than a year the whole army would assume the turban, and our soldiers soon felt the good effects of this innocent, and, under the circumstances, justifiable ruse.

Battle of Aboukir.—Toward the end of July the Mamelukes again appeared in Lower Egypt, and Mourad-Bey again descended toward Gizeh. While engaged in making my dispositions to pursue him, I heard that fifteen thousand Turks had just landed from the fleet of Rhodes at the *presqu'île* of Aboukir, and carried by assault the fort of that name. I felt the necessity for instant action. On the twenty-fourth of July, the part of my army destined for this expedition was assembled at the wells between Alexandria and Aboukir. The next day I attacked the Turks. The two lines of intrenchments with which they had secured the *presqu'île* were successively carried, notwithstanding the obstinate resistance which they opposed. At the same time Murat succeeded, by my orders, in penetrating between their lines with some squadrons, and creating a panic there. All endeavored to regain their vessels, and those who were not killed in the attempt perished in the waves ; of twelve or thirteen thousand men, only two thousand made their escape into the fort, and two hundred, with the Pacha commanding in chief, were taken prisoners. All the others were killed or drowned. Our loss was about a thousand men *hors-de-combat*. This victory fully effaced the stain which the defeat of our fleet had attached to the name of Aboukir. The fort, after a warm bombardment, surrendered on the second of August. This success consolidated my power in Egypt, so that with an annual reënforcement, it could be maintained.

Napoleon returns to France.—At this epoch more important affairs were attracting my attention. At St. Jean-d'Acre we had learned that a new coalition was formed against France. We had received by Sidney Smith many English journals and the French gazette of Frankfort, informing us of the reverses of our armies in Italy and of the Rhine, and the successive revolutions which had disorganized and disgraced the Directory. I had also received a letter from the government announcing the departure of Admiral Bruix from Brest, to combine with the squadrons of Toulon and of Spain to carry home the army of Egypt should circumstances require it. They renewed the authorization of my return to France. Bruix had not made his appearance, and it was probable that he had been driven from his course, or had given up the undertaking.

I felt myself able to restore to my country the lustre of victory and the benefits of internal and external peace. Everything now proved that the French were tired of the Revolution, and that it was time to bring it to a close. It was necessary for me to hurry back, or some one else might profit by these favorable circumstances. I had now no motive for prolonging my stay in Egypt. The country was completely conquered, and the only task left was to colonize it. The principal arrangements for this were made, and Kleber was as capable as myself of carrying them into execution. I could better serve my country in Europe than to remain here. Moreover the time was propitious. If my reputation had suffered any by the affair of St. Jean d'Acre, it was more than retrieved by the brilliant and important victory of Aboukir. I therefore set sail for France on the twenty-fourth of August, with four small vessels, leaving Kleber the commander-in-chief of the army of Egypt. I have been much blamed for this step, but unjustly. In the first place, I was fully authorized by the government. In the second, the Egyptian expedition was either desperate, or capable of sustaining itself. If a treaty of evacuation was to be signed, the lowest officer in the army was as capable of doing it as the highest; on the other hand, Kleber was fully capable of conquering all the enemies then existing in the country. This general, intelligent, enterprising, valiant, was one of the finest men in Europe. He was the *beau-ideal* of an officer ; terrible in combat, calm and cool in combination, able in administration, beloved by the soldiers ; he resembled, in all respects, Marshal Saxe. Though not among the first rank of captains, still he was capable of becoming one ; though as yet no great strategist, he was, by his genius and habit of command, pretty certain of learning the art. I will hereafter speak of the results of this happy choice. To follow the thread of events, we will now trace a rapid outline of the campaign of 1799.

CHAPTER V.

CAMPAIGN OF 1799.

Situation of Europe in 1798—Exorbitant Demands of the Directory at Rastadt —Russia in Favor of the Empire—Negotiations of Prince Repnin at Berlin— Embarrassments of Prussia—Views of Austria—Secret Convention between England and Naples—Favorable Chances for Austria—Alliance between Austria and Russia—Policy of the Directory—Affairs of Switzerland—Treaty of Alliance concluded at Paris—The smaller Cantons refuse the Oath of Fidelity—Expedition of Schauwembourg against Stanz—The Grisons call upon the Austrians—French Law of Conscription—Consequences of the Defeat at Aboukir and the Declaration of War by the Ottoman Porte—Decree for a Levy of two hundred thousand Men—Embarrassed State of the Finances— Negotiations paralyzed by the Intermission of Spain—State of the Negotiations at Rastadt—England—Russia—Spain—Portugal—Sweden and Denmark —War commenced by the Court of Naples—Joubert seizes upon Piedmont and occupies Tuscany—Ferdinand flies to Sicily—Championnet takes Possession of Naples—Erection of the Parthenopean Republic—The Russians advance toward Italy—The Directory takes the Initiative without Preparation —Massena gets Possession of the Grisons—The Archduke marches against Jourdan—Battle of Stockach—Reverses in Italy—Retreat of the Army behind the Rhine—Attack upon our Plenipotentiaries at Rastadt—Tardy Enterprise of the Archduke—Suwarrow in Lombardy—Grand Naval Expedition of Admiral Bruix—Macdonald's Army evacuates Naples—Suwarrow enters Turin—Massena driven from the Grisons—The Archduke penetrates into Switzerland—Massena evacuates Zurich—The Archduke paralyzed by Cabinet Orders—Macdonald returns upon Modena—Suwarrow attacks him on the Trebia—General State of Affairs—Dissatisfaction against the Directory— Political Operations of Sièyes—Address to the Councils—The Nomination of Treilhard is annulled—Merlin and Laréveillère resign—Consternation at the Result of the Battle of Trebia—Formation of Clubs—Talleyrand is replaced —The Directory close the Manège—New Plan of Operations proposed—

Joubert is charged with its Execution—He debouches from the Apennines—Battle of Novi—Massena recaptures the smaller Cantons—Project of the Archduke—New Plan of the Coalition—The Archduke Marches on Manheim—Plan of Suwarrow—Battle of Zurich—Korsakof retires to the Rhine—Suwarrow passes the St. Gothard and marches on the Muttenthal and Glaris—Defeat of the Austrians in this Canton—Difficult Retreat of Suwarrow—Efforts of Korsakof on Winterthour—Movements of the Archduke and Suwarrow—Descent of the Anglo-Russians into Holland—Lecourbe raises the Siege of Philipsbourg—Efforts of Championnet to save Coni.

Situation of Europe in 1798.—While we were hoping to found, on the banks of the Nile, a formidable *point d'appui* for overthrowing the English power in India, France found herself threatened upon her own territory. My departure for Egypt, instead of rendering the Directory more prudent, had only increased the desire for new conquests. Its agents treated the Cisalpine Republic as the Roman proconsuls formerly treated the nations she had conquered. In Piedmont the agents of propagandism excited such serious troubles that the king deemed it necessary to ask the assistance of the French troops to calm them. Brune, pretending to fear the dangers that might result from them to the army, required that Charles Emanuel should deliver up to him the citadel of Turin, in order to secure the public tranquillity.

Exorbitant Demands of the Directory at Rastadt.—The Congress at Rastadt, having at first recognized the Rhine as the boundary of France, after my departure took a step directly the opposite. The Directory, dissatisfied with the conditions of the treaty of Campo-Formio, soon redoubled its pretensions, and preferred, through its plenipotentiaries, the most exorbitant demands, asking the forts of Kehl and Cassel; all the islands of the Rhine; the demolition of Ehrenbreitstein; in a word, to place themselves offensively on the right of the Rhine, in violation of the conditions of the treaty: moreover, the free navigation of all rivers emptying into the Rhine was demanded, and that the debts of the countries conceded to France on its left bank, should be paid by those given us as indemnities ; this was the height of absurdity. Such demands were not the result of a noble ambition, but rather of a morbid trickery, and a love of propagandism. The composition of the Directory, the stoic Rewbel, the aristocrat Barras, the pettifogger Merlin, the fanatic Laréveillère, the poet François-de-Neuchâteau, were not men of true ambition, but of mere pretension—short-sighted politicians. Adding these exaggerated pretensions to the revolutions with which Europe was everywhere threatened, it was evident that peace could not be of long duration. If war did not immediately break out, it was because the enemy wished time for preparation.

The cabinet of Vienna, though acquainted with the dispositions of England and Russia, was nevertheless desirous of negotiating. It preferred to make its complaints, and demand redress of grievances, before resorting to arms. Negotiations were opened at Selz. Baron Thugut, who had resigned to avoid signing the treaty of peace with us, had just resumed the portfolio from the hands of Cobentzel, and the latter had come to Selz to negotiate with François-de-Neuchâteau. The special object of these conferences has not been avowed, but we may conjecture what were the interests agitated there ; it is evident that the councillors of Francis II. betrayed his confidence, if they admitted the state of Europe at the middle of the year 1798 to be equivalent to that which had been stipulated at Campo-Formio. It was true that at each of its aggressions, the Directory had openly protested its desire to maintain friendly relations with the Imperial house, as if it were necessary to assail directly a state of the first order to give just cause for war. Instead of the evacuation of Switzerland, and the reëstablishment of its entire independence, which were to be the first pledges of the execution of the treaty of peace, the recent conventions, transforming the Cisalpine Republic, Rome, and even Piedmont, into mere conquered provinces, authorized the cabinet of Vienna to demand that these states should be restored to independence, or that the House of Austria should obtain equivalents, at least, for this increase of a rival power. If we are to believe reports which have too much the appearance of probability, several provinces in the Italian peninsula were bartered at Selz as an indemnity to the Emperor for his loss of Saltzbourg and Innvierthal, and for permitting the ascendency of France over the new Republics.

Russia and the Empire.—The cabinet of Vienna, convinced by the rejection of its propositions that no accommodation could be expected with the Directory, decided to ally itself to Russia. This latter power could hardly remain an idle spectator of events which were changing the face of Europe, as the guarantee of the state of Germany in virtue of the treaty, of Teschen, it saw the German Empire threatened with destruction by the extension recently given to the system of secularization and indemnity. And even had Paul I. been but little interested, on the score of policy, in what was passing in Switzerland, at Turin, at Rome, and in the Mediterranean, still he would naturally have been drawn into these events from the affection which he had constantly shown for the Order of Malta.

Negotiations at Berlin.—The cabinet of St. Petersburg felt all the advantage of its position, and yielding to the proof of dangers which threatened the general system of Europe, it sent Prince Repnin at first to Berlin, and then to Vienna, as much to induce these two courts to desist from all indemnity in Germany, as to concert the means of forcing back the ambition of the Directory within the limits marked out by treaties.

Embarrassment of Prussia.—The first object of this mission was not difficult to accomplish, for Frederick-William found in the terms even of the treaty of Campo-Formio the means of recovering Guilderland, if the system of indemnity were rejected. But Prussia, more scrupulous on the second article, persisted in observing a neutrality. The young King, animated with a love of wealth, exaggerating the advantages of peace, directed his whole attention to repairing the breaches made in the state by the dissipation of his father. He was convinced that policy imposed on him no other combinations than that of forcing respect to his frontier and his flag, and of enriching his own country, while his rivals were devoting all their energies to mutual destruction. Severe critics have found fault with the administration of Count Haugwitz, the prime minister; and notwithstanding the eloquent defense published some years afterward by the celebrated Lombard, it yet remains to be demonstrated that the cabinet of Berlin fully appreciated all the advantages of its position. Undoubtedly this position was a delicate one; Prussia, as is usually the case with powers of the second order, was called upon to maintain the equilibrium between two superior masses just ready to come in collision. On whichever side the cabinet of Berlin took part, the balance of power might so incline as to render all counterpoise useless; and yet it was embarrassing to remain a mere idle spectator of the dismemberment of the German Empire, and the subjugation of Switzerland and Italy. An armed mediation had probably been much better than a strict neutrality. This kind of intervention, when of proper and timely application, often marks a vast and profound policy; all the logic of Lombard had not sufficed to prove that Prussia might not, by such a course, have prevented a war. By pronouncing with firmness, frankness, and moderation, she had obliged the Directory to evacuate the territories invaded since peace was declared, and the cabinet of Vienna to moderate its pretensions.

Views of Austria.—Austria on her side, however much

disposed to fulfil her engagements, could not overlook the necessity of laying the basis of the future relations of the four great powers. She could not fail to gain by doing this; for if they should fail to agree, there was every chance in her favor in a resort to arms. The news of the defeat of Aboukir and of the declaration of war by the Ottoman Porte against France, proved conclusively to the cabinet of Vienna, that in again entering the war, it would be their own fault if they did not reconquer and hold a great part of Italy. Fortune seemed again to place it within their reach. It was true that there was an army of one hundred thousand French between the Alps and the Tiber, but this army, left in want and neglect by the political administrators, and scattered over an immense territory to secure our conquests, was utterly incapable of taking the field with any chance of success. Besides the arbitrary acts of the Directory toward the Cisalpine Republic, and the despotism successively exercised by Trouvé and Brune over the magistrates of an independent Republic, had disgusted the Lombards, even those most attached to France, at the same time that it redoubled the hatred of the partisans of Austria. Brune had, indeed, been replaced by Joubert in the command of the army of Italy; but the evil had been done, and an impression made which it was very difficult to efface, especially while the original causes were still existing. Piedmont had been no better treated, and we had given abundant cause to the court of Turin for hostile feelings toward us. Far from acting with frankness toward our ally, we had attempted to revolutionize that country, as we had Switzerland, and to make her enter into the absurd system of *democratic balance* of which I have before spoken; and the occupation of the citadel of Turin, far from arresting the partisans of propagandism, only rendered them more audacious. Thus Charles-Emanuel, although he had concluded the treaty of offensive and defensive alliance, promising us an auxiliary corps of eight thousand men, could not submit, with good grace, to such treatment as he received. The Grand Duke of Tuscany, notwithstanding his desire for peace, was still an Austrian prince; this was enough to determine his course. The Directory coveted his territory, as a link to connect the Roman with the Ligurian and Cisalpine Republics. These projects could not fail to make us enemies. The venerable Pius VI., deposed from his temporal power, nevertheless exerted his spiritual influence to incite our enemies against us.

Secret Convention between England and Naples.—To these chances of success for Austria, it must be added that the cabinet of Vienna counted on assistance from Naples, this latter power being evidently of a hostile disposition toward France. A treaty signed the nineteenth of May, 1798, as a simple defensive measure, had been followed by a levy for completing the Neapolitan army. Acton did not wait for the victory of Nelson before manifesting his intention of returning to his former system of policy; the reception given to this admiral, in spite of the treaty of Paris, permitting him to be provisioned in the port of Syracuse, so as to facilitate his pursuit of the fleet which was conveying my army, unmasked the partiality of this cabinet. A secret convention, signed on the eleventh of June, by the plenipotentiaries of the two courts, had formally allied Naples and England against France. No sooner was the victory of Aboukir known than the councillors of Ferdinand IV. threw off the mask, by ordering a levy of all men between the ages of eighteen and forty-five years, to protect, it was alleged, the coasts of the Two-Sicilies against the dangers to which they had become exposed since the taking of Malta. Not only were the regular regiments filled to the complement, but a larger body of well organized provincial militia had raised the force of the Neapolitan army to sixty thousand men: a powerful auxiliary, which ought to have secured to the imperial armies a decided superiority in the Peninsula.

Chances in favor of Austria.—Under such circumstances, when the Russians and the Turks were marching in concert against the common enemy; when, on the one side, Lombardy was holding out to her its hands, and, on the other, the very heart of her states was menaced by the irruption of the French in Switzerland—how could Francis II. hesitate to act? Even if he had renounced all ambition of regaining his possessions, the safety of the Austrian monarchy imposed on him the duty of rescuing Germany from the danger threatened by the establishment of the French at the gates of the Voralberg. But be that as it may, his first care was to secure Naples from the fate of Rome, by signing the defensive treaty of May 19th. This was deemed sufficient to guarantee her from invasion.

Her Alliance with Russia.—To these alliances of simple precaution, there soon succeeded measures of more serious import: no sooner was the futility of the conferences of Selz known, than Count Cobentzel departed for Berlin and St. Petersburg, for the purpose of joining the interests of these two courts. The alliance with Russia was not difficult; and, in October, an auxiliary army, with Suwarrow at its head, entered Gallicia and directed its march on Moravia. On the other side, the Aulic Council, on hearing the fall of Berne, hastened to put the imperial armies on a respectable footing; this measure was but too well justified by passing events.

Policy of the Directory.—In fact, was there any hope left that Rewbel and his colleagues could be brought to adopt a more moderate system? Had the influence of Talleyrand in the policy of France been marked by any thing to justify his reputation as a good diplomatist? Indeed, had not all these invasions and steps of false policy been made since his installation into office?

Revolution in Holland.—The exactions of the agents of the Directory extended from the sources of the Tiber to the mouths of the Ems and the confines of Rhetia. The oppression of these tyranical proconsuls was felt wherever there appeared the slightest germ of resistance, and wherever men dared to believe that liberty did not consist in blind obedience to their pretensions. The Cisalpine Republic had hardly recovered from its astonishment at the arbitrary dismissal of its magistrates when Holland had her turn. Here, at least, the pretext was plausible. The Batavian constitution being accepted, the only thing wanting was the appointment of the new authorities. The Provisional National Assembly, such as it had remained after the twenty-second of January, had decreed on the fourth of May, after the example of the convention, that the greater part of the new legislative body should be taken from its own members, so natural is it to wish to retain authority when one has once tasted its charms. General Daendels, anxious to manifest his love of liberty, went to Paris to denounce the views of certain members of the government. These denunciations were sustained by Charles Delacroix, then minister at the Hague. The Batavian Directory hurled against its refractory general an order of arrest, and demanded his surrender from France. But Daendels, having made his court to Rewbel, returned on the tenth of June with orders to General Joubert to assist him in his enterprise. The contest soon began; the commissioners designated to replace the chambers were arrested by the Directory. The National Assembly prepared for resistance; and Daendels, in imitation of Augereau, appeared at the head of a few companies of grenadiers, dissolved the legislative body, and sought to arrest three Directors, Wreede, Langen, and Finyie; but two of these took to flight, and the third was soon released. The power was confided to a provisional government, until the constitutional authorities could properly be organized.

Affairs of Switzerland. — Switzerland was not exempt from these commotions. The constitution which had been fabricated at Paris after models entirely unsuited to the condition of the people, was everywhere rejected by the smaller cantons. The Grisons called upon the Austrians, in conformity to ancient treaties, for protection, and a division of the corps of Bellegard advanced to Coire. The unusual burdens to which the country was subjected by the cantonment of forty thousand men seemed odious: the vexatious conduct of the proconsul Rapinat at length completed the exasperation of the two parties; he had caused the dismissal of two Directors who were replaced by Laharpe and Ochs. The first hesitated to act; but the fear of being accused of having drawn his country into difficulty without the courage to extricate it, decided him.

Treaty of Alliance concluded at Paris. — A treaty between Switzerland and France was signed at Paris, on the nineteenth of August. For the honor of the negotiators, Jenner and Zeltner, as well as of the Helvetic government, we must believe that these stipulations were dictated by force, and justified by the refusal of all the neighboring powers to interfere in favor of the oppressed; for this alliance offensive and defensive imposed on Helvetia the furnishing of a contingent, and the construction of two military roads, into Italy on the one side, and into Suabia on the other. It was worse than a conquest and a formal reunion to France; for, in case of war, Helvetia would be obliged to bear all the burden of the levies and imposts, and all the consequences of being made the theatre of the war, without the slightest hope of compensation. The paltry price paid for this sacrifice was the acquisition of the Frickthal, and the promise of the evacuation of Switzerland in three months: an illusory clause, the execution of which seemed impossible, and even in contradiction to the tenor of the treaty.

The smaller Cantons refuse the Oath.—While the Helvetic Directory was thus joining its destinies to those of the French Republic, under such unfavorable auspices, the interior was threatened with civil war. The carrying into operation of a constitution accepted with so much repugnance, was not enough; they required the whole people to take a solemn oath of fidelity. This oath, taken in the greater part of Helvetia, met with a strong opposition in the smaller cantons. Schwitz and Underwald, especially, swore to die rather than submit to it. The Directory was much incensed that the sons of William Tell should dare to think themselves more free than Jacobins.

Expedition against Stanz.—Schauwembourg, resolved to stifle all resistance in the germ, directed two columns against the canton of Underwald. Two or three thousand exasperated peasants, ill-armed and ill-directed, opposed an army of seven or eight thousand veterans, victorious in a hundred battle-fields: they fought bravely, and as the men perished one after another, the ranks were filled by the women; but there was no possibility of success. After a most bloody contest, the inhabitants were either killed or subjugated, the towns and hamlets were burned, and the whole country laid waste. Let us draw the veil over these scenes of horror, so utterly disgraceful to France, who thus prostituted the blood of her brave men to impose, at the cannon's mouth, the metaphysics of a few republican fanatics on a people who had long known and appreciated the principles of true liberty.

Schwitz and Uri, to avoid the disasters of Stanz, took the required oath; but they did not less fail to experience a thousand vexations.

Call upon the Austrians for Protection.—But the fate of

the Grisons was still to be decided. Florent Guyot, the French Minister, copying the Planta and the Salis-Seevis, could not induce the patricians to submit to the popular régime and the most onerous of political yokes. Vainly did they solicit at Paris the preservation of their antique institutions and their independence: the reply of Talleyrand leaving them no hope, they submitted themselves to the councils of Salis, who, being in the Austrian interest, called upon the cabinet of Vienna for assistance. A corps of six or seven thousand men, stipulated in ancient treaties with the Emperor Maximilian, was sent for their protection; on the nineteenth of October an imperial division entered Coire.

French Law of Conscription.—The Directory, on the return of François-de-Neuchâteau, began to feel the necessity of preparation for war. Its armies were mere beggarly skeletons; the best regiments were fighting on the banks of the Nile and in the sands of Syria. Requisitions furnished no men, the old revolutionary law being no longer possible of execution. The Directory appealed to military men for some new project for recruiting the army; and General Jourdan presented one, near the end of August, for subjecting to military service, without distinction, all men between the ages of twenty and twenty-five. This levy, less harsh than the old system of requisitions, effected one entire generation; by ranging the entire military population into five classes, it permitted the calling out successively the required number of men, leaving a chance of drawing lots and obtaining substitutes.

Consequences of the Defeat of Aboukir.—The disaster of Aboukir, and the declaration of war by the Ottoman Porte, proved to the Directory the impossibility of maintaining our conquests in Egypt against the combined forces of England and Turkey. It now began to regret bitterly ever having undertaken this expedition.

Levy of Two Hundred Thousand Men.—The only course to be pursued, under these circumstances, was to press forward the levy to complete the army organization, to negotiate with moderation, so as at least to gain time, and, if the thing was yet possible, to really avoid a rupture. They proceeded to levy a part of the two hundred thousand conscripts, which a law of the twenty-eighth of September put at the disposal of the Directory. A treaty signed at Luzerne, on the thirtieth of November, stipulated for the levy of an auxiliary Helvetic corps of fifteen thousand men which France agreed to equip and support. The conscripts were levied without much difficulty, except in Belgium, where the standard of revolt was raised by a few malcontents; but it was readily put down by military power.

Financial Difficulties.—But there was still greater difficulty in obtaining money than men. The factitious representations of money were destroyed; specie had disappeared; the regular imports were almost nothing, while, on the contrary, the expenses were tripled by the premiums it was necessary to pay to procure contractors for supplies.

Negotiations continued.—Notwithstanding the activity of preparations for hostilities on all sides, either through a desire for peace, or for the purpose of gaining time, the negotiations were continued through the mediation of Spain, the Spanish ambassadors at Paris and Vienna exchanging the respective propositions. Austria, in deference to Russia and Prussia, was ready to renounce the Innvierthal, but asked in exchange Mantua, the line of the Mincio, the evacuation of Switzerland and Rome by the French troops, and the restoration of the independence of Piedmont and the Cisalpine Republic. If these demands had been made in good faith, with the intention of establishing a *bona fide* peace, we can not deny their justice. But was it not to be feared that when Mantua was once surrendered, and Italy and Helvetia evacuated, the cabinet of Vienna would provoke a new war? When a mutual distrust is established between great powers, there results only tricks of policy and diplomatic stratagems: the Directory wished to monopolize every thing that could strengthen her against her enemies; and Austria saw in these encroachments a spirit of intolerable usurpation. Thus in spite of the pacific state of affairs at the Congress of Rastadt, the increase of military forces was pushed with activity. The Russians advanced into Moravia without precipitating a step which circumstances might yet render unnecessary.

Negotiations at Rastadt.—The congress at Rastadt, during this interval, had progressed toward the accomplishment of its task, without observing that its labors were subordinate to the private negotiations between the great powers. The French had obtained almost all that they desired. The demolition of Ehrenbreitstein presented some difficulties, but the deputation of the Empire was too much inclined for peace not to consent to it on condition of the restitution of Kehl, which we had destroyed. The system of secularization presented by Roberjeot had just been adopted, the *ultimatum* of the French plenipotentiaries for the first basis was admitted, and every thing seemed to take a satisfactory turn when the news of the march of the Russians toward Moravia provoked a note from the French government, signifying that it would be regarded as a declaration of war if these troops should cross the territory of the Empire, and all negotiations would be suspended, till proper satisfaction was given on this subject. This note terminated the operations of the congress of Rastadt, which thenceforth existed only in name, for the war of the second coalition had already begun by the hostilities of Naples.

England.—To see the thunders of all the other nations directed upon France, now deprived of her ablest defenders, was a real triumph for England. This time at least her cabinet had no need of deep-laid combinations to form a new coalition, for the folly of the Directory had done more than all the agents of Albion to unite the opposing interests of Russia, the Ottoman Porte, and Austria. Nevertheless, the British minister lost no opportunity to incite them against France; for he offered subsidies, in November, to the cabinet of Vienna which refused them, it is said, on account of the negotiations then pending with the French Directory in relation to the cession of a part of Italy. The English squadrons, since the victory of Aboukir, had commanded the Mediterranean, and, for the purpose of forming a permanent establishment there, had just taken possession of the island of Minorca. The island of Gozzo had been retaken by Nelson in the name of the King of Naples, and Malta, already blockaded by sea, was soon to be invested by land.

But England did not confine herself to these external means of strengthening her power; the union of Ireland and Great Britain, with the formation of a single imperial parliament, was calculated to form a reconciliation and amalgamation of the two people, and to greatly increase the national power. The increase of military forces resulting from the detachment of five thousand men to the East Indies, and an expedition to destroy our power in Egypt, required a corresponding increase of the levies and expenses. The navy, by multiplying its stations and colonial conquests, also required proportional pecuniary sacrifices. The interest on the immense national debt was annually increased by new loans, notwithstanding the admirable system of sinking funds. But new plans of taxation added an immense sum to the receipts of the preceding year, and easily covered the annual budget.

Russia.—The wrecks of the Order of Malta, refugees in Germany, had just conferred on the Emperor Paul the dignity of Grand Master of the Order, in place of Baron

Hompesch, and the sentiments of this prince, known for a long time, left no doubt as to the value which he would attach to this title. The Turco-Russian fleets arrived in the Archipelago near the end of October, and, preceded by an appeal of the Greek archbishop to the faithful, raised the Ionian Isles against the French, who, confined in small number within the ramparts of Corfu, soon found themselves attacked both by land and sea.

Spain.—The cabinet of Madrid remained faithful to its natural alliance, notwithstanding the many sacrifices required of it by the chiefs of our turbulent Republic, and although, contrary to the real interests of both France and Spain, it was anew to hazard its fleets on the ocean, or on the Mediterranean. One had thought from its imbecility, and from the conduct of France toward Piedmont and Naples, allies of the family of Charles IV., that this monarch would have followed his political interests in connecting himself with the cabinet of St. James. But, drawn on by the course of events, Spain agreed to furnish her stipulated contingents; at the same time the efforts of her diplomatic agents at Paris and Vienna to prevent hostilities, attested that she appreciated the consequences of a maritime war.

Portugal.—Portugal was chained more closely than ever to the car of British fortune, and the victory of Aboukir was a certain guarantee that she would remain in this dependence for a long time.

Sweden and Denmark.—No change of importance had taken place in the situation of Sweden and Denmark. Although their flag began to feel the shackles placed by England upon the commerce of neutrals, they still prospered amid the universal embarrassments.

War commenced by Naples.—The signal for the new war was given, to the great astonishment of Europe, by the Neapolitans, who on this occasion seemed animated by a most unusual military ardor. The court of Naples had increased its army to seventy thousand men, and placed the celebrated Mack* at its head. This general, the disciple of Lacy, had directed with success the expedition of the Prince of Cobourg against Dumouriez, in 1793; but in the campaign of 1794 his plans were a violation of the principles of the art: he had imagination and intelligence, but was wanting in spirit and judgment. Ferdinand IV., vain of the pomp and show of his battalions, and incited on by Nelson and Acton, ventured to throw himself with fifty thousand men upon the Roman states, which were then defended by Championnet† with eighteen thousand men, scattered from the Adriatic to the Mediterranean. Mack advanced, between the twenty-third and twenty-seventh of November, on Rome, in several columns, and obliged the little army of Championnet to fall back on Civita-Castillana (ancient Veii), whose natural ramparts enabled him to wait there for reënforcements. To seek these, the general-in-chief departed for Ancona. In his absence Mack attacked Macdonald‡ and Kellermann who repulsed him with loss. Championnet, on his return, captured at Calvi an isolated Neapolitan regiment, which had ventured to threaten his communication: he afterward manœuvred to cut off the division of Damas, which had

---

* Mack (Charles Baron Von) was born in Franconia in 1752. He early distinguished himself against the Turks, and was gradually promoted, till in 1804 he became commander-in-chief in the Tyrol, Dalmatia, and Italy. He was then fifty-two years of age. After the defeat of Ulm he retired to his farm in Bohemia, and died in obscurity, in 1828.—*Encyclopedia Americana.*

† Championnet (Jean Etienne) was born at Valencia in 1762. He entered the Spanish army at the age of fourteen, but afterward returned to France, and was rapidly promoted till he became commander-in-chief of an army. He died in 1800.

‡ Macdonald (Etienne Jacques-Joseph Alexandre) was born at Saucene, in France, in 1765. He entered the army at about nineteen, became a colonel at twenty-seven, general-of-brigade at twenty-eight, and general-of-division at thirty. He was made a marshal of France on the field of Wagram. He died in 1840.

taken the direction of Viterbo. Mack being alarmed, evacuated Rome, and Ferdinand IV. retreated to Naples, ordering a *levée-en-masse*. Damas, abandoned by his friends, concluded a treaty with Kellermann for permission to reëmbark.

Seizure of Piedmont and Occupation of Tuscany.—Championnet returned to Rome on the thirteenth of December, and remained there some days, waiting to hear from Northern Italy ; for it was reported that the King of Sardinia and the Grand Duke of Tuscany had risen at the same time, and made common cause with the King of Naples. The relations between the Directory and the court of Turin were such as to give credence to this report. Joubert, on hearing of the invasion of the Roman Empire, made requisition, through the ambassador Eymar, for the contingent of eight thousand men stipulated in the treaty of the preceding year for all wars of the French Republic in Italy. The cabinet of Turin excused itself on the impossibility of immediately collecting this division, and Joubert, without waiting for the ulterior orders of the Directory, but sure of acting in accordance with its views, drew up a kind of manifesto of his griefs, united, on the fifth of December, the division of Victor and Dessolles[*] on the Tecino, and while Novara, Suza, Coni, and Alexandria were falling by surprise into the hands of the French, he directed these two divisions on Verceli. The Piedmontese troops, after a semblance of resistance, were driven in upon Turin, which city the republicans, already masters of the citadel, entered at the same time with the enemy. Charles Emanuel, humiliated and disgusted with his unstable and limited power in Piedmont, signed, on

---

[*] Dessolles (Jean Joseph Paul Augustin) was born at Auch in 1767. He entered the army at twenty-five; chef-de-bataillon at twenty-six; general-of-brigade at thirty, and general-of-division at thirty-two. He distinguished himself as chief-of-staff to Schérer, Moreau, and Prince Eugene, and as general-of-division in Italy and Spain. His great bravery won for him the name of the *French Denis*.

the eighth of December, a renunciation of all rights to the throne of that country, and went into voluntary exile, it was said, to Sardinia, merely stipulating for his personal safety till his arrival there. But no sooner had he reached Leghorn, than he published a solemn protestation against an act drawn from him by force. Having thus effected without difficulty the dethronement of this sovereign, Joubert directed a division on Florence, when his own, ready to strike, was arrested by new protestations of attachment from the Grand Duke of Tuscany, and perhaps, also, by orders from the Directory. Nevertheless, the division occupied Leghorn, and a part of the Grand Duchy. Being now certain of the submission of all Italy, Joubert hastened to announce to Championnet that he could resume the offensive against Naples, and sent him reënforcements.

Ferdinand flies to Sicily.—The ill-success of the expedition to Rome had so terrified King Ferdinand, that he left Naples, the twenty-first of December, and embarked for Sicily at night, with as much precipitation and disorder as if the French had been at the gates of his capital.

Championnet takes Naples.—But Championnet, waiting to hear from his left, which, under Duhesme, was to subjugate Pescara, and arrive by Sulmona, did not pass the Volturna and invest Capua, till the third of January. In the centre, the division of Lemoine advanced upon Popoli, overthrowing the corps of Gambs, and then proceeded to Venafro; on the extreme right, Kellerman and Rey marched by Itri on Gaeta, which important place, with a fine garrison of three thousand men, but commanded by an octogenarian officer, was basely surrendered without striking a single blow. A general insurrection ordered by the court and the priests, was near changing the entire face of affairs, for Championnet was besieged in his own camp under the walls of Capua. But the provisional government, confided by the King to

Prince Pignatelli, had so little confidence in the insurgent people that it hastened to sign an armistice, giving us Capua, Benevento, and a sum of two millions. On hearing of the armistice, the exasperated people accused Mack and the provisional government of treason; disarmed the troops of Damas, which had returned from Orbitello by sea; and sent detachments to arrest Mack. Pignatelli demanded troops of Mack for his personal protection against the infuriate mob; but the brigade of Dillon, sent for this purpose, was arrested and disarmed by the insurgents; and Mack himself sought safety in the camp of Championnet, by surrendering himself, the fifteenth of January, a prisoner of war.

Championnet, having now united all his divisions, advanced toward the capital. The population of this city and the environs, incited by the priests, ran to arms with the cry of *Viva la Santa Fede*, forced the viceroy, Pignatelli, to fly for safety into Sicily, and threatened to bury themselves beneath the ruins of Naples. In default of military courage, this people was animated by lively and tumultuous passions; the resistance was, like the excitable and fickle character of this people, obstinate the first day, but disorderly and feeble the second. Championnet entered, victorious, into Naples, the twenty-first of January. If the court of the Two Sicilies had declared war after the opening of hostilities on the Adige, there had been some reason in it, but to rush in this way blindfold to its own destruction, was an act of perfect madness. Nevertheless this fault turned to the account of the coalition by the more serious ones which it caused the French government to commit.

Erection of the Parthenopean Republic.—The Directory having one hundred and sixteen thousand men in Italy, estimated its power there by what I had accomplished with fifty thousand men; it thought to occupy all, and consequently became weak everywhere. Fifty-three thousand had sufficed to Championnet for the reduction of Naples, and if the Directory had offered Ferdinand an acceptable peace, no doubt this pusillanimous prince would have hastened to accept it, so that the army of Championnet could have returned to Mantua in time to take part in the campaign. But instead of doing this, Rewbel thought to create a Parthenopean Republic; an absurd project, requiring military force to sustain this Utopian theory against the court of Naples, the English, the priests, and six millions of people; thus depriving us of thirty thousand men on the Adige, and exposing them to almost certain ruin. Adding to this detachment, the division of Gauthier in Tuscany, the troops required for the occupation of Piedmont, the division of Valteline for securing the junction with the army of Helvetia, the division of Liguria, we have in all sixty thousand men on detached service, leaving Schérer only forty-seven thousand combatants on the Adige, and ten thousand at Mantua; a force entirely insufficient to oppose the powerful preparations of the coalition.

The Russians advance toward Italy.—Already the Russian troops, crossing Styria, are directing their march upon Italy; the Archduke Charles crosses the Inn, enters Bavaria, and advances toward Ulm. General Kray assembles seventy-one thousand Austrians between Verona and the Tagliamento.

The Directory takes the Initiative.—The Directory, like most imprudent governments, had rendered itself offensive to its neighbors, without being prepared to sustain its aggressions. It now resolved to anticipate its enemies, and charged General Lahorie, formerly aid-de-camp to General Moreau, but a man without genius, with drawing up a plan of operations. Jourdan, with the army of the Danube, hardly thirty-six thousand strong, was to move on Ulm, between this city and the mountains, while Massena, with thirty-eight thousand men of the army of Helvetia, should advance across the Rhetian and Tyrolean Alps, that is, across the precipices of the Grisons, of the Voralberg, and the Tyrol, to the Inn. At the same time Schérer, at the head of forty-seven thousand men, was to attack Verona and the Adige. In other words, Schérer was to oppose seventy-one thousand Austrians assembled under the orders of Kray, between Verona and Udina, and soon to be sustained by two Russian corps of twenty-thousand men each. Jourdan was to attack the Archduke Charles, who had at least seventy-eight thousand men, on the Lech and in the Voralberg; and Massena was, in part, to oppose Hotze, detached from this army, and, in part, Bellegarde, who covered the Tyrol with forty-four thousand Austrians. A third Russian army of thirty thousand men, under Korsakof, arriving in July, would serve as a reserve to that of the Archduke.

Massena seizes the Grisons.—Massena, notwithstanding the disproportion of the respective forces, commences operations on the sixth of March; he passes the Rhine, turns and carries the Fort of Luciensteig, and then debouches on Coire, where Auffenberg, invested with three thousand men, is forced to surrender; he now pushes the *débris* of this corps on the Engadine, where Lecourbe, coming from Bellinzona, has penetrated by Tusis. General Dessolles marches from Bormio on Taufers, at the head of the division of Valteline, designed to effect the junction; he there overthrows the corps of Laudon, who, cut at the same time by the right of Massena, loses four thousand men and saves hardly five hundred fugitives across the glaciers.

The Archduke marches against Jourdan.—The Archduke Charles, hearing of the passage of the Rhine by Jourdan, advanced against him at the head of sixty thousand men. To facilitate the operations of his colleague, Massena had, on the fourteenth of March, caused the intrenchments of Hotze at Feldkirch to be attacked; in spite of the vigorous efforts of Oudinot* the attack failed, and the French were repulsed. Hotze soon marched with the half of his corps against the right of Jourdan to assist the Archduke. Massena, profiting by this movement, renewed his attack upon the enemy's intrenchments, on the twenty-second of March, with the divisions of Ménard and Oudinot; but being again repulsed, he withdrew his troops, with considerable loss, into the Grisons and Rhinthal.

Battle of Stockach.—Jourdan, on the twenty-fifth of March, with only thirty-five thousand men against sixty thousand, gave battle to the Archduke, attacking his whole line at the same time; St. Cyr, commanding the right, debouched by Tuttlingen, and Ferino with the left by Schaffhausen, at ten leagues from each other! The Archduke from his central position overthrew the isolated corps of Soult at Stockach, and it certainly was no very difficult matter for thirty thousand men to overpower ten thousand. St. Cyr, who was within three leagues of the rear of the enemy's line, with twelve thousand men, had the good sense to seize upon the bridge of Sigmaringen, and retire in haste on the Black Forest so as to regain Strasburg. The right, under Ferino, separated from the *corps de bataille,* threw itself on Schaffhausen. Our troops made a fortunate escape, for had I commanded the enemy's forces I could have destroyed the whole army; I would have dealt with the corps of St. Cyr as I did with the corps of Lusignan and Provera at Rivoli.

Reverses in Italy.—Schérer did no better. His adversary waited, between Verona and Legnago, the arrival of Melas and the two divisions of Austrian reserve, before taking the

---

* Oudinot (Charles Nicholas) was born in 1767. He entered the army young, became a captain at twenty-three, chef-de-bataillon at twenty-four, colonel at twenty-five, general-of-brigade the same year, and general-of-division at twenty-eight. He was made marshal of France on the field of Wagram.

offensive. Favored by this state of things, Schérer found himself, with the main body of his forces, before two imperial brigades isolated in the intrenchments between the Adige and Lake Garda. He attacked them on the twenty-sixth of March with three divisions, carried the camp of Pastrengo, the plateau of Rivoli, and the bridges of Polo on the Adige; then carried his centre under Moreau against Verona, while the right extended itself toward Legnago. This last-named general here found himself opposed to Kray and the *élite* of his forces; the Austrian general debouched from Legnago, fell on Montrichard, pushed him by Auguiari on the Menago, and threatened to cut off the road to Mantua. Kray, instead of profiting by this success to draw the mass of his forces on this point, repassed the Adige in order to march to the assistance of Verona, which was now threatened by the centre and left of the French army. Moreau fought with the centre before Verona, on the twenty-seventh, but without any result. On the twenty-eighth, Schérer, who had for two days groped his way along the whole line, thought to throw the left under Serrurier across the Adige; it would advance from Pelo toward Verona, seek to turn this place, which, from its position, it was impossible to do, and then debouch in the middle of the whole imperial army. On the twenty-ninth, they found that the manœuvre was impossible, which undoubtedly saved Serrurier from total destruction.

Schérer, remembering my manœuvre of Arcola, conceived the ridiculous idea of repeating it; he assembled two thirds of his army at Ronco for the purpose of passing the Adige at that place, forgetting that, in 1796, I was master of Verona and Legnago, and that in passing at Ronco I threw Alvinzi into a *cul-de-sac*. But now the Austrians being masters of these two places, the conditions of the problem were completely changed. To throw himself upon Ronco with thirty thousand men in the midst of seventy thousand enemies who were masters of Verona and Legnago, was to pass his army under the Caudine Forks. As a climax of folly, the division of Serrurier advanced alone, on the thirtieth, from Polo on Verona in order to attract the enemy's attention, while the mass of the army filed by the right toward Ronco. Kray fell upon this compromised division, drove it upon Polo with the loss of two thousand men; the remainder only saved themselves by hastily destroying the bridges. It was most fortunate for Schérer that Kray, debouching from Verona, on the second of April, forced him to renounce his absurd project. The army returning from Ronco to Magnan through horrible mud, had its right overwhelmed the fifth of April, and was rallied under the cannon of Mantua in complete disorder. If Kray, who, from the third to the fifth, was opposed only by the two divisions of Moreau, had overthrown them before the return of Schérer, the latter would have been driven on the lower Po, and surrounded. In the battle even, the Austrians deviated from their first plan, which was a good one, and directed, *mal-à-propos*, their principal effort on the right of the French, instead of attacking the left. Nevertheless their victory had important results: Schérer could sustain himself only behind Mantua. After having completed the garrisons of this city, Ferrara, and Peschiera, he fell back in rear of the Chiesa.

Retreat of the Army behind the Rhine.—The retreat of the army of the Danube drew after it the little army of observation under Bernadotte, who had thrown a few bombs into Philipsbourg. The Directory, at the same time, accepted the resignation of Jourdan and united his troops, as well as those of Bernadotte, under the command of Massena. This unfortunate beginning proved to the presumptuous Directors the impolicy of their plan. They had begun war without having prepared the means, thinking that one hundred and twenty thousand scattered French were capable of conquering two hundred thousand concentrated Austrians. But in other respects this unequal contest was not without credit to the generals and soldiers of the Republic; and we hardly know which is most astonishing, the temerity of the French government, or the inconceivable timidity of the Aulic Council in deriving so little profit from its advantages.

Attack on our Plenipotentiaries at Rastadt. — But the stupor caused by an event so unexpected was soon dissipated by the tragical *dénouement* of the interminable Congress of Rastadt. In entering Swabia, Jourdan had declared Rastadt a neutral town, giving a safeguard to the congress. This situation favored the designs of France, who wished to detach the princes of the Empire from the Austrian alliance: already the turn of the negotiations promised the Directory full success, when the battle of Stockach and the retreat of the army of the Danube caused the diplomatic scales to suddenly incline on the side of the conqueror. From this time also the cabinet of Vienna undertook to direct the affairs of the south of Germany. Desiring to know the state of the negotiations between the princes of the German Empire and the Directory, it charged Count Lehrbach, its minister plenipotentiary, to devise some means to get possession of their correspondence with the Republican negotiators. The count could devise no surer way of accomplishing this object than to seize upon the papers of the French legation at the moment of the breaking up of the congress, and he was authorized by his court to make upon the Archduke Charles a requisition for the troops necessary for this *coup-de-main*. The Archduke at first refused to allow his soldiers to mingle in any way in these diplomatic affairs; but when Count Lehrbach exhibited the orders of his government to this effect, the Archduke felt obliged to obey, and put at his disposal a detachment of Szeckler's hussars. The colonel of the corps was admitted to the secret. The officer charged with the affair was only to carry off the French diplomatic papers, and if an opportunity occurred, to administer some blows with the flat of the sabre upon the persons of Jean Debry and Bonnier, as a punishment for their haughty bearing in the negotiations. Roberjeot, a fellow-student and personal friend of the Austrian minister, had been excepted by name from this course of treatment.

The French plenipotentiaries were to depart on the twenty-eighth of April; but, on the evening of the nineteenth, they were summoned to retire immediately, as the city was to be given up to military occupation the next day. They therefore set out the same night for Strasburg. But hardly were they outside of the town when the Austrian hussars, on the watch for their prey, surrounded the carriages; but forgetting the details of their instructions, these soldiers, the greater part of whom were intoxicated, struck the envoys without distinction of person with the edge of their swords, and left Bonnier and Roberjeot dead on the spot. Jean Debry, severely wounded in the arm and head, escaped as by miracle, and at daylight sought refuge in the house of the Prussian minister. This unprecedented violation of the most sacred rights produced in France an electrical effect. On every side was raised the cry of vengeance, and the same energetic feeling was manifested by the nation as in 1792. The Directory profited by this state of things to facilitate the levy of the conscription, and to give a degree of momentary popularity to its cause.

Tardy Enterprise of the Archduke.—In the mean time the Archduke Charles had not profited by his successes; if he had passed the Rhine at Schaffhausen with sixty thousand men, and combined an attack with the forty thousand of Bellegarde, Massena, half-buried in the Engadine, would have been lost. But they gave the French time to carry into Switzerland the entire army of Jourdan as fast as it returned to Alsace, and

Massena, who had taken the command of it, established the mass of his forces along the Rhine as far as Lucisteig, prolonging his right into the Engadine. The Austrians had committed the fault of rendering Bellegarde independent of the Archduke, and it is undoubtedly to this circumstance, as much as to the sickness of this prince, that we are to attribute the inconceivable inaction of his army from the twenty-seventh of March to the fourteenth of May.

Suwarrow in Lombardy.—During this interval, Suwarrow* arriving on the Chiesa, the seventeenth of April, drove Schérer behind the Adda. The French army was already reduced to twenty-eight thousand men by losses in battles, detachments for garrisons, and the mania of occupying all Italy. Schérer scattered what remained from Pizzighettone to Lecco. The right, under Montrichard, was even thrown across to the right bank of the Po to cover Modena and Bologna, or to enter into communication with Tuscany and Rome. The Directory, justly irritated against its general, recalled him, Moreau took command on the night of the twenty-fifth of April, and was attacked early the following morning, without having had time to rectify the position of his forces. Although the allies had employed thirty-five thousand men to blockade Mantua, Peschiera, and Ferrara, they still had fifty-four thousand on the Adda. To cover a line of twenty leagues with twenty-eight thousand men against a force double that number, is impossible: the detachments of Moreau, assailed on the twenty-seventh of April, at Cassano and Vaprio, are

---

* Suwarrow was born at Luskoy, a village of the Ukraine, in 1730. He was educated in the Military Academy of St. Petersburg. He entered the army at seventeen, and distinguished himself in the Seven Years' War. He was a general at thirty-eight. He distinguished himself mostly in the wars against the Turks and in Poland, for which services he received from his government rich rewards, and the titles of count, prince, marshal, and generalissimo of the Russian forces. He died in the early part of 1800, soon after his return from Italy. —*Encyclopedia Americana.*

pierced by the centre; and Serrurier, cut off toward the left at Verdirio, is forced to lay down his arms. Two days after, Suwarrow enters Milan. Moreau, who had reached the Ticino with hardly twenty thousand men, divides them on Valencia and Turin. Suwarrow passes the Po at Placentia to march on Alexandria. Kray is charged with the blockade of Mantua. Count Hohenzollern attacks successively the places of Peschiera and Orci-Novi, which are reduced in a few days. He is then charged with besieging the citadel of Milan, and with observing the troops which are returning from the Grisons into the Valteline. Kaim blockades Pizzighettone, which place is surrendered without opposition. Klenau, by the aid of a powerful flotilla, armed at Venice, and assisted by the defection of General Lahoz, and by the insurrection of the adjoining provinces, attacks Ferrara. The entire edifice which I had constructed in Italy is crumbling into ruins with the most frightful rapidity.

Expedition of Admiral Bruix.—The Directory, seeing the danger threatened by the new coalition, resolved upon a maritime expedition, for the triple purpose of uniting the squadron of Brest with those of Spain in the Mediterranean, of bringing home the army of Egypt, and of returning into the ocean to attempt a descent upon Ireland, which had been projected for so long a time. Some say that it was intended, at first, to embark some of our forces in Italy and reënforce my army in Egypt, but that the unfavorable turn of our affairs there, and our expulsion from Lombardy, compelled them to change this part of the project. Be this as it may, Bruix sailed the beginning of April with twenty-five vessels from Brest to Cadiz and then to Toulon. He put to sea again the thirtieth of May; formed a junction at Carthagena with the Spanish forces under Massaredo; made his cruise without having revictualed Malta, without having succored Egypt, in a word, without having undertaken any thing; and again entered Brest with the Spanish fleet. Keith, his fleet being increased by reënforcements to forty-eight vessels, sought for him in vain in the Mediterranean, and followed him to before Brest. This expedition, which had no other result than to bring the Spanish squadron as a hostage to Brest, and to concentrate all our naval means in that port to be blockaded or to rot, is still an inexplicable enigma to all naval men.

Evacuation of Naples.—While they were thus driving us from the Grisons and Upper Italy, Macdonald, who had succeeded Championnet, after fighting at Naples, in the Abruzzos and Apulia, against the *débris* of the Neapolitans and an insurgent multitude, had just received orders to return toward the Po, and was marching on Rome. Suwarrow detached the division of Ott upon Modena to observe him. A Turco-Russian fleet had reduced the Ionian Isles, and laid siege to Corfu. The destruction of the army of Naples seemed certain; to the fault of recalling it too late, they had added the new absurdity of directing garrisons to be left in the forts at Naples, at Gaeta, at Capua, at Civita-Vecchia, and at Rome. Moreau was convinced at Turin that the capital of a subjugated kingdom cannot be well disposed toward a conqueror, who reduces it to the post of a provincial city; he ought to have thrown a garrison into the citadel and to have concentrated his forces toward Valencia and Alexandria, in order to cover Genoa and the passages of the Apennines, the preservation of which, was indispensable to save Macdonald and the army of Naples. Suwarrow had followed Moreau by the right bank of the Po, and the road to Alexandria. His advanced guard took the road from Valencia to Turin by the left bank. This guard, too ardent, attempted to pass the river without orders at Bassignano, to attack the French camp near Valencia; but meeting a timely charge from the eighteen thousand men which still remained to Moreau, it was repelled with loss.

Suwarrow enters Turin.—This skirmish and the fine defense of Moreau near Marengo and Alexandria, did not prevent Suwarrow from passing the Po again at Cambio and entering Turin as a conqueror, on the twenty-seventh of May, the inhabitants of the city attacking the garrison in concert with the advanced guard of Wukassowich. Moreau arrived at Asti, surrounded by enemies and insurgents who had just surprised Ceva and thus intercepted his last communication. He resolved to unite his forces on the Apennines, opening for himself an issue to join the division of Perignon, who was guarding Liguria.

Massena is driven from the Grisons.—While these things were occurring in Italy, Massena, pressed on all sides in the Grisons, got off much more easily than could have been expected. Wearied with an inaction of five weeks, (from the twenty-seventh of March to the thirtieth of April), the Austrians had finally combined an attack upon the fort of Lucisteig for the first of May, in concert with a party of the Grisons who had asked their aid. But Hotze managed the affair so badly, that one of his columns, under the orders of General St. Julien, debouching before the others, fell into the midst of the division of Ménard, who surrounded it and forced it to surrender. A redoubtable insurrection broke out the same day in all the Alps, from Coire to Schwitz and Altorf: Massena was obliged to send the entire division of Soult to reduce these two little cantons and to reëstablish the communication with the St. Gothard.

Lecourbe, having ventured into the Engadine, sustained himself against the superior forces of Bellegarde, and covered himself with glory at Zernetz, while the small division left by Dessolles in the Valteline under the orders of Loison was exposed to the attacks of the right of Suwarrow. It seemed lost, for sooner or later the enemy would pierce by Coire on Dissentis, or by the Italian bailiwicks on the St. Gothard. Lecourbe saw that he could not do better than to first relieve Bellinzona, menaced by Count Hohenzollern. He marched on Taverna and drove out the prince of Rohan on the thirteenth of May, the very moment when a storm much more formidable was breaking out on his left. The Austrians, after having passed a fortnight in recovering from the skirmish of the first of May, had at last concluded to try, on the fourteenth, a new attack on Lucisteig, and the Archduke had sent for this purpose a reënforcement of twelve thousand men, with orders to act in concert with Bellegarde. By these powerful means they succeeded in carrying the fort, pierced the division of Menard, threw back his left on Sargans, and pushed his right, in the direction of Dissentis, to the foot of the St. Gothard. Lecourbe left Loison to defend the avenues of Airolo, and hastened to the defense of the menaced Alps.

The cabinet of Vienna, more intent upon consolidating its power in Italy than in destroying the organized corps which we had compromitted in the Grisons, had directed Bellegarde to leave only the division of Haddick to take the St. Gothard, and march by the Valteline on Milan, in order to reënforce Suwarrow, who was about to attack several of the fortifications and also the army returning from Naples. This contributed to save Lecourbe, who returned on Altorf after a retreat not less honorable than difficult ; he very much cut up the brigade of St. Julien, which had descended from Dissentis on the valley of the Reuss, and another detachment which had ventured into the Muttenthal between him and the *corps-de-bataille* of Massena.

The Archduke penetrates into Switzerland. — On his side the Archduke Charles, thwarted in some measure by the departure of Bellegarde for Italy, had at last passed the

Rhine at Schaffhausen on the twenty-seventh of May. Hotze passed the river toward Coire; Massena fell back behind the Thur, thinking to prevent the junction of the two corps, attacked that of Hotze at Frauenfeld, and gained a partial advantage which did not prevent him from retiring on Zurich two days afterward. This city has a bastioned enceinte of very thick masonry; on the south side where the Limmat, which runs impetuously from the lake, serves as ditches, the body of the place is commanded by the Zurichberg, and notwithstanding the defiladement of its works, it could not long resist a siege. Massena had caused a large intrenched camp to be marked out upon this mountain in order to connect its defense with that of the plateau of Hong.

Massena evacuates Zurich.—The Archduke attacked him on the sixth of June, but without success: an Austrian column succeeded, by gliding secretly along the lake, in reaching the gate; but it was punished for this audacity. Nevertheless the position of Massena was a critical one. At the approach of the Austrians, the mountaineers of the Grisons, of the smaller Cantons, and of the Valois, had taken up arms. The success of the allies in Italy threatened the Simplon and the St. Bernard; the St. Gothard was carried, and Lecourbe driven back on Schwitz and Altorf. It would have been imprudent for him to sacrifice his army in order to hold Zurich with a defile in rear. Massena preferred the line of the Albis, a precipitous mountain which borders the Limmat and the lake from Bruck to Utznach; he therefore abandoned the city to the Austrians.

The Archduke paralyzed by the Aulic Council.—The Archduke now received orders from the Aulic Council to attempt nothing decisive before the arrival of the powerful reënforcements of Korsakof, who was approaching with thirty thousand Russians; he therefore remained, till the month of August, encamped behind Zurich, which gave to Massena time to secure himself in his fine position, and to the Directory an opportunity to send him reënforcements.

Macdonald returns upon Modena.—In the mean time Macdonald had evacuated Naples and Rome, in order to rejoin Moreau; weakened by the garrisons which he had been directed to leave behind, but reënforced by the division which had occupied Tuscany, he advanced with thirty thousand men on Modena. Moreau detached the division of Victor on the Trebia, which formed a junction with Macdonald at Firenzuola on the fourteenth of June. Moreau himself defiled through the Apennines in order to descend into the plain. He thought to unite the thirty-four thousand men of Macdonald with the sixteen thousand which he had in Liguria. In thus resuming the line of the Po with fifty thousand men, he hoped at least to relieve Mantua, which the scattered position of the enemy's troops rendered not impossible. Nothing is more likely to cause an injudicious dissemination of troops than rapid conquests over an enemy who is himself too much scattered. The allies experienced this: at the moment that Macdonald descended from the Apennines on Modena, Kray was before Mantua, Hohenzollern and Klenau toward Bologna, Ott at Parma, Seckendorf and Wukassowich toward Ceva and Montenotte; Frolich was observing Coni; Lusignan was near Fenestrelles; Bagration had just subdued Suza; Suwarrow with the *corps-de-bataille* of Melas, and the division of Kaim, was besieging the citadel of Turin; finally, Bellegarde, having descended from the Valteline on Milan, was going to swell the forces of the Russian general in the central plains of the Bormida, and Haddick, left in the Valois, was guarding the Alps against the right of Massena. As soon as the allies heard of Macdonald's approach, they sent against him the detachments of Klenau and Hohenzollern, who marched on Modena, and were separately beaten on the twelfth of June:

the latter, quite seriously cut up, was driven behind the Po, and the former fell back in a little better order on Ferrara.

Suwarrow attacks him on the Trebia.—Suwarrow, hearing these events, left Kaim at Turin to blockade the citadel, and hastened, by forced marches, to join Ott at Placentia; he directed Kray to leave only a small division under Mantua, and also to march by Mezzana-Corte on the Po, where he hoped to collect fifty thousand men independently of Bellegarde, who remained near Alexandria to observe Moreau. Suwarrow arrived on the Tidone, the fifteenth of June, found Ott closely pressed, but relieved him and repulsed Victor. Macdonald, the next day, concentrated his scattered columns and attacked the enemy. Kray not having yet arrived, Suwarrow had collected only thirty-three thousand men, so that the two armies were about equal. A most sanguinary combat took place between these forces, animated on the one side by the remembrance of ancient victories, and on the other by that of recent advantages. Macdonald, who was waiting for Moreau at the foot of the Apennines on the left, committed the fault of directing his efforts in the opposite direction and along a river without bridges, where his army might be repulsed. Suwarrow, with better judgment, directed his efforts against the opposite wing, certain that if he repulsed the left of the French he would obtain great results. After a most memorable contest of three days, the French army, with half its number *hors-de-combat*, was driven back upon Tuscany. Its loss seemed certain; but Moreau having beaten Bellegarde in the plains of Alexandria, the army of Suwarrow being itself turned, and Kray having by the positive orders of the cabinet remained quiet under Mantua, the Russian marshal, disgusted with the conduct of his allies, left Macdonald time to return by the Corniche from Pontremoli, and to bring his army back to Spezzia; it was truly in a deplorable state, but to save it at all was accomplishing much. This diaster destroyed all hope of repairing our affairs in Italy. Suwarrow, victorious at the Trebia, had first designed to fall upon Genoa and complete our total expulsion from Italy, but the Emperor had given positive orders to the Austrians to limit themselves to the sieges of Mantua, Alexandria, and Tortona.

General State of Affairs.—In less than four months from the opening of the campaign, the French armies had been driven from all their conquests and some leagues from their frontiers. Notwithstanding the one hundred thousand conscripts which had been incorporated in the different regiments, there remained scarcely two hundred thousand men—exhausted by fatigue, discouraged by twenty defeats, in want of every thing—to oppose the victorious Austro-Russian armies, seconded as they were by the people of Italy and Switzerland, who had by this time become fatigued and disgusted with the tyrannical yoke of the Directory. Everywhere fortune seemed to have deserted the Republican standards; the army of the East, forced to raise the siege of Acre after sixty days of open trench, had returned to Egypt; in India the English had carried by assault the capital of Mysore, dividing with the Nizam this kingdom of the ancient ally of France. The King of Naples and the Grand Duke of Tuscany returned to their capitals; the King of Sardinia was recalled by Suwarrow. The coalition was triumphant, and England, who was its soul, impatient to accelerate the downfall of the French Republic, signed a treaty with Russia for an expedition to drive the French from Holland. The ascension of the Prince of Brazil to the throne of Portugal, which he had in fact occupied for the last seven years under the title of Regent, in consequence of the mental alienation of the Queen, left this kingdom not less subject to English policy.

The French Directory.—Such, in few words, was the

situation of the belligerent powers; but France had other vicissitudes than the fate of arms; and the Directory, even had it been able to overcome the external opposition caused by its absurd system of foreign policy, could hardly have dispersed the storm which was collecting against it in the very heart of the Republic. After the eighteenth of Fructidor, arbitrary power and immorality seemed to have been its only rules of conduct. It had inherited the embarrassments of the Committee of Public Safety, without being heir to the dictatorial power from which that body had derived its strength. In seeking to extend its control over the people, it had lost the public confidence; the nation regarded each step of the Directors in the career of power as an act of insupportable tyranny, formally opposed to the object of the Revolution. The legislative body took advantage of these difficulties to oppose the Directors. It accused them of "having violated the laws of nations in attacking, without manifesto or declaration, Switzerland and the Ottoman Empire; of having suppressed the primary assemblies, erected bastiles, banished whoever had the misfortune to displease them; of holding seats of justice in Holland, Italy, and Switzerland, and attempting to reduce the representatives to a state of continual servility." Under such a state of public feeling, all attempts of the Directory to carry the elections proved abortive, and the new deputies arrived with a firm resolution to overturn a tyranny which the dangers of the country and the hope of victory alone had thus far sustained.

Political Operations of Sieyes.—The nomination of Sièyes in place of Rewbel confirmed the Deputies in their project. This new Director having perceived that Merlin and Treilhard, imbued with the doctrines of their predecessors, completely controlled the feeble Laréveillère, felt the importance of destroying this majority, and conferred on this subject with my brother Lucien and Genissieux, the leaders of the

Councils. It was now determined to seize the first occasion to eliminate these Directors by a *coup-d'état* like that which had been made on the eighteenth of Fructidor, to get rid of obnoxious legislators.

Address to the Councils.—To this effect, addresses from several of the departments were sent to the Councils. The leaders attacked in a special manner the administration of the Directory, which, with seven hundred and twenty-five millions of taxes, let each branch of the public service suffer for want of funds; they accused the Minister of War of having sold at prices below their value, for purposes of speculation, one hundred and thirty thousand fire-arms from the arsenal of Paris. La Vendée was in insurrection, and Belgium was opposing, with an armed hand, the levies of men and taxes. Each day's session brought the most virulent attacks against the mediocre chiefs of the executive power.

Treilhard's Nomination annulled.—The contest might have been uncertain so long as the threatened Directors acted in concert. It was therefore necessary to begin by destroying this triumvirate; but how to do this without a direct violation of the constitution? In seeking to overthrow it, would not a pretext be given this body for attacking the national representation? In this perplexity a Deputy recollected very opportunely that Treilhard had been elected three days sooner than the law allowed : the two councils seized upon this pretext to annul his nomination. It is said that Treilhard himself acknowledged the illegality of his appointment, and left his colleagues with more pleasure than regret. This operation for some days completely paralyzed the Directory by the division of the four remaining members. But the number was soon completed by the appointment of the minister Gohier, who inclined the balance in favor of the reform party.

Merlin and Lareveillere resign.—Still it was only a half victory, for it was yet necessary to get rid of Merlin and Laréveillère. These at first attempted to make way against the storm, but being menaced with charges against them at the tribune, they sent in their resignation on the night of the sixteenth and seventeenth of June. Their condescension disarmed the violence of the legislative body, which was satisfied with merely loading them with sarcasms. They were called mere ciphers, men of small capacity, of small passions, and petty vengeances! In their places were appointed Roger-Ducos, an old conventional, and General Moulins. Sièyes still remained leader of the Directory. Bernadotte was appointed Minister of War.

No sooner were these changes effected than the news of the evacuation of Zurich and Moreau's retreat upon the Apennines, showed the necessity of more vigorous measures. It was no longer the question to investigate the deficit of the finances, but rather to devise means to supply this deficit. Jourdan proposed a forced loan of one hundred millions levied on the wealthy classes: a disastrous measure always repugnant to public opinion, and which the urgency of the circumstances alone could justify. All classes of the conscription were placed at the disposition of the Directory, and if the levy had been executed without obstacle, it would have furnished a reënforcement of two hundred thousand men. Time and money were alone wanting. Battalions of national guards were placed as garrisons in the frontier fortifications, so as to render all the regulars disposable, and to prepare for the dangers of an invasion.

Consternation at the news of the Battle of Trebia.— Hardly were these measures adopted, when the news of the battle of Trebia came to add to the public distress. So many disasters, justly merited, affected the different parties very differently: the good and patriotic French were sorely grieved at them, the republicans were enraged, internal enemies rejoiced, but all, with one accord, agreed in pronouncing anathemas against the government which had brought them upon the country. Where then are the conquerors of Turcoing, of Fleurus, of Rivoli, of Castiglione? was heard from all parts. Are not the armies composed of the same soldiers and commanded by the same generals, who formerly carried the glory of France from the Noric Alps to the confines of Bohemia? In reflecting more attentively upon the causes of former successes, it was perceived that they were produced by masses skilfully directed upon important points, rather than by mere valor and love of country, as had been supposed. Although moments of crisis and of popular excitement are ill calculated for reflection, it was, nevertheless, perceived that results had been attributed to general causes, which, in reality, were due mainly to individual skill. A universal clamor rose against Rewbel and Talleyrand for the impolitic administration and usurpation of the government. Even those who were the least capable of pointing out what course ought to have been pursued, saw evidently that the government had been ill administered.

Formation of Clubs.—The public calamities led to the formation of new political clubs. A society, worthy offspring of the Jacobins, was formed at the Manège; there, at the very door of the Council of Ancients, they declaimed about the ignorance and stupidity of the administration. To avoid the law against societies directed by presidents, they appointed Drouet *regulateur des débats*. These ardent republicans, without wishing for the triumph of the *prolétaires*, thought to turn these leaders to their own account, and soon the club of the Manège equaled that of the Cordeliers. France was threatened with an anarchy more horrible than that of 1793, for then the dictatorial power of the Committee of Public Safety, sustained by victory, remedied, in some degree, the vices of a mere popular government; but as no such authority now existed, there seemed no barrier to protect the nation from plunging into the gulf of anarchy. Already the tribune of the Manège resounded with accusations against those who directed the administration of affairs, and the populace only waited for the signal for beheading them. After Rewbel and Schérer, the conduct of Talleyrand was most severely condemned : he was formally accused of projecting the fatal expedition to Egypt, the cause of all their misfortunes. Compelled to seek some means of justification, he declared that the expedition had been planned before he came into office. This threw the responsibility upon Charles Delacroix, who, to exculpate himself, declared that although the project might have been agitated before the Revolution, it never had been made a question of discussion while he held the portfolio.

Talleyrand is superseded.—The justification of Talleyrand not satisfying his opponents, the Directory, in deference to public opinion, appointed Reinhard minister of foreign affairs, Robert Lindet to the finances, and Cambacères as minister of justice. But a change of ministers could not immediately effect a change of foreign policy, as there was no chance of negotiating a peace, and the dismissal of Talleyrand was not sufficient to dissolve the coalition. In looking at the past, they found good reasons to bitterly regret the extravagances of 1798. How different would have been the results if they had applied themselves to consolidating the influence of the Republic in Italy, in interesting Spain in it by the aggrandizement of the infant Duke of Parma, and the House of Savoy by just indemnities, instead of alienating the courts of the peninsula by the revolutions of Genoa, Rome, Montferrat! To raise a power in favor of the son-in-law of Charles IV. would have been an excellent means of proving to the queen of the Two Sicilies and to Charles Emanuel, of Piedmont, that we knew how to estimate the alliances of princes who frankly entered into friendly relations with us; it would have induced Spain to redouble her efforts at sea, and at the same time to furnish for the common guard of Italy the contingent stipulated at San Ildefonso. By this means, instead of having need to send Macdonald to Naples, and Gauthier to Tuscany, we should have had one hundred and forty thousand French, Spanish, and Italian combatants to oppose the imperialists on the Adige.

The Manege closed.—But the time for recriminations was passed. To preserve our power in Italy was no longer the question; the means of saving France were now to be looked after. The attention of the Directory was now turned to the interior of France, where the ravings of the society of the Manège threatened a general anarchy. Such disorders at the very door of the legislative palace became intolerable; the society, driven from their place of sitting, installed themselves in the Rue du Bac, under the presidency of the *regulateur* Augereau. The debates became daily more stormy; the eulogy of Babœuf, pronounced from the tribune of the society, proved that it was time to strike. Sièyes appointed Fouché minister of police; this ancient proconsul, whose business energy no one can deny, hastened to close this den of Jacobinism, at the same time that the Directory prohibited the abuses of the public press.

New Plan of Operations.—This was all well enough for the interior; but something else was requisite to arrest the enemies of France. Certain of obtaining by the new law the two principal elements of war, the Directory now occupied itself with devising the means of repelling the threatened invasion on the east. It directed the topographical bureau to draw up a plan of operations against the allied armies on the supposition of Massena's being driven from Switzerland, and to indicate the natural and artificial obstacles which might in this direction be opposed to a great invasion. Although a military officer of distinction had pointed out in a luminous memoir its natural direction in the trough of the Jura and the Vosges, General Clark, chief of this bureau, persisted in maintaining that it should be directed by Switzerland and the coast Alps on Lyons. He consequently presented a long work, pointing out all the measures to be taken for covering the frontier of the Alps. These views consisted principally in forming an army for guarding the two St. Bernards, the Simplon, Mont-Cenis, Mont-Genèvre, and the Col de l'Argentière; while the army of Italy, debouching from the Apennines, should resume the offensive to prevent the siege of Coni and raise that of Mantua, and the army of Helvetia should operate a powerful diversion on the Limmat.

Joubert is charged with its Execution.—The new Directory feeling the necessity of some brilliant stroke to save its credit, Joubert, a young general of much promise, was appointed to replace Moreau in Italy, while the latter was destined for the command of the army of the Rhine. Joubert was to reorganize an army of forty-five thousand men in Liguria and to advance anew on the Po, to relieve Mantua. Championnet, put on trial for having dared to brave the proconsuls of the Directory at Naples, descended from the prisoner's box to take command of an army of thirty-four thousand men which had been organized in the Alps. If the proximity of Grenoble and Chambery was a sufficient motive for this army, instead of sending the troops by Provence to Genoa, there certainly was no sufficient reason for appointing two chiefs to these armies and assigning to that of the Alps a part principally defensive. Mantua, but weakly blockaded for some months past, had been more strongly invested since the fall of Peschiera, and, all the preparations being made, Kray was to open the trenches on the fifteenth of July:

Latour-Foissac capitulated on the thirtieth. At the same time Chasteler and Bellegarde besieged still more vigorously the citadel of Alexandria, which capitulated on the twenty-second of July, after seven days of vigorous attack, in which the Austrian artillery very much distinguished itself.

He debouches from the Apennines.—Joubert arrived about the beginning of August and debouched from the Apennines on Novi, on the twelfth. He was accompanied by Moreau, who, called to the command of the army of the Rhine, nevertheless wished to remain with his young friend till after the battle. They hoped to have only some forty thousand men to oppose. It had been rumored that Mantua had capitulated, but they did not believe it. On the evening of the fourteenth of August, the right and centre had united on the superb plateau of Novi, at the foot of the Apennines, where they learned the sad news that not only had Mantua surrendered, but that Kray's corps, which had besieged it, was united to Suwarrow, ready to receive them in the plain. It hardly seemed credible that a place which had resisted me ten months should, in three, have been reduced by the Austrians. But Latour-Foissac had made a very poor defense. Admitting that it had been attacked more regularly and that the means of defense were much inferior to those of the Austrian marshal, nevertheless it is certain that he might have prolonged the defense for at least a fortnight, which had been time enough to save it.

Battle of Novi.—They received, during the evening, a confirmation of this disaster which placed the matter beyond the possibility of doubt. There remained now no object for our army to risk a battle against a superior enemy. It was necessary to return to the Apennines and concert some new project with Championnet; but occupying so good a position, expecting the left to join them the next morning, they did not deem it necessary to make a precipitate retreat, for it did not seem probable that the enemy would attack so formidable a position, when it was for his interest to draw them into the plain. But Suwarrow thought differently, and directed the attack to be begun on the morning of the fifteenth of August at break of day, by his right under the orders of Kray. Already the Austrian columns were climbing the slopes of the eminences which were covered with vines, and debouching upon the plateau. Joubert hastened to the threatened point, put himself at the head of the thirty-fourth regiment, repulsed the enemy, but was himself killed at the first discharge :* it was scarcely six o'clock in the morning. Moreau, who seemed in this campaign to be destined to direct all the unfortunate contests, took command of the army which was now engaged contrary to its wishes and without any object; he at first succeeded in repulsing the enemy. The battle had continued on our left ever since three o'clock, when, at nine, Suwarrow debouched against the centre at the head of the Russian corps, and seemed determined, at all hazards, to carry the front of Novi and its heights. St. Cyr, defended himself with great bravery ; twice the enemy, repulsed and taken in flank by Watrin, was driven quite to Pozzolo-Formigaro. At last Melas with the reserve, or rather with the left of the allied forces, arrived at two o'clock from Rivalta, moved along the Scrivia, made eight battalions of grenadiers ascend the reverse of Monte-Rotundo where runs the road from Genoa to Gavi, and thus turned the position. Suwar-

* The following is Napoleon's portrait of Joubert: "He was a native of Ain. He studied law, but the Revolution made him adopt the profession of arms. He served in the army of Italy and was there made brigadier and general-of-division. He was tall, slender, and naturally of a feeble constitution. But he had strengthened it in the toil of camps, and in mountain warfare. He was intrepid, violent, and active. He was sincerely attached to Napoleon, who, in 1797, charged him to present to the Directory the colors of the army of Italy. He fell gloriously at the battle of Novi, when he was yet young, and had not acquired sufficient experience. He possessed qualities which would have raised him to great military renown." He was of the same age as Napoleon.

row and Kray seconded this operation by a new effort. Retreat now became both inevitable and difficult. It was at last effected by cross roads on Pasturana, where the defile becomes almost impassable. Perignan and Grouchy, in order to give time to the column to pass the defile, fought in front of it against quadruple forces which the enemy brought against them from all points of a circle. They were wounded and taken prisoners with five or six thousand brave men, who shared their fate; a good part of the artillery fell into the enemy's hands. This fatal day irrecoverably fixed the fate of Italy.

Massena retakes the smaller Cantons.—Massena, more fortunate, gained about the same time (August fourteenth) a signal advantage. By a singular chance he had recaptured the line of the high Alps which he had lost in June, at the very moment that the Archduke Charles, reënforced at last by Korsakof, had intended to resume the offensive on the opposite side.

Project of the Archduke.—The Archduke wished to concentrate his army below Bruck in order to cross at once the lines of the Aar, the Limmat, and the Reuss rivers, all considerable streams, which united near this city. From Bruck to Arau, it was only four leagues, and on the same day the Archduke might pass three important barriers and seize the heights of the Jura which separated Arau from Bâle. This movement would have compromitted, in a great degree, the safety of the French army which was extended on the Albis as far as Glaris. The Directory, wishing to urge forward the enterprises of Joubert and Massena, had pressed the latter to resume the offensive. Lecourbe, having been reënforced, attacked the corps of Simbschen, got possession of the Grimsel, the Furca, the St. Gothard, and the Crispalt, and took four thousand prisoners. The division of the Valois drove Rohan from the Simplon. Soult and

Chabran attacked the canton of Glaris, and the left of the Linth. These partial successes, instead of being fortunate, would have led to the ruin of the army, had not the project of the Archduke failed.

Thirty thousand Austrians and as many Russians had united, on the sixteenth of August, opposite the village of Dettingen. The single division of Ney covered Bruch and the Frickthal: there were only six battalions to dispute the passage. Such is the inconvenience of having immense lines and numerous points to guard. The one hundred and twenty-two battalions and one hundred and forty squadrons which composed the armies of the Rhine and the Danube would have formed, if Switzerland had been neutral, an imposing army between Ulm and Strasburg; while now, compelled to cover everything from Geneva to Dusseldorf, they presented an active force of only seventy or seventy-five thousand men, scattered along a line of one hundred leagues; there were only eight thousand at the enemy's point of passage. The Austrians, neglecting the ordinary precautions, hoped to throw across their bridge under the protection of forty pieces of cannon which swept the bank, without passing over troops to cover the pontoniers. The brigade of Quetard, which assembled at the noise, was soon forced to retire; the Austrian howitzers set fire to Dettingen. A battalion of carbineers of Zurich threw themselves into the ruins of the houses, and by means of their excellent carbines, these brave and skilful marksmen cut off many of the enemy's pontoniers. Moreover the rocky bottom of the Aar prevented the ponton anchors from taking hold. Many hours passed in this way. Ten thousand French, under the orders of Ney, having had time to collect near the point of passage, the Archduke became discouraged and renounced his project. This failure of the Archduke to establish his bridges was the greatest piece of good fortune for the French; for had his pontoniers been successful, it is hardly possible to calculate the immense disasters that would have followed. Massena was then with the reserve in the Muttenthal, and half of his army must have been lost.

New Plans of the Coalition.—The allies, intoxicated with their victories, had seen their line for a moment compromitted by dissensions between Suwarrow and the cabinet of Vienna. The Russian marshal, on his arrival in Turin, had strongly urged the recall of the King of Sardinia to his capital. But Thugut, a more wily diplomatist, wishing to form no conclusions as yet on the future fate of Piedmont, strongly opposed this. He had already sold at Selz some of the Piedmontese provinces, and perhaps he wished to make, on the return of the king, a speculation to obtain from him the Novarais as a condition of peace, and thus to divide with the House of Savoy the title and functions of *portier des Alps*. This policy displeased Suwarrow, who, thwarted also by the inaction of Kray at the epoch of the Trebia, complained with so much bitterness as to threaten serious dissensions in the camp of the allies.

The cabinets of London and Vienna agreed to propose to the cabinet of St. Petersburg a new project; it was agreed:

1st. That all the Russian troops of Suwarrow and Korsakof should unite in Switzerland to form the centre, and to penetrate into Franche-Comté in concert with a corps of Austrians;

2d. That the Archduke Charles should move with the mass of his army on Manheim, retake this place, pass the Rhine, both to assist Suwarrow and to favor an Anglo-Russian expedition which was to make a descent upon Holland;

3d. That the expedition, under the Duke of York, composed of twenty-five thousand English, and fifteen thousand Russians under General Hermann, should deliver Holland, and, aided by the troops of the Stadtholder levied there, as well as by the diversion of the Archduke, drive the French from Belgium;

4th. That Melas should command the Austrians, now left arbiters of Italy, and complete our expulsion from Liguria and Piedmont;

5th. That the Russian fleet, after having subdued Corfu, should assist the attack on Ancona which was confided to the corps of Frœlich;

6th. That the English should aid the Neapolitans in the reduction of the garrisons left in Naples, Rome, Civita-Vecchia, etc.

The Archduke marches on Manheim.—As Suwarrow was to leave Italy and debouch into Switzerland, the Archduke had to effect his own movement on the Lower Rhine. He commenced his march on the thirty-first of August; but unwilling to leave Korsakof alone exposed to the blows apparently designed for him by the cabinet of Vienna, he left the corps of Hotze, of about twenty-five thousand men, in the smaller cantons, and that of Nauendorf, of ten thousand men, at the junction of the Aar with the Rhine, so as to cover the Black Forest and the Russian right. The Archduke, hearing at Doneschingen that General Muller had passed the Rhine at Manheim with eighteen thousand men, and was then bombarding Philipsbourg, directed the corps of General Starray to the assistance of that city, and marched himself, with fifty-five thousand men, to sustain him. Muller did not wait for him, but hastily repassed the Rhine, leaving the feeble division of Laroche to guard Manheim. The Archduke attacked it on the seventeenth of September, penetrated by the *tête-du-pont* of Neckerau, and, in spite of the efforts of Ney, gained possession of the place and fifteen thousand prisoners.

Suwarrow's Plan.—Suwarrow had a difficult task; the attempt of Moreau to raise the blockade of Tortona had induced him to defer his departure till the eleventh of September, eleven days after the Archduke, whereas, to concert matters well, he ought to have set out first. Departing from Asti three roads offered themselves to his choice ; he could debouch by the Valois in the Pays-de-Vaud to effect a diversion, but it exposed him to be beaten without a chance of coöperation ; he could cross the St. Gothard without artillery, debouch on Schwitz and unite with Hotze, while his material went by Coire ; finally, he could, from Como, take the route of the Splugen and effect his junction by the Grisons without fighting. He preferred the St. Gothard as more certain than the first, and as shorter than the third.

Battle of Zurich.—Informed by Suchet of the departure of Suwarrow for Switzerland, and knowing that the Archduke had moved the mass of his army on Manheim, Massena determined to fight Korsakof before the arrival of the marshal ; for if he waited for the conqueror of Novi, he would in all probability be driven on the Jura. He assembled about thirty-eight thousand men, and determined to make the attack on the twenty-fifth of September. Soult passed the Linth at Schœnis. Hotze and his chief-of-staff being slain at the first fire, his corps became disordered and was driven on the Toggenbourg with the loss of five thousand men *hors-de-combat*. Mortier attacked Zurich on the left bank of the Limmat. Lorges and Menard passed the Limmat at Fahr, in order to turn Zurich, and assail the Zurichberg.

Korsakof had received notice from Suwarrow that he would be at Schwitz on the twenty-sixth, and his *corps-de-bataille* was lying in front of the little town of Zurich to attack the Albis, when the cannon of Foy and Lorges thundering in the direction of Fahr, gave notice of the danger which threatened it. In the mean time the Russian general, not liking his position, pushed his left between the Zil and the lake, and repelled the false attack of General Drouet. It was not till the arrival of Massena and Lorges at the north of Zurich that he saw the perils of his position. He had a division opposite Bruck, but was cut off from it by the passage of Massena at Fahr: it was necessary to decide immediately either to penetrate by the Albis and join Suwarrow in Schwitz, or to attack Lorges with all his forces and drive him across the Limmat. Korsakof did not know how to act; the fear of disobeying Suwarrow made him reject the only wise course which he could pursue, that of falling on Lorges with his entire force. The news of Hotze's death and the defeat of his corps increased his embarrassment; he persisted in maintaining himself with half his forces between the Zil and Zurich, where Mortier and the grenadiers of Klein fought him all day without any decided results. But Oudinot and Lorges were already cannonading the gate of Winterthour, and crowned the heights which commanded Zurich on the north, the only retreat which remained to the enemy.

Korsakof retires on the Rhine.—Korsakof decided, during the night, what course to pursue. His whole army crossed Zurich and debouched on the morning of the sixteenth, to recover the road to Schaffhausen, which it succeeded in doing after having repulsed the division of Lorges. But the latter, on receiving a reënforcement, resumed the attack, and cut off the enemy's columns, while Mortier penetrated the little town of Zurich, now guarded by only a few tirailleurs. Korsakof succeeded in reaching Schaffhausen, abandoning to us five thousand wounded, two thousand prisoners, and all his artillery. He had more than ten thousand men *hors-de-combat*, and Hotze at least five thousand.

Suwarrow passes the St. Gothard.—Hardly had Massena completed this brilliant victory, when he received the news of Suwarrow's success at the St. Gothard. The marshal, delayed three days at Lucerne, had not been able to attack

Airola and the southern slopes of the mountain till the twenty-third and twenty-fourth. Assisted by Strauch, he dislodged Gudin, forced him to retire on the Furca, and bivouacked at the Hospice. A column of six thousand Russians, under Rosenberg, was to march across the rocks, the snows, and the precipices of the Crispalt to descend on Urseren, and to strike Lecourbe, should he venture to make a stand at the Devil's Bridge. This march, as audacious as difficult, attained its object: Lecourbe, hearing at the Hospice of the arrival of the enemy at Urseren, took his resolution in desperation, threw his cannon into the Reuss, climbed the almost inaccessible mountains of Geschenen, followed along their sides, and redescended to Wasen; but he learned here that another Austrian column from the Grisons was already in possession of the valley toward Amsteg; while Suwarrow, on his side, had forced the rear-guard at the Devil's Bridge, after a bloody combat, and had effected a junction with Rosenberg. The audacity of Lecourbe increased in proportion to his danger; he attacked the Austrian column without hesitation. The latter, threatened on the other side by the reserve which was coming from Altorf to meet Lecourbe, thought itself very fortunate in effecting its escape by opening a passage to Lecourbe. He then crossed the Reuss at Seedorf, destroyed the bridge, and supported himself against the mountains of Surenen and the canton of Berne.

Suwarrow then descended without obstacle on Altorf and Fluelen, but this was the termination of any practicable road, and it was necessary to embark on Lake Lucerne, which was the only means of communication between this canton and that of Uri. The position was a critical one: Lecourbe had an armed flotilla, and, moreover, had seized upon a small number of the barks found there. The Russian general had no time to hesitate; he climbed the steep precipices of the mountains of Kesseren in the Schachenthal, where no troops had ever passed before, and which even Lecourbe had considered impracticable : he lost there the few pieces of mountain artillery which he had with him, many men and horses, and arrived exhausted in the Muttenthal on the twenty-eighth, three days later than he calculated. Hearing of Korsakof's disaster, he hoped at least to be seconded by two divisions of the right of Hotze, who, in the general plan, was to get possession of Glaris and secure a communication with him.

Defeat of the Austrians.—These divisions, under the orders of Jellachich and Linken, had in fact attacked the single brigade of Molitor on the twenty-fifth. Jellachich debouched on Wesen by the difficult path which runs along the lake of Wallenstadt. Molitor imposed on him by the stand which he took, and the Austrian general, hearing of Hotze's defeat and thinking himself lost if he remained where he was, in a *coupe-gorge*, retired on Wallenstadt. The next day Linken, debouching from the Grisons in three columns by the defile of Engi and the Todiberg, descended the valley of Sernst, carried off one of Molitor's battalions isolated in the mountains, and advanced on Glaris ; but Molitor, having disposed of Jellachich, opposed to him the same resistance ; and the Austrian general, hearing of the fate of his colleagues, and fearing that he himself would be captured, returned to the Grisons. It is to be remarked that Molitor, with four French and two Swiss battalions, had thus routed twelve thousand Austrians, at the very point of their junction with Suwarrow. The localities favored it, it is true, but his firmness, activity, and resolution are not the less worthy of the highest praise.

Difficult Retreat of Suwarrow.—Suwarrow soon marched from Mutten toward the Bragel, a difficult mountain, where he still found the advanced guard of Molitor ; this convinced him that the Austrians had disappeared from Glaris, and as a climax to his embarrassment, Mortier and Massena, with the conquerors of Zurich, had just arrived at Schwitz, and the grenadiers of Klein at Einsiedlen. The least hesitation would have lost all. Auffenberg and Bragation fortunately forced the little advanced guard of Mortier at Kloenthal, on the thirtieth, and descended on Glaris. Suwarrow followed them with Derfelden. General Rosenberg, left with four battalions in the Muttenthal, was there attacked, on the first of October, by Mortier, whom he drove in the most glorious manner on Schwitz. The rear-guard, relieved by this success, reached the Bragel without loss. Molitor had fallen back to Neffels, behind the Linth. Bagration was directed to attack him on the first of October. They fought on both sides with fury; the little troop of Molitor did wonders; the enemy was not behind in bravery; at last the arrival of Soult's division, returning from the pursuit of the wrecks of Hotze into the Grisons, decided the victory. This incident aggravated still more the difficulties of Suwarrow, who had not a minute to lose. He threw himself by the path of Panix and Engi, that is, by the flanks of the Todiberg, into the Grisons, a route frightful in the best season, but which was then the more difficult and dangerous from being covered with snow. The few horses and mules which he had left were abandoned at the bottom of this gulf; many hundreds of men perished among these precipices. No language can describe the horrors of this retreat. Glory is not the exclusive price of dangers and victories, it belongs equally to those who brave the elements, nature, and privations. In this view of the subject, there are few events more glorious for both parties in this memorable war.

Efforts of Korsakof on Winterthour.—During this time Korsakof had been reënforced by some Bavarians and by the little army of Condé, who had just come from the interior of

Russia with three or four thousand *émigrés* to conquer France! This general felt that to efface the stain of Zurich, it was necessary at any price to relieve his general-in-chief from his present difficult position. For this purpose he had advanced from Lake Constance and Busingen on Winterthour; but attacked here by the reserves and the divisions of Lorges and Menard, he was forced to retire behind the Rhine and destroy his bridges.

Movements of the Archduke and Suwarrow.—The Archduke Charles had moved, as has been already said, on Manheim by order of his cabinet; he there soon received news of the disaster of Zurich, which induced him to renounce all other projects than that of saving the army; he therefore returned in all haste to Doneschingen. He proposed to Suwarrow to come and join him so as to re-enter Switzerland by Schaffhausen; Suwarrow preferred to enter from his side by Rheineck. The Austrian general opposed this double operation, and the old marshal became irritated and took the road to Bavaria, where he put his troops in cantonments.

Descent on Holland.—In the mean time the English and Russians had executed their projected invasion of Holland. Abercrombie landed in North Holland, on the twenty-seventh of August, with three thousand English, and the next day was followed by twelve thousand more. He found no other opposition than the small division of Daendels. The English squadron of Admiral Mitchel entered the Texel, and the Dutch sailors, incited by the Orange party, broke out in insurrection, and forced Admiral Story to raise the Stadtholder's flag and surrender his squadron to the English. The choice of the narrow *presqu'île* of North Holland, well suited for the protection of the first debarkation, was also favorable to the defense of Brune. This general collected at Alkmaer the French divisions of Gouvion and Vandamme, and the Batavian divisions of Dumonceau and Daendels;

which together formed an army of about twenty-two thousand men. On the tenth of September he attempted to force the advantageous position of Abercrombie at Slaper-Dyc and was repulsed. The Prince of Orange showed himself at the same time on the frontiers of Friesland, but his partisans were not numerous, and would do nothing in his favor. The Russians and English, on the sixteenth of September, landed the remainder of the troops under the direction of the Duke of York; which increased their number to thirty-five thousand. Brune also had reënforcements which carried his to twenty-eight thousand.

On the nineteenth of September the allies attacked Brune at Alkmaer; the principal effort was made by the Russians near Bergen, and the English, instead of sustaining this effort, threw the mass of their forces into the lagunes of the Zuyder Zee. The Russians divided into two columns; that of Hermann attacked Vandamme and drove him behind Bergen; but Gouvion and Rostolland, having rendered him timely succor, the Russian column, attacked in front and flank, was overthrown; Hermann himself, with two thousand men, was taken prisoner; the rest perished or were dispersed. Essen, who had advanced more to the left, being attacked in front and threatened in rear, fled behind the Zyp. Dundas, assisted by a Russian brigade, had at first beaten Dumonceau at Schoorldam; but the reënforcements which Brune sent there, soon forced him to retire with loss. At the centre, Pultney gained an important advantage over Daendels, but soon returned to his position. On the left, Abercrombie, finding only feeble detachments at Hoorn, fatigued his troops by marching over difficult roads without any result.

A new attempt was made on the second of October, at Egmont-op-Zee. But after several unimportant contests the allies were again repulsed with considerable loss. Their army was now shut up in the lagunes of Zyp; the autumnal rains increased the difficulty of their position; the disaster at Zurich left them no hope of succor from the Rhine; the Orange party did not move; England had accomplished half her object in the capture of the Batavian fleet. The Duke of York, therefore, resolved to return to London, and secured a safe retreat by an inglorious treaty of evacuation. This treaty was signed on the eighteenth of October.

Such was the state of our affairs when I arrived in Paris. Switzerland and Holland had just been happily delivered, at the very moment when the projected union of the Russian forces in the centre of operations was calculated to menace the French soil with invasion. But the successes of the allies in Italy still threatened our departments at the south, where reactionary passions began to foment in a manner truly alarming. The state seemed more than ever exposed to the rule of anarchy.

Lecourbe raises the Siege of Philipsbourg.—The departure of the Archduke from Manheim to the assistance of Suwarrow caused orders to be given to Lecourbe to recross the Rhine and lay siege to Philipsbourg; he succeeded in making the investment, but Starray twice forced him to give up the attempt. An armistice put an end to this enterprise without any direct result on the fate of the war.

Efforts of Championnet to save Coni.—An operation of still greater importance had also failed in Italy. Championnet, who had succeeded Joubert and Moreau as commander-in-chief in the Alps and in Italy, took advantage of Suwarrow's absence to endeavor to relieve Coni. In order to offer an obstacle to a siege by Melas' troops, more than fifty thousand men were put in motion from Spezzia and the Bochetta, by the Argentière, quite to Mont Cenis. Six or seven scattered corps could not easily succeed against the army of Melas, concentrated on the Stura between Turin and Alexandria, and capable of moving in any direction he might desire. It was exactly a repetition of the battle of Rivoli, on a scale ten times larger. Championnet, repulsed near the end of September in a first attempt on Mondovi, made a more serious attack at the end of October; the same fault necessarily produced the same result. St. Cyr, with the right wing, gained a very glorious success in front of Novi on the twenty-fourth of October; but the division of the centre, acting without concert on Fossano, were beaten, the third of November, by thirty-four thousand Austrians. Another combat took place on the tenth, when the French were so scattered that the siege of Coni was carried on by the enemy without further opposition; it surrendered on the fourth of December. While the centre was driven into the Alps, Kray forced St. Cyr on the Bochetta, and Klenau, debouching from the coast, attempted to carry Genoa.

While Melas was thus crowning a glorious campaign by manœuvres that did him honor, General Frœlich had been directed to reduce Ancona, where General Monnier had kept the field notwithstanding the approach of a Russian fleet, and a corps of observation, composed of Russians, Turks, and insurgent peasants. The siege was finally begun on the first of November, and, notwithstanding the good defense of Monnier and his little garrison, the place surrendered on the twelfth; the garrison of two thousand seven hundred men, covered with laurels, returned to France on parole.

Such was the issue of this celebrated campaign of 1799, so rich in events, of which I have merely traced an outline to show the state of affairs at the time of my appointment to the Consulate.

CHAPTER VI.

THE CAMPAIGNS OF 1800 AND 1801.

Napoleon's Return from Egypt—Necessity of a Change in the Government—Sièyes had long meditated a Change—Revolution of the eighteenth Brumaire—Project of a Constitution—Consular Government—Napoleon proposes Peace—Fall of Tippoo-Saëb—Maritime Affairs—Continental Armies—Plan of Campaign—Pius VI. and VII.—Project of the Allies on Genoa and Toulon—Massena blockaded in Genoa—Napoleon's Plan of Operations on the Rhine—Carnot Minister of War—Passage of the Alps—The French Army arrested by Fort Bard—Melas deceived—Combat of Chiusella—Napoleon marches on Milan—Passage of the Ticino—Disposition of Melas—Surrender of Genoa—Passage of the Po—Battle of Montebello—Battle of Marengo—Convention of Alexandria—Negotiations of General St. Julien—Disapproved by the Cabinet of Vienna—Negotiations for a Naval and Military Armistice—Kleber proposes to evacuate Egypt—He is forced to conquer at Heliopolis—Important Convention with the United States—The English quarrel with Neutrals—Rupture of the Negotiation of London—Conspiracy of Cerrachi—Expeditions against Ferrol and Cadiz—Resignation of Thugut from the Ministry—Occupation of Tuscany—Preparations on the Continent—Plan of Operations—Brilliant Success of the Army of the Rhine—Armistice of Steyer—Inaction of Brune—Passage of the Splugen—Operations of Brune—Junction of the Army of the Grisons—Armistice of Treviso—Infernal Machine—The Neapolitans beaten in Tuscany—Expedition of Murat against Naples—Armistice of Foligno—Peace of Luneville—Campaign of 1801—English Expedition against Copenhagen—Naval Battle of Copenhagen—Armistice with the Danes and Death of Paul I.—English Descent upon Egypt—Resignation of Pitt—Situation of France—Necessity of a new Religious System—Best means of accomplishing this Change—Chances in Favor of the Reformation—The Concordat—Objections made to it—Fault of my Successors—Negotiations of London—Preliminaries signed—Peace with Russia and the Porte—Acquisition of Louisiana—The Infant of Parma, King of Etruria—Expedition to St. Domingo and Guadaloupe—Provisional Reunion of Piedmont—Affairs of Switzerland and the Cisalpine—Italian Republic—The English—Lord Cornwallis Envoy to

Amiens—Debates upon Malta—The definitive Peace—Its Reception in London and France—The Tribunat abolished—Consulate for Life—The Principles of my Works—Solemn Publication of the Concordat—Reunion of Piedmont—Counter-Revolution in Switzerland—Friendly Relations with Russia—Indemnities in Germany.

Napoleon's Return from Egypt.—In tracing out the preceding campaign, I have anticipated events: we will now return to the vessel which sailed from Alexandria on the twenty-fourth of August, bearing my destinies and those of Europe. Our passage, though long, was fortunate, and, the sixth of October, I landed at Frejus. My presence excited the enthusiasm of the people. My military glory reassured all those who had been alarmed at the idea of a foreign invasion. My journey resembled a triumph, and I saw on my arrival at Paris that France was at my disposal, for every thing seemed ripe for a great change.*

Necessity of a Change in the Government.—After a revolution which had completely destroyed the social edifice,

---

* Thiers thus describes Napoleon's reception in France: "The inhabitants of Provence had, for three successive years, been apprehensive of an invasion by the enemy. Bonaparte had delivered them from this fear in 1796; but it had recurred with more force than ever since the battle of Novi. On learning that Bonaparte had anchored off the coast, they fancied that their saviour had arrived. All the inhabitants of Frejus thronged to the beach, and in a moment the sea was covered with boats. A multitude, intoxicated with enthusiasm and curiosity, stormed the vessels, and, breaking through all the sanatory laws, communicated with the new comers. All inquired for Bonaparte—all were anxious to see him. It was now too late to enforce sanatory measures. The administration of Health was obliged to dispense the general from quarantine, otherwise it must have condemned the whole population, which had already communicated with the crews, to the same precaution. Bonaparte immediately landed, and resolved to set out the same day for Paris.

"The telegraph, speedy as the winds, had already spread along the road from Frejus to Paris the extraordinary tidings of the landing of Bonaparte. The most confused joy immediately burst forth. The news, proclaimed in all the theatres, had produced an extraordinary excitement there. Patriotic songs everywhere superseded the theatrical representations. Baudin, deputy of the Ardennes, one of the framers of the constitution of the year III., a wise and sincere republican, passionately attached to the republic and deeming it undone unless a powerful arm should come to uphold it, died of joy on hearing of this event."

creating new interests and habits; a government, desirous of putting an end to the irregularities and license of popular commotions, should not only endeavor to improve the laws springing from these factions or enthusiastic commotions, but should establish a charter fixing invariably the basis of organic laws, and the principles of public liberty; leaving to time and experience to draw up the detailed laws requisite for the administration of the government, and to determine the rights and duties of the citizens. Every intelligent magistrate saw that the constitution of the year III. was detestable, and the authorities it had produced, destitute of capacity; but they were not so well agreed as to the remedies proper to be applied. It was very difficult to determine these. At first sight it might seem most proper to intrust the legislative body with reforming the constitutional part. Nevertheless it was to be feared that this body, jealous of all executive power, would endeavor to increase its own authority at the expense of the other, thus destroying the fundamental principles of the primitive institutions. If it were given, on the other hand, to the executive power, it was equally to be feared that under the pretext of public safety, this would be equally inclined to increase its own prerogatives at the expense of the legislative body. If, to avoid these two rocks, the protection or reform of the constitution were confided to a third authority, the desired object seemed but little more likely to be attained, for the same contests would continue, notwithstanding a change of name in the contending parties. Much cruel experience had shown that any important reforms, in a representative government, are attended by great danger to public liberty, and the vices introduced are frequently greater than those attempted to be extirpated.

There was one other means of reform, not less terrible than the three already mentioned, but which is not fatal to the nations which are compelled to resort to it;—I mean the force of the bayonet. Whatever mere politicians may say upon this subject, many instances may be cited where a resort to this remedy has saved the nation from worse calamities, such as the dissolution of the parliament by Cromwell, that of the senate of Stockholm by Gustavus III., and the *coup-d'état* of the eighteenth Brumaire. It may very well happen, however, as it frequently does, that these remedies are worse than the disease itself. It is not my present intention to enter into any minute discussion of these revolutionary reforms, but merely to make a few observations necessary for appreciating the course which I pursued in the important event about to occur in France.

At this epoch every body in France desired a revision of the constitution and the abrogation of the laws passed by the Assemblies. The general opinion was against the Directory, whose administration for the last two years had produced only disasters, whose despotic authority had shown, in the events of the eighteenth Fructidor and the twenty-second Floréal, but whose inefficiency and absolute nullity had been laid bare on the thirtieth Prairial. The people were equally tired of the scandalous debates which daily occurred in the Councils; and their state of permanent hostility to the executive power, caused a desire for a more just balance between the principal authorities of the Republic.

Projects of Sieyes.—Sièyes, occupying a place for the last three months in the supreme magistracy, had attentively examined the progress of public opinion. Advantageously known by the success of his diplomatic missions, as well as by his administrative talents, and still enjoying the popularity acquired by his earlier writings, he conceived the project of substituting, in place of the existing authorities, a government of more force and unity, and especially guaranteeing the property and rights of citizens. He was the more interested in this, inasmuch as the Jacobins, enraged at the closing of the Manège, had already openly denounced him in their journals and demanded that the Councils should annul his election as unconstitutional; some pretended that he had projected the calling of a prince of Brunswick to the throne of France, and that his mission to Berlin was for this object alone; others thought this crafty constitution-maker had reserved for himself the presidency for life of the Republic—an office which he thought to establish. This project was possible, though not exempt from danger; all France was in fact conspiring for the overthrow of the present system, and even the Directors themselves, though each in his own way, were working with ardor for the ruin of the edifice which they felt themselves incapable of sustaining. Many of the legislators soon adopted the project of Sièyes, particularly the members of the Council of Ancients. But the Council of Five Hundred, notwithstanding the changes of Floréal, still contained many old Republican zealots who had opposed all the recent changes of the government. Nevertheless my brother Lucien, president of this Council, had here formed a powerful party.

One of the men upon whom Sièyes most relied was Talleyrand, under whose orders, as minister of foreign affairs, he had acted while ambassador to Berlin. Besides a conformity of views, Talleyrand was as desirous as Sièyes to revenge himself for the vociferations of which a few months before he had been the object. A brilliant triumph was the only thing that could restore his former reputation, and to obtain this, no sacrifice was too great. But a revolution of this character could not be consummated without the assent of the troops; it was, therefore, necessary to gain over some military chief of renown, but docile enough to follow the course which they might mark out, and to stop when they should command him. General Moreau and Joubert were those upon whom they first fixed their attention; the first had inspired some distrust by his equivocal conduct on the eighteenth Fructidor, and death snatched away the second at the moment when they flattered themselves that he would gain by victory sufficient consideration to accomplish this great enterprise.

Effect of Napoleon's Return. — Such was the state of affairs and of public feeling when I arrived at Paris amid the general acclamations of the people. Sièyes, thinking he could do nothing without me, hastened, with Lucien, to place in my hands all the threads of the conspiracy; it was now agreed that my sword must achieve what they had conceived and prepared. Never, perhaps, were circumstances more favorable for the accomplishment of a project of this nature. The majority of the Directory was composed of three men of no importance; Barras, the only one who had any celebrity, owed his importance entirely to the day of Vendemiaire, and to some services rendered in the navy. If these three Directors had been men of any influence or skill, they might easily have baffled the conspiracy by the weapons which the constitution had placed in their hands; but their own stupor left them plunged into a state of inertia. Besides, they were not fully agreed, and Barras himself was the first to favor a change in the state, provided that he should be permitted to play a part in it.

Although the Directory had changed three of its members since the day of Prairial, still it had no authority. The leaders of the Councils knew that no one would raise a voice in favor of the majority of the Directory. Neither from abroad nor from the army could the triumvirs expect any support. The victories of Massena in Helvetia, and of Brune in Holland, were compensated by the defeats of the army of Italy, whose exhaustion and feebleness had opened the frontier of the maritime Alps. The ordinary levies were made with greater difficulty from day to day, and the state of penury in which the recently formed auxiliary battalions were left, discouraged the conscripts from joining their colors. The patriotic enthusiasm of 1792 had disappeared with the circumstances which gave rise to it; and the conduct of the government had completely extinguished its last sparks. Add to this that the victories of the enemy had again lighted up the fires of civil war in the Departments of the west, and that the vociferations of 1793, renewed at the Club of the Manège, had provoked the odious law requiring hostages from the nobles, the relatives of the *émigrés*, and the principal proprietors of the cantons designated as royalists. This unfortunate measure, far from attaining its object, had renewed the civil war and massacres in Poitou and Brittany. The finances were squandered, the public credit destroyed, and the sources of public income dried up. Thus the weakness of the government and the faults of its institutions had united to place France upon the very brink of ruin. Everybody seemed desirous to rescue the country, and each had his favorite plan. In these projects they all made me a confidant. They all counted on me, because they deemed my sword necessary to carry their projects into execution. But I counted on no one, and there was nothing to prevent my selecting the plan which I might think the best.

Fortune was about to place me at the head of the state; I was called to rule the Revolution, to prepare the future destiny of France, and perhaps of the world. I could not choose respecting a change of government; the rule of the Directory was already virtually at an end. It was necessary to place in its stead some imposing authority, and there was none more truly imposing than military glory. The Directory must therefore be replaced, either by me or by anarchy. France could not hesitate between the two. The republicans, who had at first received me with so much *empressement*, distrusted my projects. Even the presence of Sièyes did not satisfy them. He undertook to draw up a constitution; but the Jacobins feared my sword even less than the speculative pen of an abbé.

Revolution of the Eighteenth Brumaire. — All parties now ranged themselves under two banners—those opposed and those favorable to my elevation. Nevertheless, it became necessary to employ the bayonet in effecting the revolution of the eighteenth Brumaire, though I at one time had hoped that it might be made by acclamation. The signal was given in the Council of Ancients, where we had on our side all moderate men, intelligent magistrates, the crafty and the ambitious, and some of those political alchemists, called *doctrinaires*, who sought for a *balance of power* as they would seek for the philosopher's stone. But fearing a strong opposition we had procured the calling of an extraordinary session, at eight o'clock for the morning of the eighteenth Brumaire (November ninth), taking care to notify our friends first. The majority, one hundred and fifty members, met at the appointed time and voted a transfer of the Councils to St. Cloud, where they would be secure from the mob which the partisans of the Directory might incite against us. I was at the same time invested with the command of the troops, and all authority necessary for securing the transfer of the Councils and the maintenance of the public tranquillity. The measures were taken with precision; the Council of Five Hundred, when notified of the decree of transfer, began to murmur at it, but Lucien, the president, declared the session closed and the Council adjourned to meet again the next day at St. Cloud.

Immediately on being invested with the command, I established my head-quarters in the Tuileries, where a force of eight thousand men was soon collected. I passed them in review and harangued them. The most important posts were intrusted to the generals most devoted to my interests. All those who were dissatisfied with the Directory, and Moreau, one of the first, came to offer me their services and to solicit a command. High-sounding proclamations were issued to the Parisians, inviting them to remain quiet, and promising public tranquillity and security. I sent to the Directors, Barras, Gohier, and Moulins, an imperative invitation to hand in their resignations. The two *militaires* obeyed, but the lawyer refused. Barras sent me his resignation by his secretary, hoping that our former relations might induce me to give him a place in the new government. But I knew him too well to make a colleague of him. His message was received in the Tuileries, where a committee of Ancients, the minority of the Directory (Sièyes and Roger-Ducos), and the greater part of the military chiefs were assembled. I took advantage of the occasion to influence the minds of my troops and all others present. Replying briefly to the messenger of Barras, I added with a loud voice: " What have you done with that France which I left so brilliant? I left you peace, I have found war; I left you victories, I have found defeats; I left you the millions of Italy, I have found despoiling laws and wretchedness. What has become of the hundred thousand Frenchmen whom I knew? all my companions in glory? They are dead! .... Such a state of things can not possibly last; in less than three years it would lead us to despotism. ... It is time to restore to the defenders of the country that confidence to which they have such strong claims. We wish no better patriots than those brave men who have been mutilated in the service of the Republic."

The next day the legislators removed to St. Cloud, preceded by five thousand soldiers, who guarded the avenues and gates of the château. The Ancients had their session in the ancient gallery, and at the orangery. The preparations for the accommodation of the members delayed the session for a couple of hours, so that the Republicans had time to concert a plan of resistance, or rather of attack. The sessions were begun in a strong manner. I first entered the meeting of the Ancients, and proved to them the existence of a conspiracy, denouncing to them the overtures made to me by Barras and Moulins to strike a *coup-d'état* in their favor. I demanded prompt measures to save the Republic; they opposed to me the constitution, and I showed that, violated on so many occasions, it had become a mere collection of words, utterly useless, except as a cloak to factions. After strongly urging the majority not to disappoint the expectation of France, I cried out: " Shall I tremble before factionists! I whom the foreign coalition could not destroy! If I am guilty of perfidy, be ye the Brutuses; and you, ye brave grenadiers who have accompanied me here—let those bayonets, with which we have so often triumphed together, be instantly pointed at my heart. But if any orator, paid by foreigners, dares to pronounce the word *outlaw*, let the thunderbolt of war instantly crush him. Recollect that *I march accompanied by the god of fortune and by the god of war!*" It was Mahomet speaking to his faithful Seides!

These words, although addressed to my soldiers, were also intended for my opponents. I was now engaged in the contest, and I must either conquer or die. There was no middle course. But it was not from the Council of Ancients that I had most to fear; my most formidable adversaries were sitting in the Council of Five Hundred. At the opening of the session of this body, Gaudin, one of the secretaries, was charged with proposing the formation of a committee of seven members to report on the public danger, and on the means of obviating this danger. His speech was the signal for the tempest; cries of *Vive la constitution, à bas les dictateurs!* drowned his voice. In the midst of this tumult Delbrel moved that first of all, the representatives should renew their oath of fidelity to the constitution of the year III.; his motion passed unanimously. Lucien saw himself compelled, though unwillingly, to swear first. The republicans had succeeded in producing a momentary enthusiasm, and in gaining over to their party those who had not been admitted into the secret of the conspiracy. But they did not know how to profit by their first success; and, instead of declaring the country in danger and adopting a vigorous course, they consumed three hours in taking the oath and in vain debates on the resignation of Barras. At this moment I descended from the hall of the Ancients to that of the Five Hundred. I had been informed of what was passing there, and presuming that the scene would not be very tranquil, I had put the troops under arms and directed a detachment of grenadiers to be ready to aid me if necessary.

These precautions were not useless; for hardly had I crossed the threshhold of the door, when they raised the cry of *outlaws*. The Deputy, Bigonnet, sprung to the tribune, and, apostrophizing me, directed me to retire. Some crowded around the tribune, and others, by their threatening looks and gestures, manifested their intention of making me suffer the fate of Cæsar. In vain did I endeavor to make myself heard; my most furious enemies, among whom I noticed Aréna and Destrem, advanced against me (it is said) armed with poignards. Seeing that nothing could be effected in this way, I left this assembly, of which an angry sea lashed by the winds gives but a feeble image, and took refuge among my soldiers. But my departure did not restore order; Lucien, left alone to make head against the storm, had to support the invectives of a great number of the representatives who accused him of being my accomplice, and insisted upon his declaring me an *outlaw*. Every moment the disorder increased; opposite propositions were made from the different corners of the hall, and the president tried in vain to restore tranquillity. This violent state could not long continue: Lucien, seeing his command disregarded and his voice drowned by the vociferations of the most fiery members, stripped off his insignia of office and left the hall in the midst of a detachment which I had sent to his rescue.

I only waited for this signal to avenge myself for the insults I had received. But to give my conduct all the forms of legality, Lucien harangued the troops, telling them that the national representation was exposed to the poignards of a band of assassins, and, in his quality of president, requiring their aid to drive these factionists from the council hall. To these words, closing with the usual phrase of *Vive la Republique,* the soldiers responded by *Vive Bonaparte!* Twenty grenadiers advanced toward the hall, and the superior officer, who preceded them, summoned the deputies to retire. Prudon, Digonnet, and General Jourdan invoked the constitution and apostrophized the grenadiers; these, astonished at such words from one who had formerly led them to victory, opposed only their force of inertia; the slightest incident might have destroyed our projects. But Murat soon decided every thing by declaring *that the legislative body was dissolved.* The charge was beaten, new troops approached, and in an instant the hall was abandoned by the representatives. Some fled to the Council of Ancients, and denounced, at the bar of the Council, the act of their expulsion. But the Ancients paid little attention to their complaints, and were occupied with the report of the committee on the formation of a provisional consular government.

At nine o'clock they succeeded in collecting together a considerable number of deputies in the orangery, and Lucien declared the Council in majority and opened the session. Most of the opposition members were absent, and the few that were present were too much frightened to make any formal opposition. The project of Chazal passed unanimously.

Its principal features were the abolition of the Directory, the appointment of myself, Sièyes, and Roger Ducos as Consuls of the Republic, the expulsion of sixty-one deputies, noted as demagogues, the adjournment of the legislature for three months, and the appointment of two temporary committees of the two Councils, the one to make the necessary changes in the organic principles of the constitution, and the other to remodel the civil code. This law was soon sanctioned by the Ancients, and, after receiving the oaths of the new administrators of France, the two Councils, at five o'clock in the morning, closed their long and stormy session.

During the two days of these debates the inhabitants of the capital remained perfectly tranquil. Accustomed to political storms, and giving no faith to the promises of liberty given by a party of demagogues, they rejoiced at an event which promised them more quiet and happy times. No one took any interest in a constitution so frequently violated by its pretended friends. The authorities of the former government had lost all influence or consideration; all hope was placed in the coming administration. Natural partisans of a régime somewhat monarchical, the nobles and priests now looked for the end of their misfortunes; landholders for the resurrection of credit; holders of national property for the guarantee of their possessions; the army for an end of its disasters; in fine, the whole population looked for a new era of happiness and security. The abolition of the odious laws of hostages and of forced loans, soon justified a part of these hopes; and public confidence, which seemed to have departed forever, insensibly pervaded all classes of the nation. In this revolution Moreau had volunteered his assistance, and, commanding a battalion under my orders, had marched to the Luxembourg. This course of conduct does not very well accord with the title of Seide of Republicanism to which he frequently laid claim, nor with his pretended projects for restoring the Bourbons in 1813!

Project of a Constitution.—After the dissolution of the Councils they were replaced by a legislative commission, and a committee was charged with drawing up a new constitution. Sièyes amused us with the project of a Grand Elector, who should appoint two consuls, with the power of absorbing them in case they ventured to exceed their powers. One of these consuls was to be charged with the foreign policy and war, and the other with the affairs of the interior. It was the height of absurdity to think of dividing the public administration between two consuls independent of each other, as if the internal and external affairs were entirely disconnected; but what seemed still more ridiculous was an elector, without authority and without disposable forces, charged with directing, and even impeaching a consul who had at his disposal an army of half a million of men! It was evident that Sièyes intended himself for the office of *absorbing elector*, so as to govern without either the trouble or responsibility of doing so. This kind of Grand Lama for a ruler did not at all suit a warlike nation, like the French, much less a people plunged into all the embarrassments of a great revolution, and an internal and external war to which history hardly furnishes a parallel.

Consular Government.—I demonstrated these faults, and proposed a first consul, chief of the state, and two other consuls as a consulting Council. This project was approved, to the great displeasure of the disappointed Lycurgus. The first place in this trio belonged of right to me; and to avoid all rivalry, I took good care that my rivals should be neither military men nor men of ambition. I caused Cambacérès and Lebrun to be chosen. The first was a jurist celebrated for his erudition, the second had been an enlightened administrator; both were men of business but without energy—in fine, just such colleagues as I desired. The ministry was composed as follows : Berthier, minister of war ; Talleyrand, of foreign affairs ; Barbé-Marbois, and Gaudin, of finance ; Bourdon, Forfait, and Décrès successively, of the navy ; Abrial, then Regnier, of justice ; Laplace, my brother Lucien, then Chaptal of the interior ; the inevitable Fouché, of police ; the important post of secretary of state, which served as a kind of centre to all the other branches of the government, was given to Maret, who united the talents of a statesman to a thorough knowledge of diplomacy, and who passed through the Revolution with a reputation unsullied.*

The public voice had given to me the first place in the state. The resistance which might be opposed to me did not trouble me, because it only came from those who were ruined in public estimation. The royalists had not yet appeared. Had they come, they would have been instantly seized. The mass of the nation had confidence in me, for they knew that the Revolution could not have a better guarantee than mine. My strength consisted in placing myself at the head of the interests which it had created, for by making it retrograde I should have found myself on the ground of the Bourbons.

It was necessary that the nature of my power should be

---

* Hugues Bernard Maret was born at Dijon in 1763. After completing his studies, he repaired to Paris, and at the sittings of the States General became reporter for the *Bulletin de l'Assemblie* and afterward for the *Moniteur*. His first diplomatic post was secretary of legation to Hamburg; he was afterward promoted to Brussels, and in 1792 received the important mission to London. On his way to Italy as minister to Naples, he was arrested by the Austrians and cast into prison, where he was confined for nearly two years. He distinguished himself at the negotiations of Lille with Lord Malmsbury. After the eighteenth Brumaire his career became inseparable from that of Napoleon, who sent him on many important missions. He was made Duke of Bassano in 1809. On the return of the Bourbons in 1815, he was banished to Gratz, in Syria, but in 1820 was permitted to return to France and settle upon his estates in Burgundy. He has been described by all historians as a man of much intelligence, and a most unshaken fidelity. He enjoyed the utmost confidence of Napoleon, and never betrayed it.

wholly new, in order that all ambitions should there find the means of living; but there was nothing definitive in its nature. Men of theories, who wished something definitive, found fault with it. This, however, was its great merit, for it was a dictatorship in disguise, a kind of government most suitable for times of crisis and in a transitory order of things. Perhaps it would have been better to have boldly seized the dictatorship; every one would then have seen my power; this would have been of much advantage. The dictatorship would have prejudiced nothing for the future, would have left opinions in suspense, and have intimidated the enemy by showing him the firm resolution of France: but the name was objectionable, and the time for a definitive order of things had not yet come.

If by the constitution I was only the first magistrate of the Republic, I had for the baton of command a sword more formidable than the sabre of Scanderberg. There was an incompatibility between my constitutional rights and the ascendency which resulted from my character and my actions. The enlightened public felt this as well as I did. Things could not long continue so, and were naturally tending to changes which would give force and stability to the state.

The public will placed me at the head of the state. I had on my side a large body of the people; my opponents were mostly men who had lost the public confidence. In assuming the reins of power I found more courtiers than I wished; my ante-rooms were crowded.*

---

* Thiers, an ardent republican, and staunch friend of republican governments, writes as follows on the overthrow of the Directory, and the establishment of the Consulate: "Such was the revolution of the eighteenth Brumaire, on which such opposite opinions are entertained, which is regarded by some as an outrage which annulled our struggling liberty, by others as a daring, but necessary act, that put an end to anarchy. What may justly be said of it is, that the Revolution, after assuming all the characters, monarchical, republican, and democratic, at length took the military character, because, amid that perpetual conflict with Europe, it was requisite that it should constitute itself in a strong and quiet

Napoleon proposes Peace.— The present situation of France gave me uneasiness. Notwithstanding my chances of success I preferred peace. I could then offer it in good faith, for the preceding disasters were not of my making. I could come forward unembarrassed by the differences of the former administration. Mr. Pitt refused it: and never did this statesman commit so great an error, for this moment was perhaps the only one when the allies could have made peace with security. France, in asking peace, acknowledged herself vanquished, and the people relieved themselves of all their misfortunes, except that of being under the yoke of adversity. By this refusal, the English minister forced me to redouble my efforts, and in this way I extended my empire over the west of Europe. The form of this refusal was not less extraordinary than the thing itself: I had addressed

---

manner. The republicans deplore so many useless efforts, so much blood spilt to no purpose, in order to found liberty in France, and they are grieved to see it immolated by one of the heroes whom it had brought forth. But here the noblest sentiment leads them into error. The Revolution which was to give us liberty, and which has prepared every thing for our enjoying it some day or other, was not of itself, neither could it be, liberty. It was destined to be a great struggle against the old order of things. After conquering in France, it was requisite that it should conquer in Europe. But so violent a struggle admitted not of the forms or the spirit of liberty. For a moment, and but a brief one, the country possessed liberty under the Constituent Assembly; but when the populace became so menacing as to intimidate public opinion; when it stormed the Tuileries on the tenth of August; when, on the second of September, it sacrificed all those of whom it felt distrust; when, on the twenty-first of January, it forced every one to compromise himself with it by imbruing his hands in royal blood; when, in August, 1793, it obliged all the citizens to hasten to the frontiers, or to part with their property; when itself abdicated its power, and resigned it to that great Committee of Public Safety, composed of twelve individuals—was there, could there be liberty? No, there was a violent effort of enthusiasm and heroism; there was the muscular tension of a wrestler engaged with a potent antagonist. After this moment of danger, after our victories, there was a moment of relaxation. The latter end of the Convention and the Directory exhibited moments of liberty. But the struggle with Europe could be only temporarily suspended. It soon recommenced, and, on the first reverse, all parties rose against a too moderate government, and invoked a mighty arm. Bonaparte, returning from the East, was hailed as sovereign, and called to supreme power. It is absurd to say that Zurich had saved France. Zurich was

myself directly to the King of England: the letter remained unanswered; the secretary of foreign affairs wrote one to Talleyrand in which he indicated the restoration of the Bourbons as the only means of ending the war in Europe.

It was curious to see a government, which had twice, in the treaties of Lille, recognised the Republic and the Directory, now refuse to treat with an authority much more firmly established, and made illustrious by victory. It was, in fact, the very vacillating and temporary character of the Directory which constituted its merits, for, in the estimation of England, that was best which was best calculated to injure France. At the same time that I proposed peace to England, I sought also to treat with Russia. Paul I. was indignant at the reverses sustained by his troops in Holland, and cast the blame of it upon the English. Suwarrow also complained of the Austrian general for abandoning the smaller cantons at the moment that he entered them. Irritated by his disastrous but honorable retreat, he afterward disagreed with

but an accident, a respite; it required a Marengo and a Hohenlinden to save her. It required something more than military successes. It required a powerful reorganization at home of all the departments of the government, and it was a political chief, rather than a military chief, which France needed. The eighteenth and nineteenth of Brumaire were, therefore, necessary. All we can say is, that the twentieth is to be condemned, and that the hero made a bad use of the service which he had just rendered. But we may be told that he came to perform a mysterious task, imposed, without his being aware of it, by Fate, of which he was the involuntary agent. It was not liberty that he came to continue, for that could not yet exist. He came to continue, under monarchical forms, the Revolution in the world; he same to contiuue it, by seating himself, a plebeian, on a throne, by bringing the pontiff to Paris to anoint a plebeian brow with the sacred oil; by creating an aristocracy with plebeians; by obliging the old aristocracies to associate themselves with his plebeian aristocracy; by making kings of plebeians; by taking to his bed the daughter of the Cæsars, and mingling plebeian blood with the blood of one of the oldest reigning families in Europe; by blending all nations; by introducing the French laws in Germany, in Italy, and in Spain; by dissolving so many spells; by mixing up together and confounding so many things. Such was the immense task which he came to perform; and meanwhile the state of society was to consolidate itself under the protection of his sword; and liberty was to follow some day."

the Archduke Charles, in consequence of which the Russian army separated from the Austrians and retired into Bavaria. Profiting by this occasion, I endeavored to conciliate the Emperor Paul; I sent him back, without exchange or ransom, five or six thousand prisoners with a complete new outfit. This was not lost: no treaty was concluded, it is true, but the Russians took no further part in the coalition, and their army soon returned to Poland. Although its force was reduced to thirty or thirty-five thousand, its retreat was nevertheless an important event. The refusal of England and Austria left me no choice; I sought peace, but they forced me into war; it was therefore necessary to prepare to prosecute it with vigor. Although European affairs fixed so much of my attention, I nevertheless neither forgot the army which I had left in Egypt, nor the maritime means necessary for its succor.

Fall of Tippoo-Saëb.—Great events had occurred in the East: at the moment that I raised the siege of St. Jean d'Acre, our ancient ally Tippoo-Saëb fell in India. As soon as the English ministry had learned the certainty of my descent in Egypt, it withdrew from the Tagus, Gibraltar, and other ports, all the disposable forces, and set sail in all haste with a corps of five thousand men for India. The Marquis of Wellesley resolved to profit, without delay, by these reënforcements to strike a decisive blow against Tippoo-Saëb so as to deprive us of the powerful support which this Mussulman warrior might afford us in the centre of Hindostan. Certain of the alliance of the Nizam, and of the neutrality of Schindiah and the Mahrattas, the sworn enemies of the Mussulman caste, the English, under Generals Harris, Stuart, and Wellesley (afterward Wellington), attacked the states of the Sultan, and, after several combats more or less disputed, laid siege to Seringapatam which was breached and taken on the third of May, 1799, after an assualt more celebrated than bloody. Tippoo, faithful to his glory, buried himself beneath the ruins of his palace, and his estates were divided between the English company and its creatures. This important and decisive blow, joined to the probable fall of Malta which had been blockaded by the English for two years, rendered the situation of our army in Egypt extremely precarious, but not yet desperate.

Maritime Affairs.—I directed Gantheaume to leave Brest and carry to Egypt reënforcements of arms and munitions. The Spanish fleet being still confined to Brest, where (it will be remembered) it had returned with Bruix, and that of Holland not yet recovered from the disaster of Camperdown, I did not see, for the moment, any thing that could be done at sea. Ireland no longer offered the same chances as formerly under the Directory; England, taking warning by the descent of General Humbert's little detachment, had concentrated there a powerful army under Lord Cornwallis : more than forty thousand men had been successively transported to Ireland, and the greater part of the insurgents, deceived by promises which were never realized, had laid down their arms. Since 1796, the affairs of St. Domingo had taken a more favorable turn : Toussaint L'Ouverture having declared, with his blacks, in favor of the Republic, reëstablished order in the culture of the fields, defeated the mulattoes, shut up the English in St. Marc, where General Maitland, despairing of success, proposed to recognize him as sovereign of Hayti. The Directory had sent Hédouville to him, but the adroit and jealous Toussaint had forced him to return to France, and in the hope of avoiding an open rupture with us, he declined the proposition of our enemies and affected the most entire devotion to the Republic. Guadaloupe supported itself with success. Martinique had for six years been in the possession of the English; the Dutch colonies of Surinam, and Essequibo, on the South American continent, had fallen into their power, as well as the island of Curaçao.

Continental Armies.—If the maritime war offered few opportunities for my activity, the continental war occupied me so much the more seriously. The army of Italy, reduced to thirty thousand active men, had taken refuge on the rocks of Genoa. Ten thousand others were guarding the Maritime-Alps, and Dauphiny. The army of the Rhine, which amounted to one hundred thousand combatants, was cantoned in Alsace and Switzerland, from Strasburg to Schaffhausen. Our troops did not venture to recross the Alps in presence of the superior forces which the enemy had collected in the basin of the Po. It was necessary for us either to enter Germany and Italy at the same time, or to strike such decisive blows on the Danube as to enable me to reconquer the peninsula, by dictating peace to Austria. It was necessary to recapture Mantua, Alexandria, and Milan, at Vienna. This was my plan.

I called in the conscripts; I caused arms to be forged; I woke up the sentiment of national honor, which had only slumbered in the breasts of Frenchmen. I collected an army, young, it is true, but full of enthusiasm. Our reverses had again lighted up the fires of civil war in La Vendée. I sent there two divisions of the army of Brune which had been so victorious in Holland. The approach of these troops and a more moderate course on the part of the government, caused the insurgents and the royalist chiefs to lay down their arms. These forces were now disposable for operations in the south of France.

Miserable as was the condition of the army of Italy, that of the Rhine, united with the army of Helvetia, was in all respects good; I gave the command of it to Moreau, sending him a sufficient number of recruits for completing his corps and enabling him to take the offensive. The remainder of my disposable troops were collected at Dijon, where I organized an army of reserve of forty thousand men which, from this central position, could march into Swabia, Switzerland, or Italy, as circumstances might require. The divisions which had just suppressed the insurrection in La Vendée, formed the nucleus of this army.

Plan of Campaign.—The possession of Switzerland gave us an opportunity to take in reverse the enemy's lines of operation in Italy and Swabia. My first thought was to leave on the defensive the army of Massena in the Apennines, and to move those of the reserve and of the Rhine into the valley of the Danube. The constitution of the year VIII. not allowing a consul to command an army in person, my intention was to give the command of the reserve to a lieutenant, and to leave the grand army to Moreau; but in following the head-quarters of the latter, I could direct the operations of both. I wished Moreau to cross at Schaffhausen, take Kray in reverse, and drive him into the angle of the Main and the Rhine, cutting him off from Vienna; in a word, effecting against the left of the Austrian general the same operation which, five years after, I effected against the right of Mack at Donawert: we might afterward march without obstacle against Austria and reconquer Italy at Vienna. But it was impossible to overcome the obstinacy of Moreau, who wished to play some brilliant part on his own account. He at first refused to command under me, if I came to his army; and he afterward objected to my plans, pretending that the passage at Schaffhausen was dangerous. I was not yet sufficiently firm in my position to come to an open rupture with a man who had numerous partisans in the army, and who only wanted the energy to attempt to put himself in my place. It was necessary to negotiate with him as a separate power, as indeed, at that time, he really was. I therefore left him the command of the finest army which

France had seen for a long time, and allowed him to move upon the Danube at his pleasure. I myself decided to conduct my conscripts by the St. Gothard into Lombardy, securing the concert of Lecourbe, as soon as Moreau should gain his first success. Our affairs in Italy at this time seemed ruined beyond hope. England was preparing to act there with an army; Naples, Tuscany, Rome, encouraged by our past reverses, might make great efforts against us.

Pius VI. and Pius VII.—In evacuating Italy, the Directory had caused Pius VI. to be removed to France. This was certainly a great error, if nothing more. They certainly could not at that time expect to transfer the Holy See into France,* and the Directory could not hope to entirely destroy its influence. The aged Pius VI. had already one foot in the grave, and he expired at Briançon, a few days after his arrival. He appointed at his death the celebrated Chiaramonte, Bishop of Imola, who was proclaimed Pope, at the beginning of 1800, under the title of Pius VII. He was an excellent pontiff, and professed for me sentiments which never belied themselves. We both regretted, more than once, that our respective positions placed us in opposition. But the Church wishes to rule . . . . it is exclusive; the policy of the Vatican has always been the same since the time of Gregory: if it has sometimes slept under moderate and philanthropic popes, still it has always woke up under the more ambitious, and Europe should never cease to watch it.

Project of the Allies on Genoa and Toulon.—England, who had never neglected an occasion to expel us from a maritime port, had concerted with Austria a project to drive us even from Genoa! General Abercrombie, after his unsuc-

---

* The transfer of the Pope to Paris by Napoleon was a different affair: Rome was then a part of his possessions, and the removal was merely a change of the Holy See from one of his capitals to another.

cessful expedition to Holland, was directed to assemble a corps of twenty thousand English at Minorca, to assist the imperialists. It is probable that the views of the cabinet of London were not confined to Liguria, and that, full of confidence in the success of the fine army of Melas, it hoped to carry the standards of the coalition even to the walls of Toulon.

Massena blockaded in Genoa.—The Austrian general, who had an army three times as numerous as that of the French, had succeeded in penetrating, April sixth, from Cairo to Savona, and in this way cutting in two our line of defense. Massena, with the right of the army, twelve thousand strong, had been obliged to shut himself up in Genoa. Melas caused this place to be invested with thirty-five thousand Austrians under Ott, while Kaim covered Piedmont, and he himself, with the remaining thirty thousand men, moved against the left of the French army commanded by Suchet. The latter, with only eight or nine thousand, pressed in front by superior forces, and constantly turned by the left, was obliged to fall back and cover himself behind the Var.

Napoleon's Plan of Operations.—The news of these events, vexatious as they were in themselves, assured me that Melas had directed his attention exclusively to the vicinity of Genoa, and would not be prepared to parry the blow which I was preparing to strike. I felt that the propitious moment had arrived for invading Italy on the side where I was least expected. But as it was necessary to hasten to the rescue of Genoa, and as the march by the St. Gothard was a long one, I resolved to attempt the St. Bernard, leaving the first of these routes to the corps which was to march from the Rhine. I set out from Dijon about the first of May.

First Operations on the Rhine.—In order to accelerate the arrival of the reënforcements which Moreau was to send me, it was necessary to wait for him to take the initiative;

his army began to move about the last of April. It was more than one hundred thousand strong, without including the garrisons of Mayence, Strasburg, and the other places of the Rhine. Kray, who was opposed to Moreau, had as large a force, but the Aulic Council had paralyzed his left by ordering it to remain in the mountains of the Voralberg. Favored by this circumstance, which secured him the superiority of disposable forces, Moreau made demonstrations by his left toward Kehl, moved with the half of his army from Bâle on Engen, and there effected a junction with Lecourbe, who had just passed the Rhine at Schaffhausen at the head of the army of Helvetia, which was to form the right wing. Kray, encamped at the sources of the Danube, near Doneschingen, instead of operating to prevent the junction, fell into the snare, and pushed his right toward Kehl. While returning, his army encountered that of Moreau at Engen, when it was too late; it was beaten on the third of May. Lecourbe contributed most to this success by carrying Stockach, a decisive point which menaced the enemy's line of retreat. Kray was not more fortunate at Moskirch, two days later, although he had been rejoined by his right wing before the arrival of Moreau's left; he now retired on Ulm in two columns; one of these was defeated at Biberach, on the eighth of May. Having sustained great losses, he took refuge in the vast intrenched camp at Ulm.

Carnot made Minister of War. — Berthier having been made commander-in-chief of the army of reserve, the portfolio of war was given temporarily to Carnot. As soon as I thought the battle of Engen had been fought, I dispatched this minister to detach twenty thousand men by the St. Gothard on the Ticino; I myself at the same time set out from Dijon for Geneva. Moreau was greatly offended at the mission of Carnot; nevertheless, after what had passed on the subject of the plan of the campaign, how could I throw myself headlong into Lombardy before being certain that the detachment would be made without some difficulty or delay?

Passage of the Alps.—On the eighth of May, I arrived at Geneva, from whence I ordered demonstrations to be made toward Dauphiny, while the columns of the army of reserve were already defiling by Lausanne toward the lower Valois. The passage of the high Alps presented many difficulties, but I knew that they were not insurmountable. I threw my principal column, thirty-five thousand strong, on the Great St. Bernard: General Chabran, with a division of four thousand men, took the road by the Little St. Bernard; General Moncey, with a corps of fifteen thousand men, detached from the army of the Rhine, received orders to descend from the St. Gothard on Belinzona; a small column under the orders of General Bethencourt was to pass the Simplon, directing itself on Domo-Dossola; finally, in order to distract the attention of the enemy and deceive him with respect to my movements, I ordered General Thureau to assemble about five thousand men, drawn from the places of Dauphiny, and to debouch on Suza by Mont Cenis and Mont Genèvre.

These well combined movements produced the most happy results. Melas, kept in uncertainty by my stay at Geneva and the demonstrations of Mont Cenis, prolongs his stay at Ventimiglia. First thinking to march with twenty thousand men into Piedmont, he now changes his opinion, and marches later with only two strong brigades. His army is distributed as follows: Wukassowich, commanding the right wing, holds the upper Ticino, at the foot of the St. Gothard; Laudon guards the debouch of the Simplon; Briey covers the valley of Aosta with three thousand men; Haddick and Kaim occupy, with twenty thousand men, the plain of Piedmont, the debouch of Ivréa, the valleys of Suza, Pignerol and Coni: the main body of the army is fighting in Liguria and on the Var. The seventeenth of May, General Lannes, who commanded my advance-guard, leaves the town of St. Pierre and marches on the Great St. Bernard. The baggage and cannon are dismounted, and the latter drawn upon troughs or pieces of timber hollowed out and fitted to receive them. My presence and the grandeur of the enterprise animate the soldiers to overcome all obstacles.*

In penetrating these gorges of the Alps I felt the most happy presentiments. The shouts of my soldiers, echoed back by the mountains, announced to me a certain victory.

---

* Thiers thus describes Napoleon's personal passage of the Alps: "The arts have represented him bounding across the snowy Alps on a fiery charger; but here is the truth unvarnished. He ascended Mount Saint Bernard in the gray great coat which he always wore, conducted by a guide of the country; displaying, in the most difficult paths, the abstraction of a mind occupied elsewhere; discoursing with the officers whom he met here and there on the road; and then at intervals conversing with the guide who accompanied him, making him talk of his life, his pleasures, and his troubles, like some idle traveler who has no better occupation. The guide, who was quite young, laid before him, with ingenuous simplicity, the particulars of his obscure life, and above all the grief he endured for want of a little money, which rendered him unable to marry one of the maidens of the valley. The First Consul, now listening to him, now questioning the passengers, with whom the mountains were alive, arrived at the hospital, where the good monks received him with great eagerness. Hardly had he alighted, before he wrote a note, which he handed to his guide, desiring him to give it without delay to the administrator of the army, who had remained on the other side of the Saint Bernard. In the evening, when the young man returned to Saint Pierre, he learned with surprise how mighty was the traveler he had conducted in the morning; and also that General Bonaparte had given him a field and house; in fact the means of marrying, and realizing all the dreams of his modest and moderate ambition. This mountaineer died recently in his own country, proprietor of the field which had been given to him by the ruler of the world.

"This singular act of benevolence, at a moment of so much preoccupation, is worthy of attention. If it had been the mere caprice of a conqueror, distributing at random good and evil, alternately crushing an empire and building up a cottage, even such a caprice were worth the recording, if it should merely be to tempt the masters of the earth to do likewise. But such an act reveals something further. The human soul, in the moment when it burns with ardent wishes, is inclined to benevolence, and does good, as it were, to merit that good which, itself, it seeks at the hands of Providence."

The First Consul halted a few minutes with the monks; thanked them for their cares toward his army; and made them a splendid gift, to be applied to the consolation of travelers and the poor.

I was returning to Italy, the theatre of my first arms. My grenadiers, after having reached the summit of the St. Bernard, threw up their caps with their red plumes into the air, and uttered shouts of joy, the ordinary precursors of victory. A halt was made at the hospice, where through my care and that of the good monks who here devote themselves to the cause of humanity, refreshments were prepared for the columns. After a short repose they gayly resumed their arms and descended the mountain, whose southern slope offered the most smiling aspect, astonishing the eye and animating the courage of my soldiers. The Alps were crossed, and we descended like a torrent into Piedmont. We were all young, generals and soldiers. We feared neither fatigues nor dangers; we cared for nothing but glory.

The Army arrested by Fort Bard.—Nevertheless, an obstacle, whose importance we had not properly estimated, was near arresting us at the very threshold of our career! The army descended the valley of the Doria, after routing, at Chatillon, a small corps of the enemy, which was too feeble to oppose our march. But on reaching the little Fort of Bard which, situated on an impregnable rock, was garrisoned by only four hundred men, we found our passage closed. It refused to surrender at our summons, and resisted all our attempts at an escalade. Lannes, with the infantry, succeeded in effecting a passage by the mountains of Albaredo; but neither horses nor cannon could pass! It was almost maddening to see one's self arrested by a mere handful of men!

I caused a new road to be cut through the rocks for my cavalry. My soldiers like those of Hannibal, debouched by a road cut out with their own hands. But if the Carthagenian general was embarrassed by his elephants, I was no less so by my cannon. Seeing no other means of extricating myself from this dangerous position, I resorted to stratagem.

VOL. I.—21.

Covering the wheels of the carriages with straw so as to prevent all noise in their movements, we drew them, in the night, while the garrison was asleep, through the streets of the faubourg directly under the guns of the fort ! This bold but perilous operation was attended with perfect success, and, full of hope, we continued our march on Ivréa.* Lannes

---

* Napoleon was still at Martigny, when the couriers of Berthier came to inform him of the difficulties of passing the little fort. "This announcement," says Thiers, "of an obstacle considered insurmountable at first made a terrible impression on him; but he recovered quickly, and refused positively to admit the possibility of a retreat. Nothing in the world should reduce him to such an extremity. He thought that if one of the loftiest mountains on the globe had failed to arrest his progress, a secondary rock could not be capable of vanquishing his courage and his genius. The fort, said he to himself, might be taken by bold courage; if it could not be taken, it still could be turned. Besides, if the infantry and the cavalry could pass by it, with but a few four-pounders, they could then proceed to Ivréa at the mouth of the gorge, and wait until their heavy guns could follow them. And if the heavy guns could not pass the obstacle which had arisen, and if, in order to get away, that of the enemy must be taken, the French infantry were brave and numerous enough to assail the Austrians and take their cannon.

"Moreover, he studied his maps again and again, questioned a number of Italian officers; and learning from these that many other roads led from Aosta to the neighboring valleys, he wrote letter after letter to Berthier, forbidding him to stop the progress of the army, and pointing out to him, with wonderful precision, what reconnoissances should be made around the fort of Bard. He would not allow himself to see any serious danger except from the arrival of a hostile corps, shutting up the debouch of Ivréa; he instructed Berthier to send Lannes as far as to Ivréa by the path of Albaredo, and make him take a strong position there, which should be safe from the Austrian artillery and cavalry. When Lannes guards the entrance of the valley, added the First Consul, whatever may happen, it is of little consequence, the only result may be loss of time. We have enough provisions to subsist ourselves awhile, and one way or other we shall succeed in avoiding or overcoming the obstacles which now delay us."

The details of the several unsuccessful attempts to carry the place are too long for insertion. The final operation is thus briefly given by Alison: "In this extremity, the genius and intrepidity of the French engineers surmounted the difficulty. The infantry and cavalry of Lannes' division traversed, one by one, the path on the Monte Albaredo, and re-formed lower down the valley, while the artillerymen succeeded in drawing their cannon, in the dark, through the town, close under the guns of the fort, by spreading straw and dung upon the streets, and wrapping the wheels up so as to prevent the slightest sound being heard. In this manner forty pieces and a hundred caissons were drawn through during the night, while the Austrians, in unconscious security, slumbered above,

had already taken this place, and driven the Austrians on Romano. There were only three thousand of the enemy in the valley of Aosta, at the time of our passage; but more than thirty thousand were scattered in the valleys of the Ticino and the Po.

Melas is deceived.—Melas had not comprehended my manœuvres. On learning that the army of reserve was marching toward Genoa, he imagined that our only object was to make some demonstration toward the north of Piedmont, in order to turn his attention from Genoa and relieve Massena and Suchet. He deemed it merely necessary to detach from Ventimiglia on Turin, a corps of seven thousand men. However, he soon followed himself at the head of another division, leaving Ott to besiege Genoa with twenty-five thousand men, and Elsnitz to cover the Var with eighteen thousand more. Still thinking that we were merely making a diversion, and deceived by Thureau's attack on Suza the twenty-second of May, Melas sent Kaim from Turin to oppose this little column, and moreover assigned to him the greater part of the reënforcements which he had brought from Nice; he marched, on the twenty-fourth of May, to Savigliano. He thus had, to oppose the sixty thousand men I was leading

---

beside their loaded cannon, directed straight into the street where the passage was going forward. A few grenades and combustibles were merely thrown at random over the ramparts during the gloom, which killed a considerable number of the French engineers, and blew up several of their ammunition wagons, but without arresting for a moment the passage. Before daylight a sufficient number were passed to enable the advanced guard to continue its march, and an obstacle which might have proved the ruin of the whole enterprise was effectually overcome. During the succeeding night the same hazardous operation was repeated with equal success; and while the Austrian commander was writing to Melas that he had seen thirty-five thousand men and four thousand horses cross the path of the Albaredo, but that not one piece of artillery or caisson should pass beneath the guns of his fortress, the whole cannon and ammunition of the army were safely proceeding on the road to Ivréa. The fort of Bard itself held out till the fifth of June, and we have the authority of Napoleon for the assertion that if the passage of the artillery had been delayed till its fall, all hope of success in the campaign was at an end."

into Lombardy, only eighteen thousand scattered in three corps under Wukassowich, Laudon and Haddick.

I reached Ivréa the very day that Melas was at Savigliano. Chabran was left to continue the siege of Fort Bard. Thureau, after forcing the pass of Suza, established himself at Bussolino, whence he could menace Turin; Moncey, descending from the St. Gothard, penetrated into the Italian bailiwicks; Bethencourt moved against Fort Arona. My plan developed itself majestically, and the enemy was still ignorant of it!

Combat of Chiusella.—General Haddick had marched from Turin on the Chiusella, where he received the troops driven by Lannes from Ivréa; these forces together formed a corps of ten thousand men. Lannes attacked him on the twenty-second, forced the bridge of Chiusella, and threw the enemy on Chivasso. He entered here the next day, and Haddick retired to Turin and rejoined Melas.

Napoleon marches on Milan.—I had pushed my advanced-guard on Chivasso merely to make the enemy believe that Turin was my object; but I took good care not to move in that direction. To secure the execution of my projects, which tended to nothing less than to seize all the communications of the Austrians, it was absolutely necessary to manœuvre on Milan: this was a thunder-clap that would act on the opinion of the people of Italy, and strike terror into the enemy's army, at the same time that it accelerated my reunion with the fifteen thousand men whom Moncey was conducting from the army of the Rhine. I marched from Ivréa by Santhia, Vercelli, and Novara toward the Ticino.

Passage of the Ticino.—The advanced-guard under Lannes, now the rear-guard, masked my movement by marching by Crescentino, Trino, and Mortara on Pavia. The new advanced-guard, commanded by General Murat, forced the passage of the Ticino at Turbigo, on the thirty-first. General Laudon had assembled some troops for the defense of this river ; but he was beaten and lost fifteen hundred men *hors-de-combat.* General Wukassowich, hastening from the upper valley of the Ticino to his assistance, arrived too late, and merely had time to save himself on the Adda. The Austrians threw two thousand men into the castle of Milan, and fell back to the number of six thousand, to the banks of the Mincio. I entered Milan on the second of June.

Dispositions of Melas.—Melas, not yet knowing the character of the army to which he was opposed, at first thought of passing the Po at Casale, in order to attack me in rear ; but on learning from Haddick and Wukassowich that I had at least sixty thousand men in Lombardy, he renounced the plan, and thought it necessary to draw to himself the forty thousand men of Ott and Elsnitz before hazarding a battle. Elsnitz had been left at the Var with seventeen thousand men, and having, in spite of his superiority in number, been unable to force the position of Suchet on the right of that river, received orders to retreat so as to gain the head of the valley of the Tanaro, and to descend as far as Asti. Ott was directed either to close the affair with Massena immediately, or to raise the siege of Genoa, repass the Bochetta, and fly to the defense of the Po toward Placentia. The retrograde movement of Elsnitz begun on the twenty-eighth of May. Suchet, whose corps had been increased by reënforcements to twelve thousand men, closely followed him to the Tanaro, and by skilful manœuvres against his right, anticipated him at the Col-de-Tende, cut his centre, and subjected him to a loss of eight thousand men *hors-de-combat.* The following days Suchet, advancing by Finale on Savona, marched to the assistance of Genoa, but was too late.

Surrender of Genoa.—Massena capitulated on the fifth of June, after sustaining a close blockade and a horrible famine for *sixty days*. After the third of May he had several conferences with General Ott, when the latter received orders to make him a *bridge of gold* if he would surrender immediately, or to raise the siege, should he appear disposed to prolong it. This incident spared Massena from resorting to the act of desperation, upon which he had decided, rather than to surrender a prisoner of war. He had resolved to throw himself into Tuscany at the head of his famished column; the orders of Melas spared him this. The eight thousand men still remaining of the French garrison, obtained free egress; but only six thousand rejoined Suchet in the environs of Savona. Ott, proud of his conquest, hastened to throw a strong garrison into Genoa, repass the Bochetta, and march by the valley of the Scrivia on Tortona, with the intention of disputing our passage of the Po; but he was too late, for a double passage had been effected at the same time, on the sixth of June, by Lannes, at San-Cipriano, and Murat at Nocetto, near Placentia, after having easily defeated the detachments sent to oppose them.

Passage of the Po.—Matters were now hastening to a crisis. I had already established myself on the enemy's rear; but he could yet escape by the right bank of the Po by descending as far as Borgo-Forte, opposite Mantua. It was therefore necessary to cut off this last resource. I decided to cross the river with the division of Watrin, Chambarlhac, Gardanne, Monnier, Boudet, and the cavalry of Murat, forming a total of thirty thousand men; the remainder were charged with securing my own communications with Switzerland and guarding the left bank of the Po. The division of Chabran, made disposable by the capitulation of Fort Bard, moved to Vercelli, and occupied Ivréa, Chivos, Crescentino, and Trino. Bethencourt continued to blockade Arona; Moncey remained in the Milanais. One of his divisions was posted at Pavia, another blockaded the castle of

Milan, and the third occupied Crema and Brescia, so as to check the Austrian troops which were posted on the Mincio. The division of Loison blockaded Pizzighettone and the Castle of Placentia, observed the Lower Po, and covered the rear of my army. I confess that this position was too much disseminated, and that the attempt to envelop Melas by wishing to cover all was a little hazardous. It had been more wise to unite fifteen thousand men on Tortona, because, if Melas had defiled upon the Mincio by Milan, I should nevertheless have conquered all Italy by a single march, and by uniting myself to Massena, have had no further need of my communications by the St. Bernard: but success intoxicates, and I wished all or nothing. Moreover I had hoped that Massena would hold out some days longer, and that, debouching by Tortona, we should be able to form a junction by Novi.

Battle of Montebello.—It has just been said that the corps of Ott marched in all haste from Genoa to take part in the defense of the Po: he could not arrive in time, and only reached Montebello, where he encountered the corps of Lannes. Being very desirous to reach Placentia, and thinking that he had to oppose only a detachment of my army, Ott precipitated himself upon the burg of Casteggio, contrary to all the principles of war; concentration being now his only hope, all partial combats were to be avoided by the Austrians. Lannes received the enemy at the head of the division of Watrin and Chambarlhac; he even took the offensive, in order to turn him by the heights which commanded this burg and all the country to the Po. The Austrians fought with intrepidity; victory was doubtful, when the arrival of Victor with the division of Gardanne decided the battle in our favor. The enemy with both his wings turned, was completely defeated, his centre, driven to the bridge of Casteggio, was overthrown: he lost six cannon, five thousand prisoners, and three thousand killed and wounded. Ott threw two thousand men into the citadel of Tortona and fell back on Alexandria, where Melas was concentrating his forces. This event was of the greatest importance, inasmuch as it diminished the enemy's forces by eight thousand men at the very moment when he was obliged to effect a passage, and animated the courage of my soldiers on the eve of a decisive battle.

Battle of Marengo.—I continued my march on Alexandria. The twelfth of March we passed the Scrivia and debouched into the plain of San Giuliano. A rear-guard left by Ott at Marengo was routed by the division of Gardanne and obliged to repass the Bormida. I placed my army in echelons on the road from Tortona to Alexandria. The division of Gardanne established itself at Pedrabona, opposite the *tête-du-pont* which the Austrians had preserved on the Bormida. It was supported by Victor with the division of Chambarlhac at Marengo, and by Kellerman's* brigade of cavalry. In

---

* Kellerman (François-Etienne) was born at Metz in 1772. He was the son of François Christophe Kellerman, the victor of Valmy. In 1790, he was attached to the French Embassy to the United States of America, and returned to France in 1793. In 1797, he served with Napoleon in Italy and was adjutant-general; he distinguished himself at the passage of the Tagliamento and, as a reward for his bravery, was sent to Paris with the colors captured on that occasion; he was also promoted to the rank of brigadier-general. He also distinguished himself in Italy in the campaign of 1799. In 1800 he crossed the Alps with Napoleon and commanded a brigade of cavalry under Murat, which at the battle of Marengo numbered four hundred and seventy men. In the first period of this battle his command had greatly suffered and was reduced to two hundred and fifty men when Bonaparte ordered him to be reenforced with one hundred and fifty more. With this force he greatly distinguished himself in the final attack, and his brilliant charge contributed greatly toward the victory of Marengo. He was immediately promoted to the rank of general-of-division and joined the army of Brune with the command of three brigades of heavy cavalry. In 1805 he commanded a division under Bernadotte, and was wounded at the battle of Austerlitz. In 1808 he served in Portugal, but the operations here were unfortunate, and he concluded to sign the famous treaty of Cintra. In 1809 he succeeded Bessières in the command of Northern Spain. In 1813 he distinguished himself at the battle of Lutzen, and was wounded, on the eve of the battle of Bautzen. He also served with credit in 1814. On the return of Napoleon from

rear of Victor was Lannes, deployed near San Giuliano with the division of Watrin and Champeaux' brigade of cavalry. Finally the division of Monnier formed the last echelon at Torre-di-Gafaralo. Rivaud's brigade of cavalry, posted at Sale, observed the lower Tanaro and the Po on the right of the army. On our left I sent General Desaix with the division of Boudet to Rivalta, in order to prevent the enemy from defiling by his right toward Novi. Desaix was in this way to endeavor to secure communications with the army of Italy, which was descending the valley of the Bormida by Dego on Aqui. I thought that I might safely do this, as the enemy, from his indifference in the defense of the plain of San Giuliano, seemed not to wish a battle, and on the contrary was seeking so to manœuvre as to fall back on Genoa, and afterward gain Parma and Modena. Moreover I was deceived by the false information of a spy whom I believed in our interest, but who, it appeared, was acting a double part. This error came near costing me dear.

Melas had not finished assembling his army till the thirteenth. The next morning at break of day he passed the Bormida at the head of thirty-five thousand men, and attacked us with vigor. The division of Gardanne was forced to retreat: Victor rallied it to the right of the division of Chambarlhac, which formed a line from the village of Marengo to the Bormida. General Haddick, with the right of the Austrians, deployed in two lines opposite the position of Victor; Kaim, who formed their centre, placed himself obliquely to the left of Haddick; Ott was thrown on Castel-Ceriolo; the reserve under the orders of Elsnitz remained in rear of the right, on the road from Marengo to Alexandria;

Elba he joined the standard of his former general and was appointed to the chamber of Peers. At the opening of the campaign he received a command in the army, and again fought with great bravery at the head of the fourth corps of cavalry. On the second restoration of the Bourbons he was eliminated from the chamber of Peers.

but two thirds of his cavalry was most untimely detached to the south of Alexandria on the road to Aqui to observe Suchet and Massena.

We were not prepared to receive battle. I hasten to arrange my echelons in such a way that they may sustain themselves, and to recall Desaix from Rivalta on San Giuliano. At ten o'clock in the morning, I am obliged to push forward Lannes, and put him in line at the right of Victor, whose flank Kaim is preparing to turn. Victor defends with vigor the passage of the rivulet of Barbotta, which runs to Marengo: a murderous and well-sustained fire is kept up on both sides: the Austrians sustain considerable loss; Melas engages half of the cavalry of reserve which remained after his foolish detachment. This isolated brigade is precipitated into the marshy rivulet, and the enemy, who had double the number of cavalry, sees himself from the beginning of the action deprived of the aid of that arm at the very moment when it might decide the victory. Lannes succeeds in resisting the attack of the enemy's centre; but in the mean time Ott having passed beyond Castel-Ceriolo, and assisted by the cavalry of the centre under the orders of Frimont threatens to take our right in reserve. I oppose to him my grenadiers of the guard. These eight hundred brave men advance into the plain between Castel-Ceriolo and Villa-Nova and form there a square like an impregnable redoubt, against which are spent the reiterated efforts of the Austrian squadrons. Profiting by the glorious resistance of this troop of the *élite*, I direct on Castel-Ceriolo five battalions of Monnier's division, in order to expel the light infantry of the enemy. Unfortunately, a vigorous charge of the Austrians on the left of the division while on march, separates General Monnier from his troops, forces him to throw himself toward Lannes, compels the brigade of the left to retreat, and obliges that of Cara

St. Cyr to follow the movement of the line, at the moment when his tirailleurs are penetrating into Castel-Ceriolo.

Nevertheless the instantaneous occupation of this village gives a *point-d'appui* to my right and reëstablishes my affairs on this wing. But on the other wing we are less fortunate: Victor, after having resisted the enemy for several hours, can sustain himself no longer; his left yields and loses the support of the Bormida; his centre is pierced, and his entire corps is driven back on San Giuliano. The defeats of the left exposes the flank of Lannes and forces him to retreat; he effects this in good order across the plain in the direction of La Ghilina.

Already the Austrians utter shouts of victory. My generals, Berthier in particular, think the battle decidedly lost. Desaix and myself do not yet despair. This general advances rapidly on San Giuliano; the six thousand fresh troops which he brings me, can, under such a chief, effect miracles. I direct my whole attention to prolonging the movement of retreat on the left, in order to gain time for Desaix to arrive on the field of battle. The enemy, after a short halt, advance with new vivacity; but the want of cavalry which had been foolishly directed against Suchet and Massena, prevents him from profiting by the advantages of his position; if a part of his cavalry could be thrown against Victor it would complete the rout of the army, and decide the victory against us.

At last, near five o'clock in the afternoon, Desaix debouches from San Giuliano, and forms in advance of this village; Lannes establishes himself obliquely between the right of Desaix and Villa-Nova; the square of my guard connects its right with Castel-Ceriolo. The cavalry of Champeaux forms in rear of Desaix, and that of Kellerman in rear of the interval between Desaix and Lannes. Victor endeavors to assemble his battalions in rear and to the left of Desaix. The enemy advances, extending his line on both flanks. His left, under Ott, already reaches Villa-Nova ; his centre, after making a halt at the high ground of Guasca, directs its course on San Giuliano, and the right debouches from Cassina Grosa. Melas thinks himself so certain of victory that he goes to Alexandria to dispatch the news of my defeat to Vienna and Genoa, while his chief-of-staff, Zach, is to advance in column by the great road to Tortona to gather the fruits of victory. The latter has so little doubt of his success, that he marches by echelons separated by considerable intervals. The first, composed of five thousand men of the *élite*, which he conducts in person, is followed at the distance of a quarter of a league by three other corps under Kaim, Bellegarde, and Elsnitz. At the moment when the head of the column reaches San Giuliano, my artillery of reserve is unmasked and pours in its deadly volleys ; at the same time Desaix attacks with impetuosity ; unfortunately, one of the first balls strikes this brave man in the centre of his breast, and deprives France of one of her ablest defenders, and me of one of my dearest companions in arms. Our troops, exasperated at the death of their illustrious chief, redouble their efforts. Our enemies, who thought victory certain, are staggered by these attacks. Kellerman*

---

* The English translator of the American edition of Thiers' History of Napoleon, makes this Kellerman the same as the one that gained the victory of Valmy, and, to do this, makes an incorrect translation of Thiers' remarks on this affair. He then adds in his notes: "He (Kellerman) was the *real winner* of the battle of Marengo, changing it by a single charge of cavalry from a rout to a victory. For this Napoleon never forgave him." Again he contradicts Thiers in saying that Napoleon recompensed *all* his generals for their services at Marengo, and says, "He (Napoleon) did *not* recompense Kellerman. No other officer of his distinction but was made marshal of France far earlier than he. It has been always stated, heretofore, that after Desaix's fall, Zach's men were rallied, had assumed the offensive, and that the French foot were again in disorder, when Kellerman charged, *without orders*, and retrieved the fight."

Alison makes a similar statement to the above, and then remarks, "United with the great qualities of Napoleon's character, was a selfish thirst for glory, and consequent jealousy of any one who had either effectually thwarted his designs, or rendered him such services as might diminish the lustre of his own

seizes the moment to charge them in flank with four squadrons. The column is broken, the head, crushed and surrounded, surrenders. Profiting by this advantage our troops

exploits. His undying jealousy of Wellington !!!! was an indication of his first weakness, his oblivion of Kellerman's inappreciable services are instances of the second. * * * The obligation was too great to be forgiven. Kellerman was not promoted like the other generals, and never afterward enjoyed the favor of the chief on whose brow he placed the diadem."

Any one at all familiar with French history must be forced to smile at the innumerable absurdities into which these two writers have been carried by their English prejudices; the American, however, will feel mortified to see such absurd notes attached by the *English* editor of the *American* edition of so impartial and generally correct history as that of Thiers; and he will be not a little astonished, upon examining the original text, to find it has been incorrectly translated so as to make it support one of the foregoing statements respecting Kellerman. The passage we allude to is this, "*The brave Kellerman, who this day added much to the glory of Valmy, attached* to his name, dashed upon the squadrons," &c. This is made to read in the *Anglo*-American edition, "The brave Kellerman, who, on this day added so greatly to the glory *he had won at Valmy*, dashed," &c. Thiers, translated in this way, is made to support statements which he is very far from doing in the original.

The elder Kellerman, to whom the translator of Thiers here alludes, was not at the battle of Marengo, but for his victory of Valmy, won while Napoleon was a mere captain, Napoleon made him a marshal of France among the very first that were made. *No one* was made marshal "earlier than he." The younger Kellerman, his son, never was made marshal. The charge of Napoleon having neglected him is absurd. For his services in 1797 he made him a brigadier-general, and honored him with the colors taken at the passage of the Tagliamento. In 1800, the cavalry was commanded by Murat, and consisted of the three brigades of Rivaud, Champeaux, and Kellerman, that of the latter being much the smallest one. For his valuable services on the field of Marengo, he was made a general-of-division, and attached to the army of Brune, with the command of three brigades, numbering two thousand one hundred. Rivaud was also made a general-of-division, but his command was not increased to the same degree as that of Kellerman. Champeaux was killed at Marengo.

Kellerman did good service at Marengo for which he deserved and received great credit. But it is absurd to call him the "*real winner*" of the battle. On this subject Thiers very justly remarks: "Some detractors have sought to attribute to General Kellerman, the gaining of the battle of Marengo, and consequently all the results which this memorable day brought in its train. But if General Bonaparte is to be despoiled of the glory of that day, why not attribute it to that noble victim of the happiest inspiration, to that Desaix, who, divining the orders of his chief before he had received them, brought him the two-fold offering of the victory and of his life? Why not attribute it again to that intrepid defender of Genoa, who, by detaining the Austrians on the Apennines, gave General Bonaparte time to descend from the Alps, and handed them over to him already

push forward. Kellerman leaves it to the infantry to collect the prisoners, and advances against the division of Kaim, who is following Zach a quarter of a league in rear; the

half defeated? So speaking, Generals Kellerman, Desaix, Massena, could all be the true conquerors of Marengo! all except General Bonaparte! But in this world, it is by the voice of the people that glory is decreed; and it was by the voice of the people that he was proclaimed conqueror of Marengo, who, discovering by the glance of genius, what advantage might be taken of the upper Alps to burst down upon the Austrian rear, had, during three whole months, deceived their vigilance; who had brought into existence an army which had before no being; who had astounded Europe by the miracle of that creation; who had crossed the Saint Bernard without any beaten road; who had swooped suddenly upon the midst of startled Italy; who had surrounded his unfortunate adversary with unequaled art; who had, to sum the whole, delivered a decisive battle, which if lost in the morning, was gloriously recovered in the evening. And certainly, had it not been won that night, it would have been on the ensuing morning; for independent of the six thousand men of Desaix's division, the ten thousand men from the Ticino, and the ten thousand posted on the lower Po, presented infallible means for the destruction of the enemy's army. Let us suppose a case. Let us suppose that the Austrians, conquerors on the fourteenth of June, had entangled themselves in the gorge of the Stradella, that they had found at Placentia, Generals Duhesme and Loison, with ten thousand men to dispute the passage of the Po, with General Bonaparte in their rear, reënforced by Generals Desaix and Moncey—what would these Austrians have done in this narrow gorge, blocked by a well-defended river, pursued by a superior army? They would but have experienced a disaster more serious than on the plains of Bormida. The true conqueror of Marengo, therefore, is he who mastered fortune by a series of combinations, admirable for their depth and power, unequaled in the history of mightiest captains.

What shall we say, then, more? He was well served by his lieutenants. Nor is it needful to detract from any glory to make his shine the brighter. Massena, by his heroic defense of Genoa; Desaix, by his most fortunate determination; Lannes, by his matchless firmness on the plain of Marengo; Kellerman, by his admirable charge of cavalry—all contributed to secure his triumph. He recompensed them all in the most striking manner; as for Desaix, he embalmed his fate with the most honorable regrets. The First Consul ordered the most magnificent honors to be done to the man who had performed for France services so important; he took every care of his military family, placing near his own person his two aids-de-camp, who were left without employment by the death of their master; these were Colonels Rapp and Savary.

The following personal narrative of Desaix's aid-de-camp, afterward Duke of Rovigo, would seem to put this question beyond a doubt. "It was now about three o'clock, very few musket shots were fired, the two armies were manœuvring, and preparing for a last effort. General Desaix's division occupied the point which came nearest in contact with the enemy, who were advancing in close, deep columns along the road from Alexandria to Tortona, leaving the

same disorder is carried here by a brilliant and timely charge of the cavalry. The Austrians, in consternation, beat a retreat. In vain their reserve attempts to sustain itself at

latter town on their left. They had nearly come up to us, and we were only separated by a vineyard lined by the ninth light infantry, and a small corn-field, which the Austrians were entering. We were not more than a hundred paces apart, and could distinguish each other's features. The Austrian column halted on perceiving Desaix's division, the position of which became so unexpectedly known to them. The direction of its march would infallibly bring it upon the centre of our first line. It was no doubt endeavoring to ascertain our strength previously to opening its fire. The position was becoming every moment more critical. 'You see how matters stand,' said Desaix to me; 'I can no longer put off the attack without danger of being myself attacked under disadvantageous circumstances; if I delay I shall be beaten, and I have no relish for that. Go then in all haste and apprise the First Consul of the embarrassment I experience; tell him I can not wait any longer; that I am without cavalry, and that he must direct a bold charge to be made upon the flank of that column, while I shall charge it in front.'

"I set off at full gallop, and overtook the First Consul, who was causing the troops placed to the right of the village of Marengo to execute the change of front which he had directed along the whole line. I delivered my message to him, and after listening to it with attention, he reflected a moment, and addressed me in these words: 'Have you well examined the column?' 'Yes, General' (he went by this title at the time I speak of). 'Is it very numerous?' 'Extremely so, General.' 'Is Desaix uneasy about it?' 'He only appeared uneasy as to the consequences that might result from hesitation. I must add his having particularly desired I should tell you that it was useless to send any other orders than that he should attack or retreat—one or the other; and the latter movement would be at least as hazardous as the first.'

"'If this be the case,' said the First Consul, 'let him attack; I shall go in person to give him the order. You will repair yonder (pointing to a black spot in the plain), and there find General Kellerman, who is in command of that cavalry you now see; tell him what you have just communicated to me; and desire him to charge the enemy without hesitation as soon as Desaix shall commence his attack. You will also remain with him, and point out the spot through which Desaix is to debouch: for Kellerman does not even know that he is with the army.'

"I obeyed and found Kellerman at the head of about six hundred troopers, the residue of the cavalry which had been constantly engaged the whole day. I gave him the order from the First Consul. I had scarcely delivered my message when a fire of musketry was heard to proceed from the left of the village of Marengo; it was the opening attack of General Desaix. He rapidly bore down with the ninth light regiment upon the head of the Austrian column; the latter feebly sustained the charge; but its defeat was dearly purchased, our general having fallen at the very first firing. He was riding in the rear of the ninth regiment, when a shot pierced his heart; he fell at the very moment when he

Marengo : nothing can resist the impetuosity of our soldiers. The enemy retreats across the Bormida in the greatest disorder, leaving in our hands eight colors, twenty cannon, and

was deciding the victory in our favor. Kellerman had put himself in motion as soon as he heard the firing. He rushed upon that formidable column, penetrated it from left to right, and broke it into several bodies. Being assailed in front, and its flanks forced in, it dispersed, and was closely pursued as far as Bormida.

"The large masses of troops that were in pursuit of our left no sooner perceived this defeat than they retreated, and attempted to reach the bridge in front of Alexandria; but the corps of Generals Lannes and Gardanne had accomplished their movement: those masses had no longer any communication with each other, and were compelled to lay down their arms.

"The battle, which until midday had turned against us, was completely won at six o'clock.

"As soon as the Austrian column was dispersed I quitted General Kellerman's cavalry, and was returning to meet General Desaix, whose troops were debouching in my view, when the colonel of the ninth light regiment informed me that he had been killed. I was at the distance of only a hundred paces from the spot where I had left him. I hastened to it, and found the general stretched upon the ground completely stripped of his clothes, and surrounded by other naked bodies. I recognized him, notwithstanding the darkness, owing to the thickness of his hair, which still retained its tie.

"I had been too long attached to his person to suffer his body to remain on this spot, where it would have been indiscriminately buried with the rest.

"I removed a cloak from under the saddle of a horse lying dead at a short distance, and wrapped General Desaix's body in it, with the assistance of a hussar, who had strayed on the field of battle, and joined me in the performance of this mournful duty. He consented to lay it across his horse, and to lead the animal by the bridle as far as Gorrofolo, while I should go to communicate the misfortune to the First Consul, who desired me to follow him to Gorrofolo, where I gave him an account of what had taken place. He approved what I had done, and ordered the body to be carried to Milan for the purpose of being embalmed.

" Being only an aid-de-camp to General Desaix at the battle of Marengo, my personal observations were limited to what the duties of that situation enabled me to see; whatever else I have mentioned was related to me by the First Consul, who felt a pleasure in recurring to the events of this action, and often did me the honor to tell me what deep uneasiness it had given him until the moment when Kellerman executed the charge, which wholly altered its aspect.

"Since the fall of the Imperial government some pretended friends of General Kellerman have presumed to claim for him the merit of originating the charge of cavalry. That general, whose share of glory is sufficiently brilliant to gratify his most sanguine wishes, can have no knowledge of so presumptuous a pretension. I the more readily acquit him, from the circumstance that, as we were conversing one day respecting that battle, I called to his mind my having brought to him the First Consul's orders, and he appeared not to have forgotten that fact. I am far from suspecting his friends of the design of lessening the glory of either

six thousand prisoners. General Ott, who, in the mean time, has advanced to Chilina, thinks himself fortunate in regaining Castel-Ceriolo already occupied by our tirailleurs, and at last, with difficulty, reaches the *tête-du-pont* of the Bormida.

Convention of Alexandria.—This was truly a great victory, and it could not fail to produce incalculable results. As General Bonaparte or General Desaix: they know as well as myself, that there are names so respected that they can never be affected by such detraction; and that it would be as vain to dispute the praise due to the chief who planned the battle, as to attempt to depreciate the brilliant share which General Kellerman had in its successful result. I will add to the above a few reflections.

"From the position which he occupied General Desaix could not see General Kellerman: he had even desired me to request the First Consul to afford him the support of some cavalry. Neither could General Kellerman, from the point where he was stationed, perceive General Desaix's division: it is even probable that he was not aware of the arrival of that general, who had only joined the army two days before. Both were ignorant of each other's position, which the First Consul was alone acquainted with; he alone could introduce harmony into their movements; he alone could make their efforts respectively conduce to the same object.

"The fate of the battle was decided by Kellerman's bold charge: had it, however, been made previously to General Desaix's attack in all probability it would have had a quite different result. Kellerman appears to have been convinced of it, since he allowed the Austrian column to cross our field of battle, and extend its front beyond that of the troops we had still in line, without making the least attempt to impede its progress. The reason of Kellerman's not charging it sooner was, that it was too serious a movement, and the consequences of failure would have been irretrievable; that charge, therefore, could only enter into a general combination of plans to which he was necessarily a stranger."

Alison, in support of his false account of this affair, refers to Jomini, Napoleon's Memoirs, Dumas, Savary, and Bulow, not one of whom confirms his statements, which have no higher authority than the petty lies of Bourrienne, the scandal circulated in the saloons of Paris and collected by the gossiping Duchess d'Abrantes, or by Alison's esteemed friend, "*Captain Basil Hall.*" Directly opposed to these are the positive statements of the generals who fought on the field of Marengo, and of all the continental historians of acknowledged authority.

Napoleon's *jealousy* of Kellerman is too absurd to merit serious attention! Did he show this in promoting him from his insignificant command at Marengo to the rank of general-of-division, and afterward general-in-chief of a *corps-d'armée*, and by loading his family with favors? In return Kellerman served him faithfully through his whole career. He was a brave man, but his generalship can in no way be compared with that of Soult, Massena, Davoust, Suchet, Desaix, Kleber, Ney, Lannes, Oudinot, Eugene Beauharnois, Macdonald, Victor, and of many others that might be named.

Melas still had an army as numerous as our divisions which were present at Marengo, he might resume the combat the next day; but if defeated, he must pass beneath the Caudine Forks and surrender at discretion. Having a bridge across the Po at Casale, it has been said that he ought to have taken advantage of it to throw himself on the left bank, and attempt to force his way by Milan and Brescia on Mantua. This might have been very well if he had been certain of repelling Chabran and Moncey; but should these succeed in checking the heads of the Austrian columns in the low grounds of Lombardy, where the troops could move only on the causeways and dykes, would I not have had time enough to pursue him, and force him to surrender? In the direction of Genoa his chances were scarcely any better: Suchet, already at Aqui, could prevent the execution of such a project. The Austrian general was obliged to choose one of two courses—either to attack me again at Marengo, or to surrender to me the fortresses of Italy, and save to his master his army of sixty thousand men; the first was the most glorious, but the second the most certain and prudent; he would surrender fortresses which did not belong to Austria, and preserve a fine army.

The next day after the battle, Melas sent me a messenger to treat for a convention. I seized with joy this opportunity to secure, without further bloodshed, the greater part of Italy: I gave Melas permission to retire with his army to the Mincio; in return he surrendered to me the fortresses of Coni, Alexandria, and Genoa, Fort Urbino, the citadels of Tortona, Milan, Turin, Pizzighettone, Placentia, Ceva, and Savona, and the Castle of Arona. The armistice of Alexandria was shortly afterward extended to the army of Germany. Moreau, rendered more circumspect by the large detachment under Moncey, had skirmished for a month around Ulm and the intrenched camp; but, at last convinced of his superiority over Kray, he began, about the middle of June, to manœuvre to deprive the enemy of the advantages of this camp; he passed the Lech, the right in advance, took possession of Augsburg, completed his change of front to establish himself in battle array on the right bank of the Danube, and to threaten Kray's communications with Vienna: this manœuvre was a good one, and proved completely successful. The French army did not stop here, but crossed the Danube at Hochstedt, revenged, in these plains, the defeat of the French army under Tallard and Marsin, and beat the left and reserve of Kray, who was obliged to retreat to the Iser. Moreau anticipated him at Munich, and made him change his course to the Inn, where a convention, signed at Parsdorf, also put an end to hostilities in this direction.

I had reason to hope that the reverses of Austria would dispose her to treat for peace. Even from the battle-field of Marengo, I had charged St. Julien as a bearer of pacific messages to the cabinet of Vienna, giving it to understand that I was ready to treat on the same conditions as at Campo-Formio. Although my brilliant victory had not yet carried me to the Noric Alps as in 1797, still the army of the Rhine was in a much more threatening attitude than at that epoch.

Negotiations of General St. Julien.—The cabinet of Vienna sent back M. St. Julien with a letter of credence from the emperor himself, which caused me to give faith to whatever he said. The intention of his government was to negotiate in concert with England, with which power it had concluded a treaty of subsidy two days before hearing of the disaster of Marengo. The situation was embarrassing, and, in fact, to treat separately eight days after such a transaction, would have been a felony. General St. Julien having delivered his letters, I proved to him the advantages that must result to his court from treating without loss of time; for I could not consent to any delay, without requiring the strongest guarantees, inasmuch as our victories in all directions would enable me to continue operations with success; every week's delay would therefore cost Austria a fortress or a province. This officer, consulting the military interest rather than the diplomatic position of his cabinet, signed, on the twenty-fifth of July, the preliminaries of the same basis as the treaty of Campo-Formio. Duroc was sent with him to Vienna to obtain the ratification.

Disapproval of the Cabinet of Vienna.—Thugut, furious that his envoy had gone further than he wished, exiled him to Transylvania, and rejected the preliminaries, at the same time signifying his readiness to continue the negotiations in concert with the English; for in the mean time Lord Minto, the English ambassador at Vienna, had declared that his cabinet was disposed to negotiate for the common interests of the two courts. Although, under the circumstances, this resolution seemed natural enough, still I felt indignant at it, because the emperor's letter was of a character to make it binding upon his government to abide by the engagements entered into by his envoy;* because these engagements were of themselves moderate; because the intervention of England was intended to protract negotiations at a time when delay was far more advantageous to them than to me; finally, because I was unwilling to connect the cause of Austria with that of England. I therefore ordered Moreau and Brune to immediately denounce the armistice both in Italy and Germany.

Negotiations for a Naval and Military Armistice.—This had its effect at Vienna. The cabinet felt the necessity of peace; on the other side I did not wish to decline it simply because of a breach of forms, and, moreover, I had commenced

---

* The emperor's letter stated, "You will give credit to every thing which Count St. Julien shall say on my part, and I will ratify whatever he shall do."

negotiations at London by Otto for a naval armistice. I wished to gain a double advantage from my victories on the Inn and the Mincio : to obtain, on the one hand, a naval armistice which would allow me to send some frigates to Egypt and Malta with arms, men, and munitions ; and, on the other, to require Austria to give up to me the places of Ulm, Ingolstadt, and Philipsbourg. Austria consented to it ; the armistice was signed at Hohenlinden the twentieth of September, and confirmed at Castiglione for the army of Italy. England was unwilling to admit a naval armistice, in hopes that Malta, which had been closely blockaded for two years, would soon fall into her hands, and that she might prevent any reënforcements from being sent to Egypt for the purpose of consolidating our position there.

Kleber proposes to evacuate Egypt.—In fact an event had just occurred in the East which might have important consequences. After my departure from Egypt, General Kleber, looking at the dark side of things, had denounced me to the Directory. When his letter reached Paris I was at the head of the government ! I did not deem it necessary for Bonaparte the *first consul* to avenge the quarrels of Bonaparte *the general*. I answered Kleber by encouragements. In the mean time the Vizier Mehmed-Pacha, convinced that he had only to present himself to gain the victory, advanced on El-Arisch with fifty thousand men. Kleber proposed to him to evacuate Egypt, which the Turks eagerly accepted. But the English, hearing that this treaty was in full course of execution and that most of the forts had already been surrendered to the Ottoman troops, now thought best to refuse its ratification, although it had been negotiated in concert with Admiral Sidney Smith. They did not doubt but that Egypt would be entirely occupied by the Turks before their refusal would be received, and that our army, compelled to embark, would easily fall into their hands. This Machiavellic calculation turned to the confusion of its authors.

Victory of Heliopolis.—Kleber had committed a manifest imprudence; he felt the necessity of repairing his fault by victory, and, on the twentieth of March, he moved against the Vizier who was advancing on Heliopolis. In less than four hours he completely routed the Turkish army, drove it into the desert with a loss of ten thousand men, and returned in triumph to Cairo, which place had momentarily been in possession of a Turkish corps. The Vizier revenged himself for this defeat by basely procuring the assassination of his conqueror, on the very day of our victory at Marengo. The victory of Heliopolis would have consolidated our position in Egypt, if we could have sent a reënforcement of a few thousand men and the necessary means for founding a colony. Pitt and Grenville feared this, and tried every means to postpone the naval armistice. I showed them how ridiculous it would be for me to cease hostilities toward one power, over which I possessed such decided advantages, and to continue them against the other. Grenville acknowledged the force of the argument. They admitted the necessity of a naval armistice and of breaking up the cruisers; but they wished to interdict all navigation of state vessels, and to admit into Malta and Alexandria provisions for only fifteen days. With such terms it was hardly probable that peace could be made either with the two powers collectively, or with Austria alone.

Important Convention with the United States.—I profited by the leisure afforded me by this suspension of hostilities to repair to Paris for the purpose of arranging our relations with the United States. The absurd operations of the demagogue agents of the Committee of Public Safety had involved us, in 1793, in difficulties with these elder sons of French Liberty, and the disgraceful prevarications of the agents of the Directory had prevented Pinkney from establishing between us that good harmony which ought never to have been interrupted. In truth, the Americans had to reproach themselves for having consented to the right of maritime search, arrogated to herself by England; but it was not, by openly breaking with them, nor by an attempt at intimidation, that they were to be brought to other sentiments. My victories opened a new way. The deputies who had been at Paris for two years came to an understanding with my brother Joseph and Rœderer, and concluded at Morfontaine, on the thirtieth of September, a convention placing our ulterior relations on the same footing as the most favored nations, and sanctioning the sacred principles of maritime rights. The liberty of neutral navigation was here solemnly proclaimed, with no restrictions but those which result from the universal law regarding ports actually blockaded, and contraband merchandise, that is, provisions, arms, and military munitions. Finally, the principle that the flag covers the merchandise was here established, as the only one which a just and wise legislation could admit.

The English quarrel with Neutrals.—This event was of the highest importance; for in the month of August, Denmark and Sweden became engaged in serious disputes with England, who, not content with setting at naught all the rules of maritime law, did not blush to attack even convoys escorted by Danish and Swedish ships-of-war: Russia and Prussia, interested in maintaining the respect due to their flags, took part in these important discussions; and a storm which thickened on all sides began to threaten the British trident

Rupture of the Negotiations of London.—In such occurrences it was not for me to set an example of yielding to English pretensions. I was only the more firmly resolved not to treat till I could secure my dearest interests by a naval armistice. The conditions imposed by Lord Grenville not accomplishing this object, negotiations were broken off at London the ninth of October, and I declared that I would only treat with England and Austria separately.

Conspiracy of Cerrachi.—The same day that the negotiations were broken off at London, my life was threatened by a conspiracy at Paris. Some obscure factionists, comparing themselves to Brutus and Cassius, meditated in darkness the means of destroying a general whom their disordered imaginations painted as another Cromwell or an Oriental despot. I was that night to attend the Opera, and all Paris knew it. Fouché came to inform me that the conspirators, for want of a capitol, had chosen the corridors of the theatre for the execution of their bloody design. I was urged not to go. I did not follow a course so unworthy, but took the necessary measures for securing the guilty. Cerrachi and Arena were taken with poignards and arms with which they intended to assassinate me: they were tried and condemned.

Expeditions against Ferrol and Cadiz.—England, in the midst of the disputes to which she had given rise, redoubled her audacity and activity to secure all the advantages to be derived from the existing state of things; and to make the English people forget the horrors of a famine which was desolating the three Kingdoms, she carried her victorious flag to all parts of the globe. It seemed as though the English government only wanted garrisons to take possession of half the world. The loss of these colonies reacted on the policy of the European states as well as on their marine; to deprive a commercial people of distant trade takes from a nation the first elements of a military marine, and deprives it of the means of sustaining its colonial system.

For six months past Holland had been deprived of the colonies of Surinam and Demarara on the American continent; the islands of Curaçao and St. Eustacia had followed the same fate. Admiral Popham had just set sail with an expedition for the South Sea. A considerable armament, the troops of which were to be commanded by General Pultney, was preparing in part to join Abercrombie upon some important enterprise. A great maritime power threatens all at once, without the enemy's knowing where to expect the blow; it can strike when and where it pleases. The expedition of Pultney might intend a descent upon Holland which we had stripped of troops to form the army of the reserve, and afterward the Gallo-Batavian army, which was assembled by Augereau at Mayence; it might attack Antwerp, Flushing, or Boulogne; it might insult Spain, or descend upon Egypt. I assembled a corps at Amiens under the orders of Murat, with the impression that the attack was to be directed upon Holland. This corps was composed, in part, of grenadiers collected from all the garrison battalions in the interior. But Pultney sailed toward the coast of Spain, where he thought to do with the fleet of the Ferrol what Abercrombie and Mitchel had done in the Texel with the Batavian fleet. Pultney landed on the twenty-fifth of August, attacked Fort St. Philip and the heights of Brion; but Admiral Moreno, having landed a part of the equipages of his squadron, baffled a project which appeared to have been based on the hope of a surprise, and on the ordinary negligence of the Spaniards. Pultney having failed in this project, made sail for Cadiz. At the same time Abercrombie, the armistice rendering his forces useless in Italy, had received orders to appear before Cadiz; the junction of the two squadrons was effected at Gibraltar.

At the head of this new armada Lord Keith appeared, on the sixth of October, before the rich city of Cadiz, then a prey to the ravages of the yellow fever, and deserted by a considerable part of its inhabitants. Less audacious than the celebrated Essex, he at first confined himself to bombarding the city ; General Morla, who was in command, opposed him with a firm countenance. At last Abercrombie decided to land a part of his troops at the point of San Lucar, but they were soon reëmbarked, because (it was alleged) of the fear of the pestilence. Perhaps with greater energy, these two enterprises would have been successful ; it is incomprehensible that such immense means should be expended upon mere demonstrations.

Thugut retires from the Ministry.—While the maritime war was pushed with so much activity, nothing was yet decided upon the continent. Thugut, who in 1797 had resigned from the ministry rather than treat with us, again pretended, on the fourth of October, to yield the portfolio to Count Cobentzel ; but the latter, having left Vienna in a few days for Luneville, where a congress was to be assembled, the portfolio was transferred to Count Lehrbach, under whose name Thugut continued to direct affairs. He still flattered himself that he would be able to deprive us of Italy. His army was reënforced on the Mincio. The Neapolitans, having terminated their intestine wars and juridical massacres ordered by the Queen, and barbarously executed on board the vessels of Nelson, advanced to the confines of Tuscany. Abercrombie might, at any moment, make a descent at Leghorn with the little army which he carried from Minorca to the coast of Tuscany and thence to Gibraltar. The Grand Duke was organizing his militia to aid an Austrian corps commanded by General Sommariva.

Occupation of Tuscany.—I resolved to frustrate the junction of these stormy elements. General Dupont received orders to enter Tuscany, disarm the militia, and occupy Florence and Leghorn ; which he executed on the sixteenth of October after the slight combats of Barberino and Arezzo.

Preparations on the Continent.—The activity of political negotiations during the months of July, August and September, had not prevented the two parties from continuing their military preparations. I had sent into Switzerland a second army of reserve, formed at Dijon by Macdonald, of about fourteen or fifteen thousand men. Augereau assembled at Mayence a little Gallo-Batavian army of the same force. These two corps were intended to relieve my two principal armies of those accessories which trouble the flanks, divide the forces, and form the pretext of all the faults of mediocre generals. Macdonald would cover, at the same time, in the Tyrol, the left of Brune and the right of Moreau ; he might become the corps of manœuvre against the enemy and connect the two armies. Augereau would sweep the left of the Danube, check the forces which the enemy was assembling in Bohemia, and leave Moreau's fine army entirely free in its movements.

The Austrians had also profited by this interval. The Archduke Palatine had gone to Hungary to renew there the *levée-en-masse* of 1797. The Archduke Charles, who had been most unjustly deprived of the supreme command, urged forward, in the government of Bohemia, which had been conferred upon him, the organization of legions of ten or twelve thousand men who were soon to enter into the line. Recruits were collected from all the hereditary states for completing the regiments. The little army of Condé, changed from the service of Russia to that of England, and a fine Bavarian contingent, further reënforced the imperialists. The Emperor Francis, himself, repaired to his army to revive their patriotism and love of glory. Yielding to considerations for which it would be difficult to assign any cause, he deemed it his duty to replace Kray by the Archduke John, a young prince, instructed in the military art, but having neither the experience nor the genius of his brother, the Archduke Charles. They gave him for counsellors the same generals, Lauer and Weyrother, who had been the guides of Wurmser and Alvinzi in the great days of Bassano and Rivoli, and who, notwithstanding all their erudition, always manœuvred very well to secure their own defeat; for nothing is worse than erudition without correct principles. After these preparations, Austria thought it would be base for her to surrender to us Mantua, of which she was still in possession. It is rare that a state makes peace after a defeat, without renouncing some of its lost possessions as a recompense for the sacrifice of the others; a nation, preserving its self-respect, is seldom seen yielding more than it has already lost, when in a condition for self-defense. It will be hereafter shown how these natural maxims were misconceived in the conditions which they attempted to impose on me. All hope of peace having disappeared, I decided to break the armistice, in the middle of November, notwithstanding the rigor of the season. Should we give Austria the advantage of a whole winter's repose, the chances would be entirely against us; Moreau and Brune, therefore, received orders to resume hostilities.

Plan of Operations.—I had conceived a very bold project for outflanking the army of Bellegarde on the Mincio, by making Macdonald cross the Rhetian Alps so as to debouch on Trent and throw the Austrians back on the lagunes of Venice, at the same time that Brune attacked them in front. In order to execute this the more certainly, Murat was directed to march from the camp of Amiens for Italy, as soon as the destination of Pultney should render his corps disposable. I, for a moment, thought of marching with eighty thousand men by the Noric Alps on Vienna, at the same time that Moreau would arrive there by the valley of the Danube. I decided, however, not to go in person to the army of Brune, which, by the turn of events would only be an accessory one; I was confirmed in this resolution by what had occurred at Paris at the epoch of Marengo. The party conquered at the eighteenth Brumaire was not yet dead : at the first news of the success of Melas, brought by a commercial courier, the Jacobins, thinking me conquered, proposed to Carnot, the minister of war, it is said, a *coup-d'état* against me. We can only guess what course he would have taken, if an hour afterward my courier, announcing a decisive victory, had not changed the face of affairs. I deemed it more wise to direct matters from the interior of my cabinet, and Berthier resumed the duties of minister of war.

Macdonald found his task impossible of execution, and his means disproportionate to the end ; he sent his chief-of-staff to bring me his objections. After listening attentively to the exposé of this officer, I interrogated him on the presumed force and positions of General Hiller's corps on the side of Germany, and of the divisions of Laudon, Dedowich, and Wukassowich, which covered the Italian Tyrol. Taking a *coup-d'œil* of this mass of the Great Alps between the Rhine and the Adige, I analyzed the different hypotheses which this vast theatre presented for my combinations, and then replied : " We shall carry, without opposition, this immense fortress of the Tyrol ; it is necessary to manœuvre on the flanks of the Austrians, to threaten their last point of retreat ; they will immediately evacuate all the upper valleys. I will, in no respect, change my plans. Return immediately ; I am about to break the armistice : *Tell Macdonald that an army passes always, and in all seasons, wherever two men can place their feet :* the army of the Grisons must be at the sources of the Adda, the Oglio, and the Adige, within fifteen days after the resumption of hostilities ; let the report of its arms be heard on Mount Tonal which separates them ; and on reaching Trent, let it form the left of the army of Italy, and manœuvre in concert with this last on the rear of Bellegarde. I shall be able to reënforce them as soon as necessary : it is not on the numerical force of an army, but rather on the object and importance of the operation, that I estimate the importance of the command."

Brilliant Success of the Army of the Rhine.—Hostilities recommenced toward the end of November. A few days after, Moreau gained the decisive battle of Hohenlinden. The Archduke John, wishing to take the initiative, instead of awaiting us behind the formidable position of the Inn, threw himself into the woody country between this river and the Iser, in order to debouch on Munich, while the corps of Klenau, with a good part of his cavalry, debouched by Ratisbon and joined him at Dachau. The Archduke, by Weyrother's advice, on the third of December, penetrated into the great forest of Hohenlinden in four columns. Three of these columns marched by roads, difficult at best, but now rendered almost impassable by a deep snow. The principal column, composed of the centre of the army with all the parks and reserves, passing along a fine road, debouched two hours before the others, on Anzing, fell into the midst of Moreau's division, and met a warm reception. By a chance not less fortunate, Richepanse, going into the forest, engaged the left of the Austrians which had been much retarded, thus got possession of the road, and took the centre of the Archduke *en flagrant délit*, by attacking him in reverse in a defile of which Moreau was disputing the outlet. Assailed on all sides in this *coupe-gorge*, the Archduke John, after having lost one hundred pieces of cannon and twelve thousand men, was exceedingly fortunate in regaining the Inn.

This victory was so much the more fortunate as it had been gained without the right wing under Lecourbe, or the left under Collaud, taking any part in it; Moreau had called them to him as soon as he heard of the march made by the enemy on the offensive, but they had not had time to arrive. The victorious army pursued with impetuosity the frightened foe. The heads of our columns, led on by Lecourbe, Richepanse, Decaen, young warriors, full of activity and ardor, scarcely waiting for repose, pursued the enemy with that vigor of which I had given an example in 1796. The imposing barrier of the Inn, notwithstanding the three *têtes-de-pont* which had been intrenched during the armistice, and the fortified place of Brannau, could not arrest them more than a day. The faulty position of the enemy permitted Moreau to menace the right, and to pass the Inn on the extreme left near Rosenheim. The Austrians made a stand in advance of Salzbourg, and Lecourbe came near being engaged there alone on disadvantageous terms: his firmness gave him time to remedy the evil. The Salza, the Traun, and the Enns were crossed with the same vigor. Richepanse operated with great skill, and succeeded in carrying off several of the enemy's rear-guard. General Klenau, who had gone to cover Ratisbon with a pretty numerous corps, particularly in cavalry, paralyzed by the rout of the principal army, could do no better than to join General Simbschen and the legions of Bohemia, to fall upon the little army of Augereau, who, after having reduced Wurtzbourg and invested its citadel, was advancing toward Nuremberg. But the slight advantages gained by the Austrians on this secondary point, did not prevent the main army from being driven back to St. Polten in the greatest disorder. Richepanse, Decaen, and Lecourbe, in this short campaign covered themselves with glory, particularly in the passages of the Inn and the Salza, and the combats of Schwanstadt, Vocklabruck and Lambach.

The Archduke Charles took from the hands of his brother the command of a defeated and disheartened army, which in twenty days had lost twenty-five thousand men *hors-de-combat*, one hundred and twenty pieces of cannon, and four thousand carriages. Coming without reënforcements and without any immediate hopes, how could he be expected to immediately restore confidence and victory?

Armistice of Steyer.—He proposed an armistice. Moreau had orders to consent to it, only on condition that Austria would agree to separate her cause from that of England, and to treat separately, and without delay. Forty-eight hours were required for an answer from Vienna; but Moreau refused to suspend his march, certain that the results of anterior movements would give him a number of prisoners and a quantity of baggage. Finally, the cabinet of Vienna, consented to every thing, and General Grune signed, on the twenty-third of December, an armistice at Steyer, for the army of Germany only.

Inaction of Brune.—The army of Italy had remained wholly inactive. Brune had no interest in hurrying on affairs, for he was waiting for Macdonald and Murat. On the other side Bellegarde, ignorant of the destination of the two last generals, waited only for a cessation of the autumnal rains to render his movements less difficult in the lagunes of the Oglio and the lower Po.

Passage of the Splugen.—The army of the Grisons, obedient to my orders, rushed, full of ardor, across the snows and glaciers of the Splugen, at an epoch when even the traveler trembles to expose himself there with all the ordinary precautions to secure his safety. Drifted masses of movable snow, concealing frightful precipices, threatening avalanches, and a thousand dangers of all descriptions, were insufficient to arrest the brave men accustomed to despise death. The columns, after extraordinary efforts, debouched at last on the smiling shores of Lake Como. But this was not all; food was required, and the Valteline was incapable of furnishing it; it was necessary to seek supplies for the army in Lombardy. Macdonald crossed the secondary and abrupt chains of the Col-d'Apriga, less elevated than the Splugen, but more difficult, perhaps, for an army.

He proposed to Brune to send him his left wing, in order to render more decisive his attack by the mountains. The latter feared that, by weakening his forces in the plain, he would expose himself to be defeated by Bellegarde; and if he were beaten and driven back behind the Adda, that the army of Macdonald would be lost in the gulfs of the Tyrol. In some respects both were right; it was well to act by the left, but not to act in a partial manner. If I had been there, I should have marched with my left and the *corps-de-bataille* to join Macdonald, and treat Bellegarde as I did Wurmser in 1796 at Bassano, leaving only a light corps on the Adige. Macdonald piqued at Brune's refusal, went away to attack the Tonal, whose icy crests now bristled with the enemy's intrenchments, and was repulsed.

Operations of Brune.—The passage of the Mincio took place on the twenty-fifth of December; it was to have been made near Monzambano; the right, under Dupont, was to make a secondary attack at Volta. A delay caused a counter-order to be given to the centre and left; Dupont did not receive it till he had effected his passage, and thus the demonstration became the main attack. This wing had to sustain all the efforts of Bellegarde against Pozzolo. Suchet came to his assistance without consulting Brune, and our troops maintained themselves, by miracle, on the left bank. The next day, Brune passed at Monzambano; the enemy yielded every where to the efforts of our army whose victorious march was retarded but for a moment by the Adige. The left, under Moncey, ascended the river by Roveredo.

Junction of the Army of the Grisons.—Macdonald, on his side, after having left the half of his little troop under Baraguey-d'Hilliers at the sources of the Adige, passed the rocks of the Val d'Apriga, and descended on Breno, so as to communicate with the brigade of Lecchi which Brune had sent to meet him. Repulsed, as has been said, at the attack of the Tonal, he had to fall back by Pisogno and the Col de San-Zeno on Storo, cutting a passage through the thick ice, as he had done through the deep snows of the Splugen. This short campaign was memorable, especially for the fatigue of all kinds which the troops supported, and the natural obstacles overcome by their resignation, courage and devotion. History will transmit it to posterity as one of the monuments of our glory.

Macdonald, at last, effected his communication with Moncey on the fourth of January; on the seventh he debouched by the Col de Vesagno on Trent, where he was joined by Vandamme, who descended the valley of the Noss as soon as the enemy had evacuated the Tonal. The right of Bellegarde, caught at Calliano between Moncey and Macdonald, seemed lost. General Laudon saved it by deceiving Moncey with a false report of an armistice. The Austrians passed by the Brenta to rejoin Bellegarde. Moncey, who thought to enter Trent in consequence of the arrangement made with Laudon, was greatly surprised to find Macdonald already there. Piqued at having been the dupe of so old a stratagem, though almost always repeated with success, he followed Laudon and Wukassowich by the gorges of the Brenta. Macdonald followed, by Botzen, the trail of the Austrian division which had covered the Grisons and the upper Adige, and which Baraguey d'Hilliers was pushing on Meran. He was on the point of surrounding it, when the armistice of Treviso tied his hands, at the very moment when he was about to collect at least some trophies of his hard and toilsome campaign.

Armistice of Treviso.—Brune, who had advanced without energy to Treviso, took it upon himself to conclude an armistice, leaving Mantua to the Austrians and granting a free exit to the garrisons of the Forts of Verona, Legnago, Peschiera and Ancona, which they evacuated to him; this was a double folly: for Mantua was to become the decisive point of the coming negotiation with the cabinet of Vienna, and the garrisons which he allowed to escape would soon have been compelled to surrender prisoners of war. I had foreseen this, and ordered Brune, three days before, not to treat without obtaining Mantua. This order reached him two days too late. This strange convention was so much the more absurd on our part, as Murat was at this very moment descending into Lombardy, and arrived on the Po with a fine corps of the élite of twelve thousand men. I ordered Brune to immediately break this armistice, and push forward, at least till he obtained the cession of Mantua. Cobentzel, hearing at Luneville of this difficulty, consented to the surrender of this place, thus giving force to the convention of Treviso.

Infernal Machine.—Although every thing had succeeded to my wishes, nevertheless the event of the third of Nivose (December twenty-fourth) taught me that I was still over a volcano. This conspiracy was unexpected; it is the only one of which the police did not get some previous intimation. It succeeded, because it had no confidants. It was simple, for it included only my carriage as it was passing in the Rue St. Nicaise, which was to be blown up by a mechanical contrivance, denominated *the Infernal Machine*. I escaped by miracle. The interest shown by all classes in my escape, indemnified me for the risk I had run. The time was ill-chosen; for nothing was prepared in France for the restoration of the Bourbons. The guilty were sought out. I suspected only the Brutuses of the street corners. In committing crimes, the perpetrators seek to make an honor of it. I was astonished when, upon inquiry, it was ascertained that it was to royalists that the inhabitants of the Rue St. Nicaise were indebted for being blown into the air.

The Neapolitans beaten in Tuscany.—During the discussions between Brune and the Austrians, the Neapolitans, who never did any thing at the proper time, thought to drive our detachments from Sienna and to invade Tuscany. Count Damas entered there at the head of eight thousand Neapolitans. Sommariva, starting from Ancona, was to raise an insurrection in the neighboring valleys and cross the Apennines to form a communication with him. Murat was then approaching Parma. Miorlis, taking council only from his audacity, marched with three thousand Franco-Cisalpins on the Neapolitans, and completely routed them at San Donato, on the fourteenth of January. The armistice of Treviso, paralyzing Sommariva, exposed Naples to our blows.

Murat's Expedition against Naples.—Certain that peace would soon be concluded with Austria, or at any rate that the armistice would give us plenty of time to deal with Naples, I directed Brune to reënforce Murat with two divisions, and ordered the latter to march upon Rome at the head of twenty-seven thousand men. I coveted the superb harbor of Tarentum, which had served the Carthagenians as a bulwark to resist the Roman power in the peninsula, and where, with some new works, the most numerous fleets could find a refuge. It had to me a double interest at the time when Egypt was still in our possession: it was an advantageous point of departure for carrying succor to our establishment there.

Murat advanced without obstacle as far as Foligno. In the mean time the court of Naples began to appreciate the danger threatened by the consequences of the battle of Marengo. If Queen Caroline was carried away by her hatred to us, it nevertheless must be conceded that she had a superior mind. She repaired to Vienna, and thence to St. Petersburg to solicit the support of Russia, which had so powerfully contributed to her restoration to the throne. The intentions of Paul I. on Malta would naturally incline him to any project calculated to give him consideration at Naples;

but the taking possession of this island in the name of England so exasperated him that he decided to make common cause with me. He sent M. Kalitschef to Paris, and Lewaschof into Italy. The feelings of this enthusiastic prince were carried so far that Louis XVIII. was obliged to leave Mittau and repair to Warsaw.

Armistice of Foligno.—I had too much interest in pleasing Paul, and too little to gain in paralyzing the great forces at the extremity of the *presqu'ile*, not to listen to the intercession of Lewaschof. Murat, in accordance with my orders, signed, at Foligno, an armistice with the court of the Two Sicilies, which gave us satisfaction for all our complaints, and consented to our occupation of the roadstead of Tarentum until the general peace. Soult was detached with ten thousand men to take possession of it, and I directed him to immediately commence the construction of the necessary works for securing it from the English. Murat had gone to Rome where he was well received by the Pope. He assured the Holy See of my pacific intentions toward him, and good harmony was soon established between us.

Peace of Luneville.—The peace signed, February 9th, at Luneville, put an end to this second coalition; it differed very little from that of Campo-Formio. The principal amendment ceded Tuscany to the Infante of Parma, transporting the Grand Duke to Salzbourg. This clause was important as it called in the intervention of Spain in the affairs of Italy, as it was under Louis XIV. and Louis XV., and completely disinherited the house of Austria, which, possessing Verona and Venice, might have more easily entered there to the aid of Tuscany. The other principal articles of the treaty were: first, the Emperor, stipulating both in the quality of Emperor of Austria, and in the name of the Germanic Empire, cedes Belgium and all the left of the Rhine; second, he consents that Lombardy shall form an independent state; third, in exchange, Austria retains the states of Venice to the Adige, the *thalweg* of which, from the Tyrol to the sea, forms the boundary; fourth, the Duke of Modena receives Brisgau in exchange for his state, which is annexed to the Cisalpine Republic; fifth, the Grand Duke of Tuscany renounces his states and his part of the Isle of Elba to the Infante Duke of Parma, and is to receive a full and entire indemnity in Germany; sixth, France surrenders Kehl, Cassel, and Ehrenbreitstein, on condition that these fortifications remain in their present condition; seventh, the princes dispossessed on the left of the Rhine are to receive indemnity in the German Empire; eighth, the Batavian, Helvetian, Cisalpine and Ligurian Republics, being recognized as independent by article eleventh, their people are to adopt such form of government as they may deem best. This article, though conformable to the principles of public and natural law, was an inevitable germ of discord, and we soon had occasion to prove this. What is just, is not always wise and politic. All things considered, the day when this peace was signed, appeared to me the most happy of my life, for it was one of the most fortunate for France; she was again great and respected; she could taste the sleep of the Lion, and wake in an imposing attitude on the bosom of prosperity.

Campaign of 1801.—At the moment when I was terminating, with so much advantage, the war of the second coalition, important events were preparing in the north of Europe, and in Africa. To properly understand these, it will be necessary to go back a little. The great maritime power of the English had degenerated into an unsupportable despotism. Neutrals had been no more spared than the enemy. The principles of international law had in all time prescribed that convoys of merchant vessels escorted by neutral vessels of state, shall be free from visit; but that, in exchange, state vessels shall convoy neither prohibited goods, nor foreign ships. These just rules were the last refuge of European commerce in time of war. But England most unblushingly violated the most consecrated of maritime rights; she seized convoys destined for France; those carrying French merchandise, and articles useful to the Republic. She even attacked and carried away Danish and Swedish frigates for attempting to defend the property intrusted to their care, and for which their own honor, and the honor of their government was pledged; to fail in this charge was to tarnish and disgrace their flag. With such international laws, the commerce of Russia, Denmark, Sweden, Prussia, Holland, would be completely at the mercy of the cabinet of St. James, and no nation could recognize such a state of things without renouncing its independence and the principal sources of its prosperity.

English Expedition against Copenhagen.—England replied to the just reclamations of the neutral governments, *that she ought to do every thing she could to secure her maritime power, and that she could do all that she wished.* These pretensions and the usurpation of Malta by England, who took possession of this island in her own name, instead of that of the Order of which Paul I. was grand-master, offended Russia, Prussia, Denmark, and Sweden. All cried to arms against a monopoly both insulting and injurious. Preparations were making at Copenhagen, Stockholm, Cronstadt, and at Reval. A quadruple alliance was formed in the north for the preservation of their honor and maritime rights.

England knew well that after getting rid of Austria, I would direct all my efforts to the naval affairs. It was therefore important for her to attack the northern powers with vigor, before allowing time for any concert of action between us; it was necessary to attack the others while twenty-five Russian men-of-war were still frozen in their ports. The cabinet of St. James, far from yielding to the storm, sent an ambassador to Copenhagen, supported by twenty men-of-war. The *ultimatum* having been rejected through the influence of Bernstorf, Nelson effected the passage of the Sound, an operation of no serious difficulty, inasmuch as the Swedish batteries refused to fire upon him, and presented himself before Copenhagen. The approach to this place was defended by ten old hulks of vessels, a number of gun-boats, and two formidable land batteries on the right and left of the line.

Naval Battle of Copenhagen.—On the second of April, Nelson attacked this line with twelve ships and several frigates, passing along the side of the middle ground which divides the channel into two parts; one of his vessels ran aground. The combat was terrible; the right of Nelson could effect nothing against the Three Crown battery, and his centre was overwhelmed by a violent cannonade; eight or nine hundred guns were vomiting death upon his vessels. There was so little space that the vessels were certain, if dismantled, to run aground on the bank where they would be still exposed to the fire of the Danish line. The position was so hazardous that the admiral-in-chief, Parker, gave the signal for retreat. Nelson replied by the signal for deadly combat. Nevertheless the Danish hulks had greatly suffered, many of them were rendered completely unmanageable and floated out between the two fires. Nelson, who had just run aground with his own and two other vessels, now resorted to a flag of truce, under pretext of saving the wounded of the Danish hulks, which, according to him, had surrendered, but of which he could not get possession.

English Armistice with the Danes.—The prince-royal, who had covered himself with glory in defending the land batteries, and preparing to resist the English, fell into the snare of Nelson and concluded an armistice. Although the conditions of this armistice were very honorable to the Danes, it was of immense importance to the English. It is certain that had not this armistice been made, Nelson would have been greatly embarrassed to effect his escape. It is said, as a reason for forming this armistice, that during the battle the Prince of Denmark had learned of the death of Paul I., an event calculated to dissolve the Confederation of the North. This is possible; for the emperor fell on the night of the twenty-second of March, and the news might have reached Copenhagen by the second of April. Be that as it may, the success of the English at Copenhagen, and the pacific dispositions announced by the Emperor Alexander on his coming to the throne, destroyed all the hopes of the neutrals, and England, on the eve of a threatening crisis, came out victorious.

English Descent upon Egypt.—Her arms were not less fortunate in Egypt. The result of the battle of Heliopolis had shown the cabinet of St. James the necessity of taking a more decided part. The turn given to affairs in Italy rendered a large body of troops disposable. Abercrombie was appointed to lead them to the banks of the Nile. He landed at Aboukir, on the eighth of March, with sixteen thousand men, and was soon followed by six thousand others. He was to act in concert with the army of the Grand-Vizier who debouched from Syria by the desert, and the corps of Baird coming from India by Suez. If Menou had been a man of ability he would have beaten these corps separately, and driven the English into the sea, as I had previously done with the Turks. But he divided his own troops, and, contrary to the advice of his generals, engaged his corps in details. After losing the battle of Alexandria, where Abercrombie met a glorious death, the French general was forced to shut himself up in that place, while Belliard, left with too many people at Cairo, was invested there by the combined forces of Hutchinson and the Turks. As a climax of ill-luck, Admiral Gantheaume, whom I had dispatched with a reënforcement of six thousand men, appeared three times on the coast of Egypt without having the courage or address to effect a landing; he returned as often to Toulon, so that Belliard and Menou had no other recourse than to sign successively treaties of evacuation.

Resignation of Pitt.—In the mean time, Pitt had felt that there was no legitimate object for war, and that it was time to make peace. Even before the fleet of Parker set sail from Yarmouth, he had decided to facilitate negotiations for peace; he now retired, and his successor hastened to renew with Otto, who still remained at London, the negotiations which had been interrupted at the end of 1800.

Situation of France.—The Republic was prospering from day to day; on taking the helm of government, finances had occupied my first care. They were in the most sad disorder; I applied myself incessantly to regulate them. Ten destructive systems had succeeded each other since the time of M. Colonne. The annual receipts at the end of the reign of Louis XVI. amounted, according to the famous report of Necker, to four hundred and eighty millions, but there was a debt with an interest of two hundred and sixty millions. There remained scarcely two hundred and twenty millions for the annual expenses of three hundred and eighty millions, besides the interest on the debt, so that there was an annual deficit. This deficit was to be made up by loans, which only made the matter worse. The Constituent Assembly, under the pretext of economy, thought to reduce the entire expenses to five hundred and thirty millions, but the reduction was merely on paper, and never in reality took place. A milliard of assignats, hypothecated on the national domains, had enabled the ministry to get along till the end of 1791. The expenses of the war forced them to successively augment these emissions; and the second Assembly, in order to court popularity, avoided forced contributions and had recourse to paper money. The Convention made so ridiculous an abuse of the assignats that the sum emitted was carried to fifty milliards, on account of their depreciation. There was a time when the sum of from twelve to fifteen thousand francs in paper money was given for a gold piece of twenty-four francs.

The Directory had, at first, rejected this depreciated paper and proclaimed a first bankruptcy, ordering the exchange of the assignats for drafts, at thirty for one; but no one had confidence in rags which did nothing but change their names, and it was necessary to come back, in all government transactions, to specie. This transition was a very difficult and delicate operation where the country was engaged in internal and external wars, and especially when a maritime war was ruining ports, colonies, and all commerce of exportation. For ten years the public debt had been left unpaid, or paid in valueless assignats. The Directory had felt itself unable to pay in money the two hundred and forty millions annually required to pay for the prodigalities of Louis XIV., the Regent, and Louis XV. I thought, after the eighteenth Fructidor, to reduce the debt two thirds, that is, to about seventy millions funded, and ten millions floating. The remainder was reimbursed in admissible *bons*, in purchases of national property. This second bankruptcy had so shaken the public credit that the consolidated third was worth only twelve to the one hundred, and the other two thirds, payable in *bons*, were utterly valueless.

Notwithstanding this rescission of two thirds of the debt, the budget was increased to between seven and eight hundred millions, that is, three hundred millions more than under the administration of Necker. The wants of the navy and army and the expenses of the Republican government, caused this increase; in truth, the provinces of Belgium, of the left bank of the Rhine, Savoy, and the Comté of Nice, furnished to the treasury an increase from the imposts, which might be estimated at sixty millions. The Directory had never been able to raise the receipts to one half of the sum indicated in the budget; it provided for the wants of government by cutting and selling extraordinary quantities of wood from the national domain, by odious forced loans, by money brought from Italy, and by a ruinous floating debt.

To give order and facility to the public receipts, I caused them to be divided by twelfths from month to month. The receiver-generals were to sign monthly obligations for all taxes on freehold and personal property; so that the treasury, certain of its means, had, after the first of January of each year, at its disposal the capital necessary to secure all kinds of service. The order in the *comptabilité* and expense was placed on a par with that of the incomes; confidence was immediately restored. Indeed, I was obliged to establish a kind of "*chambre ardente*," to repair the squanderings which had been introduced into the supplies, the sale of the national domains, and of the wood. The pitiless Defermont was placed at the head of this liquidation, who, judge and prosecutor at the same time, cut away in somewhat a revolutionary style, but who saved the state from the disagreeable necessity of being the dupe of avaricious collectors and of ignoble usurers.

By these wise measures our budget of expenses, which, from time to time, varied from six hundred and eighty to eight hundred millions, was constantly supplied; the treasury was never embarrassed for a single moment, if we except two or three days of crisis occasioned by the fault of the minister; the *rentiers*, contractors for supplies, the civil functionaries, the army, the navy, were all regularly paid. Public credit rose to an equality to the interest of money; a sinking fund was created to increase the guarantees; and

France, whose dissolution, for want of money, the political economists in English pay were daily prophesying, was never in a more prosperous situation than at this epoch.*

Every thing in the interior was progressing equally with the public finances, the war and the national policy : the important codes were in course of preparation ; the list of *émigrés* was reduced to a thousand individuals, noted as movers of insurrection or chiefs of parties, more than one hundred thousand being recalled, and their property, which remained unsold, with few exceptions, restored. Public education, fallen into disorder, was reorganized by a decree of May 1st, 1802, and Fourcroy and Fontanes successively placed at its head. Factions seemed quiet ; so much *éclat* had silenced them. La Vendée was gradually becoming tranquil : the departure of Puisaye for America, and the death of Frotté,† who was taken and shot at the moment when he was stirring up a new insurrection in Britanny, left the party without a leader. Georges, the most audacious of all, had been forced to take refuge in England, and the others, wearied with being made instruments and victims, thought only of repose. Even the Jacobins were obliged to applaud my victory, for it was as profitable to them as to me. I had no rivals.

Necessity of a new Religious System.—To complete the entire pacification of France, it was necessary to build up again the altars, overthrown in times of the most violent anarchy. The clergy had been schismatic since the famous civil constitution of 1791, the churches were deserted and fallen into ruins. I deemed it incumbent upon me to reestablish the Catholic religion for the same reasons that had

---

* For the details of these financial operations the reader is referred to Thiers, History of the Consulate, Book I.

† Alison's account of Frotté's arrest and execution is utterly false. For the true facts in this case, see Thiers' Consulate.

induced Henry IV. to adopt it two centuries before. But if it was important to restore the ministers of the Church, it was no less necessary to bridle their ambition. It was necessary to shut out that army of men of no country, marching under the banner of a foreign chief, who, for ten centuries, in order to raise the tiara above crowns, had substituted ignorance, superstition, fanaticism, and intolerance, for the admirable precepts of the evangelist. In a word, it was necessary to reëstablish the religion of the Fénélons, and not that of the Loyolas or the Mouchys.

Means of accomplishing this Change.—There offered three different means of attaining this object : the first to again subject the Gallican Church to the discipline of the court of Rome, and so limiting its power as to prevent any interference in affairs of state ; the second, to shake off entirely this troublesome patronage, and to profit by the indifference inspired by the revolution toward all religious matters, in order to decorate a French prelate with the patriarchship, attributing to him the canonical investiture, and in other respects leaving the Catholic religion with all its existing forms ; finally, the third was to declare the Catholic and Protestant churches equally under the care of the state, and to favor the extension of the latter, which had already spread over a part of France, without the introduction of the Church hierarchy.

Chances in Favor of the Reformation.—The latter method would have been, perhaps, more suited to the future interests of France and those of the party which had triumphed in the Revolution. Some writers have thought that this would again have lighted up the insurrection in the west, and have dissatisfied that part of the Republic which it was then very important to calm. Undoubtedly their fears were well founded, if the reform had been attempted by force, for notwithstanding my power, I might well have failed where

Henry VIII. and Gustavus Vasa succeeded: great reformations in religion are the results of circumstances; to attempt to force them makes more martyrs than proselytes of the people. Mild measures alone can impose laws upon men's consciences. In the existing state of catholicism in France, it is probable that no invincible obstacle would have been offered to the introduction of a system placing the primitive religion of Henry IV. on a level with that of Charles IX.

Had I been able to foresee the events of 1814 and 1815, I should not have hesitated to pronounce in favor of the Reformed Church. It would have been one of the strongest barriers to the restoration of the Bourbons, especially if it had been adopted by the intelligent part of the nation. The Stuarts have proved the difficulty of reconciling a fallen dynasty and a nation professing a different religion. Those who have wished to form a comparison between the restoration of Charles II. and that of Louis XVIII., have not appreciated this difference of situation. But influenced by my vast projects, I sacrificed internal advantages to external policy. On the one side, all the facilities for propagating the Reformed religion were then conjectural: it was possible that the introduction of a new religious system would, in spite of appearance, excite the strongest passions. My power was still new, and it was important to consolidate it; I had greater motives than Louis XIV. for saying, *L'état, c'est moi;* every thing calculated to produce division or resistance appeared dangerous to my interests, whatever may have been its ultimate influence for the public welfare.

The Concordat.—It was on this account that the substitution of a French patriarchship for the Holy See appeared to me even less sure of success than the Reformed Church; for if the civil constitution imposed on the clergy in 1791, had caused so much opposition in France, could it be hoped that the priests of the south and west would consent to renounce their obligations to the Pope, and to recognize a prelate whom he could not fail to excommunicate? Would not this measure expose the peace of the provinces to be disturbed by a papal bull forbidding obedience? Moreover, the influence of France in Italy, Spain, and Ireland, might be weakened by any change in our religious belief. To oppose England, it was absolutely necessary to have the concurrence of Spain, which was ruled more by the priests than by the sovereign: what hope could we have of perpetuating the alliance between a state governed by monkish fanaticism, and a Republic struck by the thunders of the Vatican? It was therefore preferable to leave the church with the schism already existing, than to engage in a change so delicate and so dangerous. But as such a course was not calculated to produce the immediate result which I desired, and as I had already experienced in Italy the influence which the Catholic religion is susceptible of giving to a government, I preferred to treat with the court of Rome for the reëstablishment of religious matters on pretty nearly the same footing as they had existed previous to the Revolution. I nevertheless obtained for the Gallican Church more freedom than it had ever before enjoyed; the number of episcopal sees was considerably reduced, the government retained the power of opposing itself to the excesses of religious fanaticism, and the dangers of "ultramontane" maxims.

Objections made to this Concordat.—This transaction, as honorable to the moderation of Cardinal Gonsalvi as to myself, nevertheless encountered considerable reproach both from the partisans of the Republic and some celebrated publicists. "Bonaparte," they say, "applied himself, in vain, to destroy the remains of the Revolution, and to close all access to counter-revolutionists, since, by his concordat, he himself opened to the latter a safe entrance, and excavated the mine which overthrew his edifice." This is mere exaggeration: it was the armies of all Europe combined that overthrew my work; the spiritual arms of Rome had but a small part in it. Nevertheless I afterward saw my error in not entirely throwing off the ultramontane yoke. I was wrong in thinking to avoid the dangers of religious fanaticism by contracting its limits. By remembering how different was the religion of Gregory VII. and Boniface VIII. from that of the first bishops of St. Peter, we can judge what fanaticism is capable of doing in a short time, where it has a point of support from which to move the world. I thought that I had secured France and Europe from its pretensions, but experience proves that I was mistaken.

Fault of my Successors.—The concordat with its *articles réglementaires*, filled all the conditions of an excellent religious pact; it secured to society the means of keeping the people under laws of a pure and severe morality; it guaranteed the nation and government against the ambition of a cosmopolite clergy. Religious morality is of inappreciable value to humanity. Its dogmas may even become a powerful political lever in the hands of a statesman, when the influence of its ministers is confined within proper limits; but it often serves as a cloak to factious societies, and to destroy the authority of the most powerful sovereigns, if they neglect to restrain the influence of priests within the just limits which it should never pass. It is not easy to check the authority of a power which founds its pretensions on the mysteries of the Divinity, and thus places them beyond the reach of civil laws.

Spain and Turkey are sad examples of the evils which theocracy may bring upon a nation when the chiefs of the church are in opposition to the depositaries of the temporal authority. Russia, England, Holland, Prussia, and all Protestant countries, prove the advantages resulting from subjecting the clergy to the civil laws, and to the political authorities of the state, without permitting any foreign interference. That ten centuries of barbarism and error should keep the sovereigns of the seventeenth century under the weight of Romish influence, and under the sword of the soldiery of Loyola, we can readily believe; they could not throw off this yoke without exposing themselves to a religious revolution, always disastrous when foreign influence is made to interfere, as Spain experienced in the troubles of the League. But that the ministers of my successors should, instead of preserving the salutary restraints secured by the concordat, seek to overthrow the edifice erected for the security of the government and for France, was an incomprehensible absurdity; it was treason to the throne and to the nation for which posterity and inflexible history will hold them accountable. How could those holding the reins of authority so neglect the simplest axioms of government as to favor the establishment of the ultramontane theocracy? The first of these axioms is, that, as religion is the means of morality to the people, so should it be an element of force to the government: as soon as its ministers pass these limits they become men of ambition and factionists, more to be feared than any other class, since they have a fanatical multitude at their disposal, and place themselves beyond the reach of human power. That princes of the church, like Ximenes, Mazarin, and Richelieu, should desire a sacerdotal rule, is very natural: but such a thing is very extraordinary in a lay chief of the nineteenth century.

What has occurred since my exile has proved that, in a philosophical view of the subject, I did not pursue the wisest course. But in examining my system in a political view of our relations with Italy and Spain, it will find favor in the eyes of the statesman.

Negotiations at London.—The negotiations with England,

resumed after the resignation of Pitt and the peace of Luneville, did not progress as we desired. Egypt and Malta were a stumbling-block to the two cabinets. The English had debarked twenty thousand men at the mouths of the Nile with success; they were waiting the issue of this operation to treat more advantageously. On my side, I wished to give myself an equivalent situation by threatening Portugal and even England with an invasion. My brother Lucien, then charged with the embassy of Madrid, received orders to concert these measures with the Spanish government.

A little army assembled at Bayonne under my brother-in-law, Leclerc, crossed the Castiles, and presented himself toward Almeida, at the same time that the Prince of Peace, at the head of thirty thousand Spaniards, descended the valley of the Tagus and threatened Lisbon. The Prince Regent hastened to purchase peace at the price of thirty millions and the cession of Olivenza to Spain. This result did not accomplish my object; I refused to ratify the treaty, requiring the entire occupation of the kingdom. At the same time I had assembled a flotilla at Boulogne to menace Ireland or the coast of England. Nelson attacked this flotilla with his incendiary machines, but was repulsed with loss.

These reciprocal demonstrations had little influence on the negotiations, for they dragged along till the middle of July without any definitive results. The English did not press them because they learned from day to day the successes of Abercrombie in Egypt; but on the other side the *presqu'île* of Tarentum was occupied, Naples reduced, Portugal threatened with invasion; finally, the continental peace was daily consolidating itself, and it was necessary that this uncertainty should end. Otto, on the fourteenth of July, notified the English cabinet that I refused to ratify the treaty of Badajos between Spain and Portugal, and that I insisted on the occupation of the latter kingdom, as a means of compensation for the Spanish colonies which they (the English) retained. This declaration led to others on both sides, so that the negotiations again begun to make some progress. In a note of the twenty-seventh of July, Otto explained in these terms:

"The French government desires to neglect nothing calculated to lead to a general peace, which is at the same time for the interest of humanity and the interest of the allies. It is for the King of England to decide whether it is equally so for the interest of his policy, his commerce, and his people; and, if such be the case, whether a single island more or less distant can be a sufficient reason for prolonging the calamities of the world.

"The undersigned has shown, in his last note, how much the First Consul has been grieved by the retrograde movements of the negotiations; but Lord Hawkesbury, contesting this fact in his note of July twentieth, the state of the question is recapitulated with the frankness and precision which affairs of this importance require.

"The question is divided into three parts: the Mediterranean, the Indies, and America. Egypt will be restored to the Porte; the Republic of the Seven-Isles is recognized; all ports in the Adriatic and the Mediterranean occupied by French troops will be restored to the King of Naples or to the Pope; Mahon to Spain; Malta to its Order; and if England deems the destruction of the fortifications of this place as essential to her interests, this also will be agreed to. In India, England will retain Ceylon, and thus become complete mistress of these immense and wealthy territories; the other establishments will be restored to the allies, the Cape of Good Hope included. In America every thing will be restored to its former owners. The King of England is already so powerful in this part of the world that to require more would be to pretend to the same preponderance in that part of the world which he now holds in India. Portugal will undoubtedly preserve her integrity.

"The foregoing are the conditions which the French government is ready to sign. The advantages to be drawn from them by the British government are immense; to pretend to greater, is to reject a peace, just and honorable to both parties. Martinique not having been conquered by British arms, but having been placed by its inhabitants into the hands of the English, till such time as France should establish a government, can not be regarded as an English possession: never will France renounce it.

"It now only remains for the British cabinet to signify the course which it wishes to pursue; and if these conditions are not satisfactory, it will at least prove to the world that the First Consul has neglected nothing, and has shown a disposition to make any sacrifice to restore peace and spare humanity the tears and blood which must inevitably result from a new campaign."

The negotiation was prolonged till the beginning of September. England no longer limited her pretensions to Trinidad; she laid claim to Tobago and the Dutch possessions on the American continent; she placed obstacles in the way of the restoration of Malta. Mistress of Asia, she no longer disguised her wishes to control America and the Levant. On the eleventh of September, I caused a strong and peremptory declaration to be made, insisting upon the occupation of Portugal by my troops, if she did not close the matter.

Preliminaries signed.—This firmness had a happy effect. The English government renounced not only the possession of Demarara and Berbice, but also their freedom, which it had at first substituted for the claim to retain them. Finally, the preliminaries of this peace, so ardently desired, were signed at London on the first of October, between Otto and Lord Hawkesbury. Article first, directed the prompt cessation of hostilities both on land and sea, and the restitution of all conquests made by either party after the treaty. The eight following principal articles, stipulated the restitution to the French Republic and its allies, Spain and Holland, all possessions and colonies occupied or conquered during the war, with the exception of the Island of Trinidad and the Dutch possessions in the Island of Ceylon, of which his Britannic Majesty retained the full and entire sovereignty: the opening of the Cape of Good Hope to the commerce and navigation of the two contracting powers, which were there to enjoy equal advantages: the restitution of Malta and its dependencies by the English to the order of St. John of Jerusalem; the restitution of Egypt to the Porte, the contracting powers also guaranteeing its other possessions: the guarantee of the possessions of Portugal: the evacuation of the Kingdom of Naples and the Roman States by the French, and of Porto-Ferrajo by the English, as well as all ports and islands which they occupied in the Mediterranean or the Adriatic: the recognition of the Republic of the Seven Isles by the French Republic, etc., etc.

The news of this event spread universal joy throughout Europe: commerce, so long stagnated, received a new impulse. The neutral powers took no part against the happy pacification, although it deprived them of all chances of contraband commerce; they anticipated a better future and more friendly relations, which would indemnify them, in some degree, for the burdens imposed by the new maritime rules of the English. Even at London the most extravagant joy was exhibited; the people seemed as though they had passed from the depths of despair to the very pinnacle of fortune. My aid-de-camp, the bearer of the ratification, had his horses taken from the carriage by this people, who drew him in triumph through the streets.

Peace with Russia and the Porte.—I was this year very

actively engaged in regulating our foreign policy. A treaty was formed with the Emperor Alexander on the eighth and eleventh of October; our differences with the Porte were also terminated by a treaty; I ratified the convention of Monfontaine with the United States; finally, I regulated the affairs of the Cisalpine Republic, of Batavia, and Switzerland.

Acquisition of Louisiana.—I obtained from Spain the retrocession of Louisiana, which we had lost, in 1793, by the disgraceful peace of Paris. The position of this country, so favorable to agriculture, gave it great value in my estimation. Placed between Mexico and the United States, it might one day render me the arbiter of North America: possessing the mouths of the Mississippi, we could control the commerce of the entire country watered by the tributaries of this immense river. If we lost St. Domingo, we could find on the Mississippi the soil and climate necessary for the culture of our colonial commodities. Two years afterward I gave up all these hopes, by selling this precious colony to the United States: the fear that the English might get possession of it and form an establishment which might one day secure them an influence over Mexico and the United States, was the principal cause which induced me to this alienation of French territory.

The Infante of Parma, King of Etruria.—While they were negotiating the peace of London, I directed all my efforts to place the little neighboring states on a suitable basis. I caused Tuscany to be ceded to the Infante Duke of Parma, who was to be recognized as King of Etruria. This prince, of the Spanish branch, would bring a Spanish contingent against the Austrian branch in Italy, so often as I might deem necessary, as had been done under Philip V. and Louis XV. At the same time I drew closer the bonds of connection with the royal family of Madrid. I had need of this power for my maritime designs, and for the expulsion of England from America. Moreover, I gained by this the acquisition of the Duchy of Parma, as an exchange. As a seal to these relations Lucien proposed to me to divorce Josephine and marry Isabella, Infanta of Spain. This alliance would immediately have produced great advantages; it, nevertheless, had its objections. I thought that Lucien was actuated, in this matter, by his hatred to Josephine, and I directed him to not again introduce the subject.

Expedition to St. Domingo and Guadaloupe.—I profited by the freedom of the seas, restored by the treaty of London, to attend to our colonial affairs. On my elevation to the Consulate, I found our colonies a prey to civil war, the whites, blacks, mulattoes, attempting their own mutual destruction. The whites were nearly extinct, and the mulattoes, though full of energy and courage, numbered only forty thousand to five hundred thousand blacks, of whom twenty-five thousand men were already organized in regiments. I determined to side with the latter, and loaded them with benefits. To Toussaint, their chief, who had shown talent and zeal in fighting the English, I sacrificed Rigaud and the mulattoes, confiding to Toussaint all the interests of the colony, thinking that he would be satisfied with this. But is there any limits to ambition? Urged on by English intriguers, he published a colonial constitution, and proclaimed himself President for life, as I had made myself consul. This changed the course of my policy. I now determined to side with the mulattoes, who, from their superiority of mind and education, were the most influential men of the island. I armed thirty ships and sixteen frigates, which carried successively about twenty-five thousand men to St. Domingo. I gave the command to my brother-in-law, General Leclerc, instructing him *to restore the influence of the mulattoes, to capture a hundred of the black chiefs, the chiefs of battalion* *included, and to fill the vacancies with the mulattoes and whites.* Leclerc landed, but, influenced by the old colonists, he did every thing to exasperate the mulattoes instead of conciliating them. Nevertheless, by their assistance he succeeded in reducing the eastern part of the island, and Port-au-Prince. Toussaint, Dessalines, and Christophe resisted, burnt the towns along the coast, and took refuge among the hills. Defeated in several combats, they at last offered to surrender. On the part of Toussaint this was a mere feint to await the rains and fevers of autumn. They soon discovered his ruse, and seized him and sent him to France, where he died in prison. But Leclerc, instead of obeying my instructions, maltreated Rigaud, who had returned to the island by my orders, arrested him and forced him to fly again to France; other mulattoes were ill-treated and some were even drowned. This incited new insurrections, and the chiefs of the two castes stifled their mutual resentment in order to exterminate the whites. In the mean time the yellow fever broke out among our troops, and in three weeks carried away two thirds of our fine army. Twenty thousand men were dead, or dying in the hospitals. The new regiments lost half their number within twenty-four hours after landing. The crews of the vessels were also cut off, leaving the remnant of these brave men no means of escape. My brother-in-law had at least the consolation of not surviving this disaster: he himself died of this cruel epidemic.

At Guadaloupe, Admiral La Crosse had been no more prudent toward Pélage, than Leclerc toward Rigaud, and the colony rose in insurrection against him. Richepanse was sent there, and, more fortunate than Leclerc, his efforts were attended with success.

Provisional Reunion of Piedmont.—The prosperity of my European affairs indemnified me for this disaster at St. Domingo; Piedmont, at first organized as the twenty-seventh military division, to be afterward formally united to France, secured my empire beyond the Alps. Holland, Italy, and Switzerland equally recognized the laws which I dictated.

Switzerland and the Cisalpine Republic.—My negotiators at Luneville, guided by principles of justice, had stipulated that the neighboring Republics, which had grown up under French influence, should be free to form their own laws. Nothing could be more just than this provision; nevertheless, these states being constituted and recognized by the treaty, these expressions might apply only to their future independence, without that the state then existing and solemnly recognized should be troubled by counter revolutions. It was important that Holland, the Cisalpine Republic, and Helvetia should have charters posterior to the treaty; and that they should not accuse France of having constrained them in their choice. A new government was formed at La Haye, and I assembled a new Italian consulate at Lyons for the month of December, 1801.

Italian Republic.—The Batavian Republic centralized its power in the person of its magistrates the most devoted to France, which could not fail to extend my influence over it. The Cisalpins erected an Italian Republic, the presidency of which they conferred on me for life. Of course I was not a stranger to these different measures. Italy required a chief, and no one had a better right than myself to the title. France had agreed to form the Cisalpine Republic into a separate state; but I had not deprived myself of the liberty of accepting the magistracy of it. I know that this may seem somewhat a play upon words; but certainly one has a right to interpret treaties as much as possible to his own advantage. Austria did not think best to oppose this measure, and no other European power had any particular interest in it, for the institution was merely a temporary one.

Operations of the English.—If the preliminaries of London had excited enthusiastic joy among a portion of the English people, they, nevertheless, met with a strong opposition. The official communication having been made, on the thirtieth of October, to Parliament, the champions of the exclusive party, especially Grenville and Windham, severely criticized the conditions of this treaty, pretending that they were far more advantageous to France than to England. The latter declared *that the ministers having signed the death-warrant of their country, he knew not whether he was invited to a festival or a funeral.* According to him, they had given to France the means of disputing the empire of the seas, since they had restored her commerce, and given her an opportunity to reëstablish her navy. He also contended that the peace was neither sure nor necessary. The opposition, Sheridan for example, approved the peace, but opposed its stipulations, because, he said it would bring about the national degradation; sad prognostics for the durability of a treaty in a country where the general interest, inseparable from the national honor, is the first of virtues and the soundest of duties. This was the first time, since the beginning of the war, that the partisans of Fox and Sheridan were seen to vote with the constant supporters of the ministry. Pitt added to the public astonishment by proclaiming himself a defender of a treaty which he made it his glory not to have signed. These debates in the two houses of Parliament show how different the same thing may appear when viewed through the medium of passion. The partisans of the ministry applied themselves to demonstrate the advantage of the acquisition of Ceylon and Trinidad; the one placed as a sentinel to the vast possessions of India, and the other fortunately situated for observing South America, for a point of departure against the rich Spanish provinces of Caraccas and Venezuela, or against the French and Dutch possessions in Guiana. The sanction of the conquest from Tippoo, and the surrender of

Egypt, did not escape the notice of these apologists. Lord Spencer attacked the treaty with arguments more specious than real, but calculated to pique the national pride.

"We have gathered," said he, "but little fruit from the immense sacrifices we have made; we have restored to France and her allies establishments which have cost us the greatest efforts, and whose preservation was due to the brave men who conquered them, due to the security of the British empire, and essential to guarantee us against the aggrandisement of France on the continent.

"The protection which was pretended to be due to the allies, was a derisory excuse, since they have allowed Olivenza to be taken from Portugal, and have made no mention of the house of Orange which had sacrificed itself for the cause of England, but whose devotion has been rewarded by ingratitude and neglect.

"The cession of the Cape and Cochin will open to the rivals of England the road to India; France gains a formidable position at the mouth of the Amazon, and recovers the Antilles, while England has excluded herself from the Mediterranean, by giving up Malta."

To these exaggerated reproaches, Lord Spencer added his regret at seeing consolidated, by this peace, the principles of the French Revolution, at the very moment that I was about to destroy them! This was not the only error that he committed: the threatening possessions which he saw at the mouth of the Amazon was only a desert extending from Guiana to Cape North and to the river of Arowary, of which the preliminaries made no mention; they only knew that Portugal had yielded them to France by the treaty of Madrid. As to Cochin and the Cape of Good Hope, declared a free port, they were not possessions capable of causing any serious uneasiness respecting the commerce of India.

Lord Cornwallis Envoy to Amiens.—Notwithstanding

the many clamors, the new ministers persisted in following out the system which had been decided at the negotiation: Lord Cornwallis was sent to the Congress of Amiens, where he was to put the seal to the definitive peace, in concert with my brother Joseph, the Chevalier d'Azora and Schimmelpenninck, the latter for Holland and the other for Spain. The English negotiator was received at Paris with the most distinguished honor. Although his countrymen showed themselves sensible of these attentions, and notwithstanding that the preliminaries had laid the basis with so much precision that it seemed impossible there could be any material difficulty in the negotiations, nevertheless, at the opening of the conference at Amiens the old jealousy and inveterate distrusts seemed to preside over the most important matters of the two cabinets.

Difficulties about Malta.—Malta at first presented new difficulties: the minute precautions taken by the powers respecting its disposition prove more conclusively than any thing else the importance attached to this place. The Order of St. John of Jerusalem, to which it was now to be restored, was then scattered and in a state of schism, and, in the eyes of England, was an insufficient and suspected guardian. Lord Cornwallis observed at first that if the English language was incompatible with the rules of the order, it was necessary, through reciprocity, that the French language should be forbidden ! This matter was at last arranged ; but new difficulties arose. I then proposed that the fortifications be destroyed, and that Malta be made a lazaretto for all nations, the knights being restored to their primitive functions of simple hospitallers. England opposed this, because she hoped one day to get possession of this formidable fortress. My minister then offered to place this island under the King of Naples, as Lord-paramount, but with the guarantee of Russia, Austria, Prussia, Spain, England, and

France. If the troops of the order were insufficient, each of the six great powers should furnish a contingent. Malta would be respected in time of war, and might serve as a lazaretto to all parties.

England accepted these propositions with certain modifications; she wished the garrison, in default of Maltese troops, to be composed of Neapolitans. The palace of the King of Naples being under the guns of the British fleets, it would be easy for England, in the event of war, to force the government of the Two Sicilies to espouse the interests of the cabinet of St. James, and thus obtain, if not the retrocession, at least free egress for her squadrons. As these pretensions could not be admitted, and as I desired that the order should remain independent, I proposed that a Swiss garrison should be put in Malta, large enough to enable the place to defend itself. This continuation of the discussion, though no obstacle to the peace was made on our side, was not disagreeable to me, as it gave me time to finish the organization of the Italian Republic, whose *consulate*, then assembled at Lyons, offered me the presidency. It was of no great importance that the treaty should formally recognize me as President of the Republic, but if the matter should be consummated previous to the signature of the treaty, there could be no grounds, in case of a future rupture, to charge me with obtaining this thing by force.

Definitive Peace signed.—I at last thought best to yield to the obstinacy of the cabinet of St. James; and it was agreed that the King of Naples should furnish to Malta a garrison of two thousand men for a year, dating from the restitution of the forts, and that if the Order did not raise, by the end of the year, a sufficient force for defending the island and its dependencies, the Neapolitan troops should remain until their place should be supplied by others agreed upon by the guaranteeing powers. After some other discussions on the territory claimed by France around Pondicherry, and the fisheries of Newfoundland, the plenipotentiaries having passed over the question of the recognition of the new states of Italy by the English government, peace was formally signed on the twenty-seventh of March.

Doubts have been raised as to the good faith of the two contracting parties; certainly the treaty was very defective, and not well calculated to prevent difficulties. My own personal position was such as to cause me to attach great value to this peace, which in the public estimation added vastly to my glory; by giving a new impulse to the internal prosperity of France, it brought me very much nearer to the throne: my sincerity, therefore, could not well be doubted, especially as all the principal omissions were in my favor, and it was greatly to my advantage to leave them just where the treaty placed them. But the case was different with the English government: in avoiding all discussion on Tuscany and Piedmont, whose dethroned princes were still her allies, it must be supposed that England kept these as pretexts for a rupture. To consider the matter merely in the relation of political formalities, the Kingdom of Etruria might exist without being recognized by the court of London, and certainly the maritime peace would not have been disturbed for a century: but how could the port of Leghorn be opened to English commerce, if the ministry refused to recognize the prince who reigned there? The question of Piedmont was still more serious: after the treaty of Luneville, this country had been divided into six departments; this, indeed, was not a formal reunion, but the administration of this vast territory by General Jourdan, in the name of France, under the denomination of the twenty-seventh territorial division, was a sufficiently plain indication of its ultimate fate. England could not have kept silent, except designedly, on this important circumstance; for even supposing that the French government might for a long time postpone the formal reunion, still it was not less true that France administered the government of this country on her own account, and disposed of its revenues, troops, and fortifications.

Upon Switzerland there was a silence not less extraordinary; and, although the British trading companies and fleets had nothing to gain from the inhabitants of the rocks of St. Gothard, nevertheless, the disposition of a state connected with France by so many relations, political, commercial, and military, was a matter of much importance to the ministry of George III.

It will be seen hereafter how important these omissions were, and that the fault of them is to be attributed to the party most interested in regulating these different objects. However, the treaty differed but little from the preliminaries. The only important difference was in relation to the House of Orange, for whom the remarks of Lord Spencer were not lost, and in whose favor an indemnity was stipulated; and, on the other side, the cessions made by Portugal in Guiana, at the moment of making the treaty, were sanctioned, and the disposition of Malta settled.

Its Reception in London and France.—These modifications in the conditions of the treaty were not calculated to procure for it any better reception than the preliminaries. The English commercial community, seeing the departure of the French armaments for the Antilles, and the speedy submission of San Domingo, showed less satisfaction with this peace than had at first appeared. The aristocracy were displeased to see that a democratic and republican branch could bring forth good fruits. Every possible means had been taken to decry the preliminaries, and it was not surprising that the definitive treaty should be received by the multitude with a coldness, strikingly contrasting with the enthusiastic reception of the first. The same objections brought against the preliminaries were repeated on the reading of the treaty of Amiens; Lord Grenville attacked it with his strong and concise logic. He contended that the ministry, in restoring to France her colonies, had done nothing to diminish her preponderance on the continent. Since the preliminaries, the *consulate* of Lyons had consolidated my influence over Italy. The report of the cession of Louisiana to France, kept secret for two years, began to spread the alarm in America, as well as in England; finally, the death of the Duke of Parma caused the Duchy to fall into my hands: the Island of Elba already belonged to us. Party animosity was carried so far that Windham even reproached the ministry with having taken insufficient means to secure the independence of Malta, by placing it under the safeguard of a power whose ports were occupied, and whose capital was besieged by the French.

The minister Hawkesbury replied that the influence acquired by France over one of the secondary states of the continent, interested England only indirectly, and that, a few cases excepted, such a matter could not be regarded as a sufficient reason for engaging in an interminable war. He observed further, that the state of the continent, as sanctioned by the peace of Luneville, authorized a rupture so much the less as Russia and Prussia had recognized the changes made in Italy. The latter part of this argument was specious, for no public transaction had sanctioned the abandonment of Piedmont, nor of Switzerland, and the reunion of the island of Elba with France.

But these clamors of a double opposition did not prevent the ministry from ratifying the treaty, nor the chambers from voting, by a very large majority, the customary thanks to the King. Amicable relations were soon established between the two governments. Lord Cornwallis was appointed ambassador to Paris, and I selected General Andreossy, a distinguished officer of artillery, for the court of London.

The treaty had been better received in France, where all were scandalized at the declamations of the English oligarchy against what was called the triumph of revolutionary principles, while in fact these were daily disappearing from France.

Coup-d'etat against the Tribuneship.—In fact I had just dissipated the last cloud which had appeared on our political horizon, and turned it to the advantage of my authority. Wherever there is no centre of undisputed power, there are found men who wish to claim it themselves. Such was the case with respect to the power which I now held. My authority was only a temporary magistracy; it was therefore unsubstantial. Certain men who had the vanity to think themselves capable of ruling the state, commenced their political campaign against me. They chose the *tribune* for their place of arms. They there began to attack me under the name of the executive power. These modern Gracchi contended that all authority, that is all executive power, was hostile to liberty. Starting from this false base they regarded as praiseworthy any act calculated to oppose and embarrass the executive government. If I had yielded to these declamations, they would have been fatal to the state. It had too many enemies on all sides to divide its forces or to lose time in mere contests of words. Recent occurrences were not sufficient to silence these demagogues, who preferred the interests of their own personal vanity to those of their country. To enhance their own popularity, they occupied themselves in contesting the taxes, decrying the government, and contriving obstacles to impede its march. The consular government would have terminated like the Directory, had I not destroyed this opposition by a *coup-d'état*. I dismissed the recalcitrant tribunes.* This was called *eliminating ;* the

---

* According to the constitution of December 15, 1799, the *tribunat* consisted

word was happily chosen. Among the *eliminés* was Benjamin Constant, the favorite of Madame de Staël, a woman extraordinary and celebrated, but for whom intrigue was a necessary element; she wished to be first everywhere, and to lead in political affairs, as her peculiar sphere.

Consulate for Life.—This measure was called for, both by the situation of France and by the projects I was meditating for giving solidity to the government of which I was the head. I saw more clearly from day to day that the constitution of the year VIII. was only a transitory one, and could not last. Counterpoised authorities will only answer for times of peace; the dictatorship alone suits times of great difficulties. It was therefore necessary to strengthen the authority which had been confided to me, every time there was danger, in order to prevent relapses. *In truth a dictatorship for life would still have been only provisional; something definitive was required by the people to give them a strong attitude toward foreigners and tranquillity at home.* But in the existing state of public opinion, I could consult only the wants of the moment. It was enough for the occasion that I had the authority necessary for effecting internal quiet and prosperity, and a preponderance abroad; the name magistracy was nothing. The consulate for life, which was conferred on me the second of August, became the foundation of the edifice which I was to construct. This dignity had already been prolonged for ten years by a *senatus-consultum* of May sixth, which would have carried it to 1820; but I pre-

---

of one hundred *tribunes*, chosen by the conservative senate from the three lists of candidates proposed by the departmental colleges. The powers of the *tribunat* were very limited; it could neither initiate a law nor give it force; the first was done by the consuls, and the second by the legislative body; the functions of the *tribunat* were merely deliberative.—*Encyclopedia Americana.*

Thiers says that many of the most intelligent and well disposed tribunes were strongly opposed to the course pursued by the majority toward the consular government. Many of the demagogues who were eliminated merited their punishment.

ferred making it for life, and to wait for more permanent institutions. My task was to put the finishing stroke to the Revolution, by giving to it a legal character, so that it might be recognized and made legitimate by the legal code of Europe. I knew that before this could be effected the legislative power must be consolidated, and all excesses destroyed. I thought myself capable of accomplishing this task, and I was not mistaken.

Principles of my Government.—The principle of the Revolution was the destruction of *castes*, not that of ranks; it was the equality of *rights*, and not of classes: and on this principle I formed my laws. The excesses of the Revolution showed themselves in the triumph of *demagogue* maxims; these I destroyed; I took sides with no faction; these therefore disappeared: the excesses had manifested themselves in the destruction of religious worship; this I restored: in the existence of the emigrants; these I recalled: in the general disorder of the administration; this I regulated: in the ruin of the finances; these I restored: in the absence of any authority capable of governing France; I supplied this want by taking the reins of state into my own hands.

Few men have ever done so many things in so short a time. History will some day point out what France was when I was made consul, and what she was when she dictated law to Europe. I had no need to employ arbitrary power to accomplish these great objects. Probably this power would not have been denied me, but I did not wish it; I preferred to govern by laws. I made many laws; they were precise and severe, but just. I caused them to be rigorously observed, for that was the duty of the throne; but I had them respected. They will survive me. The civil, commercial, and criminal codes, drawn up under my direction, and in discussing which I took an active part, would be of themselves sufficient to render my reign illustrious.

I felt the necessity of restoring to the army the powerful incentive of military decorations, which had been suppressed by a fatal and abused system of leveling; I created the Legion of Honor into which all persons who should render important service to the state could enter; this order violated no principle of equality, for the only distinctions admitted were those based on the importance of the service rendered to France. Nevertheless, it was misunderstood and opposed by those captious tribunes, who could see in my creation nothing but pretorian guards: it passed by a small majority.

Official Publication of the Concordat.—The concordat with the Pope had been secret for eight months, for two reasons: first, in order to obtain the resignation of the titular emigrant bishops who seemed determined to oppose the new arrangements: second, to discuss at leisure in the Council of State regulations necessary to bring the religious system of the state in accordance with the opinions and wants of the nation. A prelude to these measures was made in establishing a special ministry for the churches, giving the *portfolio* of it to Portalis. I took advantage of the publication of the definitive peace, to proclaim at the same time this great moral and political act. It was, in the eyes of the Republicans and of the army, one of the most delicate subjects to manage; for if each one appreciated the morality of the gospel many of the citizens had a repugnance for its ministers, to whose intrigues and cabals they attributed a part of the troubles of the Revolution. Nothing less than the seventy-seven regulation-articles was required to dissipate the fears inspired by the return of the *recalcitrant* clergy into the Republic. These articles, pledge of a wise and just tolerance, regulated the relation of the different Protestant professions, and thus established the churches which had formerly been anathematized. They took from the Roman Catholics all subject of religious dispute, and rendered the concordat in harmony with the spirit of the age; but the court of Rome, to whose dogmas and influence their innovations seemed opposed, did not hesitate to secretly undermine them.

The concordat, thus modified, was promulgated on the eighteenth of April, after having been submitted to the legislative body for approval. The ceremony which took place on this occasion at Notre-Dame, attended by a pomp wholly new, offered to the astonished Parisians a striking contrast to the barefaced wickedness affected by the ruling powers of 1793. Since the fêtes of the Dauphin's birth, and the celebrated federation of the Champ-de-Mars, no ceremony had ever been so magnificent as this. The cortège, composed of the guard and of detachments from the different corps of the army, which accompanied the Consuls, the legate of the Pope, the ministers and deputations of the senate, to Notre-Dame, certainly effaced all impressions which kingly *éclat* had left upon the public mind. The studied solemnity of this politico-religious ceremony was a sinister augury to the partisans of the Republic: it was openly said that the magistracy no longer existed except in name. Several generals (Lecourbe, Monnier, Delmas and others) incurred, by their disapprobation, a disgrace, from which they recovered only by offering their services at a time when they deemed the safety of the country as necessarily connected with that of my person. By means of these organic articles, the concordat at first produced only favorable results, for it rallied to the government millions of the country people who for nine years had lamented the overthrow of the altars.

Reunion of Piedmont.—The King of Sardinia, Charles Emanuel VI., retired to his island, had, on the fourth of June, abdicated the throne in favor of his brother, Victor Emanuel IV. Piedmont was formally united to France the eleventh of September. The island of Elba had been so united some weeks before. Nothing was said in Europe on this event, for it had been foreseen, Turin having been for a year occupied as the head-quarters of a military division, and made subject to French laws. Nevertheless silence was not consent, and the sanction of treaties was required to legalize these reunions. The Duchy of Parma was also to revert to us on the death of the duke, since his son had, in exchange, just been proclaimed King of Etruria. I took possession of this beautiful country on the ninth of October, little thinking that it would one day become the heritage of a widow who would outrage my memory, and be wanting at the same time to her own glory and that of her son.

Counter-revolution in Switzerland.—But in Switzerland the desired changes were not so easily effected as in the Cisalpine Republics: the forms imposed upon this Republic by the Directory had created many malcontents. These, instigated by Austria, and thinking themselves authorized by the treaty of Luneville, took up arms and attempted to reëstablish the old Bernese oligarchy. I sent Ney with twenty thousand men into Switzerland. The Bernois and the smaller cantons, who had openly attacked the Helvetian government and driven its weaker forces to Lausanne, were summoned to disband their contingents: order was restored, and I assembled fifty Swiss deputies at Paris to consult with them on the institution best calculated to satisfy the different parties. The act of mediation of the 19th of February, 1803, was the result of these wise measures, and to which the Swiss owed their entire pacification. There was only wanting to this act some indemnity to the Bernois, and the selection of their city as the permanent capital of Switzerland, to make it fulfill all the conditions necessary for the welfare of the country.

Relations with Russia.—Every thing was now arranged except the affair of the German indemnities. I was for a long time afraid lest the eagerness of the Emperor Alexander to establish amicable relations with England might lead to a misunderstanding between us. These affairs being very complicated, there was reason to fear lest they might result in a rupture of the peace of Luneville. The moderation of Alexander seconded my views for the repose of the continent. In fact, we then had no cause for rivalry; France and Russia were at that time natural allies. If I had made conquests not yet sanctioned by Russia, the latter had acquired the best part of Poland without the sanction of France; both had concessions to make.

German Indemnities.—It was necessary to come to an agreement on the indemnities promised by the treaty of Luneville to Austria and the Grand-Duke of Tuscany; on that promised by France to Prussia for the left bank of the Rhine; on that claimed by Bavaria in exchange for the Palatinate; finally, on that of the House of Orange. To obtain all these indemnities it was necessary to encroach upon the Holy Roman Empire. Russia, as the guaranteeing power of the treaty of Techen, had the first voice in the chapter: it was necessary to act in concert, and we succeeded to my great satisfaction. Of course, I might have dispensed with the intervention of Russia in this affair; but her antecedents authorized this course, and I could not with good grace dispute with her a right which I arrogated to myself. We then agreed to act as the mediators, and to act frankly and with good faith in the great work of pacification. Austria was not satisfied with these arrangements; her intentions on the Innviertel had failed; and the Grand-Duke of Tuscany had received but half of the indemnity claimed; finally, the entrance of the French troops into Helvetia, was near creating difficulty with the cabinet of Vienna. Nevertheless these difficulties were arranged; and the good intelligence between me and my powerful ally was still further strengthened by the reëstablishment of the commercial treaty made in 1787 by Segur, between France and Russia. Finally, the great decree (*recez*) of the deputation of the old German Empire completed the continental peace : Europe again breathed freely. England alone, jealous of our prosperity, was preparing for a new contest.

Peace had given a powerful impetus to the prosperity of France. Our ports were filled to overflowing with the vessels of all nations ; Paris had become the rendezvous of all Europe ; the English, deprived for the last ten years of the pleasures of the continent, came there in crowds. Our trade in wines and other products of the country resumed its former activity; our manufactures, especially those of Lyons, gained a greater reputation from the fact that all the resources of art and science had been applied to give a greater development to the good taste as well as to the material modes of the fabrication. This Revolution, so much calumniated and misconceived, because it was soiled by abominable excesses and disgraced by demagogues, impressed on the whole nation a general movement of industry and activity, which gave promise of the highest destiny. It was necessary to consolidate its fruits, to banish its excesses, destroy its false maxims, and collect its heritage ; imbeciles only could think of making it retrograde.

APPENDIX TO VOLUME I.

THE BONAPARTE FAMILY.

WE have already mentioned several members of this family in the foot notes. But as the extraordinary career of Napoleon, and the recent elevation of his nephew, Louis Napoleon, to the imperial throne of France, has directed public attention to the origin and history of the Bonaparte family, the following sketch has been prepared by the Translator. It is compiled mainly from Appleton's "New American Cyclopædia," the "Encyclopædia Americana," and "Biographie des Contemporains."

Some writers have attempted to trace the origin of the Bonaparte family to Emanuel II., a Greek Emperor of the house of Comnenus, whose two sons, after the fall of Constantinople, fled to Italy under the name of Bonaparte. It is a historical fact that a Bonaparte family was distinguished among the nobles of Italy in the middle ages. The names of Bonapartes appear among the Florentine patricians in the "Golden Book of Bologna, and are also inscribed in the "Golden Book of Venice," and in the nobility records of Treviso. When Napoleon's ancestors first settled in Corsica is uncertain, but is supposed to have been during the contests between the Guelphs and Ghibellines.

CHARLES MARIA BONAPARTE, Napoleon's father, was born in Ajaccio, March 29th, 1746. He called himself a Florentine noble and patrician, and was educated as a lawyer in the university of Pisa. He became one of the most popular advocates in Corsica. He fought with Paoli for the independence of Corsica against the Genoese, and wished to accompany him into exile, but was prevented by the tears of his young wife. On the annexation of Corsica to France, he became assessor of the Royal Court of Justice. Count Marbœuf, the French commissioner, retained his name on the register of nobles, and also procured for his son Joseph a place at the school at Autun, and for Napoleon at Brienne. In 1779 he was the deputy of the Corsican nobility to Paris. On account of his health he subsequently retired to Montpelier where he died February 24th, 1785. He was buried at that place.

MARIA LETITIA RAMOLINO, his wife, was born at Ajaccio, August 24th, 1750. She was of Italian origin. He fell in love with her at the age of fourteen, but as her parents were of the Genoese party, while he was a Paolist, their marriage did not take place till several years later. She bore him thirteen children, eight of whom survived their father and attained majority. The names of these eight follow in the order of their birth: viz., Joseph, Napoleon, Lucien, Louis, Eliza, Pauline, Caroline, and Jerome. Madame Bonaparte, after the death of her husband, resided with her children in their country house on the sea-shore near Ajaccio. It was owned by a bachelor uncle, who lived with the family. He was wealthy, but very parsimonious. Anecdotes are told of the means resorted to by Napoleon and his brothers to wring money from the miser. Although the young Bonapartes enjoyed all the necessaries of life, their mother's means were not such as to afford them money for the purchase of those thousand little luxuries which every boy covets, but which it is often better he should not have. When the English conquered Corsica in 1793, she fled with her mother and family to Marseilles. After the 18th Brumaire, (1799), she went to

Paris, but not till after Napoleon's elevation to the imperial dignity, was she distinguished as *Madame Mère*. She was appointed general protectress of charitable institutions, and in that capacity, maintained a separate household. After the reverses of Napoleon she went to live with her half brother, Cardinal Fesch. All her property was confiscated in 1816. During the last years of her life she was blind and bedridden. She died in 1836, in the eighty-sixth year of her age. She is described as a woman of remarkable beauty, and great energy and decision of character. She always retained her original simplicity and dignity of manner, and never seemed elated by the dazzling success of her family. Napoleon, in speaking of his mother, said : " Left without a guide, without support, my mother was obliged to take the direction of affairs upon herself. But the task was not above her strength. She managed everything, and provided for everything with a prudence which could neither have been expected from her sex nor from her age. Ah, what a woman ! where shall we look for her equal. She watched over us with a solicitude unexampled. Every low sentiment, every ungenerous affection was discouraged and discarded. She permitted nothing but that which was grand and elevated to take root in our youthful understandings. She abhorred falsehood, and would not tolerate the slightest act of disobedience. None of our faults were overlooked. Losses, privations, fatigue, had no effect upon her. She endured all, braved all. She had the energy of a a man, combined with the gentleness and delicacy of a woman."

JOSEPH BONAPARTE was born at Corte, in Corsica, January 7th, 1768. He was educated at the college of Autun, in France, and at the university of Pisa. Returning to Corsica, he studied law there, and in 1792 became a member of Paoli's administration. But when that patriot declared against the French Convention, he removed, with his mother's family, to Marseilles. There he was married to the daughter of a wealthy banker, whose youngest daughter had also touched the heart of Napoleon, but was afterward married to Bernadotte, the king of Sweden. In 1797, Joseph was elected to the Council of Five Hundred, from one of the departments of his native island. On repairing to Paris, however, he was sent by the Directory as ambassador to the Papal court, where the indiscreet zeal of certain Italian republicans soon involved him in difficulties with the government, and he demanded his passports. He resumed his seat in the Council of Five Hundred, while Napoleon was absent in Egypt, and, in connection with his brother Lucien, prepared the way for the 18th Brumaire, which made Napoleon First Consul. The success of the scheme created Joseph Councillor of State, in which capacity he negotiated the treaty of peace and commerce with the United States in 1800. The following year his diplomatic skill was of service in concluding the treaty of Luneville with the emperor of Germany, and that of Amiens with England. When Napoleon assumed the imperial crown, Joseph became an imperial prince, and grand elector of the empire. In 1806, the emperor gave him the kingdom of Naples, which he hesitated at first to accept, but afterward took, acting as the mere *locum tenens* of his brother.

In 1808 Napoleon transferred him, much to his regret, to the throne of Spain, a position for which he was entirely unsuited from his want of military talent and energy and firmness of character. On the expulsion of the French armies from Spain he returned to Paris. In January, 1814, when Napoleon took command of the army, Joseph was appointed lieutenant-general of the empire, and the head of the council of regency. In this capacity, when the allied army invested Paris, in March, 1814, he authorized Marmont to treat for a suspension of arms, and subsequently consented to a capitulation. When his brother abdicated, he repaired to Switzerland, where he resided, busily engaged in political intrigues for the restoration of the emperor, until he again joined Napoleon in Paris, in 1815. During the Hundred Days he occupied a seat in the imperial senate; but on the second reverse of the emperor, he took solemn leave of him at the Ile d'Aix, and quitted France and politics forever. Assuming the title of Count de Survilliers, he purchased a splendid country-seat at Bordentown, New Jersey, on the banks of the Delaware, and lived in opulent retirement, till 1830. The revolution of that year in France induced him to write to the Chamber of Deputies, in behalf of the claims of his nephew, Louis Napoleon, who is now the emperor; but as the letter was not read in the chamber, he repaired to England in person. He does not appear to have been able to effect anything for his nephew, and after a brief sojourn in England, he removed to Florence, in Italy, where he died. Joseph was a man of entirely different constitution from his brother; he was not made for camps or councils; his ambition was moderate, and he was fond of books, of pictures, and of society. The correspondence betwen himself and his brother, which has been published since his death, is one of the most important contributions to history that has been made for a long while; for it reveals the confidential intercourse of the two brothers, and throws a great deal of light upon the details of important transactions.

NAPOLEON BONAPARTE, the second son, was born at Ajaccio, August 15th, 1769, and died at St. Helena, May 5th, 1821. The main incidents of his life are narrated by Jomini in the text of this work.

LUCIEN BONAPARTE, was born at Ajaccio in 1775. He removed to Marseilles in 1793, and in 1795 married Christine Boyer, daughter of an innkeeper. In 1796 he was appointed a commissary of war, and 1797 was elected deputy to the Council of Five Hundred. He soon distinguished himself as a popular orator and advocate of the rights of the people. Not long before the 18th Brumaire he became president of the council and prepared the proceedings of that day. After the consular government was organized, he became minister of the interior. In 1800 he was sent as minister to Spain, where he soon acquired great influence. His first wife died in 1802, and, in 1803, he married the widow of the banker Jouberthon, much against the wishes of Napoleon, and the two brothers were never afterwards fully reconciled. In 1804 he retired to Italy and took up his residence in the neighborhood of Rome, where he devoted himself to the arts and sciences. In 1808 the Pope created him Prince of Canino and Musignano. In 1810 he applied to Mr. Hill, the English ambassador at the Sardinian court for the purpose of going to the United States, and, having received satisfactory assurances from him, embarked at Civita Vecchia with his family, personal property, and a retinue of thirty-five persons. He, however, was seized on the voyage by a British cruiser, taken to England and treated as a prisoner of war. While confined in Ludlow castle, he wrote a poem, called *Charlemagne*, which was published at Rome in 1814. After Napoleon returned from Elba Lucien went to Paris on a mission from the Pope. He tried to take his seat in the chamber of peers as an imperial prince, but his pretensions were not admitted inasmuch as he had never been accredited as such; he therefore only appeared as a common peer. After the battle of Waterloo, he left for Italy but was imprisoned by the Austrians in the citadel of Turin. After his release in September, 1815, he resided on his estate at Viterbo in the neighborhood of Rome. In 1817 he solicited passports for himself and son to the United States. They were refused, but finally his son was permitted to go. He died at Viterbo, July 29th, 1840.

Lucien Bonaparte was highly distinguished as an orator, but less so as a writer, and particularly as a poet. In addition to his *Charlemagne* already referred to, he published a poem in twelve cantos, called *La Cyrnéide*. He was also the author of several other works: *Réponse aux Mémoires du général Lamarque*; *Muséum Etrusque de Lucien Bonaparte*; *Mémoires sur la Vie de Lucien Bonaparte*, etc. His eldest son, *Charles Bonaparte*, visited the United States, and in 1822 married his cousin, the daughter of Joseph, who then resided at Bordentown. He was highly distinguished for his scientific attainments, and the author of a splendid continuation of Wilson's "American Ornithology."

Louis Bonaparte was born at Ajaccio, September 2d, 1778. He went at an early age to France, chose the military career, and was educated at the military school of Chalons. In his reply to Sir Walter Scott, he speaks with great affection of the paternal care which Napoleon took of him in his youth. He was with Napoleon in the campaigns of Italy and of Egypt, distinguishing himself particularly at the bridge of Arcola. He was appointed by the first consul ambassador to St. Petersburg, but he did not go there in consequence of the death of the emperor Paul. In 1802 he married Hortense Beauharnaise, the daughter of Josephine, but the union was not a pleasant one, inasmuch as her love did not go with her hand, and he was obstinate and eccentric. Napoleon, on becoming emperor, made him governor of Piedmont, and afterward, in 1806, when the republic of Holland was transmuted into a kingdom, king of Holland. He refused subsequently the crown of Spain, although his wife, instigated by the emperor, strenuously urged his acceptance of the dignity. From the beginning Napoleon and Louis were not cordially agreed, and this refusal aggravated their estrangement. Napoleon's idea always was, that the countries he conferred on his family should be governed in the interest of himself and of France, while his brothers were apt to feel that they ought to be governed with reference to the domestic policy of each nation. Louis, as a Holland magistrate, favored trade with England, and encouraged the Dutch nobility, and when he commanded a contingent of his own troops on the continent, he did so as king of Holland, whereas Napoleon wished him to command as a mere French general. But this the stubborn temperament of Louis would not brook, and he was consequently often treated with studied contempt. When the splendid assembly of vassal princes was held in Paris, in 1809, Louis was not invited to be present. At last their disagreements came to an open breach; his wife, who was devoted to the emperor, left him to reside in Paris, and Napoleon sent Oudinot with a large force to compel him to abdicate, which he did in favor of his son; but the emperor refused to acknowledge the son, and in July, 1810, annexed Holland to the empire. Louis removed first to Toplitz in Bohemia, and then to Gratz in Styria, as the Count St. Leu. In 1813 he offered his services to the emperor, who accepted them, but gave him no employment. When the Batavians, on the downfall of the empire, resumed their independence, he asserted his right to the throne, but they refused to listen to his pretensions. His wife, in the mean time, had obtained, through the interference of Alexander, a grant of the domain of St. Leu, with the title of duchess, and he opened a suit against her for the restitution of his two sons, who were in her keeping; but the return of Napoleon put a stop to the proceedings. Louis then retired to the Papal States, where he devoted himself to literature, publishing *Marie, ou les Hollandaises*, a romance of Holland life; *Documents historiques et reflexions sur le gouvernment de la Hollande; Mémoires sur la versification;* a *Réponse à Sir Walter Scott*, **and** several poetical compositions. He died at Leghorn, July 25th, 1846, but his body was buried at St. Leu, in France.

ELIZA BONAPARTE, eldest sister of Napoleon, was born at Ajaccio, January 3d, 1777 (or, according to some biographers, in 1773 or 1774), and died at the Villa Vincentina, near Trieste, August 7th, 1820. She was educated in a convent at St. Cyr, lived with her mother in Marseilles at the breaking out of the Revolution, married at Paris, in 1797, Felice Pascale Bacciochi, a Corsican noble, was made princess of Lucca and Piombino in 1805, and Grand Duchess of Tuscany in 1808. The vigor and state with which she ruled her principality gained her the appellation of the Semiramis of Lucca. She protected literature, science, and the industrial arts, and was especially the friend and patron of Châteaubriand and Fontanes. In 1814 she retired to Bologna ; thence, the next year, to Austria, where she lived with her sister Caroline, the widow of Murat ; thence, with her family, to her estate of Villa Vincentina, where under the title of Countess of Compignano, she passed the remainder of her life. She left two sons, Jerome Charles, who died in Rome in 1833, and a daughter, Napoleone Eliza, who married Count Camerata, and whose only son, Napoleon, born 1827, killed himself March 3d, 1853.

PAULINE BONAPARTE, was born at Ajaccio, October 20th, 1780. When the English occupied Corsica in 1793, she went to Marseilles, where she was on the point of marrying Fréron, a member of the convention, and son of that critic whom Voltaire made famous, when another lady laid claim to his hand. The beautiful Pauline was then intended for General Duphot, who was afterward murdered at Rome, in December, 1797 ; but she bestowed her hand, from choice, on General Leclerc, then at Milan, who had been, in 1795, chief of the general staff of a division at Marseilles, and had there fallen in love with her. When Leclerc was sent to St. Domingo, with the rank of captain-general, Napoleon ordered her to accompany her husband with her son. She embarked in December, 1801, at Brest, and was called by the poets of the fleets, the *Galatea of the Greeks*, the *Venus Marina*. Her statue, in marble, has since been made by Canova, at Rome—a successful image of the goddess of beauty. She was no less courageous than beautiful, for when the negroes under Christophe, stormed Cape Francois, where she resided, and Leclerc, who could no longer resist the assailants, ordered his lady and child to be carried on shipboard, she yielded only to force. After the death of her husband, November 23d, 1802, she married, at Morfontaine, November 6th, 1803, the prince Camillo Borghese. Her son died at Rome, soon after. With Napoleon, who loved her tenderly, she had many disputes, and as many reconciliations; for she would not always follow the caprices of his policy. Yet even the proud style in which she demanded what her brothers begged, made her the more attractive to the emperor. Once, however, when she forgot herself towards the empress, whom she never liked, she was obliged to leave the court. She was yet in disgrace, at Nice, when Napoleon resigned his crown in 1814; upon which occasion she immediately acted as a tender sister. Instead of remaining at her palace in Rome, she set out for Elba, to join her brother, and acted the part of mediatrix between him and the other members of his family. When Napoleon landed in France, she went to Naples to see her sister Caroline, and afterwards returned to Rome. Before the battle of Waterloo she placed all her diamonds, which were of great value, at the disposal of her brother. They were in his carriage, which was taken in that battle, and were shown publicly at London. He intended to have returned them to her. She lived, afterwards, separated from her husband, at Rome, where she occupied part of the palace Borghese, and where she possessed, from 1816 the Villa Sciarra. Her house, in which taste and love of the fine arts prevailed, was the centre of the most splendid society at Rome. She often saw her mother, her brothers Lucien and Louis, and her uncle Fesch. When she heard of the sickness of her brother Napoleon, she repeatedly requested permission to go to him at St. Helena. She finally obtained her request, but the news of his death arrived immediately after. She died June 9th, 1825, at Florence. She left many legacies, and a donation, by the interest of which two young men of Ajaccio will be enabled to study medicine and surgery.

CAROLINE BONAPARTE, youngest sister of Napoleon, was born at Ajaccio, March 26th, 1782, and died in Florence, May 18th, 1839. She came to France in 1793, married Joachim Murat, January, 1800, became Grand Duchess of Berg in 1806, and Queen of Naples in 1808. She gained the affection of the people, patronized letters, restored the Neapolitan Museum of Antiquities, organized the excavation of Pompeii, and established a school for three hundred girls. Made a widow in 1815, she retired to Haimburg in Austria, and took the title of countess of Lipona, the anagram of Napoli (Naples). She was permitted to visit Paris in 1830, where she resided three months, to obtain indemnity for the castle of Neuilly, which her husband had purchased, and which had been restored to the family of Orleans. The French Chamber, in 1838, granted her a pension for life of one hundred thousand francs. She left two sons and two daughters.

JEROME BONAPARTE, the youngest brother of Napoleon, was born at Ajaccio, December 25th, 1784, and died at Paris in 1859. He was educated under Madame Campan, at Paris, and next at Juilly, and was early placed in the naval service, where he remained until 1801 when he was sent as lieutenant, to St. Domingo, under General Leclerc, his brother-in-law. Returning soon to France, as a bearer of dispatches, he received an independent command, and sailed again for Martinique. During the hostilities of 1803 between France and England, he cruised between St. Pierre and Tobago, but for some reason or other he was obliged to leave the station and went to New York. December 24th, 1803, he married Miss Elizabeth Patterson, the daughter of a wealthy and eminent merchant of Baltimore. After the empire was declared he returned with his wife to Europe; but as his marriage had not pleased the imperial will, she was not allowed to land in France. Napoleon had the marriage annulled by a decree of his council of state, but the Pope, to whom politics were not in this case a superior consideration to morals, refused to sanction the divorce. Madame Bonaparte went first to Holland, where, too, she was not permitted to go on shore, and then to England. In that country she gave birth to a son, July, 1805, who was named Jerome Napoleon Bonaparte. The father himself entered France after a while, and was given a captaincy. Subsequently he was created rear-admiral, and in 1807 was transferred to the land service, with the rank of general-of-division. He commanded a body of Würtembergers and Bavarians in the campaign of that year, and was successful in a movement against Silesia. On the twelfth of August, the same year, his brother caused him to be married to Frederica Catharine, daughter of the king of Würtemberg, although his own wife was still living. On the eighteenth, Westphalia was erected into a kingdom, and the youthful, half-educated and extravagant Jerome made the king. His government, however, though excessively lavish and prodigal, was an improvement upon that of the old *régime:* he was little more than the deputy or viceroy of the emperor; but that emperor was a greatly superior man to the conservative Germans, who before had held sway. In the campaign against Russia, in 1812, he led a corps of Germans, and considerably distinguished himself by his bravery; but having been guilty of some neglect, which disconcerted the plans of Napoleon, he was severely reprimanded by him, and went home in dudgeon. In the ensuing year, when the French were driven out of Germany, Jerome went with his family to Paris; but in 1814 they were compelled to quit France. His wife was arrested just as they were leaving Paris, by a body of the allies, but was speedily released. After Napoleon's abdication he lived alternately at Blois, at Gratz, and Trieste, and did not get back to Paris till April, 1815. He at once embraced the fortunes of his brother, and fought with him at Ligny and Waterloo. The final downfall of the family sent him wandering through Switzerland, to settle at last near Vienna, as Prince de Montfort, a title conferred upon him by his father-in-law. In 1852, when Louis Napoleon assumed the supreme control in Paris, he was called back to France, made a marshal of the empire, president of the senate, and, in the failure of a direct succession to Louis Napoleon, heir to the throne. By his first wife, Miss Patterson, he had one son, and by his second, two sons, Prince Napoleon, and one who is not now living, and a daughter.

NAPOLEON BONAPARTE II., (Francis Napoleon Charles), son of the first emperor, was born in Paris, March 20th, 1811, died at Schönbrunn, July 22d, 1832. He was the fruit of the marriage between Napoleon and Maria Louisa of Austria, and from his birth was styled the king of Rome. When the emperor was compelled to abdicate in 1814, he went with his mother to Vienna, and was educated there by his grandfather, the emperor of Austria. His title there was the Duke of Reichstadt, and he was most carefully instructed, especially in the military art. But he appears to have inherited but little of the ability of his father; his constitution was weak, and early symptoms of consumption unfitted him for the laborious duties of a military career. On Napoleon's return from Elba, in 1815, an attempt was made to remove the young duke to Paris, but frustrated by the Austrian authorities. He was made a lieutenant-colonel in 1831, and commanded a battalion of Hungarian infantry in the garrison of Vienna, but his death, when he was but twenty-one years old, cut him off before he had reached an age in which he might have displayed any abilities he possessed. During his lifetime he never assumed the title of Napoleon II., inasmuch as the abdication of his father, in his favor, was never admitted by the allies, nor was it ever claimed by the French government. But in 1852, when the resumption of the empire by Louis Napoleon rendered some title necessary, he was considered Napoleon II., and the new emperor took that of Napoleon III. The latter title, however, having been recognized by the several governments of Europe, the recognition of the former is implied.

NAPOLEON BONAPARTE III., (Charles Louis Napoleon), is the son of Louis, the king of Holland, and Hortense, daughter of the empress Josephine, who re-appears on the throne of France, from which she was expelled by Napoleon I., in the person of her grandson. He was born in Paris, April 20th, 1808. The emperor and empress were his sponsors at baptism, and he was an early favorite with Napoleon. As his father and mother soon came to live separately, he was chiefly educated by his mother, who resided in Paris under the title of the queen of Holland. After the battle of Waterloo, the family retired first to Augsburg, where he learned the German language, and subsequently to Switzerland, where they passed their summers, while in winter they repaired to Rome. The principal tutor of Louis Napoleon was M. Lebas, who being a stern republican, gave him his first but short-lived inclinations to republican principles.

For a time, however, he was at the military college of Thun, where he made some progress in the science of gunnery, but was not distinguished as a scholar. When the Revolution of 1830 broke out, he petitioned Louis Philippe to be allowed to return to France, but that adroit monarch refused the request. Louis and his brother, Napoleon, then repaired to Italy, where they took an active part in the revolutionary movements of 1831. But the interference of France and Austria in behalf of the papal authorities soon put an end to these, and the brothers were banished from the Papal territory. The elder brother, Napoleon, died at Pesaro, a victim to his anxieties and fatigues, March 27th of that year, and Louis Napoleon, also prostrated by illness at Ancona, was joined by his mother, and having in vain applied for permission to enter the French army, he spent a short time in England, eventually retiring to his mother's chateau at Arenenberg, in Thurgau. The duke of Reichstadt dying in 1832, left him the successor of Napoleon I., not by legitimate descent, but by the imperial edicts of 1804 and 1805, which set aside the usual order of descent and fixed the succesion in the line of the fourth brother of Napoleon, Louis, instead of in that of the elder brother Joseph. This opened a new career to his ambition, and he seems from that time to have set his heart upon the recovery of the imperial position and honors. Nor did he leave any means untried by which he might hope to win over the French people to an approval of his lofty project. He wrote a book called *Rêveries Politiques*, in which he endeavored to demonstrate the necessity of an emperor to the true republican organization of France. This was subsequently expanded into a larger work, called *Idées Napoléoniennes*, wherein the policy and plans of the emperor were magnified and extolled, and earnestly commended to the adoption of France. But he did not limit his efforts to the publication of books; he put himself in communication with Colonel Vaudry, and other military officers of the garrison of Strasbourg; and October 30th, 1836, he proclaimed a revolution. The soldiers of some regiments received him with acclamation, but the other regiments remained true to their duty, and the attempt resulted in a miserable failure. The prince, however, was taken prisoner, and Louis Philippe, instead of having him executed, consented, at the earnest entreaties of his mother, merely to banish him. He was sent to the United States, where he led a life of idleness for a short time, and then went to South America. The mortal illness of his mother took him back to Arenenberg in time to see her die on October 5th, 1837. As he immediately set to work defending his conduct at Strasbourg, the government of France demanded his extradition from Switzerland, which country at first refused to comply with the request, but afterward was about to assent to it, when Louis Napoleon voluntarily withdrew to England. There he occupied himself in preparing his *Idées Napoléoniennes,* before referred to, and in getting up a second revolutionary expedition. Accompanied by Count Montholon, who had been the companion of his uncle at St. Helena, and a retinue of about fifty persons, he sailed in a steamboat from Margate in August, 1840. He was tried for treason before the house of peers, was defended by the eloquent Berryer, but was sentenced to perpetual imprisonment in the fortress of Ham. His exclusion from the world gave him leisure for the exercise of his literary abilities, and he passed some of his time in writing "Historical Fragments," among which is a comparison of the French Revolution of 1834, and the English Revolution of 1688; also, an analysis of the sugar question, and an essay on the extinction of pauperism, in the last of which a decidedly socialistic tone is assumed. He published, also, *Considérations Politiques et Militaires sur la Suisse,* and a *Manuel sur l'Artillerie.* After remaining in prison six years, he managed to effect his escape by the assistance of his physician, in the dress of a workman, and went again to England. When the Revolution of 1848 broke out he repaired to Paris, and was chosen a deputy to the National Assembly, from the Department of the Seine and three other departments. Lamartine, opposing the Bonaparte dynasty, endeavored to effect his banishment from France, but after a stormy debate, Louis Napoleon was admitted to his seat. He professed to be a republican, and as such took the oath of fidelity to the republic. On December the 10th, when the election for president came on, he was found to be the most popular candidate, and was chosen by a large majority of votes. His government as president, nominally republican, was yet steadily directed to the furtherance of his personal schemes. In the beginning of 1851, Changarnier, who commanded the army of Paris, was dismissed, and the legislative assembly which refused to pass several bills urged by him, was denounced as factious and refractory. All through the summer the breach between the prince president, as he was called, and the representatives of the people was widened, when suddenly, on the night of the 2d of December, the president declared Paris in a state of siege; a decree was issued dissolving the assembly, one hundred and eighty of the members were placed in arrest, the leading ones being torn from their beds and sent to prison, and the people who exhibited any disposition to take their part were shot down in the streets by the soldiers. A decree was put forth at the same time, ordering the establishment of universal suffrage, and the election of a president for ten years. Louis Napoleon was of course elected under this decree; and as soon as he found himself firmly reseated in his place, he began to prepare for the restoration of the empire. In January, 1852, the national guard was revived, a new constitution adopted, and new orders of notability issued. On November 21st and 22d, the people were asked to vote upon a *plebiscitum*, reviving the imperial dignity in the person of Louis Napoleon. The votes were counted largely in his favor, and he was declared emperor, under the title of Napoleon III. Thus the long and eager pursuit of the resuscitation of the Napoleon dynasty was at last crowned with success. In January, 1853, Louis Napoleon married Eugénie, Countess de Teba, a Spanish lady of remarkable beauty and accomplishments, and the result of the union was the birth of a son, March 16th, 1856.

NAPOLEON BONAPARTE, Prince Napoleon, (Charles Paul), is the son of Jerome Bonaparte by his second wife, the daughter of the king of Würtemberg. He was born at Trieste, September 9th, 1822. After the revolution of February, 1848, he was elected a member of the Assembly from Corsica, and became a prominent party leader. Although a supporter of the imperial government, he encourages liberal, if not democratic measures. He has held high political and military appointments, and has traveled extensively in Europe and America. He served in the wars of the Crimea and of Italy, but without particular distinction.

JEROME NAPOLEON BONAPARTE, of Baltimore, son of Jerome and Miss Patterson, was born July 7th, 1805. This marriage was legal by the laws of the church, and was never annulled by the Pope; but it was opposed to the decrees and policy of the French empire. Hence, although the legitimacy of the Baltimore branch of the Bonapartes is indisputable, they are not admitted as members of the imperial dynasty. To have done so would have given Mr. Jerome Napoleon Bonaparte precedence over Prince Napoleon and the Princess Mathilde.

APPENDIX.

TITLES OF NAPOLEON'S MARSHALS AND OF HIS MOST PROMINENT GENERALS AND MINISTERS.

As many of Napoleon's marshals and most prominent generals and ministers are frequently mentioned by their titles of nobility, which are less known than their proper names, the reader will find the following lists convenient for reference.

MARSHALS.

Augereau,	appointed	1804,	Duke of Castiglione.
Bernadotte,	"	1804,	Prince of Porte Corvo, Crown Prince of Sweden, King of Sweden.
Berthier,	"	1804,	Duke of Neufchâtel, Prince of Wagram.
Brune,	"	1804,	Count Brune.
Bessières,	"	1804,	Duke of Istria.
Davoust,	"	1804,	Duke of Auerstadt, Prince of Eckmühl.
Grouchy,	"	1815,	Count Grouchy.
Jourdan,	"	1804,	Count Jourdan.
Kellerman,	"	1804,	Duke of Valmy.
Lannes,	"	1804,	Duke of Montebello.
Lefébvre,	"	1804,	Duke of Dantzic.
Macdonald,	"	1809,	Duke of Tarentum.
Marmont,	"	1809,	Duke of Ragusa.
Massena,	"	1804,	Duke of Rivoli, Prince of Essling.
Moncey,	"	1804,	Duke of Cornegliano.
Mortier,	"	1804,	Duke of Treviso.
Murat,	"	1804,	Grand Duke of Berg.
Ney,	"	1804,	Duke of Elchingen. Prince of Moskwa.
Oudinot,	"	1809,	Duke of Reggio.
Perignon,	"	1804,	Count Perignon.
Poinatowski,	"	1813,	Prince of Poland.
Serrurier,	"	1804,	Count Serrurier.
Soult,	"	1804,	Duke of Dalmatia.
St. Cyr,	"	1812,	Marquis Gouvion-St.-Cyr.
Suchet,	"	1811,	Duke of Albufera.
Victor,	"	1807,	Duke of Belluno.

MOST PROMINENT GENERALS AND MINISTERS.

Cambaceres,	Prince of Parma.
Caulaincourt,	Duke of Vicenza.
Champagny,	Duke of Cadore.
Clarke,	Duke of Feltre.
Eugene Beauharnais,	Prince of Venice and Viceroy of Italy.
Fouché,	Duke of Otranto.
Junot,	Duke of Abrantes.
Le Brun,	Duke of Placentia.
Maret,	Duke of Bassano.
Mouton,	Count Lobau.
Savary,	Duke of Rovigo.
Talleyrand,	Prince of Benevento.
Vandamme,	Count Unebourg.

www.ingramcontent.com/pod-product-compliance
Lightning Source LLC
Chambersburg PA
CBHW052042220426
43663CB00012B/2411